Winter Park
PUBLIC LIBRARY

Book-A-Year Endowment

In memory of
Maria Fenninger

Presented by
Chris Fenninger

HOMEWARD BOUND

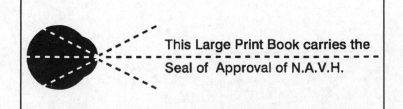

HOMEWARD BOUND

THE LIFE OF PAUL SIMON

PETER AMES CARLIN

THORNDIKE PRESS
A part of Gale, Cengage Learning

GALE
CENGAGE Learning·

Farmington Hills, Mich • San Francisco • New York • Waterville, Maine
Meriden, Conn • Mason, Ohio • Chicago

GALE
CENGAGE Learning®

LIBRARY OF CONGRESS CATALOGING-IN-PUBLICATION DATA

Names: Carlin, Peter Ames, author.
Title: Homeward bound : the life of Paul Simon / by Peter Ames Carlin.
Description: Large print edition. | Waterville, Maine : Thorndike Press, 2016. | Thorndike press large print biographies and memoirs
Identifiers: LCCN 2016040603 | ISBN 9781410494481 (hardcover) | ISBN 1410494489
Subjects: LCSH: Simon, Paul, 1941- | Rock musicians—United States—Biography. | Large type books.
Classification: LCC ML420.S563 C37 2016b | DDC 782.42164092 [B] —dc23
LC record available at https://lccn.loc.gov/2016040603

Published in 2016 by arrangement with Henry Holt and Company, LLC

*For my mother and father
And for my grandparents
Ralph and Freda,
Simon and Betty*

I go at things as I have taught myself,
free-style, and will make the record
in my own way.

— SAUL BELLOW
The Adventures of Augie March

CONTENTS

1. Real and Assumed 11

2. The Tailor 20

3. Our Song 39

4. Nowhere to Go but Up! 72

5. Two Teenagers 98

6. The Freedom Criers 121

7. What Are You Searching for,
     Carlos Dominguez 143

8. The Voice of the Now 169

9. He Was My Brother 194

10. It Means Nothing to Us 227

11. Some Dream of What I
      Might Be 263

12. Bookends 290

13. So Long Already, Artie 315

14. I'd Rather Be 348

15. That's It, That's That Groove . . . 379

16. Through No Fault of My Own . . 411

17. Swallowed by a Song 443

18. What Did You Expect? 463

19. These Are the Roots of Rhythm . . 499
20. I've Got Nothing to
    Apologize For 535
21. The Whole World Whispering . . . 572
22. Phantom Figures in the Dust . . . 601
23. The Teacher. 644
24. See What's Become of Me 677

    NOTES 691
    ACKNOWLEDGMENTS 733
    ILLUSTRATION CREDITS . . . 737

CHAPTER 1
REAL AND ASSUMED

On February 16, 1967, Paul Simon sat at a conference table in his lawyers' offices and tried to explain who he was, who he used to be, and who he had become. This would take some doing.

For while he was clearly Paul Frederic Simon, born in Newark, New Jersey, on October 13, 1941, the elder of the two sons whom Louis and Belle Simon raised in the Kew Gardens Hills section of Queens, New York, he had answered to several other names in his twenty-five years. All in the pursuit of a professional music career that took off a few weeks into his senior year of high school, when the short, dark-eyed Simon, along with his tall, blue-eyed best friend, Arthur "Artie" Garfunkel, recorded "Hey, Schoolgirl," a sprightly pop tune of their own composition. The owner of a small New York record company heard cash register bells in the boys' chiming harmonies, and within days he had their signatures on a recording contract.

The boys waxed another song for the single's B-side and then set to inventing a catchy stage name for their act. Anything to differentiate themselves from the hundreds, even thousands, of artists lobbing songs at the *Billboard* charts that week. There were other reasons, particularly their obviously ethnic names, so when record company owner Sid Prosen came up with Tom and Jerry, which played off the popular cartoon characters of the day, Artie and Paul added surnames (Graph and Landis, respectively) and crossed their fingers. *Mirabile dictu,* and by Thanksgiving "Hey, Schoolgirl" was hopscotching up the sales charts. By the end of Christmas vacation Paul and Artie's shiny-cheeked alter egos were famous. TEEN SONG-WRITERS HIT, shouted the *New York World-Telegram and Sun,* WHIZ KIDS ROCK 'N' ROLL! cried the *Long Island Star-Journal.*

The glory didn't last. Tom and Jerry recorded and released eight or so other songs in the next few months, but none of them followed the astral trajectory of "Schoolgirl." With college on the horizon and a bitter disagreement already in progress, the duo retired from the Tom and Jerry business and stepped back onto the middle-class over-achievers' path to college, graduate school, and the 7:04 from Scarsdale to Grand Central. That didn't last, either, and when the pair re-reformed as folksingers in 1963, it took just over two years for them to become extremely, wildly, imprinted-upon-a-generation famous as Simon and Garfunkel. One year and a chain of folk-rock hits later, the pop tunes by 1950s teen idols Tom and Jerry reappeared in a package decorated with the grown-up Simon and Garfunkel's poet-rocker frowns — and this was a big problem.

Tom and Jerry had been light-footed teen idols whose central, nay, *sole* concerns involved girls, school, the joys of the former, the hassles of the latter, and the travails of both. They were the boys every mother wanted her daughter to bring home. But a decade later Simon and Garfunkel were stylish folksingers whose melancholic songs surveyed the internal geographies of postadolescent malaise, social disconnection, and the euphoria that grabs you when the sun shines and you're rapping with lampposts and feeling groovy. So how could Prosen have compiled those ridiculous high school songs, slapped a recent photo on the cover, and called it Simon and Garfunkel's latest album? Outraged by the potential damage the bogus album could cause their reputations and fortunes, Paul and Artie had summoned their attorneys and gone on the attack.

The argument boiled down to this: While the original contract the adolescent Paul and Artie and their parents had signed with

Prosen in 1957 did grant the executive the right to use their master recordings in any fashion he chose, nothing in the deal gave him the right to advertise the work as the product of Paul Simon and Arthur Garfunkel. Back when they signed, Paul and Artie were unknown high schoolers who were thrilled to get any attention whatsoever. If "Tom and Jerry" was a more marketable handle than "Artie and Paul," then so be it; pop stars always changed their names. Yet when their debut record made a splash, virtually every feature written about the teen duo, in newspapers ranging from the Forest Hills High School *Beacon* to the *New York World-Telegram and Sun* to the *Long Island Star-Journal,* revealed some combination of the boys' real names, the names of their parents, and the exact name and location of their high school. And they were thrilled. They wanted *everyone* to know who they were and that they were now pop stars. It was the greatest thing that had ever happened to them!

Or so it seemed until late 1965, when the older and more sophisticated pair hit the top of *Billboard*'s Hot 100 with "The Sound of Silence." In the era of Dylan and dissent, when musicians who mattered were expected to be not just artists but also activists, generational spokesmen, and something like sages, a song like "Hey, Schoolgirl" could be

14

a career ender. In their complaint to the New York State Supreme Court, their statements are a pastiche of rage, legalese, and Blanche DuBois. The belated appearance of the Tom and Jerry album was a moral, ethical, and economic travesty: Unfair competition. Unlawful trade. A violation of privacy. An unlawful appropriation of the plaintiffs' duly established trade name, "Simon and Garfunkel."* As Prosen had learned in 1958 and as future defendants and/or aspiring plaintiffs would later discover, Paul Simon wouldn't stand for anything that struck him as a violation of his personal, professional, or economic property. He drew lines and constructed barricades around himself, particularly when it came to defining who he was. So Paul wanted everyone to get this straight. Even if Paul and Artie had been Tom and Jerry, Tom and Jerry had never really been Paul and Artie. And there were others, too — True Taylor, Paul Kane. The existence and the limitations of Paul's alter egos would be courtroom fodder for many years.

This time, the court would rule quickly in

* The affidavit puts the quotation marks around "Simon and Garfunkel," emphasizing that their surnames constitute a duly established trade name. An attorney for Prosen's side responded: "I know of no precedent in which one would call his own legal family name an assumed name."

15

Simon and Garfunkel's favor. Most every copy of Prosen's wayward LP would spend eternity at the bottom of a landfill in New Jersey or Ohio. Still, if the courtroom victory ensured Simon and Garfunkel a clear path to their future, it did little to ease the ache in Paul's muscled chest — the vivid glare of his failings, the dismay of matching eyes with the stumpy, prematurely balding creature in the mirror.

And yet millions of people adored Paul. At twenty-five, he was already phenomenally successful: a hit songwriter and performer whose popularity — Simon and Garfunkel's most recent album had sold three million copies, peaking at No. 4 on the *Billboard* charts — was rivaled only by the critical acclaim that greeted his work. Critics evaluated his songs in terms of poetry and musical innovation. Editorialists interpreted his thoughts as social commentary, statements from the heart of the surging, seething New Generation. Four years out of Queens College, three years after dropping out of Brooklyn Law School, Paul Simon had made himself into one of the most influential voices in Western popular culture. Yet his father, a former professional musician who had remade himself into an educator, couldn't stop telling his famous son that he was wasting his life.

Paul was accustomed to not measuring up

— not physically, given his tiny build and humble facial features; not musically, given his relatively thin singing voice; and not in heritage, due to being the scion of Jewish immigrants growing up in the midst of a largely anti-Semitic culture. And yet no criticism could rival his own unsparing judgment of himself: the standards he could rarely meet, the shame that would plague him after he had taken pleasure in achieving something that made him feel proud. He felt like a phony, and accused others of being the same: Dylan, with his fictional past and bogus name; Artie, Paul's tall, blond, golden-voiced brother in music, for being called a sex symbol. How, Paul asked, could there be a sex symbol named *Garfunkel*? Even while dressing himself in velvet and adding a cape, wraparound sunglasses, and elegant high-heeled boots, he swore he was finished with music and stardom. He'd stick it out another few months, maybe a year, he said, and then abandon the whole enterprise. No more shows, no more records, no more songs. He'd always wanted to be a novelist anyway. "I enjoy singing and rock and roll, but the main thing I want to do is write. That's what I'm living for in between performances. I'm always writing, trying to develop characters so that I can do the Great American Novel." Even in the spring of 1966, in the middle of his first great rush of success, the impulse to

17

be something else, not to settle for whatever or whoever he was at that moment.

Then Paul got writer's block, a months-long spell of creative paralysis that finally ended when he sensed a few chords gathering around him and teased out a thread of melody that led to a vision of a watery fellow sitting alone in the gloom of his manse — a man out of place not just in his home but also in his own skin. His girlfriend lives by her own inscrutable whims. He can barely leave the house, thanks both to the grabby vines in his garden and his skim milk constitution. Even he knows how sad a vision he truly is. "I know I'm fakin' it," he says. "Not really makin' it." Then something happens. He has a vision of himself in an earlier life: not as a washed-out member of the landed gentry, but as a shopkeeper; a man of cotton, silk, wool, and bone; a skilled creator of necessary goods, the garments that keep you warm, dry, and healthy even in the worst of conditions. "A tailor!" — a valued, even beloved, member of his community. And it's a revelation: "I have the tailor's face and hands!" he cries. "I have the tailor's face and hands!"

Recorded in June 1967, "Fakin' It" was released as a single in early July 1968 and became a moderate hit, peaking at No. 23 on *Billboard*'s Hot 100. Paul said later that he was astonished to learn that he was in fact the descendant of a tailor, a tailor who was also named Paul Simon. Simon the elder learned his trade back in the Old World, and brought it with him to the new one at the dawn of the twentieth century, working first in New York City and then crossing the Hudson River to start his own business in Newark, New Jersey. There he made a home and raised his family to be real Americans — smart, ambitious, and hardworking, their eyes locked so securely on the future that it took only two generations for his descendants to forget, or at least pretend not to remember, that he ever existed.

CHAPTER 2
THE TAILOR

Paul Simon the tailor was born in Galicia, then a part of the Austro-Hungarian empire, in 1888.* He grew up in the tight embrace of Jewish family and tradition, supported by his faith, his people, his handed-down trade. The Jews had thrived in eastern Europe for centuries, but more than five hundred years since they brought their families and their faith to the region, the nativist tribes there were again focusing their hatred on the synagogues and shtetls. By the last decade of the nineteenth century, the occasional attacks had grown into pogroms. The ancient black cloaks, the long beards, and the furred hats that had signified their belief for so long now

* Galicia has also been claimed by Hungary and Poland over the years, fueling confusion between our Louis Simon and another Louis Simon who had played violin in the Hungarian National Orchestra before moving to the United States and joining the same musicians' union to which Paul's father would eventually belong.

marked them for torment and death. The traditions that had sustained them, the tribal identity that had knit their communities into extended families, had become ruinous. Individuals, then families, and then entire communities abandoned their homes and fled.

So Paul Simon had gone. It was the spring of 1903, the year of his fifteenth birthday. Already schooled in the ways of the thread, the cloth, the pins, and the numbered ribbon, he packed his things and climbed aboard the train that would take him to the seat of his future. The journey seemed unfathomable: first to Le Havre, home port for the fleet of steamships owned by the Compagnie Générale Transatlantique. There he'd board the steerage deck of *La Gascogne* for the long journey away from the past and to the threshold of the New World — to the United States, and to the modern city at the foot of that great welcoming torch. A whisper of its name was enough to ignite the weariest of Old World eyes. New York City, the global capital of freedom, democracy, culture, and industry; home to peace, brotherhood, and a million Jews already, all of them free to practice their faith and pursue their ambitions. *La Gascogne* carried the young tailor past Liberty's fire and to the immigrants' clearinghouse on Ellis Island. Here some subterfuge occurred: the immigration records describe the Austrian

21

boy as a married forty-year-old farmer who would be met by a Jacob Aushorn, whose only known address was a post office box. That was good enough for the immigration agent on duty, and soon Paul Simon was standing at the foot of Manhattan, which was surprisingly grimy for a promised land, and noisy. But the streets were lit up at night, and the gas-powered cars were already shoving the horse and buggy to the curb — and there he was, an ambitious young man set free in the electrified modern world.

Paul Simon moved quickly. He found a place to live, and then got tailoring work. Soon he married Trieda, a spirited if stubborn Austrian immigrant who preferred to be known as Frieda. The couple moved across the Hudson River to Newark, New Jersey, and by the time the U.S. Federal Census caught up with them in 1920, Paul was thirty-two years old and living in a rented apartment on Somerset Street in Newark's heavily Jewish Ward 3. Their first child, a son named Louis, was four and a half years old, and little Rosie was just a few months short of her third birthday. The census taker noted that the primary language in the home was still "Jewish," meaning Yiddish, but Paul had already submitted his application for citizenship. The application was a formality, given that the enterprising Austrian émigré had built himself a foothold in the American economy, owning a small tailor shop that specialized in European-style wool cloaks. It had taken just ten years for Paul Simon to get from the immigration desk at Ellis Island to owning a business and, as the census noted approvingly, employing other Americans.

Paul and Frieda were happy to stay close to the pickle barrels and black-cloaked merchants of Newark's Third Ward, who had essentially recreated their old lives in a new locale. Most of their neighbors spoke enough English to get by outside the neighborhood, but the old language prevailed, as did the dedication to the synagogue and the wisdom of the ages. Then came the kids: good, obedient children, but American-born and quickly steeped in the lights and the music, the crowds, the five-cent matinees and the American pastime, the sport of baseball.

The school-age Louis became a fan of the sport, then a fiercely partisan fan of the New York Yankees. In the New York of the 1920s the sport was inescapable: the dirt-and-grass fields next to the schools, the boys playing catch in the streets and sawing off broom handles to whack balls in every direction. Baseball was on the front page of the newspaper, on the radio, on everyone's minds. It was a heavily symbolic American bonding ritual that happened to strike immediate and overwhelming terror into the hearts of old-school Jewish parents. They were thinkers, intellectuals, tea drinkers. Baseball was lawless and wild: grown men waving bats and hurling hard balls at one another's heads.

Like other kids, Louis also fell under the spell of the radio and the stomping, sloppy popular music of the day. He couldn't resist the lights and sound calling from the city on the other side of the Hudson. Not that Louis had to cross the river to hear the music. By the mid-1920s it was nearly everywhere: the scratchy signal from the radio speaker, the variety show at the neighborhood theater, the jitterbug rattle shaking the windows of the street corner dance hall. Take the Old World waltz of klezmer and add lights, streamers, and fireworks. To the adults, nothing sounded crazier. To the kids, nothing could be so heady, so alive with the heartbeat of the moment. To be the first true American in your family, to have emerged from a murky and painful past and feel the current in your vertebrae — it changed you.

And Louis could play. He had a feeling for rhythm and for melody, and when they handed out instruments in the classroom, his fingers reached for the right notes and hit them at the right time. Eventually settling on the stand-up bass, the teenager studied and practiced with the diligence of the top student he already was, and earned his first paying gigs when he was still a high school student, filling in for dance bands and orchestras that needed a last-minute player, and then getting enough regular work to become a dues-paying member of the American Federation of Musicians, Northern New Jersey Local 16-248. If Paul and Frieda Simon objected to the sound of hot jazz their boy had taken up, they couldn't complain about how he'd turned his hobby into a profitable venture.

He'd always been a studious boy, the immigrant's dream child, with the brains and fortitude to really make something of himself. Louis never diverged from his path to college. Playing music, he told his parents, was just the trade he'd found to pay his way through school. Accepted into New York University for the fall of 1935, he transferred his union membership to New York's Local 802 and lined up a slate of regular engagements on the weekends and occasional weeknight gigs. He majored in music, grounding his talents with a thorough knowledge of the internal mechanics of melody, harmony, and rhythm.

Living in the university hub of Greenwich Village, Louis met Bella Schulman and fell in love. She was trained as a schoolteacher, the youngest of the four children born to Suniel "Sam" Schulman and his wife, Ettie, a petite young woman with a sunny smile and an easygoing warmth that didn't exist in the Simons' rooms in Newark. Married in 1935, the couple lived at first near Louis's family in

Newark, and then relocated to an apartment at 1748 West First Street, in the Bensonhurst section of Brooklyn, until the arrival of their first child coaxed them back to Newark to raise the dark-eyed bundle they named Paul. The boy was small but healthy, born with his grandfather Paul's dark hair and deep brown eyes. Younger brother Eddie followed in 1944, and Louis and Belle realized they needed to find something larger than the one-bedroom apartment. They turned their eyes to the borough of Queens and the just-developing neighborhood of Kew Gardens Hills.

Rising from what had once been the greens of the Queens Valley Golf and Country Club on the edge of Flushing and Forest Hills, the mostly semidetached houses of Kew Gardens Hills popped up like an urban fantasy of suburban life: curving streets and rustling trees; freshly stamped curbs, sidewalks, and driveways; steady jobs, good schools, and playgrounds; jump ropes flashing and jacks skittering across immaculate concrete. There were people of all ethnic varieties, streets for Italians and Irish, for Poles and Asians, and even a few WASPs, though they were mostly set apart in the stone piles beneath the elms of Forest Hills. And there were even more Jews: the sons and daughters of the immigrants, still working and rising and making a place for themselves defined less by the ethnic and religious ideals of the past than by

26

the American faith in financial and social transcendence.

To be a Jew, but not only a Jew, to be whoever or whatever you chose to become — this was the dream. As the Jewish title character in Saul Bellow's landmark 1953 novel *The Adventures of Augie March* introduces himself in its opening line, he is "an American, Chicago born." Get the picture? "I go at things as I have taught myself, free-style, and will make the record in my own way." So it was for Louis Simon, as it was for millions of the American-born children of the Jewish exodus — because the journey couldn't end on Manhattan's Lower East Side, or in the modern shtetls in Newark and Brooklyn. The American promised land had never really been a particular place; instead, it was an idea, a spinning wheel, a vision of the next horizon. In the mid-twentieth century it looked a lot like the suburbs, the grander and WASPy-er, the better. And if you couldn't get all the way to Westchester County just yet, there was always Queens.

It took the Simons a few years to find the perfect home. In 1944 they lived for a time with one of Belle's brothers in a semidetached brick house at 136-63 Seventy-Second Avenue, across the street from where Jack and Rose Garfunkel had just settled in with the first two of their three boys, though the families didn't know each other then. A few months later the Simons relocated a block away, to an apartment at 141-04 Seventy-First Road, and less than two years later they moved for the final time, settling into 137-62 Seventieth Road, the right half of a compact, two-story redbrick row house on a gently sloping, tree-shaded street. It was a nice, cozy home, but surrounded for blocks with houses so identical that after a long night of work, Louis would sometimes pull his car into a neighbor's driveway and be halfway up the steps before realizing he was at the threshold of someone else's house.

Nevertheless, there they forged their version of postwar middle-class life. For Louis, tradition held little interest, religion even less. Belle felt very differently; she was a regular at the synagogue and happily enmeshed in the community and familiar rituals. Still, Louis set the tone for the boys, and when they felt the need to worship they made the pilgrimage to Yankee Stadium, where they could stand, sit, sing, and pray according to the rituals of American baseball. When Paul was well known enough for people to care about his thoughts on such things, he made it into a joke for the sports pages. Why should anyone focus on religion when there was a pennant to win? "I never saw the point," he said. "Though Al Rosen, the Cleveland third baseman, is Jewish. But I was a Yankee fan so he never really excited me."

Louis was too pragmatic to worship anything, including the romantic ideal of the musician as artist. He didn't need to waltz among the gods to draw the right sounds from his bass. He was a *professional,* sight-reading his parts with perfect rhythm and inflection the moment the music was put in front of him. Always neatly combed and dressed, his tuxedo and instrument rarely beyond an arm's reach, Louis built a diverse set of regular clients, slipping as easily into orchestral performances as he did into society dance bands. He served as a staff bassist with the orchestras of several New York–area radio stations, including WCBS, WAAT, and WOR, and played for the Ballets Russes and with the Alfred Wallenstein Orchestra. Later in his career Louis earned a staff position with the CBS Radio and Television Orchestra, helping provide music to nationally broadcast variety shows by Jackie Gleason, Art Linkletter, and Arthur Godfrey. And he did it all as Lee Simms, a man who could claim every talent, skill, and virtue Louis Simon had developed or been born with, but without the name that immediately identified him as a Jew.

You had to do it; all the big stars already had. The Russian-born Al Jolson lived the first part of his life as Asa Yoelson. Star clarinetist Artie Shaw shortened his name from the original Arthur Arshawsky. Even the songwriters did it. Irving Berlin, another child of Russia, came to America as Israel Beilin. George Gershwin started life as Jacob Gershowitz. And it wasn't just a Jewish thing. The great movie star Rudolph Valentino came out of Italy with the marquee-busting name of Rodolfo Alfonso Raffaello Pierre Filibert Guglielmi di Valentina d'Antonguolla. Tough and burly man's man John Wayne had to ditch the womanly Marion Morrison to establish his cowboy bona fides, while the Missouri actress-dancer Virginia McMath projected her natural elegance so much more clearly when she started calling herself Ginger Rogers.

Showbiz folk from all kinds of backgrounds and disciplines could find reasons to alter or jazz up their names. Yet more Jewish performers found it necessary for the same reason that Jews working in business, the law, or any trade that put them in daily contact with gentiles changed their names: America, as it turned out, wasn't entirely free of anti-Semites. It was a more nuanced kind of prejudice than Jews had encountered in Europe. Physical attacks were rare, and most Americans didn't stoop to insults — not very often anyway. Still, some colleges, including the Ivy League schools, kept their quota of Jewish students to a minimum. Major companies, particularly in the financial and legal trades, refused entry to Jewish professionals, no matter how finely educated or skilled. And even the companies that did welcome Jews weren't likely to give them the opportunities or promotions their gentile workers received. Also, Jews, no matter how wealthy, were often barred from the tonier city and country clubs where so many of their gentile colleagues gathered to raise their glasses, trade stories, and, in the way drink and elaborate food make so easy, cut their deals. Slicing a few syllables from an obviously ethnic name wasn't an automatic pass into the convivial gentile world, but it was, at least, a start.

The elders and the orthodox didn't approve. To abandon your ethnic identity, your *family name,* was at best a cop-out and at worst a self-inflicted cultural purge. Then again, most Jews already had multiple names. Observant Jews get called to the Torah by biblical names that bear little resemblance to the family name they use in daily life. And for families who trace their lineage through eastern Europe or Russia, the chances are excellent that the family name was assigned to them by a tax collector who tracked families either by where they lived or by their patriarch's profession. Names were rooted in European soil, perhaps, but not very deeply. And for Louis's cohort of first-generation Americans, adopting a fresh name and identity felt like liberation, a symbolic declaration of independence so powerful that it is in no way coincidental that *The Jazz Singer,* the

31

smash 1927 film that introduced sound to the movies and made Al Jolson, né Yoelson, a superstar, tells the story of Jakie Rabinowitz, a Jewish boy who turns his back on the synagogue and his cantor father in order to make it big in showbiz as a jazz singer named Jack Robin. It's the classic story of Jewish assimilation, lovingly told by a heavily Jewish industry that would all but ignore obviously Jewish characters for the next several decades.

In an industry peopled heavily with eccentrics, boozers, and bohemians, Louis slipped from band to orchestra to recording session so unassumingly that colleagues he'd played with for years wouldn't know he was present until they heard the agile sound of his bass. The session guitarist Al Caiola recalled Lou best for how absent he could seem even when he was standing in front of you. "Lou," he said, "was really quiet." Yet when Louis formed his own band in the early 1940s, the Lee Simms Orchestra did make a few ripples in New York's dance band scene. Aimed mostly at the society circuit in and around New York City, the band played weddings, bar mitzvahs, debutante parties, and other private affairs. It also won regular gigs at some of New York City's busiest dance clubs, playing most consistently at Club 28, a former casino near the Brighton Beach Race Track, and at the always-hopping Roseland Ballroom (capacity 3,500), in Midtown

Manhattan, where on Thursday afternoons the LSO traded sets with Latin groups. The club engagements, both of which Louis kept well into the 1960s, weren't marquee gigs, but every so often he and his band would get noticed. In the September 30, 1959, issue of *Variety,* the Inside Stuff — Music column featured an item that decried the caliber of New York's dance bands, proposing that most bandleaders could stand a class or two from Lawrence Welk on keeping things simple. The item ended with this: "I would add Lee Simms of Club 28, Brooklyn and Paul Martell of Roseland to the faculty."

There was a sadness about the boy. Even as a baby, Paul would gaze from his swaddling clothes with a look of despair in his dark brown eyes, as if he'd already glimpsed things, terrible things, things that could never be unseen. At first Louis and Belle were concerned, but soon they made a joke of it, referring to the little one as Cardozo, after the pickle-faced Supreme Court justice Benjamin Cardozo. Paul grew into a bright-eyed, inquisitive young fellow, a reader and a listener and an affectionate older brother to Eddie, who looked up to him with the same eyes and was soon big enough to catch the balls Paul tossed, and then toss them back. The boys both took on their father's willful nature and his teasing sense of humor.

Smart, athletic, and personable, Paul was a lot like the other kids at school, except in one way: he was a lot smaller. Small like a mouse. Small like a pipsqueak. Small like the punch line to every short-guy joke the other kids could imagine. Did he live in a dollhouse? Did his mom bring him to school in her pocket? They'd swipe his Yankees cap and throw it among themselves, until Paul finally balled up his fists and went after them. He might have been short, but he definitely wasn't a pushover. He was stronger than he looked, and when it came down to it he could be pretty mean himself. In fact, Paul's penchant for schoolyard fisticuffs unnerved some of his teachers. He'd get his hat back, thank you very much, and make you think twice about ever snatching it off his head again. When the bell rang, he'd march back to the classroom with a vengeance, ripping through the assignments ages before the others, acing tests that reduced other kids to sweat and tears. And he wasn't shy about pointing it out, either: "You thought that was hard? Huh. It seemed kinda obvious to me."

It was more difficult to silence the self-directed abuse, to hush the voice that reminded him just how small he really was, and just how his body's failures would always undermine him no matter where he was or what he was trying to do. And it was only getting worse. Months turned to seasons,

seasons turned to years, and while the others stretched upward, gaining weight and strength as they grew, Paul was lucky to add a fraction of an inch. That wasn't all. When he looked in the mirror, he didn't like the chubby cheeks, flat nose, and heavy beetle brows that greeted him — even then, he knew there was nothing he could do about it except to do everything as well or better than anyone else.

Paul found his archetype for triumph on Louis's knee, the same pin-striped vision that had enraptured his dad thirty years earlier: the visions of glory that were the New York Yankees. Like his father, Paul came to the sport early. When Louis had the time to sit in the kitchen and take in a game, he'd let Paul climb up into his lap and he'd regale the boy with tales of Yankees heroes Gehrig, DiMaggio, and Ruth, the mightiest baseball giants of their age, or any age, the heroic ones, the team that won when the odds were with them and when they weren't. And even if they came up short, as Lou Gehrig did when he discovered he had the fatal neuromuscular disease that would soon bear his name, they still went down in a golden cloak, speaking verse from home plate.

Today . . . I consider myself . . . the luckiest man . . . on the face of this earth . . .

Paul dreamed pinstriped dreams and wore his deep blue NY cap with a disciple's pride.

When Louis took him to Ebbets Field to see the Brooklyn team, the Dodgers, during their pennant-winning 1949 season, the seven-year-old wore a Lone Ranger mask, lest someone mistake him for a follower of the Bums, whose glorious season would end in tears at the hands of — yes, that's right — the New York Yankees. Therein lay the distinction between a soulful, hardworking team and a victory machine staffed with superheroes. If you could choose between them, why would you ever go with the also-rans? "I felt there was enough suffering in real life," Paul said later. "Why suffer with your team?"

A natural athlete, the grade-school-age Paul spent endless hours with his little brother, playing wild indoor basketball games they narrated as dramatic clashes between rival brothers George (Paul) and Mickey (Eddie) Muffchatiery, one of whom (it varied) had come out of retirement for this final fraternal battle. They wrestled and played indoor hockey, and when they felt inspired they'd organize their games into the Simon Olympics, a kind of decathlon with a complex scoring system designed to balance the scales between older and younger brother. When they got a little older they staged boxing matches, hurling punches they would pull a fraction of inch before hard knuckles hit brotherly flesh. The real victory was in outthinking and outmaneuvering each other.

When Belle called, they'd come thumping down the stairs for dinner, taking their places at a table with an empty setting where Louis was supposed to be. It was the evening, and more often than not he'd be recording half a dozen commercials in some Manhattan studio or hunkered down in the back of a nightclub or hotel ballroom, scribbling lead sheets for yet another performance of the Lee Simms Orchestra. Sometimes he missed the boys when he was right there in the house, walled off in a fog of stress and middle-aged frustration, thinking that he had made all the wrong calls in his life, that his career wasn't going anywhere, and that if he'd only gone to graduate school he could be a college professor by now: tenured, secure, and admired. Only he hadn't, and he wasn't, and for Christ's sake, where's that racket coming from? Why aren't those boys studying? They should go to graduate school, they should be the lawyers, doctors, or businessmen he didn't have the vision to become. Belle told Louis to stop being so critical; they were *boys,* for heaven's sake. Give them a chance to have fun before they grow up.

So he would. He'd tell jokes and make them laugh. He'd go outside and toss a ball for a while. But then it was time to go to work again, and he'd shoo the boys off to do their homework, change back into his tuxedo, and lug his bass down the front steps and into the

car for another evening of professional musical conviviality — and another night of knowing that he was working beneath himself and
that the time had come to discover the real
purpose of his life.

CHAPTER 3
OUR SONG

One spring afternoon in 1952 the school buses scheduled to take the kids home from PS 164 were running late. Rather than keep the students cooped up in class, the teachers herded everyone into the school auditorium. Who knew some jokes? Did any of the kids have some kind of talent? One of the fourth-grade teachers had a student who liked to sing for his classmates. Did he want to come onstage and give it a try now? Artie Garfunkel nodded eagerly and came bounding up the aisle. What would he like to sing? Well, his new favorite was Nat King Cole's "They Try to Tell Us We're Too Young." Sounds like a lovely choice; whenever you're ready, the teacher said. The slim boy with blond curls positioned himself at the microphone. When he opened his mouth, the voice that emerged was high and clear, something like bells, only warmer and incredibly rich and sweet.

They try to tell us we're too young
Too young to be in love . . .

Every note was issued without hesitation,
his confidence nearly as mesmerizing as his
voice. Everyone was riveted, the girls positively bedazzled. Hundreds of restless grade-
schoolers went completely silent and still.
Including another fourth-grader, who had
been thinking musical thoughts as of late —
and he wasn't just watching the stage. Looking around him, Paul Simon picked up on
the excitement, the feminine ardor, all because one of their schoolmates had stood up
and sung to them. It was a revelation — the
performance, the applause, the cheers. Could
he do it, too? Hard to say, but he knew one
thing for certain: someday he wanted to get a
slice of those cheers for himself.

Paul kept an eye out for this Garfunkel kid,
catching glimpses of him in the halls or on
the playground, and feeling that familiar tug
of admiration mixed with envy whenever he
popped up at talent shows or in one of the
school musicals. As Paul came to understand,
nearly everyone in the neighborhood either
knew or knew of Artie Garfunkel. He was, as
Paul remembered, "the most famous singer
in the neighborhood." Playing coy, Paul
didn't say a word to his classmate for two
years, until both boys, now twelve years old,
were cast (Paul as the White Rabbit, Artie as

40

the Cheshire Cat) in PS 164's nonmusical production of *Alice in Wonderland.*

Artie could tell that Paul was trying to start a friendship; he was so attentive and enthusiastic. They clicked immediately. Both were smarter than most of their classmates, and neither was shy about mentioning it. They had the same spiky sense of humor and a growing passion for Alan Freed's wild new show on WINS-AM. They lived just three blocks apart, so when school ended in June it was easy for them to find each other and hang out, often for hours at a time, talking about songs they'd been hearing on their radios. *Didja hear this one?* One of them would start singing. If the other boy knew the song, he'd start singing along.

A year earlier Paul wouldn't have risked going line for line with such a gifted singer. After Artie's indelible fourth-grade performance, he hadn't even dared *talking* to him. Since then, though, he'd started singing. Mostly to himself, usually when he was alone in his bedroom. Often he'd take a record player in, shut the door, put on a favorite record, and sing along. That was exactly what he was doing one day, listening to the soundtrack of Disney's animated *Alice in Wonderland* movie and piping along with focus, when his father leaned his head inside to listen. Before Paul could say anything, Louis, freshly scrubbed and knotted into his stage tuxedo, smiled down at him.

"You've got a nice voice."

It was the briefest of exchanges, but for Paul, his father's words rang like an Arthurian investiture. The man wasn't what you'd call unstinting in his praise, particularly when it came to music. Yet: *You've got a nice voice.* He could sing. From his father's lips to the core of his consciousness.

After dinner one summer evening when he was ten years old, Paul stepped outside with a ball and glove and went looking to have a game of catch. He walked around the corner and down the street a ways, maybe a block and a half, and soon he could hear the rhythmic thump of horsehide hitting leather, the easy chat of a boy and a father. When they noticed Paul watching, the father tossed the ball his way and invited him to join in. He was Charlie Merenstein; his son, Ronnie, was exactly Paul's age. They'd just moved to the neighborhood and were crazy for baseball, too. Charlie was also a top-notch coach: he had charisma, knew perfect throwing and batting motion, and had the patience to help a kid get it right. From that point, they were a trio, Charlie hauling the boys to the batting cages every other night, hurling sky-high pop flies and then wicked-fast grounders. Paul was invited to drop in anytime, to come and go like any other member of the family. Charlie lit up when Paul was around and, with Louis away at work so many evenings, Paul came to treasure Charlie's company, too.

A natural athlete with quick reflexes and a strong arm, Paul started playing Little League baseball as soon as he was old enough to qualify for a team. He held his own against the other kids, but as they moved toward junior high school and the game became more competitive, Paul was no longer eligible to play with his regular teammates. Due to his height, he would be relegated to a special league for boys shorter than five feet tall. Devastated but still determined, he made himself into a team leader, fielding with a famished glove and spring-loaded arm that picked off runners with deadly efficiency. He swung a fearsome bat, too, snapping off line drives fast and low enough to be all but ungrabbable. Paul wasn't the team's only asset, and at season's end the team had fought its way into the league's all-city classic, a single-game duel against Staten Island for the championship. The league required each player to submit to a pregame height measurement, just to make sure that neither team had snuck in a ringer. And wouldn't you know it, Paul learned he had grown just enough that summer to put himself a hair or two above the five-foot mark, which disqualified him from the championship game. Enraged by the double humiliation, he stomped to the bleachers and spent the rest of the afternoon rooting for his squad to lose — which they did, granting their exiled hero at least a shred of satisfaction.

One day in 1954 Paul tuned in to the Yankees versus Boston Red Sox game on WNEW-AM and caught the last few minutes of *The Make Believe Ballroom,* the station's pop and jazz show that had been one of the most popular music broadcasts in the nation since its debut in 1935. The public enthusiasms of host Martin Block had built careers for the likes of Tony Bennett, Dinah Shore, and many more. That day, Block was sputtering, his clipped mustache a-twitch about a song he'd heard that was already hurtling up the pop charts, a guaranteed smash hit. Only it couldn't be true, because this was the *worst tune he'd ever heard in his life.* It was so bad, in fact, that if it actually *did* become a hit, he'd eat his hat. Dropping needle on wax, the radio host died just a little bit more as the Crows, a four-man doo-wop group out of Harlem, let fly the "duh-dudu-duh-duh . . . love that girl!" opening to "Gee."

That was when Paul looked up from his scorecard. He'd been only half-listening to the music, but Block's rant had caught the boy's ear, and less than a minute into "Gee," he knew that it was the first song he'd heard Block play that he actually *liked.* Just four voices set to a jump blues quartet banging away at the velocity of a Manhattan-bound IRT express. The music was simple and the words even more so. "Hold me baby, squeeze me, / Never let me go!" For the likes of Block and probably 96 percent of the aged and/or aging *Make Believe* listeners, that made "Gee" the iciest kind of portent: the sound of a future that doesn't include you.

They were right. This new music, that pounding, jiving rhythm with its three-chord verses, four-note melodies, and horny fifth-grader lyrics, was spreading fast. The year before, 1953, onetime country swing band Bill Haley and the Comets hit No. 12 on the *Billboard* charts (and No. 11 on *Cash Box*) with "Crazy, Man, Crazy." Next came Big Mama Thornton, dominating the rhythm and blues charts for more than two months with "Hound Dog," a jump blues shouter composed by a pair of Jewish wiseasses, Jerry Leiber and Mike Stoller, already becoming the hottest pair of songwriters in the Brill Building, the eleven-story art deco building that was considered the center of New York's pop music industry. "Gee" took a little longer to break through — released in 1953, it had simmered for almost a year, creeping onto regional sales charts. The tune broke big during the summer of 1954, racking up enough sales and plays to make it a crossover smash: No. 2 on the rhythm and blues charts and

No. 14 on the pop list. By the end of that year, "Gee" had sold more than a million copies and helped launch a renaissance for doo-wop, the kind of harmony-rich group singing first made popular in the late 1930s and early 1940s by the Mills Brothers and the Ink Spots. Now, fifteen years later, those older groups' perfectly enunciated ballads had come to sound as stiff as the tuxedos they performed in. They'd sung about love with a chaste formality that seemed almost completely desexualized, the kind of lovemaking you can do while sitting on her parents' front porch. But their inheritors had moved closer to the bedroom. Spin "Earth Angel" or "In the Still of the Night" and you can hear the eroticism oozing through the swirling *ooh*s and *ah*s. This love song was slinky and silky, passionate and, if you were a boy on the cusp of adolescence, thrilling.

The not-quite-thirteen-year-old Paul Simon found just as much in the music as in the lyrics. He loved the way voices joined in harmony added up to so much more than the sum of the two or three or four parts; the way the intertwined melody and harmony connected to backing chords that moved in strict adherence to the rhythm, which, he noticed, also dictated the meter of the lyrics, but also the words' balance of consonants and vowels. The sound was so electrifying he couldn't resist presenting it to Louis. Surely

46

his father would recognize the beauty, too, and maybe even admire Paul's ability to discover new and beautiful things in pop music. But that's not quite how it turned out.

They were driving, just the two of them, when Paul started prattling on about Patti Page's 1952 version of "I Went to Your Wedding," how lovely a tune it was, with this melody he couldn't get out of his head. To illustrate his point, Paul sang a few lines. He didn't get very far before Louis cringed.

"God, that's *awful*!"

Louis might as well have slapped him. Paul's father had ridiculed his favorite song and worse, far worse, had called his singing awful, too. Or at least that's how Paul heard it. "Boy," he remembered in a 1991 interview, "I just sat back and I said, 'Well, all right. I'm not singing any more here.'"

Still, that didn't keep Paul from trying to pry out exactly what was so wrong with the music he loved. He went back to his father on several occasions, with a record or when another one of his favorite songs came on the radio. He took it for granted that Louis would get that same disgusted look, but now he wanted an explanation. *Why* don't you like it? Louis made a face. "Because it's really *dumb.*" Paul couldn't believe it. Dumb? "Earth Angel," that spine-rattling piece of vocal perfection, with that clever image of the girl being both an angel and still on earth?

47

Louis shrugged. "I just think it's dumb."

Of course that was typical middle-aged dad stuff. But the twelve-year-old Paul didn't know that. What he'd heard was derision, a fresh bulletin about his shortcomings. He never forgot it.

At the end of sixth grade, Paul and Artie were both accepted into the Special Progress program for advanced students at Parsons Junior High. Neither of them, to say nothing of their parents, would have dreamed of passing up the opportunity to study with Queens' smartest kids, but the program came with another benefit: the students would complete three years of the junior high school curriculum in just two years. The only drawback, as they soon discovered, was that the only way for them to walk the mile from their houses to the school led directly through a neighborhood claimed by the Parsons Boys, a gang of leather-clad teenage thugs who made an enterprise extracting cash from the pockets of young or otherwise helpless passersby. Paul and Artie encountered the gang within a day or two of starting seventh grade and came to call them the Hitters, after the gang members' traditional methods of intimidation. Thumpings, or promises of them, became a regular event. The two boys learned to weather the abuse as best they could.

Music remained Paul and Artie's central

fixation, and the more they listened to Alan Freed's show, to the nightly Top 20 broadcasts, and to the array of other stations crowding the New York City airwaves, the deeper their connection became. Paul was the more adventurous listener. He had become fond of the Latin dance band that shared the bill with the Lee Simms Orchestra's Thursday afternoon shows at Roseland, and now he spun through the far edges of his radio dial, constantly on the prowl for unfamiliar sounds. Artie, meanwhile, kept track of the weekly *Hit Parade* broadcasts with mathematical precision, charting each song's rises and tumbles in neatly penciled graphs, cross-indexed to reveal new textures in the weekly, monthly, and annual trends.

Artie took to the family's basement playroom to find his way through the lead and background parts of the new songs. His father, Jack Garfunkel, a wholesale representative for a clothing manufacturer, was an early technology fan and had been one of the very first owners of home recording equipment. First came a Webcor wire recording device, then a Wollensak reel-to-reel. The machines were easy to operate, so the Garfunkel boys — Jules was the eldest, Artie came next, and baby brother Jerry was last — had learned to operate the rudimentary devices without much effort. The recorders became Artie's vocal laboratory. Drawn to sentimental tunes and juicy love ballads, he'd emote his way through "You'll Never Walk Alone" or a Nat King Cole song, and then play back the recording and harmonize with his own melody part. At one point the family owned two recorders, which allowed Artie to record one part, then record himself singing along to the original tape, and finally come up with a third part while singing along with the second, two-voiced recording.

Paul started to join the afternoon basement sessions. They'd listen to a record or two, singing along at first and then by themselves, each boy locking his eyes on the other's mouth in order to sync not just the words but each syllable and intonation. "I would sit and examine exactly how Paul says his 'T's at the end of words," Garfunkel said. "And where would the tongue hit the palate exactly. And we would be real masters of precision." Kid brother Jerry Garfunkel became accustomed to getting booted out of the basement playroom so the older boys could work uninterrupted. Often he'd take refuge on the top stairs to listen to them work, chat, and goof around. It didn't take long for Jerry to notice how easily they made each other laugh, and how much it reminded him of their dad's usual patter. "I'm sure Paul's father had the same humor, too. It's Jewish sarcasm, and [some people] get insulted by it. But back then, there was no arrogance: just two kids trying to sound as good as they could."

Paul and Artie sang in public together for the first time midway through the school year, doing the Chords' doo-wop hit "Sh-Boom" at a Parsons talent show. Neighborhood doo-wop groups were popping up everywhere, and the boys teamed with a fellow student, Johnny Brennan, and sisters named Ida and Angel Pelligrini to form the Sparks. A few weeks later the quintet redubbed themselves the Pep-Tones, as a tip to the Cleftones, a junior high doo-wop group from the Jamaica section of Queens who had just scored a national pop hit with their self-composed "You Baby You." Although Paul had abandoned an early attempt at piano lessons, he asked for and received a guitar[*] for his thirteenth birthday.[†] Louis showed him

[*] Much to the bemusement of younger brother Eddie, who had excelled at guitar ever since he began lessons a year or two earlier. Eddie Simon went on to teach the instrument and open his own guitar school in New York.

[†] A three-quarter-size sunburst steel string made by the Stadium guitar company. The guitar obviously came from Louis, and when Paul broke a string while attempting to tune the instrument, he was too embarrassed to admit it and so put the instrument back in its case and didn't touch it for a few days. When he finally fessed up, Louis shrugged it off. Guitar strings break all the time.

some basic chords, and Paul soon realized how often the same two- or three-chord progressions would come up in different songs. He showed the archetypical changes to Artie, and they crafted an original doo-wop they called "The Girl for Me," a paean to a flower-bedecked dream girl whom the singer will love forever, knowing that she'll always be true. Convinced the song was just as strong a contender for the charts as any other teen-oriented pop tune, Paul got Louis to transcribe the music onto a lead sheet, which he and Artie sent to the U.S. Library of Congress in order to copyright the tune. Next they recorded a demo (probably on the acetate-cutting machine one of the Garfunkels' neighbors owned), and brought it to a handful of the publishers and record companies in and around the Brill Building on the west side of Manhattan's Midtown. No one was buying, but the company execs there might have been wise to take note of the audacity of the youngsters, confident enough at the moist age of thirteen to stride into office after office bearing their first-ever pop composition.

The other touchstones of teenage life came and went for Paul at the standard pace. Compelled by Belle and her fealty to tradition, he celebrated his bar mitzvah on his thirteenth birthday, with Artie following just six weeks later. In typical fashion, Artie not only mastered the Hebrew in his assigned section of the Torah, but also worked with the synagogue's cantor so he could sing parts of the service. When they worked on a harmonized section, the not-quite-teenage Garfunkel gave as much direction as he received, going so far as to shake off the cantor's instructions to stand away from their shared microphone, issuing the older man such confident directions that he acquiesced immediately.

ARTIE: (firmly) You keep it the same and I'll know just when to change, because it was fine before, except for one or two parts.
CANTOR: (changing position) This is okay?
ARTIE: No. You're gonna have to keep it closer.
CANTOR: Okay.

When they started singing, Artie took the higher part, his harmony closely tracking the cantor's melody for a time, sometimes in unison before closing to a standard third interval, then abruptly leaping to a fifth before tumbling back down again — his harmonies sounding very much like those he would write and perform a little later in his life.

Around this time, Paul traded in his baseball bat for a broom handle bat and took to the stickball circuit around central Queens.

He and longtime ball mate Ronnie Merenstein would venture into other neighborhoods
in search of the high-bouncing Spaldeen-
brand ball-carrying kids they could challenge
to a game. Their strategy came right out of
Hustling 101. After letting their rivals run up
a big lead during the first few innings, Paul
and Ronnie would call things to a halt. How
about starting a new game, only this time
putting some money on the line to make it a
little more interesting? Wagers made and
secured, they'd start up again. Only, now
everything was different. Toss a pitch at the
short kid and, instead of whiffing it like he'd
done through the first game, he'd uncoil and
kablammo!, the pink ball would go airborne,
sailing over two, three, sometimes *four* man-
hole covers before touching down again. The
taller guy was suddenly just as dangerous at
the plate, and when it was their turn on
defense, the short one hurled left-handed
curves that were all but unhittable. By the
time he got home at the end of the afternoon,
Paul could have as much as fifteen or even
twenty dollars stuffed in his pocket.

He would have done it all for free. "He was
a very good ballplayer because he worked
harder at it than most other people. And he
always wanted to be on the winning team,"
Ronnie Merenstein said. And it didn't matter
what sport he was playing or how low the
stakes were. When the boys played sock

basketball in Paul's bedroom, he'd lunge at the hoop as if they were playing in Madison Square Garden, sometimes with enough force to put Merenstein on the floor. But soon Paul wouldn't have time for bedroom athletics. If he wasn't working on music with Artie, he'd be shut in his room with his schoolbooks. When he finished with that, he'd pick up his guitar and work on new chords and progressions, repeating them over and over, sometimes for two or three hours, even as his fingertips cracked and blood crusted the strings and frets.

Adopting a patina of the delinquent fuck-off of teenage life, Paul and Artie took up cigarettes, trailing smoke and as much toughness as they could muster during their daily walks to and from school. They moved easily through Parsons Junior High School's accelerated program, leap-frogged ninth grade, and got to high school in the fall of 1955. After Parsons, which was cozy even for a junior high, Forest Hills High School seemed mammoth. Completed in 1941, the Georgian Revival structure was faced by red brick with limestone edging and white columns reaching toward a bell tower (a bonus feature chosen over a swimming pool). It had been designed to hold thirteen hundred students, but population projections for the area hadn't anticipated so much new construction in

Kew Gardens Hills, or the surge of child-births in the 1940s. By the mid-1950s the building had more than four thousand registered students. To serve them all, the administration was forced to divide the school into three independent programs that operated at different times of the day. As entering sophomores, Paul and Artie started their classes at noon and finished at 5:30 p.m., a schedule that meant they saw juniors for only half the day and never encountered seniors, who had to clear the classrooms before the younger kids could squeeze into the building.

No matter which grade-level students crowded into its overstuffed and understaffed classrooms, the place ran thick with academic and social ambition. Located at the hub of Flushing, Kew Gardens Hills, and Forest Hills, the school for many years had drawn from a mix of wealthy, up-and-coming, and stable working-class neighborhoods whose families demanded the best of their children. The recent influx of upwardly mobile Jews and other immigrants in Kew Gardens Hills, the quasi-suburb that represented what many of them viewed as only a midpoint on their journey to the American bourgeoisie, made the atmosphere that much more intense. These families knew that there were bigger trees to live beneath, fancier homes with lawns that sprawled and groomed hedges that hid swimming pools and private tennis courts.

To get there, they wanted rigorous classes for their kids. Not coincidentally, Forest Hills High sent more of its graduates to Ivy League colleges than any other school in the city.

Although at least a year younger than their classmates, Paul and Artie fit easily among the tenth-graders. Paul could be funny and charming, and he and Artie were often found at lunchtime singing with the doo-wop fans by the flagpole at the front of the school. He wasn't a campus hero, but Paul usually had a girl or two to flirt with: Donna, Pam, a few others. He played the field in that teenage way: obsessed one day, quivering with excitement the next, then broken up and back on the hunt. He went for looks but also required intelligence, working knowledge of baseball, and at least *some* appreciation for pop music. When he and Artie double-dated, they would play off each other's jokes and reduce one another to squinch-eyed fits of giggles. Later, the boys and their dates would head back to Artie's place, lower the lights, and settle into separate corners of the basement. The hot breathing and smooches and whispers didn't stay secret for very long — not between Paul and Artie, anyway.

When he had time to himself, Paul liked to wander. He'd wheel his bike around the borough, baseball glove tucked into the handlebars, and look for action. If he couldn't find a stickball or baseball game, he'd explore the streets and buildings, taking in the smells from the restaurants, the voices and different languages, the music drifting from apartment windows and barroom doors. Irish, Italian, Puerto Rican, the Caribbean — all those lives unfolding just a mile or three from his own front door, people living in the same place, feeling so many of the same things, only in completely different rhythms. Paul had the same experience roving the radio dial at night. New York had it all: pop, rhythm and blues, jazz, gospel, country, Latin. And when the weather was right, he could pick up signals from Philadelphia, Baltimore, Boston. In those days, every city and region had its own distinctive sound. Philadelphia soul had its own kind of swing. The rural towns in New Jersey played a reedier, twangier brand of country music, as Appalachia as it was Nashville. The patchwork spirit of the old days still survived, a quilt of rural hollers, industry towns, ethnic neighborhoods, social clubs, and large extended families.

Artie focused on the hit parade, ears tilting to a pretty love song, his schematic brain tracking the curvature of the melody, the contrasting gradients of the harmonies. The relatively obscure rhythm and blues duo Robert and Johnny ("We Belong Together") had an upside-down blend that put the melody on top and the harmony voice below. Nobody could match the streamlined Kentucky twang of the Everly Brothers, the sound of chrome-plated hickory. There were others: the Orioles, the Moonglows, Frankie Lymon.

Late into the night, Paul and Artie would be alone in their respective bedrooms, but listening to the same songs and feeling the same irresistible pull to do it themselves. They'd take what they heard into Artie's basement, or to the even cozier space beneath the Simon house, and pull it apart and put it back together again, working until they could match the singers syllable for syllable, note for note, breath for breath. Sometimes, when they pulled a song apart, they'd shuffle through the component pieces and find ways to snap them into new and slightly different forms. These were silly little songs, teenage fantasies of dream girls, silky romance, and heartbreak. Half the kids in New York were probably up to the same thing on any given day. But these two voices, so sweet and high and tightly knit, could cut through even the worst clichés. And if their run through the Brill Building two years earlier with "The Girl for Me" had turned out to be disappointing, the experience did nothing to discourage them from writing and copyrighting more original songs. Once they had a tune they figured was as catchy as anything else on the radio, they'd head back to Midtown with Paul's guitar to see if they could charm one of the gruff men lurking in one of the Brill's cell-like offices to publish or maybe even let them record it. Nothing came of it — beyond Artie's realization that he was far more uncomfortable with rejection than Paul. No matter — when they got back to Kew Gardens Hills, he would pick up his guitar and get to work on a new song. Paul and Artie copyrighted "Rock with Me Tonight" not long after, and then "Now Is Goodbye" (". . . If you have trust in me / Please know that I will love you faithfully . . ."). They were just getting started.

But where were they headed? That's what worried Louis Simon. He'd wandered down the same path when he was Paul's age, and where had it taken him? What had started as a fun way to make money for school had become his career, and now he was stuck in his cookie-cutter house on the cookie-cutter block of a working-class neighborhood in Queens. He'd lost track of who he was supposed to be. This Lee Simms character, the smiling, tuxedo-wrapped entertainer, was little more than a glorified servant: a follower of orders, a reader of scripts, a living ornament at the parties where other intelligent, ambitious men were *celebrated,* not employed. Yet Louis Simon was an intelligent man, an intellectual with serious ideas about education and philosophy. The work of his life, still ahead of him, was not going to be done with a stand-up bass anchoring him to the floor.

This realization first hit Louis in the mid-1950s, when he was still in his thirties, not too old to make a change, but definitely not a young man by any stretch of the imagination. From there the path was obvious: he would go back to New York University and, at long last, get the advanced degree he should have pursued right after he graduated from college in 1939. He started work on a master's degree in education and made steady progress, earning his MA in the early 1960s. Louis continued supporting his family with music until then, and it would take another decade for him to earn a full Ph.D. But he already felt like a new man, and wasn't shy about telling his older son how thrilling it was to realize that he wouldn't have to be a working musician for the rest of his life.

Louis Simon would be a teacher, one of the most honored professions in the Jewish tradition. Education had been a central pillar of American Jewish culture since 1889, when the primarily upscale German Jews whose parents arrived in the mid-nineteenth century created the Educational Alliance, a privately funded group dedicated to teaching both English and the fundamentals of American society and social etiquette to the waves of unschooled Jewish workers and farmers washing in from eastern Europe. It was an

61

exercise in organized altruism — one freighted with condescension. If you'd picked up a copy of the *Jewish Messenger* from that period, you'd have read pro–Educational Alliance editorials that dismissed the unsophisticated new arrivals as "slovenly in dress, loud in manners and vulgar in discourse." Louis never achieved that level of smugness, certainly not in public, but he made a point of telling his son, repeatedly, that the highest calling in life was to teach others the things you'd learned for yourself. Otherwise, you'd spend a lifetime enriching yourself to the benefit of no one else — and then what was the point of your presence on earth?

Paul was dutiful enough to listen to his dad, but he had no intention of heeding him. He had long since figured that his father's career in music was the coolest thing about him. He liked Louis's fellow musicians, who were funny, quirky guys, and he already knew he was a different kind of musician from his dad. He wanted to write his own songs and be the guy who stood in front of the musicians in the orchestra. *He* wanted to be a star. The Cleftones were on the *Billboard* charts — in fact, the music shops were full of records made by teenagers. So why them? And why not him?

Louis didn't get it — he didn't want to get it. But Charlie Merenstein did. Paul was playing less baseball these days, but he was still a regular at the Merensteins' dining room table on the evenings Louis was at work. The bond that began with baseball had deepened as Paul grew up, and if baseball was Charlie Merenstein's hobby, music was his business.

Charlie's sister Bess and her husband, Ike Berman, along with two other friends, had cofounded Apollo Records in the early 1940s. Bess had been running the small independent label for several years, but she grew sickly in the early 1950s and invited her then-unemployed brother to come to New York and take it over. Although a perennially underfinanced operation, the label had a reputation for finding and building careers for under-recognized talents, including the gospel great Mahalia Jackson, rhythm and blues singer Dinah Washington, R&B songwriter/performer Doc Pomus, and others in the African American music world.

Most of the label's biggest artists eventually abandoned Apollo for the gold-plated major labels, but Apollo's reputation for finding new hit makers persisted even after Charlie Merenstein took over in 1953. Charlie may have had no musical experience prior to that, but he proved to have excellent ears, discovering and producing records for, among others, Solomon Burke and Jimmy Jones. He cowrote Jones's defining hit "Handy Man," which went on to become a global smash when James Taylor recorded it in 1977. The

Cellos' hit "Rang Tang Ding Dong (The Japanese Sandman)," the Delroys' "Bermuda Shorts," and the Chesters' landmark single "The Fires Burn No More" bear Charlie Merenstein's mark.

Charlie had heard enough of Paul and Artie's compositions to know that Paul would eventually be as capable of writing hits as any aspiring young songwriter, though maybe not for Apollo's African American–dominated roster. Charlie did what he could to help the boy see his way into the music business — and it was just as it was with baseball, really, the other passion they shared: you needed a core of God-given talent to get started. After that, it was all hard work: honing your tools, practicing the skills, forever pushing at the boundaries of your abilities, then going right back to hone, practice, and push even harder than you did before. Actually, Paul didn't need anyone to explain that to him; he never had — which was another reason Charlie was so sure about the boy's future.

Around Kew Gardens Hills, Paul had become the kid with the guitar. He'd take it to the playground, to the park, onto the subway for the long ride to Coney Island. While his buddies tossed a ball around and called out to girls, Paul would shoulder his instrument and belt pop songs. Friends would drift over, then strangers, too. Girls, especially. He was already a good showman, witty and crowd-conscious, always happy to take requests and goof on himself when he fumbled a chord or didn't know the words. He had a strong rhythm hand, and when things really got going he'd have his friends clapping and singing along. They'd applaud when he was finished, and maybe a girl or two he didn't know would hang back later and ask where he went to school. Sometimes he'd go home with a telephone number stuffed in his pocket.

It was even better with Artie on board. When they did their Urban Everlys act at the Forest Hills High School talent show at the end of their sophomore year in 1956, the cheers were so wild they could only look at each other and laugh. Amazing! They were both famous in the neighborhood after that one, and to Paul, the feeling of being known and recognized was intoxicating. People called out to him on the street — and not just kids; the grown-ups knew who he was now, too. He started selecting his clothes with more care, and investing a bit more time in the construction of his piled-up-and-swept-back hairstyle. He felt attractive on a good day, even given his increasingly chubby cheeks, heavy brows, and thickening adult nose. On a big stage, it was still easier for him to have Artie alongside. No one was going to laugh at Artie's seraphic curls and finely cut cheekbones — and that voice! When Paul wove his ordinary voice together with Artie's dulcet instrument, he knew he sounded better than he ever could on his own. Artie had become so many things to Paul: his best friend, his partner, his musical inspiration, and increasingly his rival, too. On a darker day Paul would examine his friend from afar and feel a pulse of bile. Why had Artie gotten to be so blessed, with his height, his voice, his hair? And why did Paul have to be so dependent on him? Paul was the one who could play guitar. He didn't need Artie to help him write a song or face down a real audience — unless he did, and that need put kerosene in Paul's veins.

Paul's insecurities were every bit as clear to Artie as their shared impulse to outdo each other whenever the opportunity arose. And when Paul started bragging about his stickball heroics or the pretty girl who had all but asked him to ask her out, Artie knew exactly where Paul's fault lines lay, and how much of a tremor it would take to knock him off balance. Still, their friendship ran deeper than their rivalry, and when they were in the public eye, Artie made a point of standing slightly behind Paul, or even hunching a little to make their height disparity less obvious. Artie didn't say anything about it, but Paul was well aware of what his friend was doing — which made Paul that much more dependent on Artie, and then his cheeks reddened and he wondered again why a guy as smart, talented, and popular, goddammit, as he was should need anyone to do anything for him.

Yet who else was he going to hang out with? Who else could see the hilarity of an imaginary Fattest Girl in the School contest, then roll on the floor laughing half an hour later when Paul leaped to his feet to greet a visiting rotund girl by shouting, to the confusion of everyone except Artie, "You're the winner!" They both got sent to detention for that one, but it was worth it. Artie was still laughing about it fifteen years later, recalling that absurdist goofball humor they shared, a juvenile punch-and-kick comedy fueled by the adolescent reality of high expectations, harsh judgments, and the terror of being anything less than entirely perfect.

Taking jobs at different camps for the summer of 1957, Paul and Artie traded letters describing remarkably similar weeks of shaving cream fights, busted curfews, midnight raids, and serial romances with the female staffers. To Artie, who had never been to a camp of any sort, the experience was a revelation. He was learning how to play tennis, he had met at least two great friends, and he'd fallen in love at least three times already. So many of the girls were really "pretty and built," and out of the twenty-five at least five or six were really nice — "and that's a damn good average." That any of them was even interested in him was easy to figure: "I've been doing a lot of entertaining, and it has made me pretty popular." Paul had been up to the same thing. "You can imagine what a crazy guitar-thumpin' kid can do to these kids." When he wasn't wowing 'em with his guitar, he could do it with a racquet and a fuzzy white ball. ("I'm afraid you've had it, Garf, I'm slightly great in tennis.") After hours, he'd jump into a car with the black kitchen staffers and ride for hours, driving from town to town and cranking the radio dial between rhythm and blues stations. On a couple of occasions, he and another guy sneaked back to New York to catch Alan Freed's rock 'n' roll revues at the Paramount Theatre in Brooklyn, finding their way back to camp just in time to serve breakfast to the unsuspecting campers. And that wasn't the half of it. Paul had also gone steady with three different girls so far, and was "workin' on" another so intently it was biting into his tennis time. It's hard to imagine a better way for a highly pressured independence-starved city kid to spend his sixteenth summer, so how to account for the anger that erupts in his looping cursive script. The former pro who had been teaching Paul and another friend how to play tennis each day turned out to be "a fuck, though. I hate his guts." Turning his attention to a girl he'd met just before leaving Queens for the summer, Paul reprinted a few choice phrases from a letter she'd sent, the better to ridicule her imprecise description of a baseball game she'd seen. The girl, he concluded, was "so pitifully stupid its [sic] pathetic . . . Incidentally I really liked her."

Paul was becoming a seething young man, a slave to the invidious comparison, acutely attuned to the pleasure of dealing a truly nasty bolt of humiliation. Yet flash-forward a year, and he was back in camp, this time as a counselor to a cabin full of seven-year-olds. They were the youngest campers, not all of them entirely happy to be away from their parents, their dogs, the stabilizing comforts of home. Paul kept an eye on the quiet ones, reading the sorrow at the corners of their mouths, including them in all the cabin hijinks, keeping the jokers and bullies from making sport of the smaller and weaker. When one homesick camper peed in his bed in the middle of the night, Paul got the weeping boy cleaned up and tucked him into his own dry bed before tossing a blanket over the boy's wet mattress and spending the rest of the night sleeping there. The boy had the same accident a few nights later, and Paul responded in exactly the same way, then made certain to change the subject quickly when another camper asked why the two kept switching bunks.

Paul the counselor was warm and inclusive. He composed and sang funny songs about camp at meals and around the campfire, and reveled in the corny jokes and sing-alongs that left the kids giggling and humming at the same time. When Artie paid a visit late in the summer, Paul arranged for them to sing a set of songs for all the campers, wowing them with their tight harmonies and all-around professionalism. It was a highlight in the kids' scrapbooks, many of which included at least one snapshot of Paul, that cool counselor with the guitar. A lot of them never forgot him, even the ones who weren't music fans enough to realize, until many years later, that their former counselor had written his guitar into very different circumstances. A former camper, Helen Strassner, saw Paul and Artie perform ten or so years later and gathered with the fans and autograph seekers near the stage door after the show. When the door swung open Helen went straight to Paul and reintroduced herself. She had been at Camp Washington Lodge, he had been her brother's counselor one year, they were *so* happy for his success, so proud to have known him back when . . .

Paul shrugged. He looked through her. A summer camp? He didn't know what she was talking about. "I never went to camp." He turned away. But she had a snapshot; she'd taken it herself: of her little brother's counselor playing guitar outside their cabin, beaming into the Brownie lens, a Brylcreemed teenager having a ball on a gorgeous summer afternoon. Yet a decade had passed, and things had changed. Different times, different values, a different Paul.

CHAPTER 4
NOWHERE TO GO BUT UP!

Together in the basement they spent hours sitting nose to nose. Paul strumming his guitar and the both of them singing, each matching the other's notes and timing until both could focus on the micro-elements of vocalizing. Artie stared into his partner's mouth to see where Paul's tongue moved when he formed his consonants. Mimicking the shape his lips formed when he was singing "ooh." They'd set up a record player and listen to how the Bronx rhythm and blues duo Robert and Johnny traded parts mid-song, switching the melody between the higher and lower voices. They listened to hit records until they could isolate the discrete vocal, melodic, harmonic, and rhythmic pieces. Once they had that worked out, they'd put them back together in slightly different ways, crafting their own words and melody until they had a fresh song that sounded like something you'd hear on that week's hit parade.

Songs about dancing, about school, and about feeling like an idiot; goofy songs about girls; hushed songs about falling in love, about being in love, about breaking up and then falling for someone else — it didn't seem hard. There were only so many chords and notes in the scale, and you didn't even need to be in love to sing about it. Just figure out what everyone's already saying and say it again, only with a catchy opening riff or a funny twist to the lyric. They slapped songs together like jigsaw puzzles — the bright blue skies up here, the reds over there, the squiggly lines where the lake is. Two hours later it'd be done and they'd upend another box and start again. If one song seemed a cut above the others, they'd get Louis to write it down in musical notation, drop seven bucks to get it copyrighted, and then spend an afternoon or two shopping it around in Midtown Manhattan. The first few times they went out more or less blind, like kids who thought they were in a movie about teenagers who stumble into stardom by accident. Since they weren't in a movie, though, and had the rejections to prove it, they decided to bring their newest tunes to Charlie Merenstein so he could give them a listen.

Charlie, who rarely uttered a discouraging word in Paul's company, didn't disappoint. Yes, he *could* imagine hearing a few of those tunes on the radio. Better still, he knew a few guys in town who would give them a listen, too. So go see Sol Rabinowitz at Baton Records. If he didn't like any of them, try Ben Kaslin at Hull. No go? Well, Charlie could call Morty Craft over at Melba Records. He was a good friend, so he'd give them a fair hearing. Charlie accompanied the boys to Craft's office and stood by as they played and sang. When they were done, Craft nodded. He wasn't sure if he'd heard the right song yet, but he did think they probably had it in them, so he offered them a contract — more of a holding deal, but don't worry about that, he said. Just keep working. Whenever you've got a few new songs, come on in and we'll see if we have a single. They signed happily and then got back to writing, but they couldn't come up with anything that lit a fire in Craft's eyes. Nine months later they were out of the deal with nothing to show for it.

Then they wrote "Hey, Schoolgirl." It was the start of their senior year at Forest Hills High School, just a few weeks away from their sixteenth birthdays. The song's theme was harmless at best — charmingly devilish classroom chatter from a boy who wants a cute girl to ditch class with him. At first she fends him off. She's too young to date. She can't skip school and, besides, she's got too much homework to do that afternoon. But he keeps at it, and she thinks again. By the last verse, she's got "that gleam" in her eye.

When the period ends, they're out the door and down the street, class and homework forgotten, romance in the air, and teenage fun already in motion. The song took an hour to write, they said. It was a quickstepping tune built from tight guitar strums, tambourine slaps, and a jumping acoustic bass line. The opening vocal riff, a quickly repeated "Ooh-bop-a-lucha-bop, you're mine!" is straight out of Little Richard (see "Tutti Frutti"'s "a-whop-bobba-lu-bop-a-whop-bam-boom"), but the harmonized lead vocals, along with the hop-skip-jump turnaround between verse lines, are pure Everly Brothers. The short instrumental break pairs the rhythm guitar with the bass, and once the final verse propels the young couple out of school and down the street, the "Ooh-bop-a-lucha-bop"s send them into the sunset.

The song had the spark. When they sang it for Charlie, he clapped and said he could imagine putting it out. Louis transcribed the music for the Library of Congress forms, and with all that in hand they trooped back to Midtown Manhattan to knuckle the doors, launch into their tune, and hope the skeptical-to-visibly-impatient man on the other side of the desk would let them get through at least a verse and a chorus before barking them back into the hallway. They shopped it around for days, and no one bit. Artie was too sensitive to let the humiliation roll off his back, but no amount of disinterest could dissuade Paul. He knew they had a good song. They owed it to themselves to give it all they had. In that spirit, they put together the money required to record a proper demo of "Hey, Schoolgirl." With studio time booked at Sanders Recording Studio, on the corner of West Forty-Eighth and Seventh Avenue, they went back to Midtown on the afternoon of October 4. In the studio, they paired off at the microphone. Paul had his guitar on and miked, and when the red light ignited, they knocked off "Schoolgirl." Then they stepped through the control booth to the lounge where others awaited their turn in the studio. That group was chaperoned by a balding fellow who introduced himself as Sid Prosen. "I wanna talk to you guys when you're through," he said. Called back into the studio to take a quick run at "Dancin' Wild," which they figured as the B-side to "Schoolgirl," Paul and Artie then returned to the lounge and found Prosen waiting.

They were terrific, he brayed. The greatest thing since the Everly Brothers. He knew that; they knew that. Now they needed to let the rest of the world know it, and that's what he wanted to do for them. Prosen owned a label called Big Records and a publishing company named Village Music. He could also produce, promote — the whole deal. He knew a hit when he heard one, and when they were singing "Hey, Schoolgirl," that's exactly what he heard: a *hit,* and maybe a smash. He could make them into stars, just like Phil and Don Everly, just like Elvis, too. He knew how to do it, and he also knew that starting with a sizzling tune like "Hey, Schoolgirl" would make it a sure thing. The boys looked at each other, then back at Prosen. They'd just been through all this over at Melba Records. It was one thing to get signed, but would he actually *release* the song? Yes, that was the whole point! He'd even write it into the contract: if he didn't release "Hey, School-girl" within thirty days, that would be the end of the deal. Not that he needed a contract to tell him to do that — he knew "Schoolgirl" would be a hit. And once they were high on the charts, anything was possible: TV shows, movies, everything. Now the boys were getting excited. This sure didn't sound anything like the Melba Records deal. But they weren't old enough to sign anything on their own; Prosen would have to clear it with their parents first.

A few nights later, Prosen turned up at the Pierre Hotel ballroom, where the Lee Simms Orchestra was performing, and when the band took a break he introduced himself to Louis and showed him the contracts he had written up for his talented son and his friend Arthur. Louis was delighted, and even more so when Prosen asked if he had a recording deal for his own terrific orchestra. No? Well, how about recording some sides for Big Records? Rock 'n' roll was fine for the kids, but someone still had to make music for the grown-ups, right? So let's toss in a deal for you, too. They shook hands on that, then read over the as yet unsigned agreement committing Paul and Artie's services to Prosen as both recording artists and songwriters. As promised, Prosen would record a new master of "Hey, Schoolgirl" and release it with a freshly recorded B-side within thirty days. His song publishing company, Village Music Inc., would retain the rights to publish the boys' original songs. In exchange for this, Prosen would pay a small advance on the eventual royalties for all copies sold. And make no mistake, copies *would* be sold. It was a terrific little tune, for one thing. And he knew what went into getting a record played on the radio, particularly when it came to winning friends and influencing certain disc jockeys. Louis took the papers home, Prosen cleared the deal with the senior Garfunkels, and on October 18 they all signed the contracts.

From that moment things happened with velocity. On October 29, Paul and Artie, with Louis and his bass in tow, met Prosen and a session drummer at another recording studio and recorded finished versions of "Schoolgirl," "Dancin' Wild," and a new tune they called "Our Song." At the same time, they set to coming up with a stage name for themselves. That made it feel even more real: this was the stuff of professional showbiz; they weren't just playing the neighborhood anymore. They would need to choose a name that would make them flashy and, at the same time, beyond the reach of the disc jockeys and record salesmen determined to keep ethnic voices away from the tender ears of middle America. Prosen had already given the matter some thought. Did they know the *Tom and Jerry* cartoons, the ones with the battling cat and mouse? The show was on television every day; everyone had heard of them. Sure, Paul and Artie said. So Tom and Jerry it was. Charged with coming up with faux last names, Paul chose "Landis," after his then-current girlfriend Sue Landis, while Artie played off his mathematical whiz kid reputation with "Graph." With that settled, it took exactly a week for thousands of copies of the single, with a slight title alteration, "Hey, Schoolgirl (in the Second Row)"/ "Dancin' Wild" to be pressed and shipped to record stores and radio stations across the country.

When the first box of "Hey, Schoolgirl" singles got to the Big Records office in Midtown, Sid Prosen tucked a few copies into a manila envelope, added two hundred dollars in cash, and took it to the WABC-AM offices of star disc jockey Alan Freed. Just like Martin Block with his *Make Believe Ballroom,* the big band radio show that drew Paul's attention to the Crows' "Gee" in 1953, the rock 'n' roll–crazy Freed[*] ruled the scene like a Mercury of the airwaves, a speed-rapping potentate made from equal measures of faith, flimflam, cigarettes, and whiskey. Getting his start in Cleveland during the early 1950s, Freed followed his taste for high-velocity jazz and jump blues to rock 'n' roll, and as the music got louder and more popular, so did Freed. Launched into the New York City airwaves in 1954, the disc jockey was an instant hit. He soon went national, and by 1957 he had become the go-to radio man for any artist, manager, or record company owner hoping for a hit and willing to slip a little legal tender into a deejay's back pocket. Once Prosen provided the wax and the dough, Freed jumped on "Hey, Schoolgirl" like a cheerleader, not just adding the tune to his influential playlist but also talking up its cheery rock 'n' roll sound.

It worked. The national trade magazine *Cash Box* made "Schoolgirl" its Sleeper of the Week for its November 16 issue. Radio stations in New York, Philadelphia, Albany, Buffalo, and Pittsburgh added the song to

[*] Who had reputedly coined the term *rock and roll* in 1951 to describe upbeat rhythm and blues songs.

80

their playlists soon after, and *Variety* made the song a "Best Bet" in its November 27 edition. "Schoolgirl" hit playlists in the Deep South (New Orleans, Memphis, Oklahoma), the industrial Midwest (Cincinnati, Cleveland, Detroit), the Southwest (Dallas, Denver), and the West Coast (San Francisco), and other regions. Prosen hired an agent for the act, while Paul and Artie asked Charlie Merenstein to be their manager. Soon the boys' weeklong Thanksgiving vacation was filled with bookings for sock hops, record store appearances, and TV dance shows in Hartford and Waterbury, Connecticut, and in Cleveland, Ohio. Most thrilling of all, Paul and Artie got a slot on the biggest TV dance show of all, Dick Clark's *American Bandstand.*

Can you imagine? Just six weeks earlier, Paul and Artie were one more rejection away from giving it all up. If that last-ditch demo session hadn't led to anything, they would have been through. Now they were going to be stars — or rather, Tom and Jerry were going to be stars — so to help prepare the boys for their turn in the spotlight, Belle Simon escorted them to the Ivy League Shop around the corner from Forest Hills High School to find the flashy threads pop idols were supposed to wear. Attended by their classmate Norman Basner, who happened to be clerking when they came in, the boys bickered over colors and fabrics for only a little while

81

before settling on fire truck red blazers made from a pleasantly nubby material, with white button-up shirts and black bow ties, black slacks, and white buck shoes. Prosen sent Freed another two hundred dollars for the next week of airplay and hired a more traditional publicist for his now very much up-and-coming duo — and when their Thanksgiving vacation started in late November, he bought train tickets and sent the boys off to conquer the pop music world.

Then they were riding to Philadelphia to perform their song on *American Bandstand* — where the Everly Brothers had played, where Buddy Holly had stood, where Chuck Berry had duck-walked while still ripping those jet-powered double-stop solos from his gleaming Gibson P-90, where they would stand together, singing their song into cameras that reached into every teenager's home in the United States. They just looked at each other and laughed. *Howled,* more like it — until they got to Studio B in the WFIL-TV headquarters in downtown Philadelphia, from which *American Bandstand* originated every afternoon, where their giggles fluttered back into their stomachs. Ushered into the artists' dressing room, they first noticed a tall, knobby guy channeling his cascades of blond hair into a high-and-tight DA. Was that really . . . yes, of course it was Jerry Lee Lewis. He was on the show, too. Should they say hi? Of course they should. He was a huge star ("Great Balls of Fire" and others), and now here they were, about to appear on the same show with him, based in the same dressing room. But, wait: wasn't Jerry Lee a brawler? Didn't people call him "the Killer"? On second thought, they kept their distance. When Artie went to the bathroom, he found himself peeing next to two of the show's regular dancer/cast members just as one was asking the other about the day's musical guests. *Tom and Jerry? Who are* those *jerks*?

The boys felt far more welcome when Dick Clark called them out to lip-sync their song while the show's cast of teenagers danced and snapped their fingers along to the rhythm. The two got a big hand when it was over, and the members of the three-kid jury all agreed that "Schoolgirl" was both catchy and danceable and thus deserved a top-drawer rating of 95. When Clark stepped up to ask the still-trembling singers where they were from, Artie talked about Queens and Forest Hills High School. Bedazzled by the microphone and the cameras pointed in his direction, Paul could only think about the hometown of Little Richard, the flashiest singer of them all. "I'm from Macon, Georgia!" he piped. Artie shot him a curious look, but Clark, who had also worked under the named Dick Clay, nodded and smiled. As per union rules, Paul and Artie both earned $176 for their national TV performance, but before the show's producer gave the boys their checks, he explained that the show's policy required all guests to endorse the checks and then hand them back over to Dick Clark, who would keep the money for himself. The boys were crestfallen; they had already decided which clothes and shoes they were going to buy with their earnings. "But that's what it was, the world of payola," Paul said in 2014. "That was early rock 'n' roll."

By the time Paul and Artie got back to Kew Gardens Hills, they were both neighborhood celebrities. Kids and parents who used to walk by them without raising an eyebrow now waved and called out their names. The two made a special headlining appearance at their school, running through a few numbers, then climaxing with "Hey, Schoolgirl," much to their schoolmates' delight. Yet the thought that ordinary schoolkids could actually be on the radio struck their classmate Robert Lieberman as so far beyond the realm of possibility that he nudged a friend to tell him what a great job Paul and Artie were doing on the school stage. "Man, they sound exactly like Tom and Jerry!" Lieberman's pal could only shake his head and smirk. "Schmuck! They *are* Tom and Jerry!"

Meanwhile, "Schoolgirl" had danced its way into New York's pop music Top 10, selling well enough in the Northeast cities to lift it to No. 49 on *Billboard*'s national pop chart. That level of success (50,000 copies sold within forty-eight hours of its release, and 250,000 sold during its first month, according to the fanciful statistics released by Prosen) attracted a flock of reporters and photographers from the New York newspapers. Thoroughly briefed by Prosen's publicist, the reporters arrived with a hard focus on the boys' high-flying academic records. The *Long Island Star-Journal*'s two-page feature came with the headline WHIZ KIDS ROCK 'N' ROLL and, in tabloid style, a smaller subhead noting approvingly, BUT THEY STILL TUTOR CLASSMATES. Posed photographs captured the boys playing driveway basketball, studying in Artie's room, joyously tossing records into the air, and sipping ice-cream sodas at Addy Vallens's drugstore. The stories detailed the pair's after-school jobs, tutoring skills, and plans for college: Princeton for Tom and Harvard for Jerry.

Sometimes it got even more personal than that. Anthony Adams in the *New-York Tribune* revealed the boys' real names (along with the names of their parents), and Victoria Lee of the *New York World-Telegram and Sun* made herself the first of the hundreds, maybe thousands, of reporters to ask after the tensions that might exist in the duo's relationship. Jerry, "the guitar-playing member of the team," said that their occasional fights were easily resolved, as on a recent afternoon when they went to a clothing store to buy matching sweaters for their newly booked performances. When they got to the store, they couldn't decide which sweater to buy. After a brief argument, they simply threw their hands up. "Since we couldn't agree," Paul/Jerry said, "we ended up not buying anything." It made for a good laugh in the newspapers; ordinary adolescent boys being ordinary adolescent boys. Yet they had been friends "and collaborators," according to Paul, since they were in the fourth grade. They had already achieved so much together, and were so thrilled with what they'd done. Everything was ahead of them.

Just a few weeks before his son wrote his first hit song, Louis Simon, whose postgraduate studies still hadn't ended all of his music ambitions, came up with a new tune of his own, a novelty number titled "Water in My Ear." Soon after, he played the song with the Lee Simms Orchestra on the *Ted Steele Show,* a daytime entertainment show broadcast on New York's WOR-TV, and was so happy with how it came out that he made a recording of the performance into a demo he could shop around to the record companies and song publishers in Midtown. Then he thought again and decided to wait until Paul came home from his summer job and get him involved in the project. The boy's voice was getting stronger. And even if Paul's dedication to pop music gave Louis pause, he knew his son had professional-grade talent. As Belle reminded him, Paul was bringing home stellar report cards, so why keep him away from something he loved? Louis saw the logic in this especially given that his and his son's ambitions currently matched: having Paul's boyish voice on the demo, Louis felt, would make it easier for record companies to hear the hit potential of "Water in My Ear."

Paul passed the news to Artie in a letter to the summer camp in New Jersey where he was also working as a counselor. "You want to crack-up [*sic*]?" he wrote, and then described the "real weirdy" of a tune his dad had just written. "The kind only my father could think of." The news got even more embarrassing, Paul wrote with gleeful horror: Louis wanted *him* to be the face of the project. "He'll bring it up to some big [record] company. He's dead serious about it, too. No! That's bad!" Though Paul made fun of the old man, he couldn't resist reporting Louis's latest burst of praise for him ("According to my father my voice has improved") or remarking that it was kind of cool that his father was putting his song on hold until Paul was available to participate in it. As close as he was to Artie, and as much as they had invested in their work together, Paul saw that the world was full of opportunities. He didn't write this, but maybe because it was only too obvious. If you didn't reach for what you wanted when it was available, you had only yourself to blame for not getting it.

So Paul reached. During the Tom and Jerry contract negotiations in October 1957 the Simons pitched Prosen on adding another artist to the Big Records lineup: Paul Simon, solo artist. Paul would stick with his Jerry Landis pseudonym for his own record; after all, the guitar-thumpin' half of Tom and Jerry might have a following after "Schoolgirl." As he assured Prosen, he didn't have any plans of breaking up the duo, but he had his own ambitions, and as great as Paul and Artie were together, there were things Paul could do alone that the duo couldn't do together. Artie preferred ballads and harmony, but Paul was a rocker at heart; he could tap into that harder, Elvis-like sound and really put Big Records on the rock 'n' roll map. Prosen, who had already shaken hands with Louis to release records by the Lee Simms Orchestra, agreed to add this side contract, launching Paul's solo career even before he and Artie had sung a note on their first professionally produced record.

Somehow, in all the excitement of "Hey, Schoolgirl," Paul forgot to mention this side deal to Artie. There was a lot to distract him. Every day brought a new surprise; the excitement was dizzying. For Paul's solo record, maybe as another of Louis's weird ideas, the elder Simon took the lead on the project, not just booking the studio time but also writing the lead sheets for the session and hiring a drummer and lead guitarist to accompany his bass and Paul's rhythm guitar. Louis also composed the single's A-side, a rockabilly shuffle called "True or False." Why Paul didn't write the A-side of his own debut record — he ended up with the B-side — is unclear. Also, whatever mortification he might have felt about singing a song that his father had written didn't keep Paul from throwing himself entirely into what is without a doubt the goofiest performance he ever committed to record.

Highlighted by hand claps, a popping snare drum, fast-walking bass, and "Rock Around the Clock"–style guitar arpeggios, "True or False" features Paul hiccup-singing in a faux-southern drawl to the girl who may or may not adore him above all others. To put her on the spot, the jiving swain presents her with a pop quiz.

> You lahk to call me on-hawn the telephone, bay-buh
> Please answer "true-hoo" or "false."

More questions follow. Does she like to turn the lights off when they're alone? Would she be sad if he went away? Can she not wait until they make a date? And what of this other fellow he sees her with when they go to parties? It's hard to know, since Paul's hillbilly gurgle often veers into the unintelligible. But the girl in question is supposed to offer simple true-or-false responses, which the singer will score the moment she drops her pencil.

Weeel, I'm a-checkin' on your answers so I
  can
plainly see If my bay-bee's true or
  fah-halse to me!

The pop quiz conceit is a bit more pedagogic than you'd expect from a rock 'n' roll song, but Louis Simon's "True or False" has a goofball charm that Paul's unhinged performance nearly suits. Paul's self-composed B-side, a by-the-numbers ballad called "Teenage Fool," falls the other way. Tracing the stock doo-wop chords that Louis taught Paul just a few years before, the tune is set to tinkling piano and a doleful saxophone, with a moaning, sighing vocal that vanishes from memory (thankfully) once the needle hits the playout groove. Still, the far bouncier "True or False" was the A-side, and now that "Schoolgirl" had broken through, who knew what else was possible?

Eventually, Paul told Artie about "True or

False" and the side deal he'd struck with Prosen. He'd kept it a secret from his best friend for nearly two months but, amazingly, he still wasn't all that apologetic. It was his dad's tune, he said. It wasn't that big a deal. And even if it became a hit, what difference would it make? He and Artie were having their chance to be the Everly Brothers, and he had decided he wanted a shot at being Elvis. What was so wrong with that? A *lot,* Artie pointed out; or maybe he shouted it. Whatever the scenario, it was not a happy moment for either of them. *We're a team. You went behind my back. You* lied *to me*! This was double-dealing bullshit, and Paul knew it. It only got worse when Artie told his parents what was going on. They were furious, too, not just at Paul but at Louis and also Prosen. What kind of people behave like that? It's not as if the Garfunkels were entirely naïve. Jack was a salesman; Rose worked as a court stenographer. They knew all about negotiations and contracts, and how easy it was to get screwed if you didn't read the fine print. But to be screwed by your neighbors, people you've been friendly with for years?

Paul shrugged it all off — at least until his copies of Big Records No. 614, "True or False"/"Teenage Fool," arrived at his house in Queens. Now it was Paul's turn to be furious. Only a few weeks earlier, he, Prosen, and Louis had agreed that his solo records would be released under his new pop pseudonym, Jerry Landis. But Prosen, without telling Paul or Louis, had decided to credit the record to True Taylor. *True Taylor?* Who the hell was that? Even worse, Prosen had ignored their agreement that the composer of "Teenage Fool" also be listed as Jerry Landis. Instead, the executive had written in "by Paul Simon," thereby confusing the matter all the more. The first thing they had agreed upon when they met was that the Simon and Garfunkel names weren't going to be a part of their pop star identities. They were Tom and Jerry, high schoolers from Anytown, USA, not Paul and Artie from the most Jewish high school in the most Jewish section of Queens, New York.

Paul and Louis demanded that Prosen recall the records he'd printed and reissue them with corrected labels, but the executive wasn't having any of that. The record was already in the shops. Pulling it now would destroy its commercial momentum. And of course it was Prosen's call in the end. But "commercial momentum"? *What* commercial momentum? "True or False" received none of the publicity Prosen had generated for "Hey, Schoolgirl," and the new record's sales statistics showed it. In fact, if it sold anything beyond a small scattering of discs, Paul never heard about it. Thrown into the same marketplace that had embraced Tom and Jerry, poor old True Taylor found no love whatsoever. He and his song evaporated the moment they came into being.

Artie wasn't what you'd call broken up by his friend's failed attempt to carve out his own chunk of pop glory. But Tom and Jerry's next single, "Our Song," a chipper breakup song inspired by the Kentucky end of the Everly Brothers' catalogue, also vanished without a trace, in early February, as did "Pretty Baby," in May. At least there was still demand for Tom and Jerry to play at sock hops and concerts on the teenage circuit around New York, Connecticut, and New Jersey. Prosen shipped them to Chicago in early May to perform alongside Jimmie Rodgers, Connie Francis, and Mahalia Jackson at the Music Operators of America convention at the battleship-size Morrison Hotel, which would have seemed like a greater show of faith in the "Hey, Schoolgirl" duo if it hadn't taken place just as Prosen was preparing to release a "Tom and Jerry" single that had been recorded by two different Queens-raised singers. Indeed, "Baby Talk," the A-side of Big Records No. 621, was the work of two fellows whom Prosen had dubbed Tom Layton and Jerry Darcey, in the hope of launching them as a kind of Tom and Jerry 2.0. Prosen slapped the already released Paul and Artie–performed "Two Teenagers" on the B-side, but given the dismal performance of the two "Schoolgirl" follow-ups, Prosen had already moved on.[*]

So had Paul and Artie. They still played a few shows as Tom and Jerry, mostly for school functions or group-billed sock hops in either the city or one of the nearby suburbs, but their brief spasm of success, and the selfishness Paul displayed once it started, had webbed their friendship with cracks. They could still talk about music and their friends and get excited about the sock hop or school dance they were booked to play at the end of the week. Also, they teamed up to file a lawsuit against Sid Prosen for royalties he owed them, and would share their happiness when they received fifteen hundred dollars from him at the end of the school year. Still, the tenderness between them had faded. You can still love someone who shoves you aside, but you can no longer trust him in quite the same way.

They found other things to keep them busy. Paul had never made the varsity baseball team under Coach George Lapp, but Lapp's successor, Chester Gusick, brought the pint-size sixteen-year-old onto the squad and was impressed by the kid's speed and springlike

[*] As would Darcey and Layton, who eventually moved to Nashville and become successful songwriters under their real names, Chris Gentry and Len Chiriaka.

bat. "He was a little fella, and he could draw walks, run fast, and steal bases," Gusick says. "And he was a pretty good hitter, too." When the season began, Gusick installed Paul as his starting right fielder and lead-off batter, and kept him there all season. It was a rainy spring, and Forest Hills lost more than a few games to the weather, but Paul played well, and the team battled its way to the top of its division. His most heroic moment came on May 13, when he stole home base in a hard-fought game against Grover Cleveland High School. Paul finished that season among the leaders in the final Public Schools Athletic League averages, with twenty-seven at bats, twelve runs, eight hits, and a .296 batting average — not spectacular numbers, but good enough to earn him an honorable mention for the All-Queens squad at the end of the season.

Paul invested most of his share of the fifteen-hundred-dollar "Hey, Schoolgirl" royalties in a sporty red Chevrolet Impala, a hard-top convertible with triple carbs, twin headlights, chrome edging, a lunging front end, and a long winged rear end. The interior was spacious, the bench seats trimmed in shiny red leatherette. It was the perfect ride for a graduating honor student with a hit single in his past and his entire future lying just beyond the end of summer vacation. He and Artie would continue on their independent roads, with Artie headed to upper Manhattan to attend the city's Ivy League Columbia University and Paul staying in the neighborhood to attend Queens College, the most elite institution in New York's City College system.

The former partners wouldn't speak again for five years. At least, that's how they told their story later. Others would recall that period quite differently. Still, there was no arguing the fate of Paul's sparkling Impala, that cherry red symbol of his run as a teenage idol. Driving home through Kew Gardens Hills one evening, he was within a block or two of his parents' house when he smelled smoke. Flames leaped from the hood, and it was all he could do to pull over and jump out before the gleaming beast was filled with fire, the upholstery ablaze, a dense black curtain rising from its every crease and crack. A fire engine came, but by then it was too late. The car was a wreck, its windows smashed, its glamorous white wall tires reduced to puddles. Paul watched glumly while the firefighters picked the wreckage apart, sprayed it down with foam, and made sure there was nothing left to burn. It was his entire share of "Hey, Schoolgirl," he realized, burned, smashed, and ruined in the gutter. When there was nothing left to see, he looked up and realized he was on Seventy-Second Avenue, a short walk from his parents' house,

and within sight of the Garfunkels' front
door.

CHAPTER 5
TWO TEENAGERS

Paul got to Queens College in September 1958, an undergraduate in a dark V-neck sweater, a neatly tucked button-up shirt, jeans, and Adler elevator shoes. Maybe his dark hair was piled higher than the average undergrad, but not so much that you'd look twice. It was a faint signifier, a hint that there was a bit more going on here than met the eye. He didn't talk about his other life, not at first. If some people remembered hearing "Hey, Schoolgirl" or reading one of the newspaper stories about Tom and Jerry eight months earlier, virtually none of them connected their serious new schoolmate to the chipper teen they would have recognized from the pop song. Paul would mention it to a friend here or there, but when he perched on the stairs somewhere to strum his guitar, "Hey, Schoolgirl" was not part of his repertoire.

Queens College wasn't Columbia University, as Artie's excited talk about his new school reminded Paul. The campus was a mile from the Simons' house, an easy walk down Seventieth Road to Kissena Avenue and a short walk to what is definitely an urban campus, its grassy quad, compact plazas, and scattering of office and classroom buildings only a few blocks from the new Long Island Expressway. Still, Queens College had a grandeur of its own, as an elite kind of Roosevelt-era utopian society where the children of garbage men, maids, truck drivers, and tool-and-die operators could learn the secrets of the universe that came tumbling off the tongues of some of the nation's greatest thinkers. Admissions were strictly meritocratic. Tuition cost nothing. The usual collegiate accouterment, the gilded halls and ivy-cloaked brick, didn't factor. Most of the buildings were new and the caretakers too conscious of the mortar-crumbling damage the vines could inflict to indulge such ivory tower sentiment.

The Queens College of the late 1950s sparked with the pent energy of the young and the unleashed. Progressive idealism filled the classrooms, dissent rang from the student publications, and civil disobedience fomented in the cafeteria and campus quad. Civil rights activists were a constant presence on campus, as were labor organizers, antinuclear petitioners, and the pioneering women's libbers — all that and so much more for an incoming freshman to wrap himself around: classes and professors and pretty girls and figuring out who was who and why they mattered. Pick up the college's *Rampart* newspaper and you'd start to recognize names and faces: the president of this, the featured speaker at the rally against that, the profs who wrote the fieriest letters about the administration and its sins against thought, speech, and students' rights. You really only had to skim the thing to sense the mounting frustration. Paul kept his distance. He was there to be a student, so he focused on the classroom. He signed up for the freshman usuals and talked about following a prelaw path, but connected most with his English classes, reading widely and developing lifetime attachments to writers ranging from James Joyce to John Updike, from the modernist poet Wallace Stevens to the Jewish-American writer Saul Bellow. Paul scanned poetry with care, and when he found a line he liked, he'd copy it into his notebook and look for ways to work its words or feeling into his own writing. When spring arrived he took measure of the fraternities and pledged Alpha Epsilon Pi, a Jewish house known for its control over the student government and for having, as its rush advertisements read, the "Best Men on Campus." Paul pledged, survived the indignities of Hell Night, and was delighted to be tapped.

He was even more delighted when he

started going to the parties and the dances, hoisting a beer and goofing with the guys and chatting up the girls. He could be enormously charming and was obviously bright, so the AEPi guys put him on the fast track to leadership, a position he used in both serious and less serious ways as he started taking on authority during his sophomore year. Sometimes he'd lead off-campus romps to the beach, where he'd show the gang which fence they could climb to avoid paying the user's fee. Friends also recall his leadership the night he and another frat house head conducted a few younger AEPi brethren to Harlem, where they engaged a couple of prostitutes to relieve the younger men of their virginities.

Paul loved the typical frat boy antics, but once he soaked up the high-democratic atmosphere of the school, he made a point of introducing a more enlightened attitude to the fraternity. Appointed rush chair during his sophomore year, he persuaded his brothers to eliminate the physical abuses of hazing in favor of a Dostoyevskian panel of inquisitors who grilled the pledges on their beliefs, ethics, morals, and their philosophies on the meaning of life. He orchestrated campaigns to tap pledges from tougher, poorer, or culturally diverse backgrounds. Given the force field of his charisma, Paul's frat brothers fell easily under his influence, developing new interests in philosophy and, not surprisingly, the internal dynamics of the songs on the radio. Paul could talk you through the whole Top 40 with astonishing detail, describing why this one song was a stiff and why this other one was so fucking brilliant. In his car with a few brothers one night, he turned the radio to one of the obscure stations only he knew about and suddenly ordered everyone to stop talking: "You gotta hear this!" It was a hypnotic groove by Olatunji from his album *Drums of Passion.* It was so mesmerizing that the car went perfectly silent, and Paul pulled over so they could all absorb the African rhythm together.

Paul's influence over AEPi was most apparent when the frat set out to create its entry for the college's annual Follies stage spectacular. Held in late December, the shows were a significant event on campus, a high-profile fund-raiser for local charities and also the year's most hotly contested battle for supremacy among the school's fraternities, sororities, and the groups of independents who signed up to compete. The challenge was for each group to perform ten- or fifteen-minute skits for the college crowd and for the panel of experts who would judge each entry's entertainment value and then pick a champion. AEPi had never been a serious player in the Follies — not until Paul got involved.

Paul took control of AEPi's entire production. He wrote or edited the script and wrote the words and music to all the songs, and directed, too. Any frat brother who signed up thinking the sketch would be another fun fraternity goof learned otherwise the moment Paul walked into the first rehearsal. He was all business. "We're gonna get this right, okay?" The roles were demanding. Performers had to recite lines, emote, sing, and even dance without screwing up a word or motion, lest Paul stop everything in its tracks. "That's not it!" he'd bark, causing all eyes to swing to the now-mortified offender. Then came the sharply worded correction, often paired with a needling observation about the offender's commitment and brainpower. You didn't want to be the offender.

Year in and out, Paul's productions for AEPi were always the most complex of the night, usually multilevel satires that combined fairy tales, movies, or plain old absurdities with commentary on campus characters or the administration and the latest outrage it was attempting to perpetrate. One year, the show had a Robin Hood theme, with college president Harold Stoke transformed into "Huge Harold," a hostess in the school cafeteria. The climactic song went, in part, like this:

Huge Harold, a hostess,
Long live Robin Hood!
Huge Harold, a hostess
He got what he should.
Tyranny never pays (please return your
trays!)
Your virtue was a fable (don't sit on the
table!)

Any on-campus demonstration of academic pomposity could get a professor parodied in an AEPi sketch, as hidebound conservative political science teacher Mary Dunn, who taught her classes clad in an academic gown, learned the year Paul transformed her into "Sahara Mary":

Sahara Mary teaches poli sci
Nobody ever figured out why
In class she wears her robes so silky
Talking about her hero, Wendell Willkie

Just that quickly, AEPi was unbeatable in the Follies. At the same time, Paul's campus reputation gained a kind of gravitas. He had proven himself to be a trenchant, witty commentator on the state of the Queens College campus. What the activists were saying through walk-outs, marches, and protest speeches, Paul could put into a single verse of a satirical song performed by a character dressed as a medieval woodsman. The audience marveled at the ingenuity. They had their own Mort Sahl, a sleek-but-toothy comedian whose insights resonated far beyond the spectacle onstage. His peers got the sense that Paul could get somewhere in life.

Yet where was he going after the day's classes ended? He never mentioned it, not even to his close pals in AEPi. He didn't let anyone know that when he wasn't playing his guitar on campus, he was strumming it in a recording studio in Manhattan, working on songs they might be hearing on their radios by the end of the semester. And he certainly didn't tell anyone that the Paul Simon who jogged down the subway stairs in Queens emerged in Manhattan with another man's name and bright prospects, as *16 Magazine*'s young editor Gloria Stavers proclaimed in the January 1960 debut of her column on up-and-coming artists: *Jerry Landis is going places!*

When Paul Simon started classes as a freshman in the fall of 1958, Jerry Landis wasn't going anywhere. Less than a year since "Hey, Schoolgirl" launched him into *Billboard*'s Hot 100, the young pop star/musician/songwriter had been put on ice. Paul had no plans to kill off his alter ego; just as there was no Jerry without Paul, the reverse was also true. The problem was that each of his personae had such different visions for their joint future.

Even as he threw himself into his classes and wove himself into the social fabric of the Queens College campus, Paul had kept right on writing pop songs. Someone else's tune would come on the radio, and his ears would lock into what he was hearing, decoding the parts and reconfiguring them into his own songs about dream girls, true love, and the heartbreak of being so shy and so very lonely. All were composed with both ears turned to the teenage market, all set in the familiar milieu of classrooms, homework, Saturday night dances, and the lush daydreams of first-time lovers. He'd head over to the Merensteins' place and spend another few hours with Charlie, playing songs and breaking down the new hits. If Paul brought his guitar, they might start writing a new song. When it was finished, they'd share the credit fifty-fifty and publish it through Charlie's R&S Publishing. During those years, the two finished at least half a dozen Landis-Merenstein (or Merenstein-Landis, depending on who did the most work) songs, including the jilted lover's weeper "Please Don't Tell Her/Him," which was recorded by three different artists in the space of a few months. None charted as hits, but having three covers of one song was encouraging, to say the least.

Once Paul felt comfortable enough in college to think about resurrecting Jerry Landis, he had some new publicity pictures taken, listed Merenstein as his manager, and headed back to Midtown to push his songs, and himself, through the office doors of labels, producers, and scouts until one of them figured out that Jerry Landis had the stuff to make another hit or three. In the meantime, the steadiest work for a guy with Jerry Landis's skills came from song publishers needing a skilled newcomer to transform their contracted writers' music into lightly arranged, pleasant recordings showcasing the tunes' charms. It was tradesman's work, a flat twenty-five dollars a pop for quickie recordings. Most of the songs ranked somewhere between mediocre and daffy — what could one expect from songs called "Fortune Teller Cookies," "Up and Down the Stairs," and "I Want You in My Stocking"? — but Paul didn't care. More than money, the job gave him nearly unlimited access to the recording studio and all its electronic and instrumental gear. He learned quickly, and it wasn't long before he located new ways to elaborate on the basics: recording tongue clacks and finger snaps so they had the resonance of real percussion instruments; overloading reverb on a guitar until a simple riff wailed extraterrestrially; pairing a three-chord rocker with Latin percussion.

He did the same thing with the songs he recorded for the do-it-yourself companies (best known as song sharks) that offered amateur lyricists a chance to turn their verse into finished recordings produced by professional-grade composers and performers. It was a weird gig, but it allowed Paul to hole up in the recording studio, which had become his favorite place to be. He'd take a sheaf of lyrics to the Variety Arts Studios at 225 West Forty-Sixth Street and spend an entire day writing and recording songs, challenging himself to add an original twist to each tune: a jazzy chord change here, an unexpected burst of congas there. He could have cranked them out in a fraction of the time; no one would hear the song beyond the customer/lyricist and whomever he was romancing. Yet Paul was too absorbed in the recording process to care about the time.

It was the storied era of pop songwriting, the time of Goffin and King, Mann and Weil, Leiber and Stoller, Shuman and Pomus, Sedaka and Greenfield, Barry and Greenwich — all of them dishing up hit songs as if they were the day's social studies homework, lyrics and chords scribbled on notepaper, on the back of a shopping list, on a torn-out page from a teenager's diary. Hit after hit after hit until the pickles-and-cigar aura of Tin Pan Alley turned neon with Brylcreem and Tabu, grass-kissed sweatshirts and hairspray. People still talked about the art deco Brill Building as the Alley's main address, but the more that rock 'n' roll took its grip, the less this was true. A few younger writers may have worked the pianos in the Brill's cubicles, but the real action was a few blocks north, behind the Euro-sleek facade of 1650 Broadway, where baby impresarios Don Kirshner and Don Nevins had stationed the headquarters of Aldon Music, the umbrella name for the various enterprises that were fast becoming an industry behemoth. Once Aldon set up at 1650, a legion of others followed them there, or else set up shop across the street at 1697 Broadway, where CBS's ground-floor studio lay beneath thirteen floors of rehearsal rooms, studios, and music offices in which some of the biggest artists, bands, writers, publishers, and record companies went about their daily business.

Pop music was all around Paul, and not just in Midtown Manhattan. When he called Queens College's student tutor offices looking for help in his mathematics class during his freshman year, the service sent over a sophomore named Carol Klein, a Brooklyn girl who spent most of her off-campus hours in the Brill Building as Carole King, one-half of a rising pop songwriting team she'd made with her new husband, a fellow Queens College student named Gerry Goffin. The pair had started working together, and then fallen in love, during their first year on campus. Paul told Carole that he was also a songwriter with Hot 100 experience, and they hit it off so well that they formed the Cosines, a two-person demo recording team producing first-rate demos. Paul played guitar and bass, Carole piano and drums, and both sang lead and background parts. Paul and Carole didn't write songs together — she had her husband for that — but they were working in the music business, and as far as they were concerned it was the greatest thing in the world.

In the late spring of his sophomore year, Paul finally landed a recording contract for Jerry Landis. The deal wasn't with a record company, though; he signed with Wemar Music, a publishing company that had a side business making and selling master recordings of its writers' songs to record companies willing to pay a premium for finished material. The Wemar executives figured Paul's "Anna Belle" for a moneymaker and sent him into the studio to cut the track, along with another original, "Loneliness," for the flip side. An A&R man at MGM Records liked what he heard, and in late July the first real Jerry Landis record slipped into the stores. Publicity was minimal, and when *Billboard* mentioned "Anna Belle" in its New Records column, the writer judged its sales potential as only "moderate." Even that prediction turned out to be ambitious. When the MGM accountants tallied the song's numbers at the end of the season, its national sales added up to something fewer than one hundred copies.

Try and try again. Ten months later Paul got another Jerry Landis record into the record stores, thanks to the help of Charlie Merenstein, who convinced his pal Morty Craft to give the kid another shot on his new Warwick label. Craft signed Paul to record four sides, adding up to two 45s, front and back. Still working with the strategy of knocking off last month's hits, Paul staked his first release to his chime-adorned ballad "Just a Boy," the whispered confession of a kittenish fellow who is "unwise and full of fears," until his precious love gives him "the wisdom of many years." It was better than the B-side, "Shy," a tangle of goops and sighs and "doodle-ee-doo-doos." The 45 came out in May 1960 and fell flat. That didn't stop Craft from trying again in the fall, this time with "Just a Boy" as a B-side to a cover of "(I'd Like to Be) The Lipstick on Your Lips," which turned out to be every bit as appealing as its title. Still, the *Billboard* review was upbeat, judging "Lipstick" a "real cutie" enhanced by Paul's "delicate performance." "Just a Boy" won the most praise from *Billboard*'s critic, who heard a distinctly folk influence that disc jockeys would find "out of the common groove."

Paul was doing just fine in his literature and history classes at Queens College that term, but he still had a lot to learn when it came to producing recording sessions, which became painfully evident to the storied jazz guitarist Bucky Pizzarelli when he was booked to play a session for Paul at Astoria Studios. Louis, who had been booked as the bassist and bandleader, had written a bare-bones lead sheet for the song, but Paul kept stopping the takes, looking for a rock 'n' roll feel he could hear in his head but was unable to put into words. Even Louis had no idea what Paul was trying to say. Pizzarelli figured out later that the kid was after eighth notes rather than fours, but Paul could only flail during the session, and eventually he sent his expensive session players home so he could start fresh with musicians who had enough of a feel for rock 'n' roll to intuit what he was after.[*]

Being in the studio was magic to Paul: the microphones, the knobs and sliders on the recording console, the in-the-moment arranging, the creation and manipulation of sound. Then he could walk down the hall to the front offices and be as engaged by what he found there. As he'd come to learn from Louis and from Charlie Merenstein, the guys who ran the business could be just as wild and electric as the artists they propped up in

[*] One detail Pizzarelli doesn't recall was the name of the song they were working on. "But it wasn't 'Stardust.' I can tell you that."

the spotlight. Most of them were earthy guys, barrel-chested and bellowing, arguing and laughing, sloshing whiskey and peppering their conversations with equal measures of Yiddish and profanity. Most shared the same rough-hewn spirit of the Lower East Side operators who had bare-knuckled their way into the game back when ragtime was still king and there was big money in sheet music. The business had grown a lot since then, and some of the swifter boys had built themselves empires and fortunes. That hadn't changed the game, though, especially not for the guys who knew the value of the veiled threat and the very public display of power. Ike Berman, Charlie Merenstein's brother-in-law, had cousins who were so connected that Ronnie Merenstein could resolve any problem in New York, and later in Las Vegas, by mentioning his grandfather's name.[†] Like Charlie, most of the record men weren't mobsters but the same essential ethic, the impatience with etiquette and the disinterest in politesse, still applied. Business was business, sentiment was a luxury, and if an advantage presented itself to you, you didn't hesitate. And if someone complained about getting the short end of a deal, maybe he should be more careful next time. Everyone knew that all the

† Ronnie grew up hearing that as a toddler he'd been bounced on the knee of Bugsy Siegel.

money in the music business traveled through the front offices before it got anywhere else. The business guys structured the deals, they counted the profits, they took what they thought they deserved, and they gave everyone else whatever was left.

Over at 1697 Broadway you could wander up to Jim Gribble's office and settle into his waiting room alongside a dozen or more other hustling music people. Gribble was a southerner of the classic variety (tall, broad-shouldered, loud, forever cocooned in a blue cloud of cigarette smoke), a native of small West Tennessee town called, yes, Gribble. More important, he was a talent scout/manager/packager of rock and rhythm and blues acts, so it made sense for him to keep track of who was around, what they did, and how good they were. If he had a job for a guitarist, he'd get a couple of guys to open their cases and audition on the spot. Background singers? Let's see if that doo-wop group can really sing. Paul was a regular, so when one of Gribble's hit doo-wop groups needed to replace its lead singer in short order, the manager stepped into his outer chamber and pointed to Paul.

"Landis! Git in here!"

The Mystics was a five-man doo-wop group from Brooklyn best known for "Hushabye," a Pomus-Shuman song they had taken into the Top 30 in 1959. The band made a couple of ripples when their next single, "Don't Take the Stars," reached the lower rungs of the Top 100, but by the winter of 1960 they had lost their lead singer, and with its record company demanding new material pronto, Gribble offered the job to Paul. Was he interested? Sure! Probably! What would it pay? Gribble mentioned a number, Paul thought that sounded fine, and after a quick check-in between the manager and the executives at Laurie Records he was in. The group's members all got together to teach Paul the songs and determine who would sing what, and it didn't take much time for the others to figure out that this college boy from Queens was actually a great guy. He laughed when they teased him for being short, and he laughed again when they made fun of his high-pitched voice. Then he busted them right back, which made the Brooklyn boys laugh even harder. Gribble and the A&R guy at Laurie Records had already chosen the tunes. "All Through the Night," essentially a faster version of "Hushabye," featured a group vocal; Paul sang lead on "Let Me Steal Your Heart Away," but is inaudible on "(I Begin) To Think Again of You." The sessions went smoothly, and everyone had a fine time, but Paul had no interest in performing at any of the sock hops Gribble set up for the group, and when its original lead singer decided to come back, Paul stepped aside cheerfully. He had Jerry Landis's career to focus on.

From late 1960 throughout 1961, Paul wrote songs and found labels willing to bankroll recording sessions and release and then promote Jerry Landis's singles. The titles make Landis seem like a sulk: "I Wish I Weren't in Love," "Play Me a Sad Song." And sulk he does: "I've got no one to hold me tight." And complain: "I can't do my homework . . . the way she treats me just isn't right." And kvetch: "Everywhere I look kids are having fun, / But I might as well go read a book." And ponder the abyss: "My nights are spent in misery / Without your love I can't endure." In a lighter mood, he moans softly to himself: "I'm lonely." It would seem that something is desperately wrong with Jerry Landis — except that none of it rings true; he mouths clichés that condescend to heartbreak. The music is just as void, always the standard doo-wop ballad progression, the same *ooh*s and *ahh*s and *doodle-doo*s from the chorus; the same gulping, cooing vocal style. By contrast, you can put on a Chuck Berry record and *feel* the hum of a well-oiled Cadillac purring down the macadam, and "Great Balls of Fire" leaves no doubt that Jerry Lee Lewis was as crazy as a goose and as mean as a snake. Even "Hey, Schoolgirl (in the Second Row)" has that cooped-up, about-to-bust feeling of those slow-ticking afternoon classes. Yet to listen to the Landis

116

songs, particularly in light of everything that would happen in the near future, you guess that Jerry Landis had no idea who he was, either.

Over at Queens College, Paul Simon rose through the ranks at AEPi and was eventually elected president of the chapter. Unchallenged authority agreed with him. He was focused, cheerful, and generous with his fraternity brothers, and kept an eye out for the stragglers and outsiders. When a thuggish-looking kid found his way to a pledge party in a wise guy's shiny shoes, tight slacks, and shiny open-neck shirt, Paul's first reaction — his mouth fell open and a hand flew up to cover his astonished smile — made the streetwise recruit, the son of a troubled Brooklyn family named Brian Schwartz, suspect the worst. Instead, Paul beelined over and greeted him like a friend. After talking for a while and learning something of Schwartz's past, Paul took him around to meet the fraternity's other key members, and as the weeks went by he shepherded him through the pledge process. When Schwartz got tapped to join, he was certain Paul's efforts had had everything to do with it.

Paul's star continued to rise among the college's most influential students, his renown stemming from his reputation as a campus performer, as the impresario behind AEPi's golden Follies entries, and increasingly as the guy most likely to whip out his guitar and hold forth for anyone and everyone within earshot. Given free time between classes, he would find some stairs where he could sit and strum his guitar for a while. Every so often he'd get up in the cafeteria and sing a few pop songs, often with frat brothers Schwartz, Ronnie Pollack, and Elliott Naishtat hauled in to sing the Belmonts' parts while Paul put on his best Dion for "The Wanderer." They harmonized on Kingston Trio hits, and Paul was particularly expert at the group's "Scotch and Soda," always a crowd favorite. Assigned to make a presentation about his hopes for the future in a speech class, Paul delivered a paper that cast his Tom and Jerry experience as the first step in a life he was determined to build around music. Richard Milner, a classmate Paul had gotten to know over a few terms, came away from the recitation feeling both impressed and inspired. He'd never met someone his age with such a clear and confident vision of what, and who, he wanted to be.

One day between classes, Paul took Milner to an empty hallway to sing a few songs he had just written. Who knew that these songs would soon be released as singles on MGM Records? Milner certainly didn't. Neither did Joan Tauber, one of Paul's college friends. Ron Pollack, an AEPi brother who worked closely with Paul on multiple Follies productions, had no idea that his friend had recorded anything between his high school hit and the mid-1960s. "I wasn't aware of Jerry Landis," Pollack said to me after a puzzled silence. "I've never heard that name before."

Another time, Paul took Milner by the arm during a class break to tell him about an extraordinary thing that had happened to him the day before. Paul's subway train had been held at an uptown Manhattan station. When he heard singing coming from the platform, he hopped off to investigate. He followed his ears down a stairway and, at the landing, found a five-man clutch of doo-wop singers, all black, all his age, all locked in harmony. Paul listened for a while, and when they got to a tune he knew, he started singing along. He sang tentatively at first, but when one of the singers picked up on what he was doing, he moved aside and gestured for Paul to join them. Paul stepped in eagerly and was immediately one of them. Heads bobbing together, fingers popping to the same beat — the moment of harmony triggered something in Paul he couldn't put into words. He just shook his head in wonder. "The niggas let me sing," Milner recalled him finally saying. He uttered the word with a tentative hush, trying it out on his tongue like Cinderella slipping the crystal shoe over her callused heel, wondering if the previous day's magic

119

could possibly have been real. *The niggas let me sing!*

CHAPTER 6
THE FREEDOM CRIERS

One night in the late spring of 1961, Paul went to a talent show at Forest Hills Jewish Center. He was in Jerry Landis mode, a persona now looking to become a pop mastermind. Sitting among the parents, neighbors, and friends, Paul looked for glimmers of real talent, measuring the singers' sound and presence, imagining them on a bigger, shinier stage and himself in the wings, tapping his foot to the clang of the cash drawer. He watched act after act, some of them decent but still so young, so hesitant, so not ready. Then came four kids from Parsons Junior High, of all places, three boys and a girl (shades of the Peptones!) singing doo-wop with real flair — rich voices, strong harmonies, a gleam in their eyes. After the show, Paul introduced himself. They knew they were really good, right? Did they ever think about making records? Well, he knew exactly how they felt because he'd come out of Parsons just a few years back, already knowing he had what it took, but with no idea how to show it to the right people. But he worked at it and then — do you guys remember Tom and Jerry, "Hey, Schoolgirl"? Yeah, that was me. So how would they like to do the same thing, only without the years of frustration he'd endured? He could guide them, step by step. All they had to do was everything he told them to.

Some of them weren't even in high school yet; they were just a bunch of kids having fun. Lead singer Marty Cooper and his garrulous pal Mickey Borack were just finishing up at Parsons. Falsetto whooper Howie Klein and Gail Lynn were in high school. Cooper had the richest voice; he could sing sweet on the love songs and then summon Dion's streetwise edge for the foot stompers. But they all had strong voices, and with Borack's big personality leading the show they had a spark.

To make sure they could gather and hold a crowd, Paul trailed them to a street corner singing session. Then he sat them down to explain how it was going to work. He'd write the songs, produce the records, and manage every aspect of the group's career, working in tandem with his new business partner, Bobby Susser, a super-enthusiastic kid he'd met while visiting his college friend Judith Tauber in the Jackson Heights section of Queens. Susser took care of the business, and Paul took care of the music, scheduling regular rehearsals in his parents' basement. In search of a group name that would stand out among the Fleetwoods, the Impalas, and the Coasters, Paul combined his favorite record label (Tico) with a flashy sports car (Triumph) and, ta-dah! Tico and the Triumphs. Cooper, as lead singer, would be Tico, but they were all in this together, Paul told them when they were together. Don't worry about it. Yet when they weren't together, Paul would tell Cooper a strikingly different story.

Paul opened the first rehearsal by handing out lyrics for a song he had just written called "Motorcycle." A fast-paced rocker built to showcase the group's harmonies with engine-evoking chants of *Brrrrr-mmmm-boppa-boppa-a-boppa-bop-bop.* The tune was the hardest, and best, song he had written since "Hey, Schoolgirl," and he wanted it sung just so. When Gail got through a few rehearsals and realized she wasn't all that interested in the showbiz life, Paul stepped in to round out the vocal parts and, now that he thought of it, take over the lead on "Motorcycle," which he performed with a raw-throated fierceness he'd never achieved on record. Even the B-side ballad, "I Don't Believe Them," was several notches above the typical weepy Landis fare, thanks to a soaring chorus and a soul-stirring vocal from Cooper. After a few weeks of practice, Paul was satisfied enough to go to Charlie Merenstein for the cash he'd need to finance a proper recording session (something like a thousand dollars, according to Cooper), then shopped the finished master around Midtown until he found a buyer in Larry Uttal, whose Madison Records released the 45 in October 1961.

Kicked off with the throaty blast of a revving engine (Paul's car, not an actual motorcycle), "Motorcycle" got to a quick start in New York, where it made the playlist of WINS-AM and nearly stole Murray the K's Record of the Week contest from Boris Pickett's novelty hit "Monster Mash." Sales leaped across the Northeast, but just as the sparks started to fly, the record disappeared from the shops. Already short on cash, Uttal couldn't scrape together the money to keep the printing plants stamping out the vinyl 45s. When the label declared bankruptcy, Paul snatched back the master and ran it over to Amy Records, where Charlie's friend Arthur Yale took it straight to his printers and had them stamp out thousands of new copies. By the time the new discs found their way to stores in November, the momentum for "Motorcycle" had faded. It had a brief run on a few regional Top 20s, even topping the charts in Baltimore and, a few months later, in Puerto Rico. But those wavelets of interest weren't enough. Tico and the Triumphs' debut only just managed to crack

Billboard's Hot 100, spending a week in the No. 99 slot.

Feeling they'd come agonizingly close with "Motorcycle," Paul traded the car engine sounds for the thump of a steam engine and switched the revved-up *Brrrrr-mmmm-boppa-boppa-a-boppa-bop-bop* for the *Wooo-wooo* of the rails to come up with "Express Train," which rocked just as hard as its predecessor, but with a more complex rhythmic texture and more inventive chord changes. Released by Amy Records in April 1962, Tico and the Triumphs' second single once again fell short. In fact, so few copies of "Express Train" were sold that its B-side, a deliberately exotic number called "Wild Flower," went all but unheard. But listen to it now, knowing where Paul's long journey through the musical cultures of the world would take him, and you get a very clear preview of the revolutionary work he'd do decades hence.

The seed of "Wild Flower" arrived in "The Lion Sleeps Tonight (Wimoweh)." At the time that Paul composed "Wild Flower," the Tokens, another New York doo-wop group, had been riding high on the *Billboard* pop charts for months with a lyrically enhanced, retitled cover of "Wimoweh," a nearly wordless South African song that Pete Seeger's folk quartet the Weavers had launched into the pop charts in 1949. The song, based on a Zulu chant that had been a big hit in Africa

125

in 1939, had gained English lyrics after that, but it was the odd cadences and harmonies of the tribal original that ignited Paul's imagination.

Thus came "Wild Flower," the story of a free-wandering girl set to a grab bag of Bo Diddley beats, acoustic guitars, a pair of soprano saxes making like snake charmers, and a faux-Hawaiian tribal chant ("Manga-wey-ah-poola-wey / Hada-ma-la-hada-ma-ley / Hey!") that Paul and the group constructed from random syllables. The production doesn't quite make it — the Diddley beat is too familiar to power a journey to distant lands — but you can hear what Paul is after: the allure of the world beyond, the threads linking there to here; everyone moving to the same *lub-dub;* the fear and the ease of love; a world filled with beasts and friends, risk and revelation; the lion in the jungle; the myths and miracles; the radio signal; the long distance call.

When the record fell flat, so did Paul's interest in the group. The other members of Tico and the Triumphs were fine singers and good guys, but the more Paul worked with them, the more he realized that most of the talent in the band resided in its lead singer, Mickey Cooper. Paul had gotten to like him. He could hear the power in Cooper's vocals and see the hunger in his eyes, and he concluded that Cooper didn't really need those other guys. In fact, they were in his way. If Cooper really wanted to make it, Paul said, he should be a solo singer. Cooper wasn't so sure. Mickey Borack was his best friend; they'd been like brothers for years. How could he toss him to the side now? Paul shrugged and found subtler ways to make his point. Tico and the Triumphs became Tico *with* the Triumphs. Then became, simply, Tico. Cooper wasn't proud of himself; he knew he was double-crossing his pals. But he was the son of a cabdriver; nothing had come easily in his family. And here was Paul taking Cooper out to buy him a sporty new jacket, tight pants, and bright, silky shirts, and then accompanying him to the Bruno's of Hollywood photography studio to make publicity pictures. How many people got that kind of treatment? And once it was offered, who in their right mind would turn it down?

Paul set up recording sessions and didn't invite the others. Cooper sang the leads, Paul sang the background parts, and by the time Borack and Beck heard the title of Tico's next single it was already finished. When the rest of the group figured out what was happening, the eruption was as ghastly as it was inevitable: Borack stopped speaking to Cooper. In any case, Paul's new songs for Tico — a dance tune called "Get Up and Do the Wobble," "Cry Little Boy, Cry," "Cards of Love," and "Noise" — all flopped. Cooper, in whom Paul had invested so much time, energy, and money, didn't become the pop star Paul envisioned.

Paul moved on. By the end of 1962 his entire look had changed. He draped a scarf around his neck and took to wearing it nearly everywhere, one end hanging down his chest and the other strung loosely around his throat. Life on campus, and especially the many hours he'd spent with James Joyce, Wallace Stevens, and all the other great authors he'd studied, had combined with his growing interest in folk culture and music to end his appetite for schlocky pop music. Not the good stuff, though — he still couldn't get enough of Dion, the Everlys, Elvis, the real masters of the form. Still, by the early 1960s, the Top 40 had turned to cardboard, the charts dominated by the Frankies and Annettes and the other Hollywood phonies. All the interesting people Paul knew in college were stuck on folk music, and not because they were trying to escape to some far-off land of maidens and soldiers and corn-cracking farmers. No, the folk that mattered was about real people and real life, as much about tomorrow morning as about yesteryear. And it wasn't just a college fad, either: the Kingston Trio, the Brothers Four, and the Chad Everett Trio were all over the charts. You could still make a few bucks in pop music, sure — Paul had another song or two brewing for the teeny-bopper market — but whenever a new song grabbed him these days, it almost always came in a cloud of dust, sweat, and purpose.

When he cut things off with Cooper, Paul also told Bobby Susser that he was done trying to be a showbiz magnate and would be shutting down their jointly held management and publishing companies, effective immediately. Nothing they'd tried had worked, and now things had changed and he didn't need a partner anymore. Susser was dismayed, but Paul said they should still be friends, and so they were. The next time Cooper saw Susser, he was also sporting a loosely draped scarf and urging the singer to follow Paul's example. "You've gotta start singing folk songs! That's what Paul's doing now."

At Queens College the folk musicians gathered on the upper floor of an old cafeteria that had been replaced with a modern facility a few years earlier. The upstairs of the Old Caf, as they called it, was snug and smoky, just the out-of-the-way place to haul out your guitar or banjo or washboard and raise a voice to the slaves and the workers, to the great protests and to Woody Guthrie's ramblings across the parched fields of the Great Depression. And none of it felt old because the pursuit of justice never ends, and you didn't have to look any farther than this very campus to see it for yourself.

Given the school's antielitist philosophy and the progressive tilt of so many New Yorkers, politics electrified the Queens College campus. The dialogue on campus was like a nonstop debate about the entire contents of the day's *New York Times.* College politics, particularly when it came to the school's administration, ran even hotter. The first major controversy at the college broke out in the early fall of 1958, just days after Paul sat for his first class. Noting the near-complete absence of minority faces among their ranks, faculty members accused college administrators of mounting an organized effort to keep black and minority academics out of the school's faculty. The administration tried to fend off the charges, but students rallied with their professors, organizing a successful college-wide walkout. After a solid year of criticism, newly arrived president Howard Stoke moved to shut down the student newspaper, the *Rampart,* to punish its staff for covering the controversy with such vehemence for so long. Stoke did the same to the school's even more antagonistic newspaper, the *Crown,* declaring that both would be replaced in the fall with a new and, presumably, less radical campus newspaper. But as Stoke somehow failed to anticipate, the new publication, the *Phoenix,* was staffed almost entirely by ex-*Rampart* staffers, who displayed their anger by covering the top of the premiere issue's front page with the text of the censure the National Student Editorial Affairs Conference had slapped on the Queens College administration for its attempt to silence the students' collective voice.

There was so much more to resist. Queens College became the focal point for a student protest against New York City rules banning Communists from speaking on public school campuses, including at the city colleges. Female students, still forbidden from wearing pants on campus, protested the school's treatment of women. Students organized by the nation's most powerful civil rights activists made Queens College a hub for recruiting and training students to be Freedom Riders, busing down to the Jim Crow South to help the black communities build the schools, libraries, and voter rolls they needed to exercise the basic rights they hadn't gained after the Civil War.

The walls of the Old Caf rang with talk of all these movements and initiatives — but not with the guitar or voice of Paul Simon, who kept almost all his political sympathies out of sight. As much as he liked the subtextual meanings in folk music, Paul preferred songs that didn't sound like editorials set to music. The music he connected with most closely were the folk ballads and quirky old-timey tunes that came from the likes of the Kingston Trio and the Brothers Four. So he did most of his strumming in the new cafeteria, entertaining the other students with a few frat brothers in tow, whipping through some familiar folk and pop tunes before closing with his popular cover of the Kingston Trio's arrangement of the little-known cocktail jazz tune "Scotch and Soda." That always got a big hand, but not from everyone. When newly elected student body president Mark Levy, who had campaigned with a promise to launch an on-campus folk festival, agreed to let Paul audition for his show, he balked at Paul's pop-folk pleasantries. "I was reaching out to blues players and Appalachian players. Some old guy who played the dulcimer," he says. "All Paul had were these silly romantic songs. Nothing political, nothing ethnic, nothing that, in my limited mind at the time, qualified as folk. So I wouldn't hire him."

Though too bourgeois for the hard-core folkies, Paul also wasn't entirely clean cut. He smoked marijuana enthusiastically and often. What bugged his close friend Brian Schwartz was that the stoned Paul wasn't anywhere near as forthright or reliable as the sober Paul. Sometimes pot made him giggly; other times he became prankish and heedlessly sharp-tongued, much like his new hero Lenny Bruce, the so-called sick comic whose unsparing and often lewd social commentary was as liberating to some as it was offensive to others. Paul's sense of humor evolved accordingly, and like Bruce, who spent most of the last decade of his life fighting obscenity charges in New York City and elsewhere, it sometimes got him into trouble.

Paul had a severe distaste for academics who condescended to the students, particularly when the student happened to be Paul. He'd already hung a few of his professors out to dry in his Follies skits, but he could also take a much more direct approach, as he did in a class on Middle English taught by a professor notorious for his leather-patched tweeds and his gratingly stentorian boom. Assigned to read a section from the original text of Chaucer's *Canterbury Tales,* Paul used his ear for music and rhythm to great effect, gallivanting through the six-hundred-year-old meter and pronunciation with no problem. When he finished, the professor jumped to his feet, the better to drape his student in garlands of claps and bravos: "Magnificent, young sir!" Paul responded with a shrug: "Yeah, well, we speak Middle English at home." The other students laughed. The professor didn't. Cheeks ablaze, he nodded curtly and called on the next student. At the end of the term, the professor paid Paul back for his impertinence by giving him an F for the course. Brian Schwartz, who was also in the class, was enraged on Paul's behalf. He was vice president of the student body; he could launch an official protest with the administration and get Paul the grade he deserved. Paul waved him off. He'd suck it up — better that than becoming best known for being a victim.

The only problem was figuring out how he *did* want to be known. Paul continued working as Jerry Landis through 1962, but from a greater and greater remove. That guy, with his shiny white bucks and shimmering hair helmet, was a projection of Paul's high school fantasies of the music business. Four-plus years and nearly his entire college education later, Paul had taken on an entirely new palette of feelings and ideas: serious thoughts about identity, morality, and the pursuit of justice. He had read the timeless writers and studied the great philosophers. Like many others on campus, he'd been influenced by the work of Queens College's increasingly well-known philosophy teacher John J. McDermott, whose analysis of the existentialism lurking beneath America's faith in assimilation and self-determination touched the core of Paul's conflicted, post-immigrant consciousness.

The small-time music industrialists in Midtown Manhattan couldn't have cared less about Paul's consciousness — they had no idea who Paul Simon was. When they needed someone to record a bunch of demos or come up with a cheap but plausible stab at a pop radio hit, they called for Jerry Landis. That's the guy they knew, the Tom and Jerry guy who had written and produced the Tico and the Triumphs records, the guy they saw pictured in the ads for his occasional solo singles. But when he sat down to write his own songs, Paul's mind flashed to images much darker and deeper than the high school romantic Jerry Landis could ever imagine. The months of playing folk music led his fingers to new chords and less frantic rhythms. His interior geography was shifting; everything he had learned at college had started to give voice to feelings that had evaded expression for too long. At least one other guy in New York, a newcomer, even, had poured similar feelings into a raw but gripping album of folk songs that Paul's hipper pals at school and in Midtown couldn't stop talking about. Then Paul got his own copy of Bob Dylan's self-titled first album and heard it, too.

By the time Dylan's debut on Columbia Records came out in the early spring of 1962, his reputation as a performer — he had barely started writing songs — and interpreter of Woody Guthrie's free-ranging spirit had made him a kind of superhero to the folkie demimonde in the city. Guthrie was the lanky outlander who had blown across the prairies and highways of the real tumbledown America, collecting old stories and songs that revealed as much about modern times as they did of the old. Dylan's own story was a bit of a mystery. He told some people that he was part Native American and others that he had spent his childhood traveling the nation with a circus. He didn't tell anyone that his real name was Bob Zimmerman or that he had been raised in a middle-class Jewish family in Hibbing, Minnesota, but all that would emerge later.

Paul had already listened to the Dylan record a few times when he dialed up Al Kooper, a neighborhood guitarist he'd met at the height of the "Hey, Schoolgirl" moment, when both their groups were playing the same sock hop. Kooper's family lived just four blocks from the Simons in Kew Gardens Hills, and they had stayed friends. Kooper had skipped college to focus on his music career, so when Louis asked Paul to play a few dance numbers for the kids at Lee Simms Orchestra gigs, Paul often called on Kooper to play the lead guitar parts. It made for a dull evening for the boys, except that Louis paid exceptionally well — Kooper recalls earning one hundred dollars a night — and when they weren't playing, he and Paul could talk about records and bands and, on this one night in the spring of 1962, the much-talked-about record by this Bob Dylan kid.

Of course Kooper had heard the record — and had quickly dismissed it because, as he told Paul, he couldn't stand Dylan's exaggerated prairie whine. At this, Paul waved his hand. "Don't listen to the *singing.* Listen to how he plays the guitar!" Paul dropped the needle on his copy of the album, and after a track or two Kooper knew what he was talking about. Rather than strumming the strings like nearly all the other folk guitarists, Dylan was fingerpicking in a driving, bluesy style that gave the songs a crunch forceful enough to make the Kingston Trio's sweaters unravel. Kooper went home a convert, and altered the course of his career accordingly.[*]

Paul followed Dylan closely after that, and Dylan's influence on him grew even more powerful when Paul started writing his own songs. There was an intelligence to Dylan, a literary sophistication that came through not just in his performances but also in how he carried himself. He didn't waste time trying to mimic other artists' hits; he sang what he

[*] Not an exaggeration. When Kooper wrangled an invitation to observe a Dylan recording session a few years later, he insinuated himself into the studio and wound up contributing the soaring organ line to "Like a Rolling Stone." Dylan tapped Kooper to play keyboards in the group that brought electric music to the Newport Folk Festival, and Kooper played sessions with Dylan for many years after that.

wanted to in exactly the way he wanted to and wound up winning the support of John Hammond, the Columbia Records A&R man whose discoveries included Benny Goodman, Count Basie, and Billie Holiday. And Paul was still trying to pump out hit songs for Jerry Landis?

When the Queens College spring term ended in 1962, Paul packed his acoustic guitar and a few other essentials and traveled to California. He explored the cities and visited friends here and there, but he focused much of his time and attention on finding and connecting with the folk clubs and musicians. He'd go to shows and introduce himself to the players and their friends and hang out for a while. If he was lucky, he would find a sofa to sleep on, and then they'd be up all night, drinking wine, smoking dope, and talking politics, poetry, songwriting, and anything else that seemed to matter. He'd play open mics at folk clubs, and if he connected he'd approach the owner and see if he could play a full set. A few days later he'd be doing it again, in a different town — Berkeley one night, San Francisco the next, and so on. By the time he got back to New York to prepare for his next, and final, term at Queens College, he had found a new voice and the stirrings of a new identity.

Many of those late-night talks in California

during the summer of 1962 touched on the civil rights movement and the stand-off between the Kennedy administration and the state of Mississippi over African American student James Meredith's right to attend the publicly funded University of Mississippi. The constitutional arguments for integrating the school seemed obvious, but some hearts beat a crooked rhythm in a nation built on slave labor, so Mississippi governor Ross Barnett planted himself in the doorway and swore and swore. For so many of the students and folkies Paul met that summer, just as for the friends he would soon see again at Queens College, the civil rights movement had become the central battle in the war between the nation's past and its future. When the news came on, they'd sit together and watch Barnett and his fellow racists blocking the doorway at UMiss, another reminder of the ugliness of institutionalized prejudice — which, as Paul knew, was also practiced by the national leaders of his own beloved Alpha Epsilon Pi fraternity.

It was right there in the fraternity's charter, and they'd all lived with it ever since: the fraternity would not open its doors to black men. But wasn't AEPi supposed to be the house for intellectually enlightened Jewish men? Paul had kept his distance from the fist-in-the-air types, but now he saw something he could do, a significant change he could

139

make within an institution by maneuvering its parliamentary process. With a national meeting of the AEPi chapters scheduled for the end of the summer in Buffalo, Paul launched a nationwide effort to strip the offending rule from the organization's charter. Tapping a few Queens College brothers to help him work the phones and tally votes, he and his friends pushed their issue to the threshold of victory — the frat's active members voted to pass the measure — until a cabal of alumni, known as "grandmasters," only just managed to tilt the balance toward the "no" votes.

At that point Paul and his brothers could have escalated the fight. They could have organized a walk-out from the convention or gone even further and recruited like-minded chapters into a full-scale revolt, tearing up their AEPi charters and forming their own fraternity, one that stood for equal rights and equal admissions for qualified pledges no matter their racial or religious background. But no one joins a fraternity because they're itching to tear down institutional structures. These were organization men, adherents to Robert's Rules, willing to wait until the times tilted in the right direction.

When James Meredith was finally allowed through the door of the University of Mississippi that fall, Paul performed in Queens College's celebratory folk hootenanny, playing guitar and harmonizing with fraternity brothers Brian Schwartz and Larry Mandelker and an African American student, Pat Dagler, in an ensemble the *Phoenix* called the Freedom Criers. Although the show was set to take place in the campus's central quad, a rainstorm chased it into the cafeteria, where the tidy group — Schwartz wore a three-piece suit, Mandelker buttoned a clean white shirt beneath a blazer, Dagler chose a skirt and blouse, and Paul wore a less formal V-neck sweater and T-shirt — sang impassioned versions of Pete Seeger's "If I Had a Hammer," "We Shall Overcome," and all the songs of hope and deliverance a guitar player could sing with his chest out, his mouth wide, and his eyes raised to the light in the sky. Everyone sang along, and cheered for James Meredith, and for President Kennedy and the men in his federal brigade, and also for the movement as a whole, the arc of justice, and the strength of their own voices and convictions.

Some of them were already working for justice and some were about to start. Student body president Ron Pollack invited the civil rights movement's leading activists to use the college as a central organizing spot for the Bus Project, an effort to send sympathetic college students from the northern states to join the effort in the most racist corners of the Deep South. Paul's AEPi brother Mark Levy, past president of the Queens College

141

student body, traveled to Mississippi to help prepare the students' organizational and survival tactics. Classmate and AEPi brother Michael Schwerner signed on to ride, and so did Paul's friend June Tauber, who bused to Prince Edward County, Virginia, for the summer of 1963 to build schools and register voters. When she got back, Tauber spoke at churches and college campuses to recruit more Riders. After one presentation at Queens College, a younger student named Andy Goodman came up to ask her what the experience had felt like. Tauber knew him already: he was a theater student, a sweet-faced young man who was more artistic than political, a soft-spoken outsider who couldn't stand bullies or unfairness of any kind. Face flushed with the overwhelming sense of purpose the work had given her, Tauber gazed into Goodman's eyes and put it as clearly as she could.

"It's the most alive you'll ever feel in your life."

It was the last time she saw him alive.

CHAPTER 7
WHAT ARE YOU SEARCHING FOR, CARLOS DOMINGUEZ

Originally scheduled to graduate with his class in the spring of 1962, Paul opted to stay for another semester. He spent part of the time boning up on the subjects he'd need to get a quick start in law school, the destiny he had predicted for himself since he'd started talking about what his future might hold. When he wasn't at school that fall, he was writing and recording an upbeat novelty called "The Lone Teen Ranger," a silly song based on the popular *Lone Ranger* TV Western. The tune begins with pistol shots and then a doo-wop-style *Brrrrr-bop-bop-bop-Brrrrrrr-bop-bippy-bippy-bop* vocal to set up a galloping Jerry Landis plaint about the masked TV cowboy who has stolen his girl's affections. "She even kissed the TV set / Oh, it's a crying shame!" It's hard to hear the Wallace Stevens influence here, but a catchy novelty tune could go a long way in those days, so the industry trade journals gave the song a thumbs-up. "Teen Ranger" earned pick-hit status from *Billboard, Cash Box, Variety,* and a dozen other publications and radio tip sheets. Once again, though, Paul's best efforts couldn't carry him past the lower rungs on the Top 100. "The Lone Teen Ranger" climbed to No. 97 on *Billboard*'s Hot 100 in the early weeks of January 1963 and then faded to nothing.

Paul finished his bachelor's degree in January 1963 and then turned his attention to starting law school in the fall. It was an easy call to make, a natural fit for an ambitious young man with the intelligence and work ethic he'd always shown in school. It was also a future he knew Louis and Belle wanted him to pursue. A serious career in a profession that could take a hardworking young man nearly anywhere he might want to go.

Paul certainly overflowed with aptitude for the practice of law. He was fast on the uptake, a poised communicator, seethingly competitive, and naturally argumentative. The only necessary thing he lacked was any real interest in being an attorney. Yet how could he ignore his parents' wishes without at least giving it a try? So he'd long since accepted the law as his destiny: he wrote "Law" in the space beneath his graduation headshot in the Forest Hills High School yearbook where you're supposed to describe your future, and told the admissions office at Queens College that he planned to be a prelaw student. Then the towering marks he received on the law boards clicked the lock once and for all. When Brooklyn Law School accepted his application for the fall of 1963, his future was set — for the time being anyway.

With eight months left before he had to return to the lecture halls, he went back to producing demo recordings, many for the large and enduring Edward B. Marks Music Company. Most were the same bland pop tunes he'd always worked on, but with increasingly recognizable flair. He recorded the folky tunes with a single voice and guitar accompaniment, dressed up others with Latin percussion, still others with an airy bossa nova treatment, and sang one updated Latin traditional, called "Coplas," entirely in Spanish.

Without thinking about it, Paul had started constructing a bridge between the English major and pop songwriter holed up in the opposing hemispheres of his brain. Forget the lovesick teens, sock hop dance songs, and TV cowboys; forget the billowing strings, guitars, and tinkly pianos. Now he was dreaming songs carved from a voice or two and acoustic guitar, with plainspoken lyrics about the world and the internal riddles of the soul. The first of these songs he took to Midtown was "Carlos Dominguez," a Spanish-style ballad of an "unhappy man" who wanders the world in search of truth and comes home empty-handed. The gently fingered "The Side of a Hill" draws a wartime parable from the imagined land of Somewhere, where a single cloud weeps upon the grave of a child killed in a battle over something no one can remember.

The more intriguing "Bleecker Street" describes the seamier side of Greenwich Village, the seat of New York City's folk renaissance, in strikingly biblical terms ("it's a long road to Canaan on Bleecker Street") and with a melodic grace that points to much of what would follow. But the real knockout was the most direct of them all, a protest song so in tune with the times that the event it describes wouldn't happen for another year. So much lay ahead. But in the spring of 1963, "He Was My Brother" stood out only as Paul's best attempt at writing in the journo-poetic tradition renewed by Bob Dylan. And what a great distance it was from the black-and-white TV frontier of "The Lone Teen Ranger" to the crimson dirt of America's Deep South. A reckoning was coming somewhere, but for Paul in Kew Gardens Hills, the most significant collision that year came in the form of Artie Garfunkel.

It was late spring, somewhere in the midst of Paul's transformation into a modern folk singer-songwriter. He has described it again and again — how he was out for a walk in the neighborhood, crossing a bridge over a pond, and looked up to see blond curls and a familiar smile. Oh wow, Artie. Had it been a while? Was it in fact the first time the old friends had shaken hands since they swiveled their tassels and walked out of Forest Hills High School for the last time? That's how they both recall it, and it is a pleasingly romantic vision. The boyhood besties who made it big, fell out, and then by *kairos* were brought together again. Crossing a bridge from opposite directions, lingering for a little while against the railing, ducks adrift below their feet, and then walking off together, back to their brotherhood and to the creative union they were born to serve.

Then again, maybe it didn't happen exactly like that. Maybe they had been in touch throughout their college years, not seeing each other nearly as much as before, but still seeing each other. And maybe they still worked together, too, earning good money for playing pop hits, dance numbers, and a few of their own songs as Tom and Jerry. They definitely performed for some very impressed campers at Camp Washington Lodge where Paul worked in the summer of 1958. They also played the La Salle Junior High School's GO! dance in the fall of 1962. Both were well-received performances, still recalled by the kids who were there, most of whom left with memories of fast-moving shows that seemed quite well rehearsed.

Or maybe it really had been five years, and maybe Paul was both surprised and delighted to hear that Artie had also fallen for folk music, getting heavily into Dylan and the disarmingly beautiful California priestess Joan Baez, whose songs were far more political, and whose voice was so much stronger, than those of Greenwich Village's footloose idol. When Paul pulled out his guitar to play his new songs, Artie tapped his foot to each one. Yet "He Was My Brother" was the one that made his eyes gleam. Inspired by the growing violence directed against civil rights workers in the South, the song tells an imagined story of a Freedom Rider's death at the hands of racists. As personal as it is political, "Brother" packs a punch other protest songs often lack, particularly during the tune's final moments, when Paul's lyrics transform the notion of brotherhood to include all humanity: "He was my brother / And he died so his brothers could be free . . ."

They sang it together a few times, and Paul's face lit up — that voice, that blend. Though Artie was planning to spend his summer hitchhiking through California with little brother, Jerry, and while Paul already planned to travel through Europe, they resolved to sing together when they got home in the fall. Both had visions of singing their way through their travels, and both did. And the thing

Artie noticed that summer was that whenever he got up to sing folk tunes for his friends or at open mics, the song that got the biggest response was always the one he had just learned from Paul, the song about the murdered civil rights worker, "He Was My Brother."

Flying into London with his guitar, limited cash, and no contacts, Paul scuffled around the city for a few days, singing to empty street corners and seeing only disinterest in the faces of the passersby. Paris proved far more hospitable, however, and he fell happily into the wandering bohemian folkie life, learning the tricks of the busker's trade — how to position yourself in a storefront entrance so its windows become an amplifier, the benefit of drafting a cute girl to pass the hat — until he could reliably draw a crowd and squeeze a few francs out of their pockets. If he collected enough to buy food, he'd eat; if he got enough for a hotel room, he'd sleep in a bed. If he didn't, he'd sleep on the bank of the Seine, beneath the Pont Neuf, and when tourist boats full of wealthy Americans puttered past he'd holler, "Capitalist pigs!" at them and laugh when they gaped back at him. When he wasn't busking, he took in the sights, sticking out his thumb to catch a ride to a cathedral or a particularly lovely garden, and then hang around for a while, taking it all in.

He was doing just that, kicking back on a garden lawn somewhere, when he noticed another young traveler speaking English to a companion. The thin, dark-haired guy spoke with a British accent and wore the jeans and sweater of a proper college man, so Paul sidled in closer and, with a companionable smile, introduced himself. They chatted for a few minutes, the basic "Where are you from?" and "How long have you been around?" and "What have you been up to?" stuff. Then, with a casual grin, Paul asked his new friend if he had any grass on him. The fellow smiled approvingly and Paul shook hands with David McCausland, a college student from Essex, England, a patchwork of farms and suburban villages about thirty miles east of London. McCausland was a folk music fan, too, and the co-owner and co-manager of his own folk club, so when Paul told him he was a folk musician busking his way across Europe, McCausland wrote his name and address on a scrap of paper and invited Paul to stay with him and his family when he got to England.

It was a dreamy summer, even given — no, *especially* given — his dusty hand-to-mouth existence. For those precious weeks, Paul went wherever the wind and whimsy took him. Europe was full of young travelers, many moving by thumb, and if you were on the circuit of the roadways, hostels, coffee shops, and folkie college pubs, you'd start recognizing faces. "Didn't I just see you in Amsterdam? I didn't know you were going to Copenhagen, too!" — a whole continent full of places he'd barely heard of, places he knew nothing about. Imagine poor old Carlos Dominguez on his tragic quest for truth, only Paul was having a ball, and finding what he was looking for nearly everywhere he went. And it was all new, and completely detached from where he'd been and whom he knew. It was a kind of liberation he'd never experienced before, which only made it that much more painful to go back to Queens at summer's end with nothing but law school awaiting his return.

At least Artie was waiting for him, too. One year into Columbia University's graduate program in mathematics, he was back living at home, so there they were, once again living just a few blocks apart. They started singing together in earnest, working out harmonies for Paul's new songs, Artie encouraging him to write more, the two of them trying to create their own arrangement of Orlande de Lassus's a cappella "Benedictus." They mastered a few folk standards, and also the camp song about the dog named "Bingo," for which Paul had an inexplicable fondness, and then started to think of places where they could perform. Greenwich Village was the center of the scene, so why start anywhere else? They got their names on the list for the Cafe Wha's Monday night hootenannies and sang into open mics at the Gaslight Club and Gerde's Folk City. On October 22 they landed their first scheduled show in Greenwich Village, supporting the vintage Tennessean banjo player Clarence "Tom" Ashley and the Clancy Brothers-esque Irish Ramblers. Unheralded and not quite in their element among the downtown hipsters, the clean-cut duo Kane and Garr did their best to seem at home.

Those were the names they used when they first relaunched themselves as folksingers. Paul was still Jerry Landis when he ran the Tin Pan Alley circuit, and when he hired on as a song plugger for the large and enduring Edward B. Marks. It wasn't a bad job; he earned $150 a week to take the latest crop of songs by the company's staff writers to the producers and record companies who had the power to make them into hits. The entry-level job came with a lofty pedigree. Both Irving Berlin and George Gershwin had been song pluggers before they hit it big as songwriters. Still, Paul could barely stand it. He had very little interest in selling songs written by other people, especially when the songs didn't suit his taste. How could he sell products he didn't believe in? He couldn't, really — a failure he couched in a know-it-all swagger that drove some colleagues to despise him. But it was steady work, and as his bosses made clear, they would be happy to publish whatever marketable new songs he might have to sell. And that's what Paul did with his new folk songs, selling to Marks "Carlos Dominguez," "He Was My Brother," "Bleecker Street," "The Side of a Hill," and his and Artie's new arrangement of "Benedictus."[*]

Paul would come to regret that decision later, but his most immediate lament that fall and winter involved his decision to go to law school. As he had feared, you could have all the aptitude in the world for law and still be out of place in law school. The intricacies of torts and civil procedures dribbled across his skull like water torture. Not even his appreciation for a cannily drawn subclause could fuel an interest in contracts. In the evenings, he would study among his friends

[*] Talking about his brief Edward B. Marks era to *Rolling Stone*'s Nicholas Dawidoff in 2011, Paul said he agreed to let Marks publish his songs only because he felt so bad about being such a lousy salesman. Yet that's a farfetched interpretation, given his inability theretofore to write a hit song that wasn't "Hey, Schoolgirl," and even that was only a middling success. Swagger indeed, even five decades later.

at the Queens College library, and when Brian Schwartz saw how quickly his once-inspired mentor fell asleep over his new textbooks, he started urging Paul to toss the books, and law school, into the garbage. Paul had shared his new songs with Brian, and Schwartz knew exactly where his friend's passion lay, and how far it might take him. "Focus on your music," he urged when Paul drove him to the subway every night. "That's your path! That's what you're meant to do!" Paul shrugged it off for a month or two, but when the As and Bs he earned during the first quarter sank to Cs and Ds at the end of the semester, he knew something had to change. But what? And at what cost?

One evening that fall, Paul took his guitar into the bathroom, locked the door, and turned on the sink's spigot. The sound of the water soothed him, and kept the music from echoing into every room in the house. Usually he'd switch off the light and sit on the tile floor, the coolness against his haunches, and strum a chord or two to see what came into his mind. Or maybe, on this gloomy night in late 1963, he was more interested in getting things *out* of his head — the ongoing disaster of law school and the dread that settled over him whenever he thought of giving up. The dismay on his parents' faces and then the guilt that would surely follow. And then there was everything else in the world. The murder of President Kennedy; fires, bombs, and bullets raining down on civil rights activists in the South. Could he really risk it all on his guitar and the second-rate Dylan songs he was trying to write? He struck a minor chord and followed it down.

Hello darkness my old friend,
I've come to talk to you again . . .

Then it all started to come, a nightmare tumble of dreary weather, chemical street-lights, throngs of human automatons, ignored wisdom, and soul-sucking isolation — all of it cloaked in silence, a suffocating hush deep enough to still tongues and deafen ears. Wisdom can be found; it's literally written on the walls. Yet if anyone bothers to look, they still can't see it; if anyone speaks it, no one listens. The hush is paralytic. The creeping tendrils of a living death. So speak up! "Hear my words that I might teach you / Take my arms that I might reach you." The singer shouts it to the skies and receives only an echo in return. Hear my words, take my arms: Is he offering comfort or begging for it? Is he addressing a single person or society as a whole? A lover? A parent? A child? Or maybe he's talking to himself, to the gloom in his own soul, to his guilt and anger, to his stymied connection with friends, a woman,

155

an audience. Paul called the song "The Sound of Silence" and built it on a spare sequence of chords designed to fit a melody line that moves repeatedly from flat to vaulting to towering before sinking down again — a song desperate for attention, that would not be ignored, that would change his life.

Yet first he needed to get away. Memories of his European summer had sustained him through the fall, and with more than a month between the end of fall classes and the start of the winter term at Brooklyn Law, he calculated the cost of flights and set his sights on England. Particularly on London and its bustle of folk musicians and its pubs, nightclubs, and social halls where audiences gathered to hear them sing. Better still, London was only a short train ride from Essex, where David McCausland, the hospitable fellow he'd met in that Parisian garden a few months back, lived in his parents' meandering suburban home. And hadn't McCausland said he ran a folk club? Paul wrote a letter to the address he'd been given and started preparing for his journey.

When Paul's letter got to England, its recipient was flummoxed. McCausland certainly remembered Paul, and also his invitation to come visit him in Essex, but now the American was expecting to play in his Brentwood Folk Club, and not just once. Paul's letter proposed that he start a full residency in the club, performing each week he was in Essex, for a full five pounds a show. Five pounds was a decent rate for an established musician, but McCausland had never seen or heard Paul perform. He had no idea if the guy could even carry a tune! McCausland passed the letter to his musician friends to see if any of them had ever heard of this Paul Simon bloke. They were all mystified, but when he got to Martin Carthy, the guitarist urged McCausland to book Paul. Carthy had seen American musicians before. Most British folksingers tended to plant themselves behind the microphone with shoulders hunched and eyes closed. But the Americans, even the ones who weren't very good at music, all seemed to know how to *entertain.* They told funny stories, and they knew how to play and sing loud enough to be heard in the back of the room. Carthy figured the Americans must teach it in their schools. "So I told David he'd probably be great," Carthy says. "And if he wasn't, he could always sack him."

So Paul had a gig. In England he grew close to David and his parents, who enjoyed the American's excellent manners and his eagerness to turn dinners into long conversations about the United States, philosophy, and religion, which he loved to discuss even if he couldn't believe in it. In the evenings, David took Paul to his friends' parties, where Paul charmed and joked and entertained with his ever-present guitar, belting out the latest Dylan or Tom Paxton and, once the ale had been flowing, his favorite pop hits by Elvis, the Everlys, Dion, or whatever got his new friends clapping, singing, and dancing. They'd all laugh and applaud and slap him on the back, and when the time came for the next Brentwood Folk Club show at the Railway Pub, they came flocking out to see him and hear some more.

The Brentwood Folk Club met weekly in an empty room above the Railway Tavern, one of those cozy neighborhood pubs where the owner pulls pints of ale, bitter, and stout for his customers without having to ask who wants what. McCausland had cofounded the folk club with David Rugg, a young accountant he'd met at the folk clubs around Essex. Unlike London, where folk clubs were regular nightclubs that booked performers night after night, the suburban folk clubs met only once or twice a week. They ran like any other club, with membership fees, faithful attendees, and the easy conviviality shared by the like-minded. Noting the lack of a club near Brentwood, McCausland and Rugg had made an arrangement with the Railway Tavern's owner, posted notices in the other clubs to spread the news, and signed up enough members to book their first show in early 1963. They didn't fill the room's eighty-person capacity that night, but they brought in enough cash to pay for the next week's booking, and with local performers happy to play opening sets for free the club thrived.

At one of his first shows that winter, Paul sat at a table with friends while his opener, a guitar-playing husband-and-wife team, performed the requisite British country ballads with the crisp locution of the educated middle class. The room warmed once the chairs filled and the pint glasses started thumping onto the tables. The duo closed with a few bawdy tunes about whip-happy coachmen, randy barmaids, and so on, and left to a nice hand, making room for Paul, who stepped up to solid applause and cheerful shouts from pals in the room. He strummed a few chords and seemed to be starting something, but then stopped abruptly.

"Ha. It's good to be here at the fabulous London Palla —"

A voice called out, "You'd never hear Pete Seeger say that!"

"Well, if you see Pete, make sure to tell him about all the political things [I] said tonight!"

He launched into Dylan's "Don't Think Twice, It's All Right," got halfway into the first verse, and then cut off abruptly.

"Ooh! Sorry, Nigel, I lost my head, played a Bob Dylan song!"

He got back into it, strumming another few

chords before cutting it off again.

"Aw, I don't like that one anyway. Let me think . . ."

Next came "Man of Constant Sorrow," delivered in a variation of Dylan's parched prairie voice, the *I*s coming out like *Aaaahhh-hh*s, and then more joking, which turned out to be a central part of Paul's act that evening. Did anyone want to hear his new poem? "Oh, yes, let's have your poem!" a woman shouted back, so he took a dramatic moment to compose himself. Then:

> My name is Fred. I sleep in a bed.
> I used to have to sleep in a cot but when
>   my mommy saw how big I got
> She knew I couldn't possibly fall on my
>   head. So now I sleep in a bed.

That bit of nonsense earned great cheers, which Paul acknowledged with a shrug: "A little existentialism with your folk music." Then came a kid's song or two, then a request for an original — "One of your new songs, Paul!" — and then the opening guitar figure to "The Sound of Silence" brought all the tittering to an abrupt halt. He sang quietly at first, then with gathering intensity, biting down so hard on the final verse that it took a moment for the crowd to start what became a loud, sustained ovation.

So it went whenever Paul stepped up to a

microphone that winter, starting in Brentwood and then moving to the other suburban clubs, and then into the London clubs, the permanent fixtures such as the Troubadour and Les Cousins, where he could sign up for a floor spot, a two- or three-song mini-set delivered from wherever you were standing. He'd perform the same blend of traditionals, kids' songs, a Dylan cover or two — they were basically required from all but the most hidebound folk musicians at that time — gospel songs favored by the civil rights movement, and then these stunning bolts from the blue: "Sound of Silence," "He Was My Brother," "Bleecker Street," the just-composed "Leaves That Are Green," and a growing list of others that would silence the crowd and pin them to their chairs, breathless. The music was accompanied by a comedy shtick lampooning intellectuals, folkies, mainstream showbiz, and, increasingly, Bob Dylan, whose overwhelming authority among the folk music circles had clearly become an aggravation to Paul.

He sounded talented, thrilled, and a little bit terrified. Could he really remake himself into a folk performer? Each night marked another step in his transformation, a herky-jerky combination of showbiz gags, folk traditionals, satirical bits about existentialism and psychology, kids' songs — "A Dog Named Blue" and "Bingo" were favorites — deliberately bad poetry, and then, like a gem tumbling from the sky, one of his own songs. Maybe a brief introduction, a spare guitar figure, a series of chords, then melody flowing across perfectly measured lines about isolation, love, or mortality. When it was over, the applause came with new intensity. Other guitarists and songwriters caught each other's eyes and shook their heads. *The fucking guy knows what he's doing!* Always neatly trimmed in his black corduroys and black sweaters, with that fast-talking, blurt-it-all-out manner of speaking, Paul had a way of filling up every room he entered, despite his size. The poetry-reading urban rustics around London took notice. They mentioned his name, wondered if you'd heard him, suggested that you make a point of doing so, because he could really play guitar and had these songs that were nothing like Dylan's, but still so stunning. He had his own thing, did Paul Simon. He was worth knowing.

Paul made friends with other folk musicians and became particularly chummy with Martin Carthy, the influential guitarist who had urged McCausland to hire him. Paul got a few bookings, five-pound-a-nighters that kept him busy and spread his name that much farther. And then there was Kathy. He'd spotted her the moment he walked into the Railway Tavern and made for the stairs to the club room. She was new in the area, a friend

162

of a friend of McCausland and Rugg's who had volunteered to help out at the Brentwood. Kathy Chitty came from a small village in Wales, and though she'd had courage enough to leave her family home and travel alone to London when she was barely twenty, she was also shy, with a soft pair of eyes behind dark brunette bangs. When McCausland brought Paul to the club, he said hello to her and smiled. She smiled back, and it didn't take much time for Paul to ask her out and then fall in love.

They struck some as a curious pair, given Paul's bluff American charisma and the Welsh girl's near-invisible public demeanor. Many of the friends who grew used to seeing her with Paul rack their brains to recall if they ever heard her utter a word in their presence. But Kathy's timorous facade hid a rugged soul. The Welsh winters were raw and long; the mountainous terrain there offered little but physical labor, much of it in the calamitous mines crawling into the earth's crust. Death was not a stranger in Wales. But there were also the lush green hills and jagged mountains, the rock-strewn coastline and the bittersweet, poetic hearts all that roughness nurtured. If Paul could be tough and gloomy, if he could rage at the world and at himself, if he could reach out and all but consume her with his need, Kathy understood. She could gird his spirit in the morning and draw him back to earth in the evening. A mother, a confessor, a lover, a mirror, a muse — Kathy was everything Paul could possibly need. He could look her in the eye — she was close to him in size — and when he spoke to her, his entire being seemed to soften. "I stand alone without beliefs," he would soon sing of her. "The only truth I know is you."

Then Paul's time ran out, and he had to go back to New York, back to everything he had been so happy to escape just a few weeks earlier. So much had happened since then. He'd glimpsed a life that had nearly nothing to do with everything he'd known growing up in New York, an existence free of expectation. But once he stepped through his parents' door, once he found himself not quite fighting off sleep in those downtown Brooklyn classrooms, England might as well have been a dream. He was back in his childhood bedroom, walking the same old streets, trudging back into those soporific law books, and then to the dusty old Edward B. Marks offices to bear the aggravation of selling other people's songs. Still, at least that job came with a few advantages — particularly now that he had a new crop of songs and a renewed partnership with Artie.

They were getting serious about their music again, continuing their Washington Square Park busking and open mic rounds, and also knuckling the Midtown office doors in search of a recording contract. But that process had become no easier than it had been nearly a decade earlier. An unknown pair of folksingers would never get through the doors Paul had come to know so well as an emissary for the Marks corporation. It was hard to resist the temptation to pitch one of his own songs along with the others, but Marks had so many songwriters on its staff that it had had to construct a strict intra-office law to make sure that kind of thing didn't happen. One slip, and you were finished. Then again, this was showbiz, and as Paul had been taught so many years ago, if you had an advantage to work you used it.

It didn't take long: a couple of weeks, maybe a month. Holding a sheaf of songs for Columbia Records, Paul was ushered into the office of A&R executive/producer Tom Wilson, a statuesque black man with stylish clothes and an air of sophistication that drew as much from the jazz-and-poetry underground as from the lecture halls of Harvard, from which he had graduated with honors in 1954. When Columbia's preeminent talent scout John Hammond needed a staff producer who could understand and nurture his latest discovery, he had paired Wilson with Bob Dylan, with terrific results. Just a few albums later, the impact of their collaboration had altered the course of folk music and was still radiating outward. Now seen as a kingmaker among folk producers, Wilson set out to create the Pilgrims, a pop-folk vocal trio that could serve as an African American answer to Peter, Paul, and Mary.* By early 1964 he had found his three singers, recorded a handful of songs, and was looking for the right song to make the group's debut single when Paul came knocking with the entries from Edward B. Marks. Wilson passed on all of them and was about to dismiss him when Paul offered something else. He was a song-writer, too, he said, and had just written a song that might be a better fit. Did the producer have time to hear it? Wilson shrugged. Sure, why not.

When Paul got a verse or two into "The Sound of Silence" Wilson started nodding his head. When it was done, he positively beamed. Yes, that *did* sound like the right kind of song. Why didn't Paul go make a demo recording and bring it back so Wilson could play it for the others? Paul hopped the D train for Greenwich Village and tracked down his new friend Jim McGuinn (who later changed his first name to Roger), a guitarist and singer who was one of the more experi-

---

* The Pilgrims included Robert Guillaume, the actor who would become quite famous on a variety of television series, including the top-rated *Benson* in the early 1980s.

166

enced young musicians on the scene, to help oversee the recording session. When it was done, he brought the disc back to Wilson, who once again declared himself impressed. In fact, "The Sound of Silence" would be the perfect single for the Pilgrims. Once again, though, Paul had another idea. He'd formed a singing duo with a friend from Columbia University, and they'd worked out a great duo arrangement for the song. Could they at least sing it for him together before Wilson gave it to the other band? Wilson said sure, and when Paul came back with Artie a day or two later, Wilson had to hear them sing it together only once. He booked time in the Columbia Records studio, asked a young staff engineer named Roy Halee to roll the tape, and watched from the control room while Paul and Artie harmonized their way through "The Sound of Silence," "He Was My Brother," "Bleecker Street," and one or two others. Not long after that they were offered a recording contract with Columbia Records.

That was the end of law school. Studying music industry law, as it turned out, had not only failed to deepen Paul's interest in the legal world, but crystallized exactly why he didn't want to be there in the first place. "I thought, this is completely backwards," he said. "I want to be a musician who *hires* these lawyers. So I'm quitting." The elders at Edward B. Marks didn't give him the opportunity to quit. Once they learned that their song plugger Jerry Landis had pitched and sold his own tune during a work trip to Columbia Records, they fired him on the spot.

And with that, Jerry Landis, the walking vision of Paul's pop music fantasies, breathed his last. Or so Paul thought.

CHAPTER 8
THE VOICE OF THE NOW

Now Columbia Records recording artists, Paul and Artie made their presence known in Greenwich Village. Hanging in the clubs, taking measure of the other musicians and songwriters, mentioning their new deal, and shaking hands all around. When they saw expert banjo player and multi-instrumentalist Barry Kornfeld play a set at the Gaslight Club one night, Paul had a flash: he'd seen that goatee and those horn-rimmed specs before. During his freshman year at Queens College, when Kornfeld was finishing his degree at the school, Paul saw him with a guitar case on the subway platform near campus and struck up a conversation. The train arrived in short order, and they'd never spoken again, but when Kornfeld finished playing that night in early 1964, Paul reminded him of their earlier meeting and this time they had a much longer talk.

Kornfeld was only four years older than Paul and Artie, but he had been playing folk music in Greenwich Village for more than ten years, all the way back to the early 1950s, when the entire scene amounted to Sunday afternoon jam sessions in a corner of Washington Square Park and smaller gatherings at the one or two Village lofts whose musician residents invited friends over to sing and play. Kornfeld was then best known for his work with Rev. Gary Davis, accompanying the great bluesman on banjo and guitar while also serving as a conduit between the older blind musician and his growing fan base among young folkies. Along with playing solo shows and in various folk groups, Kornfeld also did session work, so he was all ears when Paul told him about the album he and Artie were about to start recording. Both Paul and Artie had been impressed by his show, Paul said. Would Kornfeld like to do some playing at their sessions in the Columbia Studios? Kornfeld was happy to do it. He didn't care if the duo's scrabble was hard enough for Village idealogues, for one thing, and he had a union card, and enough experience to know that Columbia Records would pay its session musicians union scale. So just say where and when.

Paul started bringing his guitar to Kornfeld's apartment at 190 Waverly Place to rehearse, and they soon became friends. There was so much music to talk about, and Kornfeld couldn't help but be impressed by his new chum, not just by the quality of Paul's songs and his guitar playing, but also by his gleeful tales of the many hours he'd spent learning the tricks of the recording studio. They'd talk for hours, passing a joint and digging deep into music and literature, politics and the folk music history. And Paul was funny — not just witty but deeply and endearingly silly, quick to crack a joke, quicker to burst out laughing. Kornfeld's building was a hub for Village musicians and writers — his neighbors included Dave Van Ronk, the soft-spoken army veteran Tom Paxton, and the Irish Native American singer-songwriter Pat Sky, and most of them would stop by and end up hanging out to jam with Kornfeld and his friend.

Still seeing the world at least partly through Jerry Landis's eyes, one day Paul came to Kornfeld with a proposition. The Village was overstuffed with songwriters, but hardly any of them knew how to publish their songs. At the same time, the cigar smokers in Midtown were eager to find folklike songs to appeal to the new market. He and Kornfeld should launch their own folk-centric publishing company. They'd be equal partners, with Paul providing the business expertise and Kornfeld bringing in the songwriters and matching the company's songs, including Paul's of course, to other performers in Greenwich Village and beyond. Kornfeld saw the logic of it

171

immediately. They called the company Eclectic Music, and registered its address as Kornfeld's apartment on Waverly Place. The first song on their roster was the still-unrecorded "Sound of Silence."

The recording sessions began at the Columbia Records studio on March 10, with Paul on guitar, Kornfeld on guitar and banjo, and jazz bassist Bill Lee, a favorite for many folk musicians, on an acoustic stand-up. Given the simplicity of the arrangements and the extent of Paul and Artie's preparation, the work went quickly. "Bleecker Street," "The Sound of Silence," and a cover of Dylan's "The Times They Are A-Changin' " were finished by the end of the first day. The group reconvened a week later to nail down "He Was My Brother," "Wednesday Morning, 3 A.M." and covers of Ed McCurdy's "Last Night I Had the Strangest Dream" and the British songwriter Ian Campbell's "The Sun Is Burning." Gathering for a final time on March 31, they finished the album with versions of "Sparrow" and "Benedictus," and covers of Bob Camp and Bob Gibson's gospel thumper "You Can Tell the World"; the standard "Go Tell It on the Mountain"; and the tragic British love ballad "Peggy-O."

Released more than six months later, the album, which they titled *Wednesday Morning, 3 AM,* was both prim and impassioned, a product of its fading era and a signpost to the one about to start. The album's cover illustrates the moment vividly: Paul and Artie together on an empty subway platform considering the lens as a silver train bullets past. The station is gritty,[*] redolent with the exhaustion of the endless night. Still, the duo look daisy fresh, their charcoal suits pressed and ties knotted tight. Both lean against a black girder, but Artie stands taller, his face open and confident. Paul keeps his back against the steel, a guitar around his neck, gloom tugging at his boyish features. The songs inside project the same contradictions. Opening with the exuberant neo-gospel "You Can Tell the World," they make like glimmer-eyed Christians ("He brought joy, joy, joy into my heart!"), but snap the mood immediately with the faux-naïveté of "Last Night I Had the Strangest Dream" and its fantasy world in which war has been outlawed. The instrumentation stays constant: Lee's stand-up bass holds down the rhythm while Paul's and Kornfeld's guitars twinkle and strum with tasteful reserve. If the duo's cover of "The Times They Are A-Changin' " is fairly rote, the five Simon originals and the Simon-Garfunkel arrangement of "Benedictus" veer into far more distinctive terrain.

* A large but unnoticed FUCK YOU that had been scrawled on the wall behind them had to be airbrushed from the final image.

"Bleecker Street" sounds just as tidy as the other tunes, but the lyric tells a more complex story. Fog hanging over the streets becomes a shroud dividing a shepherd from his sheep. The people are shadows, their verse crooked and their love furtive. Apartments rent for thirty dollars a month, pace the thirty pieces of silver Judas earned by betraying Jesus. Once a paradise of art and ideals, Greenwich Village has become a moral desert. It's a dire portrait but, strikingly, no villains emerge. The blight is existential, a function of humanity's innate flaws. Church bells signal hope, but the ringing is faint, righteousness still on the far side of the desert.

The bleakness continues on "Sparrow," the wintry parable about a bird dying from the forces of greed, vanity, and indifference, then takes a turn for the self-pitying on the title track, whose narrator must abandon his lover due to an impulsive decision to rob a liquor store. "My life seems unreal, my crime an illusion / A scene badly written in which I must play," he observes, in the style of a poet who needs to learn a bit more about the psychology of crime.

The heart of the album, and the best indicator of all that would follow, starts with "The Sound of Silence" at the end of the first side and continues through "He Was My Brother," which leads the flip side. At twenty-two, Paul had discovered the essence of his mature voice. Both songs are free of artifice. Rather than hiding behind the new idiom, he absorbs it deeply enough to use it as an expression of his troubled soul, his own experience, the fragile balance of perception, passion, dread, and joy that would fill his art and consciousness for the rest of his life.

The night before the final recording session, Paul and Artie played at Gerde's Folk City, sharing a three-way bill with Chicago blueswoman Tracy Nelson and the Even Dozen Jug Band. It was their first major appearance since they started recording for Columbia, and to stir up excitement, Tom Wilson rallied some of his hipper friends and colleagues to the show. The producer was there, of course, as were Kornfeld and some of his living room regulars. Yet the real prize was Bob Dylan himself. He came a little late, perching at the bar next to the *New York Times* music critic Robert Shelton. They'd had a few drinks; maybe they'd blown a little grass. Whatever, Dylan was laughing, hand in front of his mouth, head down, shoulders heaving — "Haw-haw-haw, oh my god" — and you could hear it. Paul and Artie played in a hush: one guitar, two voices, and delicate strands of melody and harmony. The power was as much between the notes as in the notes themselves, and it begged close listening. And everyone knew that beaky high plains honk.

"Haw-haw!"

In a career whose every twitch and twang has been anatomized for personal, literary, political, and biblical magnitude, the meaning of that Dylan guffaw remains unfathomed. Shelton went to his grave insisting that the laughter — he was giggling, too, only more quietly — had nothing to do with what was happening onstage, that whatever had spurred the laugh riot was completely detached from Paul and Artie's performance. It was just bad timing that whatever he and Dylan were talking about that evening — and Shelton never identified what it was — had popped their corks just then.

There was more to Shelton's story, though. Dylan and Paul had met for the first time only days earlier, and the encounter had gone badly. Despite having so much in common, including extended visits with the same folk musicians in London, the two couldn't find anything to say to each other. So they traded the smallest of small talk. Neither pretended to be delighted, or even all that interested, in meeting the other.

Oh yeah, how's it going? You're Kornfeld's friend, right? So, yeah. Hi. Okay.

Then back to their separate corners, separate friends, and separate visions of the world and their rightful place within it. Maybe it was the same place, and maybe there was room for only one of them in it. This may be why Shelton described that night at Gerde's as "an encounter typical of New York's paranoia and instant rivalries," which makes his claims of innocent snickering seem a wee bit less convincing.

Dylan wasn't the only Village folkie rolling his eyes at Paul and Artie that night. "Their ethereal harmonies," Shelton wrote, "sounded out of place at Gerde's, home of weather-beaten ethnic songs." Indeed, the folk ethic in Greenwich Village, and throughout the revivalist scene, was governed by a traditionalist notion that defined a musician's authenticity by the dust in his guitar, the sweat on her banjo, and the songs of chains and ropes, hammers, shovels, and pickaxes; of rounders and ramblers; of hard luck and midnight trains; of the blues and the bottle; of deceit, death, and the glory of God. It was the homegrown, yet exotic, sound you heard then from cowboy singer Ramblin' Jack Elliott or the modern scalawag Dave Van Ronk or, of course, from Dylan, who had blown into New York like a folktale in boots, telling tales of a childhood spent on Indian reservations, in a traveling carnival, and among the hobos riding freight trains and holing up in the ghost towns of the wind-blown Southwest.

Compare those real-world vagabonds to the soft-cheeked boys from middle-class Queens, with their Windsor knots, college degrees, and bourgeois *agonistes.* No wonder their songs sounded so self-important and so very melodramatic. "Hello darkness, my old friend"? For a time that spring, you could march from apartment to apartment on Macdougal Street and get a laugh in all of them by summoning your inner stentor and reciting the opening phrase of "The Sound of Silence." *Hello, darkness* . . . To the beatniks and the leaflet distributors, the purists and the deeper-in-the-gutter-than-thou, it was easy to see how phony these boys were: rich kids pretending to be the real folks.

Oh, but the crazy irony of it all! Because self-styled rodeo rider, steer-driving, country-wandering Ramblin' Jack Elliott was actually raised as Elliot Adnopoz, the son of a well-to-do doctor in the Flatbush section of Brooklyn. And you know who thought that was truly and deeply hilarious? Bob Dylan, of course, who was sitting with Kornfeld, Paul Stookey (Paul from Peter, Paul, and Mary), and a few others at Le Figaro coffeehouse when Kornfeld told the tale. The hilarity stayed with the folksinger for the rest of the evening, so whenever Kornfeld leaned in and whispered, "Adnopoz," Dylan would lose it all over again. Soon he'd be laughing out of the other side of his guitar, because the *Little Sandy Review,* a small folkie magazine published by strict constructionists in Minneapolis, would pull the rug out from beneath his own vagabond tales, revealing that the part-Cherokee carny hobo with the name of a poet was actually Robert Zimmerman, a nice Jewish boy whose father owned a successful electronics store in Hibbing, Minnesota. And those wild tales about Dylan's family and his drifter's childhood? He'd lifted all of it from Woody Guthrie, adopting the legend's fantastical past for his own.

None of it mattered, though, not for Dylan and not for Ramblin' Jack, either, just as it hadn't mattered for Gershwin, Berlin, Lee Simms, Tommy Graph, Jerry Landis, or any other showbiz-savvy performer who knew how to shake off the limitations of family and religious history. So what names would Paul and Artie choose to be their sophisticated-but-folky alter egos? When Paul sold "Carlos Dominguez" and "He Was My Brother" to Edward B. Marks, he was still using the Landis imprimatur. But when he published the first of his folk songs, he felt that it was time for a change. He credited the songs to a new alter ego he named Paul Kane, and when Tribute Records released the tracks as a single in August 1963, the (solo) performances were credited to an imaginary group that was called either the Voices of Paul Kane (the credit in *Billboard*) or the Paul Kane Voices (per *Variety*), as if the bare-bones guitar-and-voice arrangements were performed by a folksy chorale. When Paul and

Artie started playing their folk material that fall, they called themselves Kane and Garr. Then Paul's success under his real name in England convinced him to continue using it at home. So they were Simon and Garr through the winter and spring of 1964. Then Artie got tired of Garr and said he wanted to use his real name, too. Paul shook that off. For all that Simon was a Jewish name, it was also short and easy to say. But *Garfunkel*? No, no, no — too long and too clumsy. People would assume they were comedians, or tailors, even. So how about Garfield instead? They kicked that around for a while. Artie didn't like it, but he knew how show business operated; he'd never worked or recorded under his real name. Eventually he gave in. Simon and Garfield it was.

Except Tom Wilson didn't like it. He'd bitten his tongue whenever Paul and Artie debated names and pseudonyms or when the Columbia executives who consulted on the names of acts and records called to talk about the name of the company's new folk duo. The execs didn't like the duo's real names, either — Simon and Garfunkel just didn't sound like a name that could catch on with anyone. At first the execs thought they could sidestep the problem by calling them Paul and Artie, but then someone remembered that just a few years earlier they had released an album by another pair of young folksingers who went by Art and Paul.* So they considered other young protest types and proposed another approach: how about the Catchers in the Rye? Paul and Artie just laughed at that one. Paul, now with Artie's support, went back to Simon and Garfield, and that was when Wilson put his foot down. He'd loved "The Sound of Silence" the moment he heard it, but it was "He Was My Brother," the impassioned civil rights anthem, that had convinced him to invest in their future. Paul wrote so powerfully about civil rights and justice; they both sang the songs with a righteous fury that was really stirring, particularly for Wilson, a black man who had lived with racism his entire life. So how was it that they were so gutless about their own ethnicity? Were they really going to let the bigots tell them that there was something wrong with having a Jewish name, just so they could sell more *records*? Well, they'd done that before, so, yes, that's exactly what they were going to do.

The publicity guys at Columbia felt the same way, all of them telling the same story: the duo's real names would be off-putting to the anti-Semites behind the radio dial, along with all the average folks who just felt more — how can I put this? — *comfortable* around

* *Songs of Earth and Sky,* by Art & Paul, Columbia Records, 1960.

less ethnic types. But the world was changing, Wilson protested. There were hardly any anti-Semites left! That last argument was more aspirational than factual, unfortunately, but when Wilson and the other executives laid out the dispute to Columbia executive vice president Norman Adler, he let out an exasperated sigh. "Gentlemen, it's 1964," he snapped. "They're Simon and Garfunkel. Next record?"

With the Columbia recording sessions finished and the release date still months in the future, Paul returned to London to resume his career there and his love affair with Kathy Chitty. This time he got his own place, in Hampstead, a bottom-floor studio apartment in a house three doors down Haverstock Hill Road from the Belsize Park tube stop. Folk guitarist Martin Carthy had lived there for months but was moving at precisely the right time. Paul figured he'd stay there through the spring and summer. Starting with shows back at the Railway Inn in Brentwood, and at many of the other clubs he had played earlier in the winter, he threw himself into the serious business of building his reputation in London and beyond. Not the least bit shy about publicizing himself and his work, he launched a one-man campaign of telephone calls and neatly typed letters, all noting his previous appearances at the London clubs, the upcoming American album to be released by Columbia Records (Dylan's label, of course), and his new asking price of seven pounds per show.

His first break came at the Troubadour Club, on the Old Brompton Road, near Shepherds Bush. The Troubadour was arguably the most important folk club in London. Bob Dylan beelined to the place when he got to town in 1962. Paul had played a handful of floor sets there during his first visit to England and made enough of an impression to land a booking soon after his return in April 1964. The new songs he'd written that winter were just as popular as the ones he'd played a few months earlier, but "The Sound of Silence" was always the highlight. It was also the song that hit hardest for record company artists-and-repertoire man Bill Leader. "This terribly well-written song, meaningful, hung together beautifully and played on the guitar in an extremely competent way," Leader said. Paul also knew how to connect with his audiences, making eye contact, projecting his voice and the driving feeling inside the song, unlike so many of the mumbling British folk performers. He stood out in other ways, too. He'd buzz to gigs in a red Sunbeam Alpine sports car, and dressed almost entirely in black. Leader, who worked for Topic Records, Britain's most significant folk music label at the time, also noticed the fans who came to see Paul every time he performed, and the fact that they started turning up even when he wasn't on the bill, just in case he put in a surprise appearance.

After seeing two or three shows, Leader introduced himself to Paul. Did he have a record deal in the United Kingdom? Well, how about recording an album for Topic? Paul definitely wanted to do that, so a few days later he took his guitar to Leader's home. His host led him to a back room where he had set up the portable Revox tape recorder and microphone. They spent a few minutes figuring out the sound levels and microphone angles, then Leader turned on the machine and Paul got to work, singing his latest songs over the rumble of the buses and trucks just outside the window. The noise didn't disturb him. He nearly burst the seams of "The Sound of Silence," jabbing at the chords and spitting the words with a raw force that collapsed to a whisper at the end of the third verse, only to rise again in the final lines. He went in the opposite direction with the just-written "April Come She Will," a hummingbird of a song he'd based on a three-hundred-year-old British nursery rhyme. Borne on a sparkling guitar pattern played high on the neck, and sung in Paul's moist, boyish voice, the tune traces a love affair from the dawn of spring to the first chill of autumn, with the tinge of mortality lurking at the edge of every verse.

Leader took the tape to the next executive meeting at Topic, figuring the handful of songs he'd recorded were finished tracks for an album he and Paul would complete in another session or two — Paul had already updated his pitch to club owners: "I also record for Columbia Records in the States and will cut my first LP for Topic Records over here," he wrote to one regional booker on June 12 — but the other Topic executives who heard the Revox tape shook their heads. How could an American songwriter possibly be a Topic artist? Founded as the publishing wing of the Workers' Music Association in the late 1930s, the label had been created specifically to serve the British labor movement. Simon's songs about American racism and civil rights had a spark of protest to them, but very little to do with Britain or British laborers and even less to do with proper British folk music. So, no, thanks.

Leader was less surprised than exasperated by his colleagues' reactionary thinking. But that's how the folk music world ran in Britain, where rules for what constituted a legitimate folk song, or an authentic folk performance, of a song that was part of British folk culture, were dictated almost entirely songwriter, scholar, and unapologetic Stalinist Ewan MacColl.

Born as James Henry Miller to socialist

laborer parents in Lancashire, England, in 1915, MacColl became a Communist during the Great Depression. He devoted himself to left-wing theater until the late 1940s, when he came across a copy of American folk historian Alan Lomax's book *People's Songs* (cowritten with Pete Seeger) and decided to start playing folk music. Although he had grown up in England, both of MacColl's parents had been born and raised in Scotland. Given that connection, he adopted his parents' Scots heritage for himself and changed his name to Ewan MacColl. In 1953 he cofounded the club Ballads and Blues — its name was eventually changed to the Singers Club — which grew into a capital for England's most influential folk musicians and scholars. MacColl's Marx-inspired disdain for popular culture and anything else that seemed to violate the established doctrines of British folk music came to define the scene. Eventually he formed a committee to set criteria for defining folk styles and judging which musicians could be trusted to perform truly authentic folk music at his club and every other serious folk club in the British Isles.

MacColl was less successful at ridding folk clubs of the long-standing tradition of floor spots — when audience members can stand and do a song or two, and there was always the chance that someone might play something impure — but his loathing of popular music was shared by folk aficionados around the Western world. Some also rejected the idea that any modern songwriter could contribute to the folk culture, though Mac-Coll, who wrote songs himself, figured that was okay, as long as the songs weren't intended to be commercial. No one could rival his disdain for American popular culture, whose influence over Britain since the end of World War II struck him as catastrophic to the nation's history and character. An entire generation, he proclaimed, "were becoming quasi-Americans, and I find it monstrous!" Never mind that the inspiration for his devotion to folk music had come from a book written by two Americans, or that he was now married to another one.* No matter: Mac-Coll's tastes reigned, and to a generation of folk aficionados, including the executives at

* Irony compounds over the years. MacColl's love song "The First Time Ever I Saw Your Face," which he'd written for then-paramour Peggy Seeger (half sister to Pete), became an enormous hit for popular American singer Roberta Flack. Written in 1957, the song was covered quickly by the Kingston Trio, the Chad Mitchell Singers, and other pop artists in America, but it reached an unexpected zenith when Flack's version topped the *Billboard* charts for six weeks in 1972 after it was used in the Clint Eastwood–directed film *Play Misty for Me*.

Topic Records, the likes of Paul Simon, an American songwriter bred on Elvis Presley, was anathema. Just like Greenwich Village, just like every other self-selecting society, the MacColl-inspired British folkies played things by the book: the contempt for outsiders, the blockading of the bridges, the loathing of the new and the different, the feverish testaments to "authenticity" and "legitimacy," the worship of credentials. As always, though, the calcification of the institution only clarified and strengthened the revolution.

By the time Paul was digging into the British music scene, Dylan's gravitational pull had sent compasses spinning, particularly for the new generation of fans. For them, the old songs were less a destination than a foundation for songs that still needed to be written, the songs that would document their lives, their loves and lusts and loathing, their growing belief that it was up to them to set things straight and change the world. And though Paul had been too buttoned down to impress the Greenwich Village regulars, their counterparts in London saw him as positively dashing. He didn't dress like the British folkies did. His boots were stylish, as were his woolen donkey jacket and black V-neck sweaters. Paul could be serious but also hilariously funny; his wit filtered through a postcollegiate sophistication. And even if his banter fell flat, it was impossible to ignore

188

those finely wrought, emotionally piercing songs.

"I'd never heard anything like him," says singer-songwriter Harvey Andrews, who first glimpsed the American singer at a club in Birmingham. "His guitar work was better than anybody I'd ever seen." Fifty years later Andrews still remembers the songs he heard that night. " 'A Church Is Burning,' 'He Was My Brother,' 'Sound of Silence' and 'Most Peculiar Man.' That [last one] was a story song, and a very interesting one, very different. 'Sound of Silence' — well, there had never been anything like *that* in a lyric. And 'He Was My Brother' — I'd never heard one like that before, either. When he was finished I was sort of gobsmacked. What is this? *Who* is this?"

Who, indeed. Without knowing of Paul's travel plans, the UK-based Oriole Records had purchased the rights to release the "Carlos Dominguez"/"He Was My Brother" single from Edward B. Marks and released it on May 8 as a Jerry Landis record, with the songs credited to Paul Kane. Not much of a calling card for Paul, but the record did gain the interest of a rising middle-of-the-road singer named Val Doonican, who included "Carlos" on his 1964 debut album, *The Lucky 13 Shades of Val Doonican*. The long-player hit No. 2 on the British charts and stayed on the list for six and a half months, but neither release did much to enhance Paul's reputation. No matter, he kept working.

Soon he had played all the leading clubs in London. The Troubadour, of course, and also the Black Horse, the Roundhouse, and the Enterprise. The more friends he made, the wider his network became. Dolly Terfus, who had come to know a huge swath of musicians and club owners while working the door at the Troubadour, helped him book dates all over the United Kingdom, then called on friends to put him up when he got to their town.

So off he went, to Hempstead, Chelmsford, Leicester, Cambridge; then south to Romford and Bexhill-on-Sea; then north again to clubs in Hull, Liverpool, Birmingham, Widnes, Birstall, and Edinburgh, Scotland. Most often he took the train, which clanged by fields and factories, smoke-stained homes, going from one concrete platform to another, then carrying his guitar and bag of clothes, shoes, and notebooks to the next smoke-draped club, to have a pint with whoever else was playing that night — the chances were increasingly good that it was someone Paul knew. The shows always seemed to go well, even when he made a crucial mistake, as when he arrived at a hard-won show at the Jug O' Punch club in Birmingham precisely a week after he'd been booked to perform. The club's owner, musician Ian Campbell, had another performer booked that night and at first refused to allow Paul even to do a floor spot between sets. Campbell eventually relented, allowing his apologetic guest a four-song set, and when the last notes of "The Sound of Silence" faded from the air, the crowd leaped to their feet to cheer.

In London, the hipper musicians were migrating into Soho, the glittery if sometimes sinister, nightlife district. Introduced to the scene by Redd Sullivan, a sailor turned musician with flaming hair whose broad frame housed a decidedly outsize personality, Paul hustled to draw crowds and juicier gigs. While the bigger clubs had barkers calling passersby to their evening shows, Paul and Sullivan promoted their sets with impromptu sidewalk performances that began with Sullivan calling Paul a towering figure, the largest talent in London, the biggest thing in England and all of the United Kingdom, too. When enough people had gathered to catch a glimpse of this great artist, Sullivan would spread his arms and stand as tall as possible as the relatively elfish Paul leaped from behind him, smiling impishly and already strumming his guitar.

That was business as usual around Soho in the mid-1960s, where mobsters retailed somebody's goods from the backs of their trucks; where the elderly street performer known as Meg the Busker was always welcome to belt out a tune no matter who was performing onstage; where Curly Goss, a cheerfully incompetent crook and part-time porn movie actor (or so he claimed) put on unlicensed folk shows in an ever-changing series of abandoned basements, the addresses of which were so secret that even the musicians wouldn't know where they were playing until Goss took them there. It was all a revelation to Paul, who planned to stay through the end of the summer, when he'd fly back to New York to reteam with Artie and gear up for the release of *Wednesday Morning, 3 AM* in October.

Artie spent much of the summer scootering around France, and on August 28 he took the ferry across the Channel to visit Paul and get a look at his life in London. Paul had shows set up for the next few evenings, and incorporated Artie into the act, adding his harmonies to the *Wednesday Morning* songs he'd been performing solo and working out parts for one or two of his newly composed works. Paul's last show for the summer was set for September 1, at the Troubadour Club. He sang a new civil rights song called "A Church Is Burning," a meditation on aging called "Leaves That Are Green," and "The Sound of Silence" before calling for his friend to join him on their arrangement of "Benedictus." When it was over, a motherly forty-year-old woman approached Paul and with a plummy, if vaguely exotic, trill thanked him for his music. "I think you're a very great artist," she said. Paul smiled and shrugged. Oh well thanks a lot, and all that, it's lovely to meet you. And you are . . . ?

The real answer to that question was a whole other adventure, so Judith Piepe kept it simple. She was a social worker at St. Anne's Church, the particularly liberal outpost of the Anglican Church in Soho. A German refugee after the war, Piepe had spent quite a bit of time in the district's nightclubs, particularly the ones that specialized in folk and other socially conscious forms of music, and her constant presence in the scene, along with her network of friends in and around the music community, gave her an air of influence. Piepe's feelings for Paul ran even deeper than she had been able to tell him that first night. "I knew this was a true prophet," she said. "This was the bloke nobody had ever heard of. And I knew this is the voice of the now."

CHAPTER 9
HE WAS MY BROTHER

The news about Andy Goodman reached the Queens College campus the same day it hit the national news, on June 24, 1964. Less than a week earlier, Paul's younger school-mate had boarded a bus with several dozen other Bus Project volunteers going south to register black voters in rural Mississippi. They reached their home base in Meridian, a small town on the east side of the state, their destination on the morning of June 21, the same day Goodman sent a postcard home to his family. "This is a wonderful town and the weather is fine," he wrote. "The people in this city are wonderful, and our reception was very good."

The same couldn't be said about the village of Philadelphia, Mississippi, where a few days earlier a Meridian-based CORE (Congress of Racial Equality) worker named Michael Schwerner, a recent graduate of Cornell and a member of its AEPi chapter, had led a voter registration meeting at the black Mount Zion

United Methodist Church. Ku Klux Klan members rallied to burn Mount Zion to the ground the day after the meeting, and Schwerner, along with an African American CORE staffer named James Chaney, planned to return to Philadelphia to check in with the minister and his flock. Goodman arrived in Meridian just as the other two were about to leave, so they gave him enough time to stow his bags and stretch his legs, then they all piled into a station wagon and started the hour-long journey northwest to Philadelphia. When they got there, the police were waiting. Deputy Sheriff Cecil Price arrested Chaney on a speeding charge, and hauled all three to the Neshoba County Jail. Released at about 10:30 that night, the three CORE staffers were escorted out of the county by Sheriff Price. Rather than taking them to safety, though, Price delivered them to two carloads of Klan members waiting just a few miles down the road. Chaney's burned-out car was discovered three days later, with no trace of its occupants. The Neshoba County sheriff refused to investigate, and the disappearances blew into a national controversy. When the FBI stepped in, it took forty-four days for the federal investigators to find Goodman, Chaney, and Schwerner's bullet-torn bodies buried in a swamp.

The tragedy shook Queens College and Paul's circle of friends, but Paul hadn't known Goodman very well. Still, Paul and Andy were similar in many ways. Both were New Yorkers from Jewish families, both dark-eyed and left-handed. Both were lifelong baseball fans who developed into solid hitters. Both were drawn to music, though Goodman ultimately pursued acting. Both studied at Queens College; both felt passionate enough about the civil rights movement to put their thoughts into verse. If Goodman's poems were less accomplished, they overflow with the same moral fervor. "We close our eyes and choke our sighs, / And look into the dreadful skies," he wrote in "Corollary to a Poem by AE Housman," citing a poet whose work would inspire Paul's writing in the coming years. But while Goodman's beliefs set him on a collision course with violence, Paul glorified the righteous in song, including in "He Was My Brother," the 1963 song he'd written about a civil rights martyr. When Goodman disappeared under such grim circumstances, Paul's performance of "Brother" and his other civil rights songs gained a new fervency.

In September 1964, Paul sat down to record an audio letter for his British girlfriend, a forty-five-minute tape of news, guitar pieces, complaints, and familiar songs performed alone and as a duo with Artie. "And also two new songs," Paul promises at the start of the tape. "One of them is the song

196

I wrote you about. The other is about two days old." He sounds sweet and vulnerable on the tape, and exceptionally needy. Kathy's most recent letter, he complains, "*ruined* my day" because it wasn't as long as he'd hoped. Paul was just as hurt that David McCausland hadn't responded to his most recent letter, and he asks his girlfriend to confront their friend about this neglect. ("Don't ask Margaret. Ask David.") Paul's mood lightens when he starts singing. A delicate version of "Leaves That Are Green" leads off, followed by a bluesy take on "Patterns." He shows off polished covers of "Anji" and two or three other instrumental pieces by British guitarist Davy Graham, whose records served as master classes for the United Kingdom's most accomplished guitar players. Then Artie shows up, and they take a run through "Benedictus" and "The Sound of Silence." When Artie takes a telephone call, Paul starts playing the opening chords to one of his newer works, a fast-moving civil rights tune in which hooded racists burn a black church to the ground. A close relative to "He Was My Brother," "A Church Is Burning" makes the same lyrical feint in its final verse, in which the horrific image of smoke and flames rising from the sanctuary becomes a symbol of redemption — two hands held together in prayer. Like its predecessor, "A Church Is Burning" is designed to be a rouser, a jolt of

197

righteousness to bring a crowd to its feet.

When Artie returns asking what they're doing next, Paul strums the chords again. "I've already done the whole introduction," he says, pausing for the punch line. "I don't know if you ever heard this introduction about Andy Goodman." Oh, Artie had heard it before, many times. They both crack up, then move into the first verse. They sing together, Artie's harmony shadowing Paul's voice exactly, until just before the line about freedom being a dark road, when Paul's voice flutters, he stifles a laugh, and then, as Artie loses it, too, collapses entirely, rendering the next line — "the future is now, it's time to take a stand" — nearly incomprehensible. When they get to the final chorus, Paul shifts to "America the Beautiful," which they both laugh through before turning back to belt the final verse of "Church" with the outsize gusto of chorus boys in a Broadway showstopper. "Thrilling!" Paul declares when it's over. "A thrilling work!"

It had been less than a month since Goodman's decomposing body was discovered alongside those of Schwerner and Chaney. The murders shook the nation and then catalyzed the civil rights movement, becoming one of the signal moments in America's bitter history of racism. And it was only the start of Paul's complicated relationship with the memory of Andy Goodman.

Columbia Records released *Wednesday Morning, 3 AM* on October 18, 1964, to lukewarm reviews. *Billboard* noted only "moderate" sales potential, and that proved to be an understatement. Of the one thousand copies sold during the album's first eight months, the vast majority sold in New York City. "So that was a bomb of great magnitude," Tom Wilson said years later. "Mega-tonnage, as far as Columbia was concerned."

Neither Simon nor Garfunkel had the time to fret. Artie was already in his third year of graduate-level mathematics at Columbia, earning extra money by tutoring high schoolers. Paul still felt the buzz from his successful spring and summer in England, and passed the fall writing songs and setting up club dates, concerts, and a new place to stay for his return to London on January 15. Considering his prospects for the future, he had bought a one-way ticket. Given the number of friends he had in England, his passion for Kathy, and his growing reputation in the folk music world, it was hard to imagine what could compel him to return home.

Back in London in January 1965, Paul launched into a schedule of dates he'd arranged that fall with a great deal of help from the friends and contacts he made during the previous year. The biggest leap in his British career had been engineered by Judith Piepe, the church social worker who had approached him at his final show in September. Piepe's prominence at St. Ann's and the Soho district in general had earned her a show on BBC Radio, *Five to Ten,* a lightly religious thought-of-the-day type of broadcast heard each day at 9:55 a.m., right between *Housewives' Choice* and *Music While You Work,* two of the network's most popular programs. After meeting Paul, Piepe had gone to work on her bosses at the BBC, insisting that this young man's songs examined the same social and moral issues her program always pursued. She won them over, and less than a week after his return Piepe ushered Paul into the BBC studios to record songs she would play on a week's worth of *Five to Ten* episodes.

In an hour or two they had taped a handful of songs for the BBC's consideration: "The Sound of Silence" along with "Bleecker Street," "April Come She Will," "Kathy's Song," "I Am a Rock," a new song about drug addiction called "Bad News Feeling," and "A Most Peculiar Man," which Paul had written after reading a four-line obituary of a suicide victim. Paul voiced introductions for the songs, describing how he'd been inspired to write them, as a commentary on current events and the widespread social issues troubling the world at large. Not all aired, but the ones that did, just a week or two later, made an immediate impact. "Coming between *Housewives Choice* and this general light music thing [*Five to Ten*] was the spot where people go to put the kettle on for a cup of tea," Piepe said. "One had the feeling of thousands of people standing in the doorway, kettle in hand, listening almost reluctantly. And we got snowed under with letters from people who wanted to know who was Paul Simon and where could his songs be bought on record."

When an A&R man at the British division of CBS Records asked the same question, he was surprised to discover that the path led back to his own company. Columbia Records in the United States was owned by the CBS corporation, so the British CBS label already had the right to release Simon and Garfunkel's *Wednesday Morning, 3 AM* in the United Kingdom. Not certain if the interest kicked up by *Five to Ten* was strong enough to rate an entire album release, the CBS-UK executives cherry-picked four of the songs Paul played by himself on the *Five to Ten* performances and released them as an EP (an extended-play single, which was very common in England in those days). The company also contracted Paul to record a solo album for release that summer. Paul got a British publishing deal with Lorna Music (the company responsible for getting "Carlos

Dominguez" to Val Doonican), and soon other artists started recording his songs. Guitarist John Renbourn covered "Leaves That Are Green" with American folk singer Dorris Henderson, singer-songwriter Harvey Andrews recorded "A Most Peculiar Man," and the Irish pop group the Bachelors would soon take their melodramatic arrangement of "The Sound of Silence" to the UK Top 3. Paul also signed up with a young talent manager named Graham Wood, whose connections at the London music newspapers, in British television, and at clubs and concert halls around the Isles started paying off almost instantly.

Yet Paul owed his greatest debt to Judith Piepe, who soon gave him an open-ended invitation to move into her East London flat. Rent was not a problem. The multibedroom apartment was subsidized by her employers at St. Ann's Parish, provided she could take in some of the young drifters who turned up at St. Ann's in search of lodging. The standard-issue drifters generally wound up on the living room floor; Piepe reserved the spare rooms for needy musicians who had impressed her with their talents. And Piepe had good ears. She had supported Cat Stevens during his struggling days, and when Paul moved in, he joined a fair-haired nineteen-year-old songwriter named Al Stewart and future Fairport Convention singer

Sandy Denny, who was dating the heavily scarred, hard-drinking American singer-songwriter Jackson C. Frank, who also had a room.

A lot of talented people ended up crashing in Piepe's flat during the 1960s, but once Paul came through the door in 1965, it didn't take long for them all to realize who was their den mother's favorite. The day Paul told Piepe he'd be delighted to move in, she knocked on Al Stewart's door and told him he had to move into the smaller, darker room on the same hallway: Paul preferred a room with good light. Piepe's guests made a habit of playing different games in the evening, but when it turned out that Paul liked to play Monopoly, all the other games went back up on the shelf. And if there were enough folks around to make a communal dinner, they didn't settle on a menu until someone asked Paul what he felt like eating. Even Piepe's eleven-year-old daughter, Ariel, who lived with her father in South-sea, could tell that Paul outranked her in her mother's eyes. "He was the favored child, he got all the love and attention," she says. Tempted to hate the interloper for taking her place, the girl decided instead to follow her mother under Paul's spell. "In a completely Oedipal sense, if I wasn't going to kill him, I had to love him," she says. "If I was going to square up in my own life with her, somehow he had to be worth it."

What Ariel didn't understand was how much her mother had in common with the American visitor. Born in 1920 to a well-to-do German couple named Fritz and Eugenia Sternberg, Judith had spent most of her life avoiding, and then revising, the facts of her past — and no wonder. Her mother committed suicide when Judith was three. Her father, a political economist and theorist who was still in his midtwenties when his wife died, was too busy building his career to tend to his daughter, so he left her in the care of her mother's parents. Fritz's leftist writings, along with his Jewish heritage, made him a natural target for the Nazis, and he soon fled to the United States, leaving his then-teenage daughter to make her own escape. Judith married young, divorced quickly, got a job teaching at a girls' school, danced ballet, had an affair with the *London Telegraph*'s dance critic, and birthed and then lost his child. When that relationship ended, she married Tony Piepe, a much younger man with whom she had Ariel, in 1951. A distracted and unhappy mother with no community to rely upon, Judith converted to the Anglican Church and found a spiritual home at Soho's socially progressive St. Ann's Church.

Along the way, she had traded her German accent for the delicate elocution of the educated British middle class, though she never quite got the weight of the Fatherland out of her vowels. Piepe didn't mind exotic. Despite her stern mothering of Ariel and her old-school policies about keeping the unmarried couples apart at night, Judith smoked hashish with cheerful abandon and preferred the company of eccentrics. When someone asked about her childhood, she would speak at length about her past, describing her time in a Nazi concentration camp in the 1930s and then her daring escape to the Swiss border, which nearly came to a tragic end when she was captured by German police officers, who concluded, after a brief interview, that she would be executed in the ditch where she stood. Instead, she explained, a mysterious last-minute deal allowed her to cross to safety. Piepe had a whole other set of stories about her perilous days of driving battlefield ambulances during the Spanish Civil War, and they were every bit as thrilling — and, like her stories about Germany, complete fiction.

In June, Paul reported to Levy's recording studio on Bond Street, where CBS staff producers Reginald Warburton and Stanley West oversaw the recording of his first solo album. The sessions couldn't have been simpler: Paul played guitar and sang, and if it seemed necessary he'd tap his foot for percussion. On the EP, only "The Sound of Silence" and "He Was My Brother" repeat from *Wednesday Morning, 3 AM.* The rest of the songs had emerged during his months in England. And if the bare-bones production seems flat compared to the rerecordings that would come, it's fascinating to realize that beyond the pair of civil rights tunes and the unfunny take-down of Bob Dylan that Paul called "A Simple Desultory Philippic," all *Songbook*'s narrators and characters either confront or symbolize the meaninglessness of individual existence.

The suicide at the center of "A Most Peculiar Man" makes such little impression on the world that his neighbors have next to no idea he was even alive. The heartbroken narrator of "I Am a Rock" has chosen to be just as isolated, and the narrator of "Flowers Never Bend with the Rainfall" not only can't tell the difference between truth and illusion, but can't recognize his own image in the mirror. "Patterns" compares the singer's life to a rat stuck in a maze: "And the pattern never alters / Until the rat dies." The antiwar song "The Side of a Hill" describes the accidental killing of a child in a bullet-pocked land, while "April Come She Will" and "Leaves That Are Green" portray the crumbling of love and life as being as inescapable as the changing of the seasons. Still, none is quite as cutting as "Kathy's Song," the most obviously autobiographical song on the album.

Here Paul speaks directly to Kathy Chitty, the sole source of truth in his life. Without her presence, his intelligence, his talent as a musician and songwriter, his knowledge, his thoughts, and his beliefs fall to nothing. Alone, he peers into the void of a rainy night, notices the water dripping across the window-pane, and sees himself. "I know that I am like the rain," he sings. "There but for the grace of you go I."

So sad, and yet so afire with energy, ambition, and self-assurance. A regular in the Soho clubs, particularly at the just-opened Les Cousins, a basement club beneath a restaurant on Greek Street that became a rallying point for musicians, Paul continued honing his image, which drew even more attention to his songs and performances. "He was creating a package," recalled fellow musician Harvey Andrews. "The little man with the chip on his shoulder, who was lonely, lost, and in need of mothering. And he was going to be immensely successful." Paul had always imagined he'd be the reigning champion of something, but the more songs he wrote, the more his *Five to Ten* success swept through the increasingly packed clubs he played, the more confident he became. When Brentwood Folk Club co-manager David Rugg booked him to open a theater concert in Chelmsford for the popular American folksinger Buffy Sainte-Marie, Paul took the gig happily, but showed up that afternoon beneath an angry little cloud that he took straight to Rugg. Now Paul insisted that he be the headliner; he had constructed an entire argument about it. Obviously, Sainte-Marie was an out-of-towner. He, on the other hand, was the local hero with a loyal fan base. Clearly, Sainte-Marie should open for *him.* Rugg could only stare. Sainte-Marie was an international star; the club had sold out the four-hundred-capacity Shire Hall on the strength of her name. So no. Of course not. Paul didn't push the point much further, but the moment resonated. "He was very friendly, and an outgoing sort of person," Rugg says. "But he had these ideas about where he was going and how important he was." And if you didn't pick up on that by yourself, Paul wasn't shy about telling you all about it. "If I'm not a millionaire by the time I turn thirty," he told suburban Liverpool folk club manager Geoff Speed, among many others, "I shall be very disappointed."

Paul didn't like to be disappointed. If someone in an audience was talking too loudly while he was playing, he'd stop mid-verse and deliver a scolding. If someone had the gall to heckle him, he'd shout him or her down with arctic efficiency. When he got to a scheduled gig at Soho's Les Cousins club only to discover that the blues singer Long John Baldry had also been booked for his slot, both musicians went after each other, their ensuing argument was so loud and bitter that people still talk about it. When manager Graham Wood managed to book Paul to play "I Am a Rock" on the hit pop music TV show *Ready, Steady, Go!* a few months later, Paul responded to the producer's last-minute instruction to play only half the song — the live show was running long — by stubbornly performing the entire tune, thus forcing headliner P. J. Proby to cram an abbreviated version of his current smash, "Let the Water Run Down," over the show's closing credits.

Among a set of musicians whose shared ethic valued humility and understatement, Paul's audacity amused some and infuriated others. Bert Jansch, perhaps the most influential British guitarist of the mid-1960s, shared stages with Paul on many occasions and had more than a few opportunities to hear him predict the glories of his own future. "Very American! He used to say stuff like 'Oh I'm gonna be really big one day and make lots of money, I'll invite you all over to America!' He did of course make it very big, but never asked us over," he said. Some musicians found nothing to like about Paul, as guitarist Ralph McTell recalled. "He had a reputation as a miserable little man and was not popular among the other musicians." Things would get only more strained as Paul's fortunes rose due to the help of a generous friend whose grasp of business wasn't nearly as sharp as Paul's — but that was still a year or two off in the distance.

Still, Paul could also be remarkably generous, as both an informal guitar tutor and a songwriter with a deep understanding of musical and lyrical structure. If another musician needed help getting to a show, Paul would volunteer his car and his own chauffeur services. And when he started earning headliner's wages, he would end a long night of performing and jamming at Les Cousins or the Troubadour by gathering up every musician in sight and leading them to the Golden Egg diner, where he would treat everyone to an early breakfast. He spent a third of his ninety-pound advance for his solo album from CBS-UK to produce an album for Piepe flatmate and fellow American songwriter Jackson C. Frank, who Paul thought deserved a much larger audience than he'd been attracting. The sessions weren't easy. Frank, who had nearly died in a school fire when he was a child, was so terrified of the recording studio that he would play only behind a barrier that blocked the control room window's view of him at the microphone. Paul took the time to ease him through the sessions, paid cash to sign the songwriter to a publishing deal with Eclectic Songs, and then made sure the record got released in England. Frank's record didn't find an audience, but Paul's generosity continued through the decades, especially after his friend's emotional troubles became debilitating. Paul didn't show that side of himself to everyone. And sometimes the side he did show made it seem impossible for such kindness and compassion to exist within the consciousness of the same man.

Committed to staying in England through the summer, Paul was on hand for the release of CBS-UK's four-song distillation of *Wednesday Morning, 3 AM* tracks in June, and also for the release of his first solo album, *The Paul Simon Songbook,* when it emerged a few weeks later. The album was fronted with a photo of Paul and Kathy sitting on a cobblestone street next to the Thames, both playing with children's toys. The picture could be interpreted in several ways, either as a romantic portrait of young love or as a reference to the famous shot of Dylan and his girlfriend Suze Rotolo on the cover of *The Freewheelin' Bob Dylan.* It might also have been a parody of Dylan's cover, or just an image Paul dreamed up thinking it would look cool in a record store. The liner notes on the back open with a self-lacerating essay by Paul that leads with the admission that "I start with the knowledge that everything I write will turn and laugh at me." That thought

211

introduces a brutal conversation between Paul's creative and critical voices, both answering to the same name, with the more vulnerable voice in boldface.

> PAUL: *(Reading notes of LP)* Who wrote this junk?
> PAUL: You know very well who did it.
> PAUL: *(In mock astonishment)* Don't tell me it was you.

More self-directed criticism follows. Paul calls himself a phony; he dismisses the older songs as juvenilia ("I don't believe in them as I once did"), then concocts another fantasy dialogue, this one between himself and a poppy seller. Next comes a song-by-song analysis by Piepe, who shares none of Paul's stated antipathy toward his work. Most of the mainstream British music publications ignored the *The Paul Simon Songbook* altogether, though *Melody Maker*'s critic took the time to dismiss "I Am a Rock" as reheated Dylan ("Sorry, this guy is trying to take off Bob Dylan in every way"). Still, the British folk publications covered the album, most of them in generous terms. Those reviews helped attract more folkies to Paul's club shows, while his manager, Graham Wood, tried to interest the mainstream music magazines by emphasizing Simon's connections to Dylan and the Greenwich Village scene in

New York. Wood's work paid off, and a few reporters started to pay attention. The *New Musical Express*'s Keith Altham went to Paul ("A small, dark, intense man from Greenwich Village") to ask about Dylan and Joan Baez and then quoted him extensively in the resulting story. Unsurprisingly, Paul had more praise for Baez, who he said had succeeded "naturally," while Dylan had been borne up by a tidal wave of publicity. And when good old Ewan MacColl lashed out at Dylan in September, Paul played both sides of the fight, agreeing that his fellow American's lyrics were lousy ("rehashed Ginsberg"), while also arguing that Dylan had "written some very good songs."

Paul's attitude toward publicity was simple. If he had an opportunity to promote his work or himself, he took it. It got tricky only when he needed to explain to others how he'd somehow become a party to such naked displays of self-promotion. Performing at the Red Cow in Cambridge soon after his *Ready, Steady, Go!* appearance, Paul turned his TV spot into a joke, a comedy of errors whose central benefit was that it gave him an opportunity to call cohost Cathy McGowan a "nit" on the air. He had done no such thing, of course — his rebellion had been stealing airtime from the hapless P. J. Proby — but the club audience howled like mad at the story, then redoubled when Paul fretted that he would no longer be able to play "I Am a Rock" now that it had been corrupted by its appearance on a mainstream pop music television show.

When Artie came to spend a few weeks that summer, he moved into Piepe's flat, too, and he and Paul set to crafting duo arrangements for his new songs, working out a solid set of tunes they could perform together in the London clubs. Feeling penned in the apartment, they took to rehearsing at the launderette down the street. The first time, they came with their laundry and played around while their shirts and pants and socks spun behind the glass. But when they heard the ringing acoustics in the tile-and-steel-filled storefront, they went back the next afternoon with nothing but Paul's guitar. When the neighborhood ladies started applauding, they made it a daily ritual, spreading the word among their friends, telling everyone that even if they knew Paul's songs and had heard him play, they really needed to hear him play with Artie at the launderette; it was a completely different experience. Friends started to show up, and it wasn't long before they were telling more people about what they came to call the "launderette sessions." They ran like open rehearsals, with Paul and Artie playing through a few songs the crowd already knew, then working on something new for a while, then performing the new arrangement. Most days, they went on for two or three hours, with customers and friends cycling in and out. Most of the customers came to adore the boys, even if some of Paul's friends thought it was a bit, you know, *too much*. "Typical brash Americans, I thought initially," says Hans Fried, a fixture on the London folk scene. "Even though I was sort of bohemian I still had a certain amount of that English reserve in me."

Paul started bringing Artie to shows he'd booked as a solo act, sometimes demanding that the club pay a premium for having the duo rather than a solo performer. The two always did well, and it wasn't long before audiences began to show up expecting Artie to be at Paul's side. One night near the end of Artie's stay in September 1965, Paul started gabbing about the new pop hybrid that people called folk-rock music. "So you have the Byrds doing Bob Dylan, Manfred Mann doing Bob Dylan, Bob Dylan doing Bob Dylan." The crowd tittered, and Paul kept on because, wouldn't you know it, their own producer, Tom Wilson, also the producer of Dylan and so many others, turned out to be the guy who was behind the whole thing. He had even proposed that Simon and Garfunkel do some folk-rock, and they had agreed to give the new genre a try. They weren't selling any folk records, right? So,

215

Paul continued, they had taken the lyrics of the song "Wednesday Morning, 3 A.M." and "we put it into a beat thing. So we'll give you a taste of that." He played a few descending minor chords, and together he and Artie sang the familiar lyric, only now with a bluesy edge that made the once guilt-racked lover seem thoroughly unrepentant. He wasn't mourning anything — just gathering the loot and getting out of town before the cops showed up.

A few people laughed after the first line or two, and more giggles struck when Artie's voice cracked, purposely it seemed, on his high notes. So they were making fun of folk-rock? Maybe so. And maybe that was why Paul strummed a few bars of "Twist and Shout" afterward, then proclaimed "Lahhhk a Rollun' Stone" in his best dull-witted Dylan voice. A few people laughed at that, too. But none of this is as significant, or as surprising, as the one thing the audience did, with no hesitation: they applauded the song as if it weren't a joke after all, as if blending a folk sensibility with rock 'n' roll urgency actually sounded pretty good, as if Tom Wilson might be on to something after all.

Nearly everything Paul said onstage that night in London was true. After *Wednesday Morning, 3 AM* flopped so spectacularly, options for the duo's future had dwindled

216

toward zero. When Paul came back to New York City for a visit in April, he and Artie scheduled a meeting with Tom Wilson, who filled them in on the latest excitement around Columbia and the New York industry: Dylan had hired a rock band to play with him on his just-released album, *Bringing It All Back Home,* while the just-signed Byrds had released their own sparklingly electric cover of Bobby's "Mr. Tambourine Man." So much more was on the near horizon, and just as Paul would tell his audience in London a few months later, Wilson popped the question: Why don't you guys give it a try, too?

If Paul had any reservations about keeping his folk music pure, they didn't keep him from getting to work on this new assignment. Starting with the opening chords of Davy Graham's "Anji" and the "Wednesday Morning, 3 A.M." opening lyrics, he came up with the swaggering "Somewhere They Can't Find Me," which they recorded with a full rock band, percussion, and a horn section. They spent the rest of the session on another minor chord rocker, sung this time by a lover determined to keep his baby from leaving him because, as the title asserts (with notably eccentric spelling), "We've Got a Groovey Thing Goin'." The second song runs on an appealingly funky keyboard riff, and the more prominent horns give it a kick, but the paper-thin lyrics ("I never done you no wrong, /

Never hit you when you're down / Always gave you good lovin', / Never ran around . . .") make it the slighter work, a B-side if ever there was one.

With that, they satisfied their producer's request and pushed the Simon and Garfunkel ball as far as their record label would allow. Still, Columbia Records didn't issue that or any new Simon and Garfunkel single. As far as Paul and Artie could see, their career as a duo was over, at least for the time being. Paul went back to England. Artie spent the summer traveling in Europe and prepared for another year of labor on his PhD in mathematics. The Beat sound of *Bringing It All Back Home* took Dylan to *Billboard*'s top three, while the Byrds' version of "Mr. Tambourine Man" lodged itself at the top of the singles charts. Tom Wilson's reputation soared, too, and not just in the Columbia offices. But he was still sensitive about the colossal flop Simon and Garfunkel had made for him, and when Stan Kavan, the label's chief of promotions, buttonholed him in the hall to tell him that *Wednesday Morning, 3 AM* had sold a thousand copies, the producer grimaced. He'd heard that sad number months earlier. He knew the record was a flop. No need to rub it in now, man. The executive laughed. He wasn't talking about *that* thousand copies. He was talking about the thousand copies the supposedly dead-as-a-doornail album had *just* sold in Miami. Did Wilson have any idea why that had happened?

A few months later *Billboard* made the chain of highly unlikely events into a feature article, an object lesson in how good intra-company communication can lead to the most unexpected, and delightful, places. Not that it didn't take a while. Reports of a burst of *Wednesday Morning, 3 AM* sales in Dallas that February didn't impress anyone in the label's New York headquarters; nor did early news of the Miami outbreak in early May. Instead, they told Southeast region distributor Mark Weiner to forget about that folk music flop and spend his time on records that actually had a chance. But Weiner wouldn't shut up about it. As he knew, the trigger in Dallas and in Miami was "The Sound of Silence." It was a very simple calculus. Once a radio station started playing the song, listeners rushed out to buy the album. Yet there was no "Silence" single on the market. The big execs still didn't believe it, but when Weiner saw Wilson at a company meeting, he gave him a crucial suggestion. Instead of releasing the original "Silence" as a single, they should get some electric guitars and drums on the track and make a folk-rock record out of it. That got Wilson's attention.

At a Dylan recording session a few weeks later, Wilson asked a few of the musicians to stay late to help him on another small project.

219

He played them the original acoustic recording of "The Sound of Silence" and gave them a little while to figure out parts for electric guitar, electric piano, bass, and drums. Once they had the feel, it took only a few tries to get it onto tape. Wilson, who hadn't needed his artists' permission to alter their record, waited until the session was over to tell Artie what he was up to. At first Artie shrugged it off. He could tell they were trying to turn Simon and Garfunkel into the Byrds, and as far as he was concerned it sounded kind of cute. "I was mildly amused, and detached with the certainty that it was not a hit." He passed the news of the recording session in a letter to Paul in London, who had almost exactly the same response. "I was at that point sort of successful on the folk scene in England," he recalled forty years later. "No, more than sort of successful. I was *very* successful; I was one of the most sought-after performers."

He'd found a kind of success, for sure. But, really, he had no idea. He really didn't.

Columbia released the "The Sound of Silence"/"We've Got a Groovey Thing Goin'" 45 on September 13. The record broke across the Boston radio stations a few weeks later and soon spread to other cities. It made the lower reaches of the *Billboard* national charts in October, and as it drew closer to the Hot 100 in November, Artie called Paul to say that something had started to happen. Paul was delighted — or he didn't pay much mind, or else he was deeply offended and thoroughly outraged. His recollection of that key moment in his career depended on where he was, whom he was talking to, and when the conversation was taking place.

When Paul's copy of the record was delivered to Piepe's address that fall, Al Stewart was there to experience his flatmate's anger and angst. He was *furious*! Columbia was so determined to make him and Artie pop stars they had taken Paul's very serious song and dressed it up in a clown suit. Argh! Actually, Paul's biggest problem with the record that afternoon was that he couldn't get it to play correctly. The house record player had only the thin 33 rpm spindle, and because all British records were designed for that size, they didn't have one of those plastic doodads that fill in the wider hole of American 45 rpm discs. Stewart helped Paul fashion a 45 adapter with coins, beads, and other random bits, but it was far from perfect. You could see the disc going a bit wobbly on the turntable. No matter. Paul thumbed the needle into the groove. And of course it sounded off: the drums quavering, the guitars out of tune, and everything going *geeerrrr-wahhhh* and *eee-ew-waaaaang*. Paul's cheeks went

221

red. *What the fuck is* that? When the song ended he plunked the needle back to the start, and got even angrier. *Fucking hell!*

With Stewart watching, Paul dialed the Columbia Records offices in New York and demanded they withdraw the offending record from the shops as soon as possible. He could do a much better job electrifying the song himself; just give him a shot. The voice on the other end tried to soothe him: did Paul know that the record was No. 1 in Boston and catching fire all over New England? They couldn't pull the plug on it now, even if they wanted to, which they didn't. Why didn't he take a week to think it over? Seven days later he called back, and this time the record executive laughed at him. Now "The Sound of Silence" was No. 1 all over New England, had jumped into *Billboard*'s Top 50, and was a good bet to hit No. 1. Instead of complaining, he needed to get his ass on an airplane, get back to New York, and climb aboard for the ride. "So that's when it sort of hit him," Al Stewart says. "And then he did get on an airplane and buggered off for New York."

In another room with someone else, Paul shrugged it off with a smile. "I don't feel it at all," he told a *New Musical Express* reporter within a day or two of his raging around Piepe's flat. "I'm here in England, and I'm goin' to folk clubs, and I'm working like I was working always. It hasn't changed me at all. Oh, I'm happy, man. I've got to say I'm very pleased. It's a very nice gift!" Two years later he couldn't even remember being angry about anything. "I wasn't violently against it. It sounded okay after a couple of hearings. I didn't think it was great, though. I didn't say, 'Oh, they screwed up my song.' . . . I was pleased with that. It grew on me. Now I strongly prefer the electric version."

In 2006, Paul described the episode as an old-fashioned hero's journey, recalling how he'd monitored the *Billboard* charts from London, noting the jump "Silence" made from 111 to 101 and realizing that the next week's chart held the key to his future. If the song hit the Hot 100 above the No. 80 spot, it would come in with a bullet, *Billboard*'s symbol for fast-rising records, which would guarantee far more radio station pickups and a chance to climb a lot higher. He was headed to Denmark to play some clubs that week, and after taking an overnight ferry from Arhus to Copenhagen that landed at 6:00 a.m., he realized he had to wait four hours until he could get into the offices of his Danish publisher and check the new numbers in *Billboard*'s international edition.

Paul spent the time walking past the towering glass-fronted skyscrapers and comic book–colored wooden structures and feeling his future hanging in the balance. When

10:00 a.m. finally arrived, he skipped to the publisher's door and followed the secretaries inside. They handed him the morning's *Billboard,* and he fingered his way to the Hot 100 with his heart fluttering in his chest. The suspense was excruciating. He figured he'd focus his search by starting with the lowest twenty slots, Nos. 100 to 81, knowing that if "The Sound of Silence" wasn't there, it meant one of two things: the song had either collapsed entirely or jumped high enough to earn bullet status, a crucial designation for a rising hit. After not seeing it there, and feeling optimistic, he checked the 79–70 segment. Nothing. Then he started taking it slot by slot, up through the 60s. Still no "Sound of Silence." "I said, *'Shiiiit.'* It didn't make it. I'm really dragged, you know." But he couldn't give up now; he had to keep looking, just to see.

And then he saw it. "The Sound of Silence" had leaped all the way to No. 59, where it resided next to a bullet. A *fifty-two* slot leap.

"I remember this very clearly," he said. "I'm alone in the Danish publishing office, and I thought, *'My life is irrevocably changed.'* "

One of those versions of the story has got to be true. Or maybe none of them is, or maybe all of them are. What mattered is that "The Sound of Silence" was exploding in the United States, and no matter how successful he'd been in England and Europe, no matter his many friends, no matter how free and happy he'd been there, no matter his love affair with Kathy, he had just discovered where his destiny lay. But knowing it didn't mean he knew how to accept it.

Not yet, anyway. He still had shows to play, fans to win over, a perfectly happy existence to live, doubts about American pop stardom to entertain. After Copenhagen, Paul headed to Holland, where CBS's affiliated record company Artone had set up a show at a folk club in Haarlem, to draw attention to its releases of *Songbook* and *Wednesday Morning, 3 AM*. Harry Knipschild, the young executive who had set up Paul's visit and accompanied him as he made his rounds to a newspaper interview, a seasonal Sinterklaas (Santa Claus) event, and then to the night's gig, listened to Paul vent about that "Sound of Silence" single. The thing was, Paul hated folk-rock — Dylan, the Byrds, Sonny and Cher, all of it. Folk wasn't supposed to be commercial; that was the whole point. "I'd rather not have a hit at all than hit with a folk-rock song," Paul declared.

That evening, a sparse audience of maybe twenty people greeted Paul at the Haarlem club owned by Dutch folksinger Cobi Schreiber. He wasn't going to earn anything for his work, but he gave the show his all, playing a set list packed with, yes, folk-rock songs. By the end of the evening, Knipschild had seen enough of the chest-first way Paul walked, the confidence in his voice, and the assurance in his playing and singing to understand one thing: no matter how much he complained and fretted about fame, Paul already had the kingly bearing of a star.

CHAPTER 10
IT MEANS NOTHING TO US

The legend puts Paul and Artie in the front seat of Paul's car, parked beneath a tree on a dark corner one chilly Sunday evening in late December. Paul has been back in New York for a few weeks, and they're both living in their parents' houses, so they have to sneak off somewhere to get stoned. This is why they're in the shadows of 70th Road and 141st Street, passing a joint between them as they listen to the week's top hits march to the No. 1 spot, just as they'd been doing for more than a decade. Up to the top of the charts! The king of the mountain! Who would it be this time? Actually, they already knew. This was the week "The Sound of Silence" reigned at No. 1. It was still too strange to take it in. So they sat there listening to the song, passing the reefer, and gazing silently through the cloudy windshield. A minute or two into the song, Artie exhaled drily.

"Simon and Garfunkel."

"Yeah," Paul said.

"Number one in the nation."

"Incredible."

"I bet those guys are having a great time right now."

"Yep."

Was it really them? That the electrified record sounded nothing like the tune they recorded made it feel even less real. Back in London, Paul couldn't bring himself to cancel his remaining shows, pack up his life, and fly back to New York until he picked up a telephone and dialed a familiar number he hadn't called in months. It was dinnertime in Queens, and all the Merensteins were at the table when the ringing phone pulled Charlie's wife, Harriet, to her feet. She handed the receiver to her husband, and there was the prodigal surrogate son Paul, looking for a little more career advice. He explained what was happening, how he'd been minding his own business overseas and now everyone at Columbia was yelling that "The Sound of Silence" was going to be huge, that he had to abandon his life in London to come back home. It all sounded great, but there was so much bullshit in the music business. Now Paul needed an honest answer from the only music guy he could really trust. Was "The Sound of Silence" really that big a hit? Yes, it was, Charlie said. "You've really got a hit record."

Paul responded immediately. "Okay. I'm

coming back. I'll call you the moment I get home."

He left London in a rush, packing up his clothes and shoes, finding a place to leave his car and everything else he couldn't carry on the airplane. Promising everyone that he'd be gone for just a few months, he canceled only a few shows, rescheduling others for a visit he was already planning to make in February. Talking to friends and fans, he shrugged off his American star turn as a brief distraction he'd get out of the way by the spring. He'd stay only as long as it took to make the money he'd need to live in London for a year or two without having to hustle for gigs. Then he'd be right back to the folk clubs to play music that really mattered.

But for the time being, there were so many other important things to do in America, so many decisions to make, so many problems to fix. Not long ago Paul would have handed it all off to Charlie without a second thought, but back in New York, he came to realize that things were different now. "The Sound of Silence" was on track to sell a million copies. *A million copies.* A huge number, and with it came huge opportunities that presented questions and potential problems of equal magnitude. The Columbia executives were already demanding a new album, one that sounded more like the electric "Sound of Silence" than the buttoned-down acoustic *Wednesday*

Morning, 3 AM. Tom Wilson, who had left Columbia to take a bigger job at MGM Records, was no longer available for guidance, and Paul and Artie had no idea who their next producer would be. Was Charlie really equipped to navigate the hazard-pocked terrain just ahead?

Apollo Records had struggled throughout Charlie Merenstein's tenure as its chief. He'd had his successes, but he'd also made some crucial mistakes, particularly when it came to enforcing his contracts. Charlie was a quirky guy. When he made deals with an artist, he was also making a friend, starting a personal relationship that was as much about trust and loyalty as it was about whatever deal they signed. Charlie knew he'd live up to his end, and he expected his artists, his friends, to do the same. But it hardly ever worked out that way in the music business, particularly when an Apollo act scored a moderate hit record or two. That's when the guys from the major labels would come swooping down from the tall buildings, beaks ruffling with bigger, richer contracts. And that, far more often than not, was the end of that up-and-comer's days at Apollo. Because even if a musician was already signed to Apollo for another two or five or ten records, Charlie could never bring himself to hold an artist back. Because: if they don't wanna do business with me, I don't wanna do business with them. He'd rather have let the big companies work out a small settlement, or maybe he wouldn't even take it that far. If he had a friend who turned out to be a rat, why spend any more time thinking about him? Fuck 'em. Move on.

Only, you can't run a record company, or any kind of company, like that, and when Bess Berman finally lost her patience with her brother in 1959, he left the company and, after a few years of living off the settlement Bess gave him, bought a route as a pretzel distributor in New York, dragging his still-athletic body out of bed before dawn six days a week to drive his pretzels. He kept a hand in the business, usually managing and producing an artist or act somewhere, but that was a part-time pursuit, and sometimes much less than that. As he told his sons, the product he sold in his new business was so much easier than what he dealt with in the music industry. Pretzels, he explained, don't talk back. Paul never called. Charlie wouldn't hear his young friend's voice again for more than twenty years.

Whether Paul had ever intended to reinstall Merenstein as his manager isn't entirely clear. Charlie was Jerry Landis's guy, a good navigator through the Midtown pop factories. Now Paul was an artist of musical, poetic, and social sophistication, and also the creator of a million-selling No. 1 hit single. Whatever happened before this moment no longer mattered. In fact, it mattered so little that it probably hadn't happened at all.

Paul and Artie had hired a new manager not long after they signed with Columbia in early 1964. Producer Tom Wilson had recommended Marvin Lagunoff, who also managed the Pilgrims, the African American group Wilson had hoped to equip with "The Sound of Silence" when Paul first played it for him. Lagunoff's real specialty was in movies and television — one of his first ideas for the *Wednesday Morning, 3 AM*–era Paul and Artie was to make them hosts of a *Hootenanny*-style folk music TV show. Nothing came of it, or from anything Lagunoff might have done to promote the release of *Wednesday Morning, 3 AM.* He wasn't involved with the overdubbed/hit version of "The Sound of Silence," either, so it had been easy to forget about him, or at least expect that he was as through with them as they were with him.

Having reported to Columbia's offices in Midtown to meet with the label's chief of promotion, Gene Weiss, Paul and Artie were on their way out the door when label president Goddard Lieberson stopped them and congratulated them on their success. They must be on top of the world, Lieberson proclaimed. The whole nation was talking about them! It was nice to hear, but they didn't feel like they were on top of anything, given that the only show their booking agent at William Morris had been able to set up for them was a two-night, four-show gig at the Coconut Grove nightclub in Miami, for which they would be paid the not-terribly-grand sum of a thousand dollars. Obviously they needed help, a new manager, pronto. Lieberson couldn't recommend anyone in particular, since whoever they hired would be the guy he'd be dealing with when they had disagreements. But since they obviously needed to focus on younger fans, Lieberson advised, they'd be smart to talk to a couple of managers who had the college circuit down cold. The first was Albert Grossman, who handled Peter, Paul, and Mary and Bob Dylan, among others. The second was Mort Lewis, who had the Brothers Four, the jazz pianist Dave Brubeck, and a few more. Paul, who was well aware of Grossman's tight bond with Dylan, had one question: "What's the name of that second guy again?"

Born and raised in Minneapolis, Mort Lewis was a jazz fanatic who had found his way into the industry when he got back from World War II and started managing artists in the early 1950s. Tall and broad-shouldered, he was smart and hardworking, and also a ladies' man, with a freewheeling panache that earned him friends ranging from Duke Ellington to Lenny Bruce.

When Paul called, Lewis invited the two

musicians to meet him at his east Midtown apartment that evening. After shaking hands and handing off his coat, Paul noticed the copy of Bruce's latest album propped up against Lewis's hi-fi. The comedian had just sent it over with an inscription on the cover — "To Morty, I hope you like it! Lenny" — and the sight made Paul's eyes pop. "Wow! You know Lenny Bruce?" Lewis nodded, and Paul looked over at Artie. *Cool.*

They sat down to talk about Paul and Artie's new set of problems and opportunities, and Paul brought up one particularly maddening thing: when they walked onstage at some venues, they'd find only one microphone, which they would have to share. It was a pain in the neck, literally, given their differences in height. Their vocal blend suffered, too, but somehow there was nothing anyone could seem to do about it. Lewis shrugged. Just write it into the contracts. If someone wanted to book them, there was always an agreement about how long they should play and how much they'd get paid, right? Just add a clause that says the contractor must supply two microphones, state-of-the-art, preferably.

"It's that easy?" Paul asked.

Lewis nodded. "If you know what you're doing."

They continued the conversation over corned beef sandwiches at the Hole in the

Wall deli, near Lewis's apartment. When the waitress brought the coffee, the manager sketched the terms for a two-year management contract on the back of a paper napkin. The next day, the three of them met with their lawyer, Harold Orenstein, and Lewis predicted that Simon and Garfunkel should and could be earning as much as ten thousand dollars a week. Orenstein, who also knew what he was doing, proposed adding a clause that fixed the number into the deal. If they *weren't* earning ten grand a week after six months, then Paul and Artie could call off the contract. Lewis agreed, and the deal was done. Back in his office, Lewis quickly pulled together some college shows for the next weekend. Paul called Barry Kornfeld, a young guitarist named Tom Dawes, an old frat brother who could play the drums, and a few others to serve as a backup band. They met up that Friday afternoon and hit the road. When they rolled back into the city on Monday morning, they had earned slightly more than ten thousand dollars.[*]

[*] Here's how that worked. After chewing out the William Morris agent, Lewis booked three nights of shows, starting with a Friday evening show at Brown University that paid $2,500. On Saturday, they went to Rensselaer Polytechnic in Troy, New York, earning $2,000 for an opening slot on a show with Little

From the start, they performed mostly on weekends, a restriction set by Artie's post-grad classes at Columbia University. Taking a break, or dropping out entirely, might have made more sense if the military draft and the Vietnam War hadn't been waiting to claim him should he have lost his college defer-ment. Paul had nothing to worry about from the U.S. Army — he had been diagnosed with a slight heart murmur that barred him from any kind of military service. The university's Christmas break freed them up to work on their second album, a hurry-up project pushed into immediate production by Co-lumbia Records executives made ravenous by the unexpected success of the "Silence" single. Rereleasing the acoustic *Wednesday Morning, 3 AM* wasn't going to cut it. Simon and Garfunkel were folk-rock artists now, so

---

Anthony and the Imperials. But then Little Anthony never showed up, which spurred a storm of stomps, claps, and hollering from the three thousand students in the Field House, which the college's activities director now imagined might not survive the night — not unless he could get Paul and Artie to go back and play a second set. And of course they would — as long as they got the $4,000 the school had planned to pay Little Anthony. On Sunday they got $2,500 at the State University of New York in Oneonta.

that's the kind of music they needed to deliver. A dozen tracks that ran deep but also rocked hard — and that could be finished within, say, three weeks or less. A lunatic demand, really, particularly for a group with a solitary songwriter who was not known for working quickly.

But first they had to record a follow-up single, and immediately. If they wanted to capitalize on the success of "The Sound of Silence" they'd need to get the new song out while the old one was still on the charts. Just after Paul got home from England, he met Artie in their old workshop in the Garfunkel family basement to strategize. The new single, they felt, had to be as strong as "The Sound of Silence," but in a different way. "To show people [that] it wasn't a fluke," Artie said. "And show that we could make an interesting record in a whole other vein." They settled on "Homeward Bound," a road song Paul had written and performed during his most recent residency in England. It was a pretty simple song, an acoustic tune with just bass, drums, and piano accompaniment. But they took care with the recording, tossing out a first attempt that didn't sound quite right for a second take they cut with local musicians in Nashville. Indeed, "Homeward Bound" had a very different sound from "The Sound of Silence," but connected as solidly as they hoped when it was released in

January, rising to No. 5 on the *Billboard* charts. But they still had a whole new record to make.

Fortunately, Paul had a backlog of songs, most of which he'd been polishing on the English folk circuit for the last year. He and Artie had worked out harmonies during those launderette sessions the previous summer, so all they needed to get going was a producer who could take over for the departed Wilson. Columbia assigned them Bob Johnston, who had also taken over for Wilson in Bob Dylan's recording sessions. Unlike his predecessor, who defined sophisticated cool, Johnston had a little crazy in his eyes. A Texas-born shouter and arm waver, he had a wild admiration for the headstrong artists he worked with (including Dylan, Johnny Cash, and Aretha Franklin), and made a point of deferring to their inspirations and whims. "Dylan or somebody would come up to me and ask what they ought to do," Johnston told me a year before his death in 2015, "and I'd say, 'Fuck you! *You're* the genius! *You* tell me what you want, and I'll make it happen!' " What Paul and Artie wanted was to make the best-sounding record possible, the fewer limitations the better. Message received, Johnston urged them to look for good musicians in other cities, pointing them first to Nashville, then cleared the way for them to head to Los Angeles to work with the studio players there who would be known eventually as the Wrecking Crew. Of the eleven songs on the new record, five were revised versions of songs first heard on the UK-only *Paul Simon Songbook,* while "The Sound of Silence" appeared on both that album and *Wednesday Morning, 3 AM.* "Somewhere They Can't Find Me" and "We've Got a Groovey Thing Goin' " came from the first folk-rock session with Wilson in April, leaving only "Richard Cory," "Flowers Never Bend with the Rainfall," "Blessed," and Paul's solo cover of his favorite guitar piece, Davy Graham's "Anji," as new songs.

Dressed up in folk-rock's Beatles-sharp threads, the songs sparkle here and snarl there, at times leaping in unexpected directions and then veering back to Dylan-worn paths. A few songs ("Kathy's Song," "April Come She Will," and "Anji") are left in purely acoustic form, but given Paul's years of studio experience, it's not surprising to hear how winningly the other songs incorporate the new sounds. Perhaps the most glaring exception is the jangling harpsichord that overwhelms the sweet melancholy of "Leaves That Are Green." "Blessed," by contrast, profits enormously from the electric guitars that wail and chime in the space between the circular drum pattern and the singers' fierce harmonies. The contemplative "A Most Peculiar Man" makes do quite nicely with light percussion, a mostly unheard electric guitar played well beneath the chords held on a quietly seething organ. The guitars, organ, bass, and drums give "I Am a Rock" a reined-in variation on Dylan's "Positively 4th Street" sound, while the snapping snare, organ riffs, and a growing bass riff add a sooty funk to "Richard Cory."

Thematically, the album covers the sweep of Paul's previously established subjects. "Blessed" contrasts the blessings Jesus bestowed upon the powerless and impoverished with images of the deprivation and decadence so common in London's Soho district, while "Kathy's Song" identifies the singer's lover, rather than God, as the sole source of grace in his life. But even love is something less than pure. The larcenous narrator in "Somewhere They Can't Find Me" seems quite comfortable trading his girlfriend for the spoils of a liquor store heist. "Somewhere" conveys a sense of wicked fun, what with all that creeping down the alley and flying down the highway and leaving the cops scratching their heads, but it's still of a piece with the bleak lives described in "A Most Peculiar Man" and "Richard Cory," both of which read like case studies in the existentialist's handbook. The nameless suicide at the center of "Peculiar" takes form only by dint of his self-destruction. And while the high-flying heir Mr. Cory (whose tale is borrowed from a poem of the same name by Edwin Arlington Robinson) is renowned for his wealth, looks, and elegant manners, the only thing that truly humanizes him is the bullet he shoots through his head.

"I Am a Rock" portrays the same internal despondency as the repurposed "Sound of Silence," and together the collection of songs creates a loosely interlocking narrative that bonds the writer's personal angst with the overarching social and philosophical concerns of the moment. To the children of the Cold War, now coming of age in a decade that still seemed so full of possibility, the desperate love at the core of "Kathy's Song" took on the gravitas of philosophy, while the sociological abstractions in "Blessed" felt as broken-hearted as a tale of lost love. It was as if Paul's most intimate sorrows, fears, and hopes had come to express the feelings of an entire generation.

Released on January 17, 1966,[*] *Sounds of Silence* (the plural underscoring that it's an album of songs) jumped immediately onto the *Billboard* album charts, peaking at No. 21. Not quite a chartbuster, but still light-years beyond *Wednesday Morning, 3 AM*. And in an industry still defined by singles, it was

[*] About five weeks after Paul returned to the United States, to give you a sense of how extremely quickly it all went.

241

far more significant that "Homeward Bound," released just two days after *Sounds of Silence* (though it wasn't included on the album), catapulted its way up *Billboard*'s Hot 100, hitting No. 5 on April 2, before falling back to make room for "I Am a Rock," which jumped into the top three. The back-to-back-to-back hits quickly established Simon and Garfunkel as incisive social commentators, yearning romantics, and prophets of alienation and disillusionment. They were, in the words of their official Columbia Records bio, "rather intense, though hardly solemn, young men with literary interests that ranged from Joyce to 'kids who write on subway walls.' . . . They are both twenty-three, direct, witty and very hip."

The full-page ads Columbia put into the trade magazines to promote *Sounds of Silence* and "Homeward Bound" were dominated by a shot of the duo huddled together in matching pea coats and striped scarfs, peering down at the lens with cigarettes smoldering between their fingers. Artie's blond curls and soft eyes give him a poetic air, while Paul's hooded eyes and the debonair pose he strikes with his cigarette suggest a louche Austrian count, a young man with a castle and personal problems. None of Columbia's bios or press releases hint at their Tom and Jerry days, or at the quantity of songs Paul wrote, produced, and released under different names. Speaking to the *San Francisco Chronicle*'s Ralph J. Gleason, the first American music critic at a major newspaper to write seriously about rock 'n' roll, Paul told a version of the breakthrough story of "The Sound of Silence" that made it seem that he was completely unaware of the single's existence until he stumbled upon a copy of *Cash Box* in Copenhagen and discovered that his song was in the Top 10. "How could this happen?" he said, adopting the gee-whiz voice of an artist-naif. "It was quite an experience." Gleason was impressed. "These two young men are excellent songwriters and fascinating performers," he wrote. "They ring changes on almost all the top people in the 'New Sounds' and 'Top 40' field."

Touring as much as Artie's class schedule would allow, the two worked their way through the college field houses and concert halls, and also drew crowds to theaters and clubs in major cities coast to coast. Reviewing Simon and Garfunkel's first nonclub appearance in New York, an afternoon show at Columbia University's McMillan Hall on May 1, 1966, the *Times*'s music critic Robert Shelton (the same fellow who had accompanied Dylan to the notorious Gerde's Folk City show two years earlier) began his rave review by noting how the duo seemed to speak "to, and perhaps for, their student audiences." Back in the Bay Area a few weeks later, they played a May 28 show at the Berkeley Community Theatre, where the already enthusiastic Ralph J. Gleason noted the "almost biblical morality" of Paul's songs, with "their concern for the fundamentals of love and justice and beauty and salvation in the midst of corruption, [which] reflects the attitude of much of the New Generation."

Simon and Garfunkel came on like musicians-artists-statesmen, two young men in dark suits and ties, singing from an austere stage whose two microphones, two glasses of water, and single stool underscored the stark heart of their songs. Onstage, they took their music and themselves seriously, both lasering into the heart of each note and syllable. They brooked no interruptions or shouted requests. Offenders suffered the lash of one or the other's furious tongue, then were gang-stomped by the crowd's laughter and applause. You idiot. You're supposed to pay attention; these songs are broadsides from the heart of the youth movement. The action on the streets, the life of the mind, the writing on the motherfucking wall. "Pop music is catching up with film as the leading medium in which to make some comment about the world for a large audience, just as film caught up with literature," Paul told the *New York Times*'s Shelton. "Pop music is the most vibrant force in music today," Artie told *Time* magazine. "It's like dope — so heady and alive."

They could be funny onstage, and even self-effacing, but as the *New Musical Express* proclaimed to British fans, Simon and Garfunkel were rock 'n' roll's first intellectual sophisticates. "Their intellectual prowess and less-than-consuming interest in music separate them from the 'normal' performer," wrote Tracy Thomas, who went on to (mis)-identify Artie as an architecture student, which only used to be true, and Paul as a writer who only sort of dabbled in music. "No matter how successful we are," Paul told her, "I'll quit in a couple of years."

It would be harder to quit than Paul thought. Riding high on the charts, higher still on reams of critical acclaim, and from the *right* critics, and traveling on jets and in limos to sing truth to power, he would have to figure out where to store the sacks of money people kept hurling their way. Back in London in the spring, Paul couldn't help talking about the absurd numbers he kept seeing on the checks they got each night, even giving the *New Musical Express*'s Keith Altham a specific figure. "Do you know how much we earned last night in a concert in America? $4,300!" And that was just one hour-long show. "Art might turn to me after a couple of concerts and say, 'We earned $13,000 this weekend.' I kinda shrug and say,

'That's a good two days' work!' " But then he'd shrug and roll his eyes, because what difference did it really make? Nothing meaningful. "I just can't grasp it — it means nothing to us."

In the early fall of 1965, when Artie was studying mathematics in New York and Paul was an up-and-coming folksinger in England, Paul went to the London Palladium to meet the Seekers, a pop-folk vocal group that had relocated to England after making several hits in their native Australia. Paul had heard from the group's publicist, Allan MacDougall, that the group was looking for material. With the electric "Sound of Silence" still weeks away from being released (or even entering his awareness), Paul was happy to pitch a song or two to a group riding high on three straight hit records. The Seekers' Bruce Woodley, tall, bespectacled, and as authoritative as a successful young musician of the mid-1960s could be, handed Paul his guitar and said, "Sing!" Paul did just that, *la-la*-ing a song that bounded genially through some interesting chord changes. Woodley and his bandmates were impressed. Come back with some lyrics, he said, and that's something we can work with. Three weeks later Paul returned with a song now called "Someday, One Day," and the Seekers recorded it as their next single.

The song took the Seekers to No. 11 on the UK pop charts, but Woodley, who also wrote songs for the group, didn't wait that long to ask Paul to collaborate on another tune or two. Their first attempt, a yearning love song called "I Wish You Could Be Here," also got tapped as a single for the group. Next Woodley pulled out an upbeat, pop-smart number that lacked only a set of lyrics, and Paul said he'd be glad to scratch something out. He composed lyrics for a song that came to be called "Red Rubber Ball," a cheerfully bitter sendoff to a lover who was never all that into him in the first place. "The roller coaster ride we took is nearly at an end," he proclaims. "I bought my ticket with my tears, / It's all I'm gonna spend." When the dawn lights the horizon, the rising sun is as bright and carefree as a child's playground ball. Another swing, another home run. That's how it struck Woodley, who figured he had just heard another Seekers single. When Paul offered to publish the song through his own company, Woodley shrugged and said sure. They'd share the writers' royalties fifty-fifty either way. They went to a studio to record a demo, and Paul sent it to Eclectic Music's office in Barry Kornfeld's living room on Waverly Street in Greenwich Village.

"The Sound of Silence" pulled Paul home after that, but Woodley came to New York in early January 1966, and Paul met him at

Kornfeld's place. After a bit of mood-enhancing conviviality, they got to work. Woodley presented a simple riff with a melody built on an inverted C chord, and when Paul started playing and *la-la*-ing a melody, he repeated the word *cloudy . . . cloudy.* In search of a good third chord, he fingered a diminished F-sharp, which jolted the tune into a new, if similarly relaxed progression through a misty northern California afternoon. The smoke in the air put them in a trippy mood, a tableau of finger-painted smiles, mind-bending sun breaks, and low-hanging puffs whispering *why*? When it was done, they both blinked and nodded and were quite happy. Another good song! Who knew where it was all going to lead? "Paul Simon is getting in our groove now," Woodley told a *Melody Maker* reporter a week or two later.

The Seekers weren't the only performers drawn to Paul and Woodley's new songs. When Kornfeld brought the "Red Rubber Ball" demo to the Cyrkle (an American group whose members included the same Tom Dawes who had accompanied Paul and Artie, along with Kornfeld and the drummer from AEPi, on their first ten-thousand-dollar weekend) they grabbed it. Originally named the Rhondells, Dawes's group had recently been signed as clients by Beatles manager

Brian Epstein, who changed their name* to the Cyrkle. The tune clicked for Dawes and his bandmates, and they made it the title track for their first album. Released as their first single, the record detonated on impact, taking the group to No. 2 on the *Billboard* list, and ultimately selling more than a million copies.

Even in the midst of Simon and Garfunkel's first run of hits, it was a huge deal. Another entry for Paul's hot streak and, it went without saying, a new gusher of royalties, money he would split evenly with Woodley, according to their handshake deal. But there was a catch. Instead of registering "Red Rubber Ball" to Eclectic Music in the United States, Paul had assigned the rights to his self-owned British publisher, Pattern Music Ltd., which, as per long-standing music publishing tradition, automatically took 50 percent of every song it published — meaning that Woodley's 50 percent share in the song actually added up to only 25 percent of its proceeds. The other 75 percent went to cowriter/publisher Paul Simon.

Who knew the song would become such a huge hit? Or how Paul's casual proposal that they publish it with his company would so drastically alter how the profits were calculated? When Woodley got his first royalty

---

*With the help of John Lennon, according to legend.

check, he assumed there'd been a mistake. Paul had never mentioned that his British publishing company would siphon off such a huge chunk of money from their joint composition; surely he intended to respect the spirit of the fifty-fifty split they had agreed upon. But he didn't.

It was Music Industry 101, what he'd learned during his days in Tin Pan Alley: if you could find an advantage, you took it, and a deal was a deal. Yet his logic didn't cut both ways. When the overwhelming success of "The Sound of Silence" made the fifty-fifty deal he'd made with Barry Kornfeld to run their co-owned publishing company Eclectic Music seem far too generous, Paul took Kornfeld out for a cup of coffee and proposed reducing the split to something more appropriate. Say, ninety-five–five, in Paul's favor. More than a little chagrined — Paul had approached him about cofounding the company with the very terms he was now calling unfair — Kornfeld refused to commit to anything. Instead, he applied one of the music industry lessons he'd learned on his own and immediately hired a lawyer.[*]

* Both pledged to keep their friendship separate from the business disagreement, and continued to enjoy each other's company even while giving affidavits and sitting across from each other while their respective lawyers debated the points of their

It was a lot of wheeling and dealing for a fellow who talked so much about how little money mattered to him — but, in a sense, Paul hadn't been lying about that. On one level, he really *didn't* care that much about money and the things it could buy. Sure, he liked having a sporty car and would soon buy himself a two-level Upper East Side apartment that looked over Gracie Mansion and the East River. But the decor was minimalist: a single guy in his mid-twenties who traveled a lot had little use for expensive furnishings. As long as their business manager sent him his seventy-five-dollar weekly allowance and paid the bill for his credit cards, he was fine. "All I need is somewhere to eat and sleep, and buy guitar strings," he said. "I haven't had any real need for money yet." But there were other aspects to the money side of the business. If numbers couldn't define the entirety of a man, Paul had read enough box scores to know that they could tell you who was winning and who was losing.

The Seekers' "Red Rubber Ball" wasn't released as a single but the success of the Cyrkle's version was overwhelming enough

---

case. Eventually, Paul and Kornfeld worked out a settlement and went their separate ways as friends — friends who hardly ever saw each other after that, but still.

to make the song a part of Simon and Garfunkel's stage act for the next year or two. Artie set up the tune with a comically rueful tale, telling the crowd how he and Paul had recorded virtually all Paul's original songs, except for the one of which the Cyrkle ("who used to be good friends of ours") had gone and sold 890,000 copies,* ha ha. "Red Rubber Ball" always got a good ovation, but something about the tune grated against Paul's skin. When he had come calling at the Seekers' dressing room at the London Palladium in the fall of 1965, they were the stars and he was just another songwriter hoping to land a song with an act that could push it into the Top 10. But now that he'd had hits of his own — all of them far more serious and significant than anything the Seekers had done — his attitude was different. For all that British critics celebrated the group's instrumental prowess and exquisite singing, the Seekers came off like sleek entertainers, their songs crowded with horns and strings, all rough edges buffed to a high sheen.

Had Woodley actually said that Paul was getting into *their* groove? That kind of talk made Paul recoil. So did the melodramatic cover version of "The Sound of Silence" that the mainstream group the Bachelors made so popular that Simon and Garfunkel's version

* The actual number was just north of a million.

252

barely dented the UK charts. "What kind of image are we getting with our songs being recorded by groups like [the Bachelors and the Seekers]?" Paul complained. "I think it strange that the Bachelors should choose to record a very hip song when their style is so conflicting. I feel that some artists never get as much out of a song as I have put into it."

To say nothing of what he was putting into his public image, which was fast evolving from thoughtful young folkie to enlightened hippie oracle. His hair now bristled past his ears, and he took to wearing capes, psychedelic ties, and high-heeled black boots, the garb befitting a young man who had in just a few months become a leading voice of his generation — like Dylan, people kept saying, much to Paul's chagrin. "Unfortunately, I'm always being compared to Bob Dylan," he told the *New Musical Express* that spring. "Our philosophies are different. He is always dumping [on] people more than I do. It's really easy to put somebody down. The biggest thing Dylan has going for him is his mystique."

Not that Paul was beyond a little mystique creation. About a year into his UK residencies, he had developed an English accent, layering the tony Londoner's misty vowels (*cahhn't* for *can't* and so forth) and precise diction on top of the muddy bray and aggravated consonants he'd absorbed on the

253

streets of New York. It was an unlikely blend, and he didn't always remember to do it; on *Sounds of Silence* his accent is most audible on "A Most Peculiar Man" (*mahhn*) and "Richard Cory" (who "owns one *hahlf* of this old town") and is only slightly evident on "Patterns." All these were songs he wrote and set in Great Britain. You can feel the tug of the Thames here and there on the coming *Parsley, Sage, Rosemary and Thyme* album, too, though not at all on the New York fantasia "The 59th Street Bridge Song (Feelin' Groovy)." But Paul used it so consistently onstage that it took years for some fans to figure out that Simon and Garfunkel weren't part of the Beatles-sprung British Invasion.[*]

An accent wasn't the only souvenir he brought back from England. At the same time that he joined Britain's serious guitarists in mastering the finger-knotting intricacies of Davy Graham's "Anji," Paul followed his peers in the pursuit of Martin Carthy's unique arrangement of the British folk standard "Scarborough Fair." Dating back to at least the late seventeenth century, the wistful ballad had been a pillar in the British folk catalogue for centuries, usually played with

[*] "We used to have to explain that we were American," Paul recalled in 1990. "I don't think that it helped that I came back sort of affecting an English accent, either."

the most minimal of instrumental accompaniment. As per Ewan MacColl's typically faithful rendition on his 1957 album *Matching Songs of the British Isles and America,* the standard performance set the vocal against basic chords strummed only once or twice per change. Carthy, however, sang "Scarborough" to a kaleidoscopic finger-picked pattern central enough to serve as a countermelody. Entranced, Paul saw Carthy at a club and asked for, and received, a private tutorial on the new arrangement. Another friend did him the favor of writing down the lyrics, and when the time came to start work on Simon and Garfunkel's third album, Paul added the song to the list of potential tracks.

The writing rarely came easily. Paul usually couldn't compose on the road, not even in the hush of a hotel room. He needed things to be familiar, and comfortable, to know that he wouldn't be disturbed, that nothing would break the spell of creation. Even under the best of circumstances it took time. When he sat down to write, it might take him three days just to get started. He'd never been a good contract writer; when he tried to write to a formula, the melodies flattened and the lyrics rang false. You couldn't believe a word out of Jerry Landis's mouth when he sang; even the teenyboppers could hear the difference. Now it was all real, every word an expression of a resonant feeling, a memory that rippled, a thought that had pierced. The wanting and the needing; the anger, jealousy, and contempt; the love and the loneliness; the fleeting moments of ease and happiness — all of it swirling around while he strummed and picked at the strings, until a thread emerged and wove into another, and then another after that. But the frenetic pace of concerts, interviews, and parties, along with the weird way fame and money had of disrupting and realigning even the most long-standing relationships, made it all the more difficult for Paul to connect with the vital core of his muse.

He had only three new songs to offer, but happily he still had a few tunes left over from his time in England, as well as the hit single "Homeward Bound." He also had arrangements for two folk standards, including "Scarborough Fair," so he didn't have to panic about filling the required twelve tracks. This time around, it was much more exciting to think about the recording process. It would be their first chance to really settle into the studio, to explore the songs and produce them with the same care and feeling that Paul put into his writing and composing. It was his first opportunity to build on the skills he had learned during all those hours he'd spent recording publishing demos and those custom-made vanity records. With Bob Johnston sticking to his do-whatever-you-want-you're-the-fuckin'-genius production technique, their primary studio collaborator became Roy Halee, the Columbia Records staff engineer who had worked the knobs on every song they had ever recorded.

A linebacker-size fellow who had grown up in a musical family — his father provided speaking and singing voices for cartoon characters, including Mighty Mouse and Heckle and Jeckle — Halee had started his career as a production assistant for CBS-TV in the late 1950s. His background as a student of the classical trumpet helped get him started in the network's audio department and launched half a dozen years of working on live broadcasts of *The $64,000 Question* and other CBS programs. Told that his job would be moving, along with most television production, to Los Angeles, Halee decided to stay in New York, and took a job at CBS's Columbia Records, where he spent a torturous few months at a tape editing desk, slicing up whatever was handed to him. Pop, folk, classical — it didn't matter. Exquisitely bored, Halee was working his way into record engineering when Tom Wilson scheduled the Simon and Garfunkel audition in late 1963. As the low man in the department, Halee got tapped to record the duo's studio audition and found himself falling in love with what he heard. Wilson was so impressed with the sound of Halee's recordings that he began hiring the engineer for Bob Dylan sessions. It made sense that Halee would engineer Simon and Garfunkel's sessions for *Wednesday Morning, 3 AM.*

The simplicity of the first album and the frenetic pace of the sessions for the second hadn't allowed for much sonic experimentation. It was all they could do to make sure one song had stuck to the tape before they moved on to the next. But with four months to produce the third Simon and Garfunkel album, neither Paul nor Artie had any intention of rushing things, and as long as his bosses were willing to pay the bills, Halee was happy to spend as much time as it would take to help them make a truly distinctive recording. The sessions went on for nearly three months, but only on a handful of days scattered across the summer, with most of the work completed over five busy days in June, a single recording date in July, and two days in August.

They kicked things off on June 8 with "Patterns," a song that had first appeared in a solo acoustic arrangement on *The Paul Simon Songbook* a year earlier. This time they underscored the panic in the lyrics — the realization that life is as preordained as a rat's path through a maze — with jumping bass notes, fast-slapped bongos, keening organ notes, and acoustic guitar runs that veer from bluesy whimpers to sitar-like exotica. Artie limits his harmonies to shouts on key words ("Casting . . . And the light! . . . my death! . . . Like a rat!") and when Paul gets to the climactic phrase ("until the rat dies"), his voice is filtered to invoke an oppressive *1984*-esque authority. Each song has its own flavor. The whimsy of "Cloudy" comes through with bells, finger snaps, and harmonized double-guitar runs evoking a bouzouki player in a Greek restaurant. Artie doubles Paul's lead vocal, but his voice is much more prominent on the rainbow *ooh*s he adds to the second half of the verses, a counterpoint as airy and drifting as the clouds in the title. Paul's urban feel-good tune "The 59th Street Bridge Song (Feelin' Groovy)," for all its hippie cheer, got its bounce from bassist Gene Wright and drummer Joe Morello, both members of the Dave Brubeck Quartet. Much of the production is relatively understated. An acoustic guitar, an electric bass, percussion, and organ for "Homeward Bound" and a more driving variation on the same to draw out the rattling subway cars on "A Poem on an Underground Wall." A basic rock combo serves for the album's pair of glib social commentary songs, the newly written "The Big Bright Green Pleasure Machine" and the revised (and far more hostile) Dylan rip "A Simple Desultory Philippic." The yearning "For Emily, Whenever I May Find Her," requires only a twelve-string guitar to anchor Artie's fervent solo.

On some tunes, they strain to match their own reputation as poets-slash-commentators. The closing track, "Silent Night/7 O'Clock News" attempts, but falls well short of, profundity by superimposing a newscaster's dismaying recitations (Lenny Bruce's death, civil rights protests, House Un-American Activities Committee investigations into Vietnam protesters, et cetera) over a sweetly harmonized "Silent Night." The biggest miscue, however, is easily the melodramatic "The Dangling Conversation," which mistakes literary pretense — she reads Emily Dickinson; he prefers Robert Frost: "And we note our place with book markers that measure what we lost" — with profundity while harps sigh and an overexcited string section wails in mourning.[*] But the album's failures still can't compete with its high points, particularly "Scarborough Fair."

While the song has been performed for centuries with the weather-beaten rumble of

***

[*] Both Paul and Artie called it their favorite song, not only on the album but in their entire careers. Released as a single, the tune stalled at No. 25, much to their surprise and chagrin. "It was above the kids," Paul mused to the *Record Mirror*'s Norman Jopling. He revised his opinion later, conceding in 1993, "It's a college kid's song, a little precious."

a lonely farmer, Martin Carthy's quicksilver guitar arrangement points "Scarborough" in a more mystical direction. The singer's demands of his former lover — she must perform a series of miracles in order to regain his affections — along with the repeated refrain of "parsley, sage, rosemary and thyme," seem to describe the rituals of some mysterious village sorcerer. To emphasize the song's transcendent spirit, during their vocal sessions Paul and Artie placed candles around the studio and had Halee turn out the lights. Paul slid his capo seven frets up his guitar neck, giving the notes a crystalline ring that combines with a spinning harpsichord and bells to move the song's setting from the fields to something like a cathedral, the notes echoing off the stone walls. Retitled "Scarborough Fair/Canticle," Simon and Garfunkel's version adds an original countermelody that is actually an entirely different song, a revised version of Paul's antiwar ballad "The Side of a Hill." As rewritten by Artie, the song's new melody plays in perfect counterpoint to the "Scarborough Fair" theme, while the words, revised into a series of dreamlike visions, move in and out of focus with all but a few phrases ("the child of the mountain . . . order their soldiers to kill . . . long ago forgotten") more felt than heard.

Released on October 10, 1966, the album they called *Parsley, Sage, Rosemary and*

Thyme came in a cover that portrayed the artists in a flowered garden. Artie is sprawled in jeans and a royal blue sweater, while Paul rises just behind, the modern poet-troubadour clad in cambric and shadow, the both of them elite practitioners of a new pop art form that, as described in a back cover essay by Ralph J. Gleason, projects "the prevailing philosophical current of the New Youth which is that of creativity AGAINST the machine and, thus, FOR humanity." Poets. Visionaries. Sages. "The songs in this album are songs for all time," Gleason concludes, and the New Generation agreed. Rising quickly to *Billboard*'s top five, *Parsley, Sage, Rosemary and Thyme* became Simon and Garfunkel's first smash hit album, selling strongly enough to stay on *Billboard*'s charts until the end of the decade. It ratcheted their fame to a new level, and solidified their reputation as artists and celebrities, while also touching off another unthinkable geyser of cash

"People say I'm a dollar millionaire. I don't know. It could be," Paul said to *Disc*'s Penny Valentine a few months later. "All I know is I'm a lonelier person than I ever was at the beginning. It's a lonely life being part of this business. People watching you, looking at the things you do. It's been bad lately."

CHAPTER 11
SOME DREAM OF
WHAT I MIGHT BE

When Louis Simon set up his first classroom at La Salle Junior High School in the fall of 1961, he brought his double bass and set it on its stand in a corner near the chalkboard at the front of the room. Mostly the thing stood alone, a symbol of a life his students' English teacher had lived before he found his way to the front of their class. They were an elite group, part of the first batch of fourteen-year-olds to join the Special Progress Enrichment Program, an experimental advanced study project housed within a Hell's Kitchen junior high. Louis was a soft-spoken instructor whose gentle ways cushioned his strict standards. The program's designers had taken care to recruit some of the district's most sophisticated educators to work with the special students. Louis's advanced training — he was close to earning his master's degree in education from New York University and was working for a PhD in special education — made him an easy hire.

He did not disappoint. He helped edit the school's literary magazine and encouraged the students to read widely and think deeply about what each author had to say and how he or she was saying it. "He had this ease of getting across things that could have been complicated, but weren't," recalls Daphne Maxwell Reid, who would eventually become a successful stage and television actress in New York City. "And you didn't see him fly off the handle. He was such a patient and serene person." Louis didn't talk much about his past or his family, but when the students started planning an all-school dance in the fall of 1962, he mentioned that his son Paul and Paul's friend Artie were experienced pop musicians who were always eager to play school dances. The boys were famous, too: they were the Tom and Jerry who'd had a pretty big hit song just a few years ago. The dance planners liked the sound of that, so Paul and Artie, one a college graduate and the other in his final term, played the best of their Tom and Jerry songs, along with the hits of the day and a few duo renditions of Paul's better Jerry Landis tunes. The kids had a great time, dancing like crazy, and Mr. Simon was there for the whole thing, standing by himself in the corner, gazing up at his son with a proud smile.

Five years later, with his PhD under his belt and a new job as a lecturer at the City College of New York's Graduate School of Education, Louis was much less supportive of Paul's career in music. Interestingly, Louis's disapproval grew all the more pointed as his son became more successful. Even after Paul had earned millions of dollars and been celebrated as a poet and generational spokesman, his father continued to shake his finger. All the boy saw were the lights, the cheering throngs, and the adulation from the teenyboppers. "Is this all you want?" he'd ask, "to be a rock star?" Paul barely knew what to say to that. "I said, 'Yeah! Why not? What am I supposed to be?' " Louis always had the same answer: a teacher. But Paul loved making music, and people loved the music he made. What could be wrong with that?

Plenty, the grumbles in his own gut insisted. It had all come so easily to him, the playing and the singing and the songwriting. Paul felt wonderful when he did it, that he was in the right place at the right time doing precisely the right thing. But later the voice of his father would echo through the silence. If it was that easy for him, how could it be valuable? Important things should never come easily.

Then again, Louis had never achieved what Paul had. Not even close. The Lee Simms Orchestra did well enough for a local dance band, but they were never going to make a real impact by playing other bands' songs.

Louis logged countless hours trying to write original material, but almost never came up with something that fit his own standards. He kept trying, but the one record he did manage to get released, the "Blue Mud/ Simmer Down" single that Sid Prosen put out as part of the contract with Paul and Artie for "Hey, Schoolgirl," had flopped. So maybe he was jealous, and maybe contempt was the only way to assert his superiority over his brilliant son. Paul's songs might be at the top of the charts, his name celebrated by leading critics around the world, but it didn't mean much, Louis said. Not compared to what really mattered in the world.

"Teach! Teach!" Louis insisted. "That's the *only* important thing!"

As work on *Parsley, Sage, Rosemary and Thyme* continued through the summer of 1966, Paul called Bruce Woodley in London. As Woodley recalled, a few months had passed since they spent that long winter night writing songs in Barry Kornfeld's bedroom, and now Paul was thinking about "Cloudy," the bittersweet tune they had set around a hitchhiker's meanderings in northern California. He'd played it for Artie, and now they were both thinking it'd be a great addition to their new album. And wasn't that great news for Woodley? Paul knew it was. Simon and Garfunkel had become one of the hottest acts in pop music. Having a copyright on their new album, even half a copyright, would create a burbling income stream even if the song never made it as a single. There was just one hitch. If "Cloudy" was going to be on a Simon and Garfunkel album, Paul needed it to be credited to Paul Simon alone. Woodley's name would stay on the copyright, and he'd get all the royalties due to a cowriter, just not the spotlight. So would that be cool? Well, no, of course it wouldn't be *cool,* Woodley recalled. In fact, it was an insult. But once he calculated the value of the copyright, which could have been in the tens of thousands of dollars, he sighed, and agreed.

At least Woodley got something out of the deal. Martin Carthy, whose arrangement for "Scarborough Fair" was so crucial to Simon and Garfunkel's version of the song, received nothing for his contribution. Worse, the composer's credit on *Parsley, Sage* didn't even acknowledge that "Scarborough" was a standard folk song. Instead, it credited Paul and Artie as coauthors, as if the centuries-old tune had emerged entirely from their imaginations. And while Artie deserved credit for composing the "Canticle" melody, the British guitarist couldn't get beyond the sight of Paul's name where "Traditional" should have been, and where the credit for the arrangement should have been at least partly his. Carthy couldn't resist grumbling about it, but even if he hadn't, all the other British folkies knew what he had contributed to the song. Like Paul, many had gone directly to Carthy to learn how to play it themselves. Word that Paul had taken the credit, and all the money, for himself cemented the sour impression many of them had been left with since the American appeared in their midst.

What none of them knew, Carthy included, was that Paul *was* sending royalties to the guitarist. At least, he thought he was. For, as it turned out, the guitarist's publishing company, Sparta Florida, had already filed a copyright for Carthy's arrangement of "Scarborough Fair." Lawyers representing the company contacted Columbia Records soon after the release of *Parsley, Sage* to demand payment. Charing Cross Music, the company Paul set up after he folded Eclectic Music, had been sending royalty checks ever since. Only, none of the money ever got to Carthy. Like so many young artists, he had been less than canny about negotiating, or even taking a close look at, the contracts he'd signed over the years, including the one that relinquished all his financial claims to "Scarborough Fair." Oh, it's just a court thing, he recalls being told. "It's not important." Carthy had been steeped in folk culture for most of his life, and believed strongly that the public domain was less an archive of precious artifacts than an open warehouse for do-it-yourselfers. Step inside and you could hear the voice of the ages singing into your ear. Listen, sing along, or take it apart and put it back together to fit the world around you and leave it for the folks still waiting to be born.

As Paul would soon learn, there's a difference between engaging in folk culture and making yourself a part of it. Once you work your way into the spotlight, you become a part of the public domain, too — not just your work or your ideas, but your life: where you grew up, what your house was like, what your parents did for a living, whom you might be screwing, what you're smoking, and why you keep answering those questions with one breath and then using the next to insist that you're a very private person who can't bear talking about your private life — once you become part of the public domain, you no longer have control. Whatever you've carved off for the marketplace is set loose in other people's imaginations to represent this and symbolize that. And by the time you realize what's happening, it's too late to do anything about it except kick yourself and wonder what you were thinking when you said so much to that reporter and why you already know you'll blurt out just as much to the next one who comes knocking.

Now Paul faced the many demands and pressures running through his days: to turn his deepest feelings into hit songs, to both woo and face down the press, to serve his fans' appetites, to be the best version of himself every time, all the time. Eventually it all ran into a blur. "They're not yelling at me," he told the *New Musical Express.* "They're screaming for what they think I am — some dream of what I might be." Paul would hear himself singing on the radio and have no idea what he was singing about, even though he had not only composed the song but written it about his own life and the people who mattered most to him. Asked about "Homeward Bound" in 1967, he raised his palms to the ceiling. "I don't know how I wrote that," he said. "It's not even me." Even the praise began to get under his skin. He scorned the critics who called him a poet. "The people who call you a poet are people who never read poetry. Like poetry was something defined by Bob Dylan," he said, tossing his rival into the fire for good measure. Had none of these people read Wallace Stevens? Did they have the slightest idea what real literature was?

He'd see pictures of himself with Artie, examine their public smiles and sulks, see how they draped their scarves around their necks; or, worse, he'd catch up with what they had been saying about themselves to reporters. It was like seeing a movie about himself written by someone he'd never met and starring an actor who had never turned an ear to his music. "Simon and Garfunkel are fictitious characters," Paul insisted. "How can anyone have a joint identity with anyone else? And there's a big difference between me and the Simon of Simon and Garfunkel. He's a songwriter and performer and so am I, but otherwise he's a fictitious character." And the only thing that aggravated him more than praise was his suspicion that anyone who glanced at a picture of the duo would automatically assume that the guy with the sparkling blue eyes and halo of blond curls had to be the one who'd written all those delicately constructed songs. He was the one with the angelic voice, wasn't he? "He *should* have been the one who wrote the songs," Paul said in the mid-1980s, still steaming twenty years later "That body *should* have contained the talent."

Then someone would call Artie a sex symbol, and Paul would go wild. For fuck's sake! He'd known Artie since they were eleven years old: Artie with braces, Artie with zits, Artie with a yarmulke on his head surrounded by all the bearded old Jews hoisting the Torah around the synagogue in Queens. Talk about absurdist *fiction.* "Can you imagine girls all over the country writing love letters to someone called Garfunkel? Or chicks spending the cold winter nights up in New England towns stitching 'Garfunkel' on a pillow?" Paul would break up, his cackle a ratcheting crow's caw. "Man, the whole idea of people accepting Garfunkel as a sex symbol. Can't you picture it? Someone in Hollywood saying, 'Get me a new sex symbol like Garfunkel!' " Paul snorted just as derisively to think there could actually be a folk-poet act called Simon and Garfunkel. "It's like the greatest put-on. Some music publisher or agent gets on the phone and says, 'Bring me something for Simon and Garfunkel!' Man, it's funny."

For all *Parsley, Sage*'s success, the singles from the album, and the ones that followed, failed to make a real connection with the New Generation of record buyers. "The Dangling Conversation" stalled at No. 25, "A Hazy Shade of Winter" did a bit better at No. 13, and "At the Zoo" got as high as No. 16, but "Fakin' It" could manage only No. 23. After more than a year without a visit to the Top 10, you might begin to wonder if your public folk tale was coming to an end. And if that happened, if the world stopped paying attention to Paul Simon and Simon and Garfunkel, where did that leave you?

Paul didn't want to quit anything. All that talk about quitting music to be a novelist was just another layer to add to the Paul Simon mystique. The cooler version of himself, the one who really was a step ahead and several sizes larger than the dumpy critter he recog-

272

nized in the bathroom mirror every morning. If you were going to be any Paul Simon, he was really the one to be.

Except that guy was a songwriter, and now Paul was lost in the grim latitudes of writer's block, just when he needed to write more and better. Yet it wouldn't come. All that music in his heart, all the thoughts rattling across his brainpan, all of it stacking up and waiting for release — and still nothing. It was a classic case of creative block, a toxic confusion of desire, pleasure, and shame. As if artistic expression were reprehensible. As if the catharsis it spurred were a mortal sin. As if the artist's need to reveal himself in his art, and the pleasure he took in his creation, were an embarrassment. And wasn't that what Louis Simon couldn't resist pointing out? "Okay, you made all this money, you gave it to everyone in the family and everyone loves you," he'd tell his son. "But that's not the purpose." Paul traced his father's words in the air and felt their bite. "My father," he said many years later, "is the person who most influenced my thinking and my life."

Not long after Paul wrote "Sparrow," his avian variation on Thomas Hobbes's bleak vision of life, he started introducing the tune with a story about, as he put it, one of "my many neuroses." That always got a laugh, and the rest of the tale went on in that vein. He'd caught himself checking out his reflection in a mirror and decided that digging yourself, as he put it, was a terrible vice, and he vowed never to do it again. "I'm like shaving with my eyes closed, you know," he said. The kick went on for months until he was walking past a drugstore at the corner of Broadway and Fifty-Second Street in Manhattan and caught a glimpse of his face in a blacked-out window. It had been a year since he'd seen himself, so he stopped to take a look. "I was digging myself for about forty-five seconds, an intense dig." And he would have kept right on digging if it hadn't been for the sparrow perched on a wire above his head, which, the moment before taking his leave, uncorked a bomb of his own devising that landed atop the crown of the self-digging fop below. Splat. "All I can think of is, 'There goes a happy bird,'" Paul said, waiting for the chorus of laughs and applause to boil down to toss out the capper: "Don't dig yourself. Relative to nothing, this is a song called 'Sparrow.'"

It was all related, his alienation from himself and his grim sense of the world, people, and the forces that shove them together and yank them apart. On tour, Simon and Garfunkel could fill concert halls across the United States, and were even more beloved on the stages in England and Europe. While so much of the pop music scene was dominated by the Doors, the Who, and all the other decibel-banging bands pushing the line between cacophony and chaos, Simon and Garfunkel presented each note with care, even if the emotional landscape in Paul's songs was nothing if not chaotic. But you had to listen closely to absorb the nuances, where all the tumult of the age could ring just as clearly in a hushed portrayal of a broken love affair. Not everyone got it, and some critics dismissed the duo out of hand, much like the widely admired jazz and pop critic Nat Hentoff, who called the neatly tucked S&G "a cul de sac" in popular culture. "Rock 'n' roll for people who don't like rock 'n' roll," added Robert Christgau. Future *Rolling Stone* founder Jann Wenner, then a music columnist for the University of California–Berkeley's student newspaper, raised his generationally savvy snout, too. Simon, he wrote, "is neither a poet nor even an accurate observer of the current youth scene."

Most critics, along with the other leading musicians of the midsixties, disagreed, including Mamas and Papas leader John Phillips and producer/record label owner Lou Adler, who in early 1967 came to Paul to help them put together the first festival for rock 'n' roll, and for the New Generation, which they hoped to mount that June on an outdoor stage at the Monterey County Fairgrounds in northern California.

■ ■ ■

When Phillips and Adler started planning the Monterey Pop Festival they made one of their first calls to Paul, who quickly agreed to put up fifty thousand dollars seed money. Though they had conceived it originally as a business venture the two founders soon opted to make their event a nonprofit benefit for musical education programs around the country. Paul soon agreed to sign on to their board of directors, joining an all-star lineup that included Mick Jagger and Brian Jones of the Rolling Stones, the Beatles' Paul McCartney, the Beach Boys' Brian Wilson, and Smokey Robinson, among others. Simon and Garfunkel agreed to headline the first of what was to be a three-day festival, anointing themselves in the first blossoms of the psychedelic moment.

Organizing the festival was a long and occasionally bumpy road. Some musicians, including Chuck Berry, refused to donate their services, as all the artists were asked to do.* Dylan manager Albert Grossman wouldn't allow his other hot act, Mike Bloomfield's blues freak-out group the Electric Flag, to play unless the festival also

* Only Ravi Shankar was paid for his music; the rest worked for expenses, which some artists, frankly, stretched to outrageous extremes.

booked his completely unknown group the Paupers. Similar quid pro quo deals popped up among other headliners.[†] As a board member, Paul's most important mission turned out to be brokering peace between the festival's contingent of industry-savvy Los Angeles artists and the underground freaks from San Francisco. With Phillips, Adler, and their top aide, Derek Taylor (most famous for his long association with the Beatles), deep into the LA fabric, they sent the New York–based Paul as an emissary to the epicenter of San Francisco's music scene, the Grateful Dead House at 710 Ashbury Street. The trip was a success: Paul helped resolve the tension, and by the end of the evening the members of the Dead had invited Paul to partake in an LSD ritual to make the rest of the evening really special. Paul begged off, but scooped up a handful of the tabs to take back to New York, where he could freak out by himself in the comfort of his high-rise apartment.

The festival didn't disappoint for sweetness, surprise, or sheer oddity. While hippies and some celebrities drifted through a lysergic fog, the hotel lobbies and backstage passages choked with lawyers, managers, and A&R

† Paul insisted that they book his British folksinger friend Beverley Martin, whose voice can be heard on "Fakin' It" asking Mr. Leitch about his day.

men, many of them negotiating rich deals for unknowns, including Janis Joplin (Columbia Records), the Grateful Dead (Warner Brothers), and the Steve Miller Blues Band (Capitol). Columbia president Goddard Lieberson (now elevated to CBS Inc. group leader) came along, too, and when Paul and Artie invited him to get high with them in their hotel room, he accepted enthusiastically, an aficionado of the evil wog hemp since he'd started hanging out with New York blues and jazz artists in the 1920s. Paul, meanwhile, sought out the reality-bending guitarist Jimi Hendrix, with whom he played a little acoustic blues before the festival-opening Friday night show began.

The first night's performances began curiously with the sleek LA vocal group the Association ("Here Comes Windy," etc.), who led off with a robotic narration describing each group member, all standing and moving with mechanized herky-jerking, as if they were widgets in a musical machine, which either commented directly on their industry-friendly style or was just a weird bit of shtick someone thought would be cool. Albert Grossman's Paupers played a surprisingly raucous bit of rock 'n' roll, setting the stage for the Neil Young–less Buffalo Springfield, whose remaining members elected to fill in their sound with the guitar and harmony singing by the Byrds' David Crosby, marking the first time he would perform with the group's co-lead guitarist Stephen Stills. The Grateful Dead played a short version of their acid blues freak-out, followed by the epochal American debut of the Jimi Hendrix Experience, blazing Stratocaster and all. Singer-songwriter Laura Nyro came next, belting a surprisingly soulful set of rhythm and blues–inflected songs. The singer Lou Rawls, still neck deep in Chicago blues, stirred things up again, followed by the patience-testing pop singer Johnny Rivers. Then, finally, came the night's headliners, the collegiate folk duo from New York City.

John Phillips, tall, hip, and in control, a fur cap perched on top of his head, made the introduction at 1 a.m. on Saturday morning: "We'd like to introduce to you at this time, two very, very good friends of mine and two people who in the music business are respected by everyone, Paul Simon and Art Garfunkel." They came out in turtleneck shirts, Artie's a golden yellow, Paul's cream with thin horizontal red stripes. Standing close enough for their elbows to touch, they opened with "Homeward Bound," then sang "At the Zoo," a particularly high-spirited "59th Street Bridge Song (Feelin' Groovy)," made extra giggly by the light director's decision to bathe the stage in red lights, a bit like an old-fashioned house of ill repute, a comparison Paul couldn't resist making at the start of the song. "Ah, you dig the red lights . . . associated in my mind with, uh, for another good time." The crowd laughed, picking up immediately on the naughty reference. "Very Pavlovian." Their "Sound of Silence" sounded a gentler warning in the soft California night, and "Benedictus," introduced by Paul as "a blessing for you," did seem to elevate the day's activities into the spiritual ether, as if they all were blessed by their own company, as if all the forbidden smoke and sex and lightning bolts to the brain were a passage to a higher consciousness.

When the ovation died down, Paul played the opening riff for "I Am a Rock," thought better of it and switched to the as-yet-unheard "Punky's Dilemma," capping the evening with its hip stoner's menagerie of self-aware cornflakes and stumblebum hippies. Another ovation and a hail of excellent vibes followed them offstage, and then to the limo park, where Paul recognized the British music journalist Keith Altham, a friend from his UK days, preparing to jump into a car with Jimi Hendrix's entourage. "Keith!" Paul shouted. "Make sure to tell 'em what's going on here when you get to England!"

The Graduate began as a lightly salacious satirical novel by Charles Webb, a recent graduate of Williams College. Its tale of an affair between a listless college graduate and a bored friend of his parents rattled some Updike-ish chimes upon its publication in 1963. As reenvisioned by Mike Nichols, whose ascendance as a stage and screen director followed a decade-long career as half of the gently subversive comedy team he'd formed with Elaine May during the 1950s, the story became an arch critique of both the older generation and upper-class American values: the moralizing, the hypocrisy, the primacy of appearances in the absence of actual thought or feeling. After a three-hit streak as a director on the Broadway stage and then a smash Hollywood debut as the director of the acclaimed and hugely popular film adaptation of *Who's Afraid of Virginia Woolf?* Nichols came to *The Graduate* with the ambition and industrial juice to do whatever he pleased.

Nichols took chances from the start, commissioning a script from an untested screenwriter named Buck Henry (née Henry Zimmerman), then steering away from familiar movie actors to cast New York theater actors. Most daringly, Nichols decided to cast as the film's central character, described in the book as a golden-haired WASP, the short, dark-featured, and distinctly Jewish stage actor Dustin Hoffman. The actor was shocked to be considered, but Nichols was adamant. Even if Benjamin Braddock came from WASP stock, surely he could be "Jewish *inside.*" At that point Hoffman relented, and Nichols's vision, one that was rooted deeply in the Jewish immigrant experience, was locked in place.

Nichols was born in Berlin to Russian-Jewish parents. (His birth name was Mikhail Igor Peschkowsky.) His father, a successful doctor, changed the name upon the family's settling in the United States in 1939, escaping the Nazis days before they stopped all departures. Still, it wasn't long before their luck ran out. Dr. Nichols died of leukemia in 1942, and his widow tilted into bitter eccentricity. Being a fatherless foreigner would have been trouble enough, but Mike had also suffered a severe reaction to a whooping cough inoculation that destroyed his ability to grow hair on his head. He wore wigs throughout his life, and the childhood humiliation of being a heavily accented foreigner who also happened to be as hairless as a seal never left him.

Nichols's realization that Ben's alienation from his parents' world of privilege was similar to the immigrant Jewish experience in America girded the film's generational commentary in feelings that had nothing to do with youth and old age. Presented in the midst of unprecedented social upheaval, *The Graduate* turned on its head Hollywood's long-established tradition of de-ethnicizing characters, turning author Webb's WASP character into the unmistakably Jewish Dustin Hoffman without raising a ripple. Indeed, when the *New Yorker* published a ten-thousand-word analysis of the film the summer after it was released, the wide-ranging essay didn't mention it at all, even though *The Graduate*'s soundtrack, widely acknowledged as being every bit as innovative and daring as the narrative and visual aspects of the film, had also emerged from the Jewish perspective of two other New York–raised artists.

The director's fixation on Simon and Garfunkel began about midway through production, when his younger brother sent him a copy of *Parsley, Sage, Rosemary and Thyme.* Struck immediately by the delicately rendered songs of social and romantic isolation, Nichols recognized a connection between the introspective folk-rockers and the internal monologue of his movie's disillusioned protagonist. No traditional dramatic picture had ever been scored with rock 'n' roll music,[*] but that made the idea only more appealing.

Nichols got producer Larry Turman on the case, and though Paul and Artie were initially dubious (gloss-and-glam Hollywood being the opposite of rock 'n' roll coolness), a meeting with the brilliant, hilarious Nichols changed their minds, and they agreed to

[*] Movies starring rock 'n' roll artists don't count.

provide three original new songs for the soundtrack. It wouldn't happen immediately. Their calendar was packed with concerts, including the Monterey festival that Paul was also helping to produce, and they were already overdue on the next album they were expected to deliver to Columbia Records. Unmentioned, but even more troublesome, was Paul's creative incapacitation. It had been six months since he'd written a new song, and the psychic ice age showed no signs of thawing. Maybe this new assignment, and the addition of another deadline, would spark something good.

At long last, a trickle: "Punky's Dilemma," the puckish vision of pothead life in the midst of middle-class society that they would soon debut at Monterey, seemed to fit the montage of shots alternating between Ben lazing in the Braddock family pool and his assignations with Mrs. Robinson at the Taft Hotel. Then came "Overs," a stark portrait of a collapsed love affair. Nichols rejected both of them. Not because they weren't good songs; they just weren't the *right* ones. So what else did Paul have? Nichols's time was nearly at an end: months had passed; he was nearly finished making a final edit of the film. He didn't need to panic: he'd been using "The Sound of Silence," "April Come She Will," and "Scarborough Fair/Canticle" as placeholders for so long that he'd come to realize that he already had exactly what he needed. Those quietly despairing songs seemed to crystalize Benjamin Braddock's consciousness: his intelligence, his bitterness, his detachment from his surroundings, and his yearning to connect with someone whose spirit was untethered from the reality that the older generation had perpetuated for so long. But if he could have just one new song, something upbeat to use as the movie's theme song, that would really do the trick. Paul could only shrug. If he had something else ready to go, he'd be happy to hand it over. But as of that moment, he had nothing finished and so nothing to offer.

Except that there was this one fragment: a few chords, a melody, but no words. Paul hadn't mentioned it to Nichols during their meeting. But when Artie had a moment alone with the director, he spilled the whole story: that Paul actually did have another song, an incredibly catchy song, in fact, which Artie knew better than anyone because he'd been listening to Paul fiddle with it for months, playing the chords and *dee-dee-dee*-ing the melody. Artie could already imagine it on the radio: it really did have that indefinable *zing*. Paul had come up with only a few words, a single line that he repeated: "Here's to you, Mrs. Roosevelt." Of course Nichols picked up immediately on the fact that "Mrs. Roosevelt" had exactly as many syllables as "Mrs.

Robinson," the name of one of the film's central characters, so when Paul returned, Nichols issued something between a suggestion, a plea, and a command: "Get to work on that song." Change its title to "Mrs. Robinson" and finish it as quickly as possible. Paul agreed to try his best.

The synergy between Paul's songs and Nichols's movie is so perfect it's easy to imagine Benjamin Braddock as another one of Paul's alter egos. Dustin Hoffman, while more traditionally handsome than Paul, shares the songwriter's compact frame, dark hair, and Semitic features, along with the intelligence and melancholy in his gaze. The chain of scenes showing Ben viewing the world through glass (a fish tank, scuba mask, dark sunglasses, and the see-through partition overlooking the sanctuary in Santa Barbara's First Presbyterian Church) summons the same sense of isolation fueling so many of Paul's songs in the early and mid-1960s. Buck Henry came from similarly upper-class circumstances in Los Angeles, and with Hoffman in the starring role *The Graduate* contains a philosophical undercurrent that extends quite a distance from the stone-walled manors of upper-crust Pasadena.

Paul finished the music for "Mrs. Robinson" in time for the last edits on the finished movie, but he still lacked a full lyric, a problem Nichols resolved by having Paul and

Artie record several acoustic guitar and harmonized *dee-dee-dee* pieces to fit different sequences as Ben pursues Mrs. Robinson's daughter, Elaine, from Pasadena to Berkeley and back again. The only words Paul managed to write for the song appear briefly, just as Benjamin's car thunders across the Bay Bridge on his way to claim Elaine for his own, defying the commands of his elders and the expectations of the American establishment.

And here's to you Mrs. Robinson,
Jesus loves you more than you will know,
Whoa, whoa, whoa
Stand up tall Mrs. Robinson,
God in heaven smiles on those who pray,
Hey-hey-hey, hey-hey-hey.

As the film's final fifteen minutes play out, the increasingly frenetic action is underscored by Paul's percussive guitar strokes, a raw sound that projects Ben's growing desperation, climaxing with a triad of ringing chords that announce the character's arrival at the church where his fate will be decided. When the happy ending comes with the well-timed arrival of a city bus, the couple sprints to the final row of seats, where their delighted smiles fade slowly as "The Sound of Silence" rises around them and the film fades to black.

As much as Paul and Artie were pleased by

the finished film, neither of them wanted anything to do with a soundtrack album for *The Graduate.* Columbia Records president Clive Davis had raised the matter after becoming aware of the enormous buzz surrounding the movie in the weeks before its opening in December 1967. As Davis knew, Goddard Lieberson had pioneered Broadway cast soundtracks, allowing Columbia to make a fortune whenever a musical hit big. Movie soundtracks had done well, too, but the appearance of the rock-dominated *The Graduate* felt like a huge opportunity to Columbia's barely fledged new president. Even though the one new Simon and Garfunkel song on the record was closer to an outline than a finished tune, they could pull together the older songs that had dominated the movie and sell them to the movie audience along with fans willing to buy anything with S&G's imprimatur. If *The Graduate* was even half the hit that the studio executives and other observers expected, they would make a fortune for doing nothing beyond signing off on the project. Nothing to lose, everything to gain, right?

Not the way Paul and Artie saw it. They were still laboring over their follow-up to *Parsley, Sage, Rosemary and Thyme* and didn't want to do anything to delay the album's release or, worse yet, dilute the demand for new Simon and Garfunkel music.

Davis insisted that none of that would be a problem. He'd release the new album the moment it was ready to go out. And if the soundtrack did make it to the top of the charts, then that would be the best possible thing that could happen. And Davis had no doubt that the next Simon and Garfunkel album would be a hit no matter what. Just imagine the publicity they'd get out of having two hit albums at the same time! Paul shrugged that off, too. What sort of artist releases an album with just a shred of a new song on it? And how could they get a full album out of that and the four other songs in the film? Davis had an answer for that one, too: jazz composer Dave Grusin had provided incidental music to the film, so they'd throw that on there, too. Paul still resisted. Why force his new music to compete with his older music? But Davis kept cajoling, pleading, and insisting, and eventually Paul and Artie gave in. *The Graduate* soundtrack appeared a few weeks after the movie's premiere and proved an instant hit, quickly becoming the first Simon and Garfunkel–related album to reach the top of the charts.

All Paul had to do now to complete their real new album was to finish writing the last song or two, get back into the studio with Artie and Roy Halee, and see if Davis's predictions kept coming true.

CHAPTER 12
BOOKENDS

Just as the four Beatles seemed to merge into one perfectly balanced system of personalities, intellects, spirits, and skills, Simon and Garfunkel seemed like two halves of one creature. While Paul's songs explored the outer limits of structure and lyrical meaning, Artie kept his ear on the pop mainstream, making sure their records didn't wander too far from their audience. While Artie, still moonlighting as a PhD candidate in mathematics, often came off as airy and a tad eccentric, Paul spoke to the world in well-measured declarative statements. One was tall, the other short. One was dark, the other fair. One kept his straight hair short and carefully combed; the other let his curls spring in every direction at once. Like so much of the New Generation's educated middle class, they loathed the war in Vietnam, reflexively questioned authority, and didn't hesitate to say that they smoked marijuana, had experimented with LSD, and had had run-ins with the same authoritarian cops who hassled all the kids. They had been called generational spokesmen since "The Sound of Silence" topped the charts. Now they truly were, in a voice so distinctively their own that the comparisons to Bob Dylan had all but disappeared.

When the successful British pop band the Hollies visited New York, they came to the CBS recording studios to pay their respects to the American duo and watch them at work. For the group's co-leader Graham Nash, the experience was like a master class in the art of making groundbreaking pop music. When Paul started talking up a Bulgarian choir album (*Music of Bulgaria,* recorded in 1955 but only just released in the United States, by Elektra Records), Nash took the copy Paul handed him and studied it like a text. Al Kooper, their guitar-playing neighbor who had been elevated into the rock 'n' roll aristocracy by the golden hand of Dylan, carried his copy to Los Angeles, then took it to the Beach Boys' Brian Wilson to play it for him inside his hashish-perfumed Arabian tent, stationed not so far from the living room sandbox that held his magical piano.

Such was life for those mid-to-late-1960s rock heroes, all abustle in their Arcadian fantasies: Wilson in his hilltop planetarium, Dylan channeling galactic truth in his deep-woods hideaway in the hills of Woodstock, the Beatles sailing the Grecian isles in search of their own utopia. As per the middle-class realism that guided most of their songs, Paul's version of communal paradise took them to the leafy Berkshire Mountains of western Massachusetts, where well-to-do New Yorkers had spent their summers for generations. In the spring of 1967, the young musician rented a vacation home in the town of Stockbridge, where you could stumble upon longtime resident Norman Rockwell or have lunch at Alice's Restaurant, already canonized in song and legend by Woody Guthrie's twenty-year-old son Arlo.

Actually, *vacation home* doesn't quite paint the picture. Owned by a former American ambassador to England, the house was a baronial estate with a marble-lipped pool, hand-cut stone patio, and an emerald sweep of immaculate lawns. The ambassador stocked the house's entryway with a gallery of personalized photographs from colleagues and friends, including Presidents Johnson, Kennedy, Eisenhower, and Truman; various secretaries of state; and foreign leaders. When visitors arrived, Paul made a point of showing off the pictures and saying he would soon replace one with a framed portrait of Lenny Bruce. Paul even grew a Lenny Bruce-ian beard, as if to summon the recently deceased comic's subversive spirit.

Looking more like teenage house sitters

than anyone who could possibly reside in such white-shod splendor, Paul and his friends took full advantage of the sprawling house, inviting friends from the city for country weekends so they could all swim, sun, play tennis, drink, and smoke pot in the manner to which none of them ever dreamed they'd become accustomed. And apart from the greenish tinge of smoke over their heads, they lived a lot like the place's real residents, taking their meals (prepared by the twenty-two-year-old Irish housemaid whom Paul had hired for the season) around the grand table in the ambassador's formal dining room. Maybe they weren't quite as sophisticated as their absent landlord: one evening the maid filled their dinner table wineglasses with sherry, mistaking the sugary dessert wine for the earthy red that would have matched with their meal. They all loved it anyway, empty-ing bottle after bottle before migrating back to the patio to smoke more joints, spin records, and laugh and laugh and laugh at the wonderful time and their excellent fortunes.

When word of Simon's, and often Garfun-kel's, presence crossed the road to the home of Chuck Israels, the highly trained jazz bass-ist recalled that his guitarist friend Stu Scharf had worked with the duo, and gotten on particularly well with Paul. Eager to escape the music camp his parents ran on their property, Israels walked over one afternoon and rapped on the heavy wooden door. Paul came out and, when he heard Stu Scharf's name, invited Israels in. After introducing him to Artie and their weekend guests — lawyer Mike Tannen and his writer wife, Mary, and Artie's architect friend Paul Krause and his wife, Elaine — Paul told Israels to hang out for the rest of the day: go for a swim, get up a game of tennis, or just lie around, eat and drink, whatever he wanted, and be part of the gang. Israels stayed until midnight, leaving with an open-ended invitation to come back whenever he pleased. And so he did, including the Saturday night that became a highlight of the summer.

Paul hatched the idea just before a three-day weekend. They should have a party! A proper affair, with lots of friends and food and fun, and no strict sense of when it would end. He jumped on the telephone and started issuing invitations: Peter Yarrow from Peter, Paul, and Mary was an instant yes; so were the members of the Cyrkle; and a legion of other musicians, friends, and near strangers, including a sixteen-year-old Carly Simon, already gaining attention for her folk club appearances with her sister Lucy. The sky was cobalt, the sun white hot in the afternoon, and the party stretched out for a lazy golden drift into the evening. It was just right for

Paul, who was thrilled to elevate his tastefully freaky flag on a whitewashed pole right there in the heart of the moneyed establishment.

The days in New York City often seemed just as dreamy. Talking to a reporter at the Stockbridge house, Artie described the partners' daily routine as a dual existence, both of them starting their days in the late morning, when they'd meet up at manager Mort Lewis's office to drag him off to a luncheonette for hamburgers and fries. After lunch Mort would go back to work, and the singers would hang out with a friend, grab a bite at another diner, and then head to Paul's apartment — it was larger and more comfortable than Artie's one-bedroom bachelor pad a few blocks away — either to check out what he was working on or to listen to the album of the moment or whatever obscurity had pricked up Paul's ear most recently. Paul and Artie had the same taste in friends, and just ten years after high school each could still spur hilarity in the other with a well-timed wince or slight widening of the eyes. Their photographs telegraphed their closeness in the easy way they posed, arms thrown over one another's shoulders, or in the midst of a crackup, mouths wide, faces crinkling in the same burst of laughter.

They also shared a taste for ridicule, particularly of people who invaded their need for autonomy and creative sanctuary. When

The Graduate soundtrack exploded and Paul and Artie still hadn't finished the new record they had titled *Bookends,* Clive Davis began talking about putting out a full greatest hits album to give fans, new and old alike, something to buy for the summer of 1968. Both aggravated by Davis's penchant for squeezing money from their work, they asked for a meeting with the label president, and smuggled in a tape recorder they had used to capture the executive's attempts to convince his treasured artists to help him satisfy his board of directors' financial expectations. They took the secret recording to their next studio session and played it for everyone in the room. This led to derisive shrieks just like they had made on that high school afternoon when Paul jumped up to congratulate the unsuspecting winner of their Fattest Girl in the School contest.

In the recording studio, Paul's and Artie's roles meshed with the same trusting intimacy. Paul did the songwriting, and usually came into the studio with strong ideas about how the tunes should feel and sound. More often than not, though, he played his new songs to Artie before they went to recording sessions, and took his partner's thoughts and suggestions seriously. Artie might tinker with the words or suggest a revision to the melody or the meter of a line, his ear tuned to making the lines more singable or open to different harmonic possibilities. Paul didn't always take Artie's suggestions, but he always listened, and usually came up with a way to resolve Artie's concerns. While Paul played guitar or sang his parts, Artie would oversee his work from the control booth, guiding his partner with a stream of advice, coaching, and, when needed, criticism. To Eddie Simon, a regular observer of his brother's recording sessions, Paul and Artie worked together like a great pitcher and catcher. Paul had the magical arm, but he still depended on Artie to call for the right pitches and haul in his wayward throws.

At one 1967 session for "Punky's Dilemma,"[*] the duo started by laying down Paul's guitar part, and when that sounded okay Paul went back to the studio to work on his lead vocal. Somewhere between jazzy, jokey, laid-back, and bemused, the tune called for a warm but gently teasing tone, a voice balanced somewhere between graceful and conversational. It was more a mood than something you could put into words, and, as Paul sang, Artie monitored him through the glass, responding to his partner's attempts with advice on the nuances of tone and giving specific notes on his rhythm and intona-

* For which Artie recalls writing the verse about being a Kellogg's Corn Flake, etc.

tion. Frustration mounting — "It's no good, I'm not into it" — Paul took off his headphones and suggested they work on some of the quirky sounds ("personality fills," Paul called them) they wanted to scatter across the track. When Paul went out for a cigarette, Artie pressed John Simon[†] to make certain the finger snaps he'd asked for were recorded as if they were sonically translucent. Make it light, he instructed. "Almost as if it's not there."

Once Paul and Artie had gained enough authority to take creative control over their records, they formed a production trio with engineer Roy Halee, whose mastery of sound and technology was matched by his eagerness to push the outer limits of recording techniques. They had come up with some distinctive techniques on *Parsley, Sage, Rosemary and Thyme*, but the *Bookends* sessions flew far beyond all their earlier recordings. Even after Paul had completed the bulk of

† Hired as a producer for the *Bookends* sessions, John Simon was unpleasantly surprised to see his credit reduced to "production assistance" on the album credits. His predecessor Bob Johnston suffered the same fate on the songs he'd overseen, including the ones that had already been released as singles listing him as the sole producer. Asked for his feelings on the matter, John Simon shrugs. "Revisionism sucks," he says.

the songs, he and Artie made a point of taking their time on every session, devoting hours to experiments that often led nowhere, then making it up to the studio musicians by taking them out for long, chatty meals with the union clock still running. When bassist Bill Crow — a contemporary of Lou Simon, whom Paul had hired for a few sessions — apologized for how little they had achieved that night, Paul just laughed. Columbia was paying for the sessions, and he was happy to stick it to the company given how little time it had allowed for them to record their first two albums.

Both Paul and Artie went into the studio determined to give each song some new wrinkle in sound that would make their listeners shake their heads in wonder. This was increasingly de rigueur in that paisley year of the Beatles' *Sgt. Pepper's Lonely Hearts Club Band,* the Jefferson Airplane's *Surrealistic Pillow,* and Jimi Hendrix's *Are You Experienced?,* but Paul had been experimenting with sound textures since the late 1950s and was no stranger to the workings of the control board. If it took time to figure out whether coat hangers on vibes, brushes across a tambourine, or maybe just a nice little trombone part would be a better fit for this bit of "Punky's Dilemma," they were not going to give a thought to how long it would take or how much it might cost.*

Looking for a mod new sound for "Save the Life of My Child," they got in touch with Robert Moog, an audio scientist who had created a computerized synthesizer that could make a wide array of unearthly shrieks and whines and burps you could play through a keyboard set to the twelve-note scale. Moog had never recorded with the thing before; he might not even have taken it out of his laboratory. And no wonder — the thing was huge, a miniature cityscape of switches, wires, and black boxes, all of which had to be connected just so before the speakers would emit the first yelp. It took hours to set up, with a good deal of connecting, disconnecting, reconnecting somewhere else, and on and on. But once Moog had it prepared, he could crank out astonishing new sounds: a kind of deep fuzz, an even deeper synthesized bass part that was halfway between an organ bass and an earthquake, a cell door–like crash, a kind of descending whistle, and more. And when they added Paul's acoustic guitar, hand claps,

* Because they were signed originally as a two-man folk act that could knock out songs in just as much time as it took to play them into the microphone, Columbia had generously agreed to cover the costs with its end of the proceeds. It hadn't anticipated that the folk kids would mature into ambitious art rock record makers.

percussion, cymbals, and a few snippets of a gospel choir, the record sounded like a 3D kaleidoscope, a furious tangle of red lights, radio squawks, anger, wonder, and something like terror, all revolving around the cry of a panicked mother.

When they finally delivered the album to Clive Davis, just in time for the summer of 1968, he was so delighted with what he heard that he decided to enhance the package with a full-color poster, and also a brand-new price tag that was a full dollar above every other album in the record stores. Davis called it "variable pricing," the basic notion of charging a premium for in-demand products. Paul and Artie, on the other hand, called it an outrage. "They were concerned about the consumers which was laudable," Davis wrote in the mid-1970s. "I was concerned about the increasing cost of recording and a shrinking margin of profits." So, as it turned out, Columbia wasn't going to pick up the tab for all that time they'd spent in the studio, not by itself, at any rate. And maybe there was nothing Paul and Artie could do about it. But if their records were worth that much to the company, it was definitely time to start renegotiating their contract.

Davis knew it was coming, and that was fine: business was business. But their attitude dismayed him. He loved their songs, for one thing: when he got home at the end of the day, the Columbia Records president would play Simon and Garfunkel albums like all the other fans, because Paul's songs spoke to his soul. Davis was a few years older, but they had all followed the same path, outer-borough kids who had gotten themselves educated — Davis grew up in Brooklyn and had attended New York University and then Harvard Law School — fought their way into the record business and then to the top of their fields. Paul and Artie had resisted everything Davis proposed to them over the last year, but when they finally did go along with his plans, and every one of the executive's far-fetched predictions — that *The Graduate* album would be a smash, that *Bookends* would follow suit, and that they'd come out of 1968 as superstars — came to pass, neither of the musicians ever acknowledged, let alone declared their appreciation for, what he had done for them. Instead, they had manager Mort Lewis renegotiate their contract, one that guaranteed them, among many other things, the then-exorbitant royalty rate of fifty cents per album sold.

Released on April 3, 1968, *Bookends* came into the world a day before Martin Luther King Jr.'s murder and eight weeks before the killing of the surging presidential candidate Democratic senator Robert F. Kennedy. It was the year of the Tet Offensive, of race riots, of the antiwar demonstrations that spurred a bloody police riot outside the Democratic National Convention in Chicago. In November, the Republican candidate, Richard M. Nixon, won the presidency, due in part to his promised "secret plan" to end the Vietnam War, a scheme that required more guns, bombs, and anger. So, hey, look, what's that sound? In 1968 it was nihilistic outrage amplified until it looped back on itself, the Doors' psychedelic carousel spinning into the Who's exploding guitars, the Grateful Dead's acidic feedback jams, and the morning-after dissonance pervading the Beatles' *White Album* — a collection of rock 'n' roll songs that would soon be twisted into one madman's vision for mass murder in the hills above Los Angeles. If all these happenings didn't eat at your faith in the nation, society, and the existence of God, you probably weren't paying attention.

Bookends is a product of these same times, but its perspective, and anger, are refracted through layers of intellectual, artistic, and emotional remove. It was intended as a concept album about life's course from childhood to adulthood to senescence, but the narrative structure never quite takes hold, due to Paul's inability to produce the songs necessary to tell the story. Indeed, for an album many fans and critics call Simon and Garfunkel's best, *Bookends* is a surprisingly grab bag affair. Of the twelve tracks on the record, only eight were previously unreleased, and one of them isn't anything like a song ("Voices of Old People"). Two are different takes on the same tune ("Bookends Theme" and "Bookends"), and one ("Mrs. Robinson") is an expanded version of a song from *The Graduate* soundtrack. Yet *Bookends* is packed with riches.

Released as a single two days after the album, the finished "Mrs. Robinson" bulleted through the Hot 100 to the top spot, which it occupied for three weeks in June. Driven as much by its unexpected musical and lyrical textures as by the nation's ongoing obsession with *The Graduate,* "Mrs. Robinson" played on AM radio's maximum rotation for the entire summer and later became the first rock 'n' roll tune ever to win Record of the Year honors from the starchy members of the National Academy of Recording Arts and Sciences.[*] Like so many era-defining hits, the record sounded nothing like anything else in the Hot 100. From the start, the music feels slightly off-kilter, the opening guitar riff spiraling out of a Latin shuffle that pulls the verses through a loop of spiky chords that take flight into the ringing "Here's to you,

[*] "Mrs. R" was ineligible for the movie industry's Academy Awards because it hadn't been intended solely for *The Graduate.*

Mrs. Robinson" chorus, which holds until the *whoa-whoa-whoa*s pull us back to the slap of the congas. The song's lyric extends *The Graduate*'s story in flights of cryptic satire. Mrs. Robinson has been relocated to a vaguely Orwellian mental institution. "We'd like to help you learn to help yourself," the doctors promise, but what's waiting for her on the other side of the wall? Politics, religion, society's empty rituals — welcome to the America of 1968. Only, it wasn't always like this, not back in the not-so-long-ago times when the nation's ideals were alive all around us, even (especially?) in the great American ballpark, back where the uniforms were baggy but backs were strong, eyes clear, and spirits pure. Of course Paul's mind spun back to Yankee Stadium. Gehrig, Mantle, DiMaggio — they don't make 'em like that anymore, do they? "Joltin' Joe has left and gone away, / Hey hey hey."

The same yearning animates "America," the other great highlight on the album. While "Mrs. Robinson" is social commentary dressed up as a character study, "America" is the opposite: an internal journey that presents itself as a portrait of a spiritually lost, post-idealistic nation. The lyrics — which contain a total of zero rhymes, for which Paul is proud, and rightfully so: the narrative is so consuming that the structural obligations cease to matter — open on a tale of two casual lovers jumping a Greyhound bus from the upper Midwest. Paul sings in the first person and identifies his lover as Kathy, as if he's confiding details from an actual journey taken with the girlfriend who meant so much to him during his prefame days in London. And there they are, stocking up on junk food, magazines, and cigarettes, then finding their seats as the bus rumbles out of the station and onto the highway. They chat, read, and watch the scenery pass, all in pursuit of some indistinct vision of the American ideal. But as we reach the final verse, he confesses that the crisis of faith he's experiencing is rooted within, not around him. "Kathy I'm lost," he tells her. "I'm empty and aching and I don't know why." Empty and aching and unable to connect to anyone or anything — he can confide in Kathy only when he knows she's asleep. And when he notices the drivers of the cars around him, realizing that they're all speeding toward New York City, the traditional destination for immigrants, pilgrims, and other seekers, he realizes that the one thing that connects them amounts to *E Pluribus Unum* in reverse: an entire nation bound only by its citizens' alienation from one another.

There it is again, that same sense of desolation, the emptiness within, the bleakness without, the nauseating understanding that your entire existence amounts to little more than a cloud of dust and static cling. "Voices of Old People" is an audio vérité montage of elderly folks talking about their lives, the shattered stretch that leads to the end of the road. More interesting in concept than in execution, the Artie-curated snippets go on for two minutes and twelve seconds that would have been better spent on nearly anything else. There are grimmer revelations to come: the spiritually withered heir in "Fakin' It," the young codger shivering through "A Hazy Shade of Winter," and the couple in the surgically precise description of a terminal love affair in "Overs" ("We're just a habit, like saccharine"). The desolation becomes most vivid in the mini-suite of the title track and in "Old Friends," both of which at least *sound* like they could be about good times and sweet memories. But of course not.

"Old Friends" opens with acoustic guitar and distant strings that grow steadily more elaborate before gaining horns and percussion to fill a lengthy instrumental break that veers from melodrama to *Metropolis*-like horrors before fading into the background. The intensity in the orchestral arrangement (by conductor/arranger Jimmie Haskell) is drawn from the lyrics, which describe a pair of septuagenarians sitting together in a city park. Given no sense of their lives, we know the men only by their desolate appearance. Paul's lyrics are dense with subtext. The old men don't notice the newspaper scuttling through the grass. The shouts and honks of their inheritors float by unheard. The men wear old-timey shoes and overcoats like funeral shrouds. "Winter companions . . . waiting for the sunset." Remember the lonely drivers on the New Jersey Turnpike? Here they are again, too old to do anything of an afternoon but share their silent dread of the approaching darkness. Paul turns the feeling outward as "Old Friends" ends and the "Bookends Theme" rises. Singing in close word-for-word harmony, Paul and Artie mourn a sweeter moment, "a time of innocence, a time of confidences," that describes the start of their own friendship, a love affair, or something much larger than that. Are they using "confidences" to describe secrets once shared between friends, or the assurance of a society still basking in its hard-won triumph in World War II? Ultimately it doesn't matter: as the old friends can attest, everything that matters to you will soon vanish. "Preserve your memories / They're all that's left you."

But the zenith of Paul's infatuation with nothingness comes in "Save the Life of My Child," the small epic that opens *Bookends'* first side. As befitting their sonic backdrop, the lyrics begin in a recognizable urban scene and end in surrealism. A boy on a rooftop has threatened to jump. A mob gathers beneath, and the scene is soon bristling with police, firemen, and predatory tabloid reporters. We've seen this before. The barricades and orbiting red-and-blues, the electrified crowd, the wails of the panicked mother. Someone passes out and is carried away. The crowd blames drugs, cops blame the kids these days, and there we are again, poised on the threshold of a nightmare and unable to do anything except argue about whose fault it is. "Oh, what's becoming of the children, people asking each other."

Go back a decade, read Philip Roth's short story "The Conversion of the Jews": the same rooftop, the frantic child, the mob, the cops, the hook-and-ladder, firefighters, and lifesaving nets. But while "Save the Life of My Child" focuses on contemporary social problems, Roth's vision traces the boy's crisis to God and the irreconcilable contradictions of religion. The story focuses on Ozzie, a bar mitzvah student who wants the rabbi to explain why God would be capable of creating heaven, earth, and light — Ozzie is particularly hung up on light — in six days and yet not be able to impregnate a mortal woman with His son? And if so, how can we say Jesus couldn't possibly be the son of God? Unable to answer Ozzie's question, the rabbi, the boy's mother, and other authority figures lash out physically and emotionally, until the boy bolts from class and finds refuge on the roof of the synagogue. Cue the crowd, the cops et al., and when Ozzie realizes how desperate they are to keep him alive, he orders the rabbi, his mother, and the entire crowd to fall to their knees and declare their belief in Jesus Christ. Transformed into a prophet, Ozzie leaps into the night, falling securely into the bright yellow safety net the firemen have been holding up to spare his life.

Published originally in the *New Yorker* (and then as the second story in Roth's first collection, *Goodbye, Columbus*), "The Conversion of the Jews" was greeted by many observant Jews as apostasy, a work troubling enough to require debates, public forums, and repeated denunciations. Yet, as signaled by Ozzie's infatuation with light, the story celebrates even its most hidebound Jewish characters as true people of God. Given the choice between the strictures of their faith and God's creation, they choose the boy, an act of mercy that affirms God's presence even as it reveals the flaws in the conventions of His followers.

The nameless boy in "Save the Life of My Child," cut loose from religious symbolism to become a symbol of generational conflict, performs the same leap with far less affirming results. Cut loose from gravity, he simply soars off into the night, his departure as mysterious as his initial motivations for self-destruction. There's no meaning to his flight, other than as a surreal way to resolve a story of social alienation. While Ozzie lands safely in the embrace of his community, Paul's miracle child has become just another celebrity, borne up on spotlights until he vanishes in the night, an airborne wraith with nowhere to land.

In early 1968, David Oppenheim, once an influential documentarian at CBS-TV but now at the helm of the *Public Broadcast Laboratory,* a live Sunday evening program from what was then called National Educational Television (later the Public Broadcasting System), worked with Paul and Artie to put on and film a college concert at the University of Moscow in the USSR. The hope was to create cultural understanding between the two rival nations by exposing the Soviet students to the United States' most sophisticated, and popular, pop acts. "They are both college boys, very intelligent and sensitive," Oppenheim wrote to Boris Sedov, a counselor[*] at the Soviet embassy in Washington, DC. "The idea of going to the Soviet Union reflects a real interest in your country." Oppenheim sent copies of *Sounds of Silence* and *Parsley, Sage, Rosemary and Thyme,* along

[*] Plus a Soviet intelligence agent, though that wasn't known at the time.

311

with a set of lyrics translated into Russian, but for whatever reason the project fell apart.

Simon and Garfunkel drew increasingly large and adoring fans back at home. Critics described wild crowds, endless cries for encores, and "two of the finest singers of the age, prophets and balladeers at one and the same time." Were they really prophets? How about generational spokesmen? "Nobody is talking for this generation. Nobody says, 'If you want to know what I think talk to Simon and Garfunkel,' " Paul told a reporter from *Time* for a cover story titled "Rock! What a Gas!" "Everybody has got his own ideas. I don't consider myself a poet. I'm a song-writer" — one, nevertheless, with a serious purpose. "Why is it I feel compelled to write about this pain I see? I could split and be free and do whatever I want. I said to myself, well, why don't I? Because I'm here, that's why."

Performing to a sold-out Hollywood Bowl on August 23, 1968, Paul and Artie were greeted like heroes, and beloved all the more for their cheery, down-to-earth response to their fans' adoration. Playing without a backing band, they led off with a spirited "Mrs. Robinson," went back a few years for "Homeward Bound," and then stopped everything when they noticed a metal lunchbox sitting by itself on the symphony-size stage. Artie grabbed the thing and brought it into the spotlight with them.

"It looks like somebody's lunch," he reported. Clicking open the latch, he looked within and reported his findings. "It *is* somebody's lunch!"

Now peering into the box too, Paul turned back to his microphone.

"Did anybody lose a tuna fish sandwich?"

Without missing a beat, Artie continued the thought. "On white?"

At that, Paul started laughing. "Did you just . . . On *white*!"

Just a couple of old friends with the same sense of humor, a shared career, and shared fame.

They sang beautifully that night, their amplified voices rising into the soft summer air above the Hollywood Hills. Their repartee stayed light even when the songs got heavy, and as they moved toward the last few songs, Paul set up Artie's most popular solo with another joke.

"There's been a change of identity, or roles, in our group," Paul said, sounding only slightly put out as he described how their media image had changed in recent months. "In our new capacity I am now the heavy of the group. I make nasty comments and, uh, kick kids, and uh, do things like that."

He paused to let the laughs boil down.

"And Art has now become our sex symbol in this group."

A swell of female cheers interrupted him, and then he got to the punch line.

"One newspaper referred to him as a frightened gazelle. At this juncture, the frightened gazelle will sing 'For Emily, Whenever I Find Her.'"

Chapter 13
So Long Already, Artie

Mike Nichols had a great idea. Sketching out his follow-up to *The Graduate,* a film adaptation of Joseph Heller's satirical war novel *Catch-22,* he thought again about Simon and Garfunkel, and how perfectly their sensibility fit into his new film's vision. He began to think of them as part of *Catch-22*'s expansive cast, and when he got in touch with Paul and Artie both of them were delighted. Now they could stretch themselves in a completely different direction, and who knew where it could lead? Of course they'd do it; just say when and where.

A few months later, Nichols called Paul with less happy news. His working script had expanded beyond all reason. He'd had to cut it, and unfortunately Paul's character had fallen out of the movie. So that was the end of Artie's role, too, right? Recalling the incident for the Rock and Roll Hall of Fame in 2013, Paul said he set Nichols straight immediately. He and Artie didn't have to do

315

everything together, and Paul knew how eager Artie was to dip his toe into acting. The shooting schedule required Artie to be in Mexico for only a couple of months, so of course Artie should be in the movie.

Paul had plenty of other things to keep him busy during Artie's absence. The best one was his new girlfriend, Peggy Harper, whom he'd met in late 1965 when he and Artie first met with Mort Lewis in his apartment. Mort, to whom Peggy was married at the time, was thirteen years her senior; they met when she was the twenty-year-old girlfriend of Brothers Four member John Payne, whom she'd met when the group gave a concert on Atlantic City's Steel Pier. The daughter of a troubled, very religious family in the rural village of Bybee, Tennessee, Peggy had come north as a teenager, eager to start a life as far from her parents as possible. Young, tall, and beautiful, she was drawn to the suave older man, and she married Lewis in 1961.

For a time, it was perfect. Lewis was sweet and funny, and though Peggy had a lot to learn about the city and the rest of the world, she was smart and independent enough to pursue her own career, first as a model, then as an editor in a film production house, and then in a graphic arts studio. But the more she became a part of her husband's packed social life, the less she enjoyed it. He liked going out and having a big time; she really

316

didn't. She often balked when he wanted to invite friends home for dinner or cocktails. "I liked people, and she didn't," Lewis says. Their marriage was drifting by the time Paul came into their lives, and though Lewis knew his client was smitten with his wife, he says he had no reason to think Paul was making a play for her. But when Lewis and Harper divorced in 1967, Simon and Harper quickly came together. It was a little awkward from time to time. Some friends and colleagues averted their eyes or whispered urgently, asking what the hell was going on between Paul and Mort's wife. Drummer Hal Blaine, who had recorded with Simon and Garfunkel for several years before joining their touring band in 1969, went straight to Lewis, who gave a breezy shrug. "We're divorced," he explained.

Just as Kathy had helped stabilize his moods five years earlier, Peggy gave Paul a sense of security. Two and a half years older and instilled with the discipline common to adults raised in chaotic families, she made certain, as their relationship grew, that Paul didn't let his fame, wealth, or power distance him from the real world. When he drifted too far into the weird vapors of the bohemian artist, Peggy would strongly suggest he take out the garbage, walk the dog, or do *anything* that would get his ass off the sofa, for crying out loud. That was good; that was the same advice he'd grown up hearing from his father.

Success was fine, but it wasn't the point. And if you weren't doing something that would be useful to others, what *were* you doing? And why?

Finally, Paul's muse thawed. After so many months of struggling to wrench out new songs like a dentist going after a molar, he started feeling the melodies drift to him again. Words, phrases, and stories fell into his head, then tumbled onto whatever scrap of paper he had to write on. On a flight to a concert in Portland, he borrowed a pen and scribbled on the pages of the in-flight magazine. He started with a few phrases. "Little and poor." "Rock with easy motion and sing a humble song." "My quests are such men daughters and sons I'd like to know." "Here for workman's wages, down the long aisle of the ages." He was reading the Bible then; his phrases felt earthier, from some other time. Settled into the Benson Hotel in downtown Portland, he added more lines and started stringing them into verses. "I am but a poor song / Crying" — the rest is crossed out — "In the company of strangers / In the quiet of the evening / I will sing to you." A page later, he had a better idea: "I am just a poor boy though my story is untold / How I squandered my resistance for a pocketful of mumbles."

"The Boxer" fell together quickly, so they

decided to record it before Artie took off for Mexico, thinking it might make a good single for the spring. The music was fairly simple, a basic folk progression played on acoustic guitars supporting close harmonies. But the staunch voice of the "poor boy" at its center, the battered young man who won't stop fighting for himself, seemed to require something more than a light acoustic treatment, a sound that would fit the biblical language that informed Paul's writing. A thunderous noise, even: skies opening, a tempest unleashed upon the streets, thunder and sheets of black rain, and their voices above it all, ringing through the clamor.

When Artie left for his two months of *Catch-22* filming at the end of 1968, they had already settled on how the next year would unfold. Paul would write songs and record some basic tracks with Halee until Artie got back in late winter, at which point they would work together as usual to produce the next Simon and Garfunkel album while also playing concerts around the country. Even though he'd been passed over, Paul wasn't unhappy about Artie taking his shot at the movies. For the first time, Artie had a high-profile gig he could do on his own. That could only be good for his friend: maybe Artie could burn off some creative steam doing something that had nothing to do with the guy he had depended on for so long.

Then the two months passed and Artie didn't come home — maybe for a short break or two, but the filming was taking much longer than Nichols had expected, so Artie had to go back to the remote Mexican village where they had been filming. And did he mention what a ball he'd been having down there? He was meeting all kinds of cool people, actors and writers and others; and when they weren't working, they hung out at the pool or explored the hills, smoked dope, had a great time. And his acting was going great! Nichols kept telling him he could be a leading man if he really wanted to pursue it. Amazing, right?

Well, sure. How could Paul begrudge his partner's success as an actor? Pretty easily, as it turned out. After years of dictating the wheres, whens, and whys of their relationship, Paul now had to compete for Artie's attention. And now that he had new songs, they needed to record — and they *did* have an album to get out, after all — he didn't want to hear Artie saying he wasn't available. And in such a deliberately wounding way! It was as if Artie had been planning it all along, taking all his advantages over Paul (his looks, his height, his charm) and running off in a direction Paul had been barred from going. Worse, Artie's absence meant that Paul couldn't do *his* work. They were Simon *and Garfunkel*. Paul couldn't make an entire album without

Artie's voice and ideas. He was the only guy, with the exception of Roy Halee, who could listen to one of Paul's songs and know what Paul was hearing in his head, and how to help make it real. And now Artie had something better to do? Well, fuck him.

The resentment would flare up from time to time, particularly when Paul found himself alone in the studio trying to anticipate what Artie might think of this or that approach, or when he came up with a harmony arrangement that clashed with the guitar part he'd just recorded. Other times, he just missed his friend, his partner, the only other person on earth who knew how it felt to be a member of Simon and Garfunkel. He wrote letters telling Artie everything he and Roy had been up to, and how eager they were to have him back. Feeling lonely one day, Paul started writing "The Only Living Boy in New York," a loving ballad addressing Artie as Tom, his name from way back in their Tom and Jerry days, when they sang in the basement and took their dates for sodas at Addy Vallens's candy store. He describes his loneliness, admits to the sorrow of being the one left behind. But the point of the song is reassurance, a farewell hug and a benediction. Then the anger would well up again, and there were no words, let alone melodies, to express that.

It had always been part of their friendship,

even when they were thirteen, comparing grades and pop song expertise while walking home from school, each of them angling for some measure of dominance, some point where they could prove, for the moment at least, which one was truly in charge. They'd spent the next four years sharing everything, staring so deeply into each other's mouths that Paul had memorized the topography of Artie's teeth, gums, and soft palate. Yet the fractures caused by Paul's backroom deal with Sid Prosen hadn't really healed, even when they went back to singing together. Strangely, the underlying tension had become part of their public mystique. The first promotional biography Columbia Records issued for them in January 1966 made the teenage breakup* a central part of their narrative, quoting them in unison calling it a "dig-yourself competition" that ended when they "got over it and got back together." Whatever the Columbia publicity office's reason for including the story in publicity, it only added tension to their comfortable harmonic identity: a hint of coming danger, a reminder that beauty never lasts, that the sound could always fade back to silence.

You didn't have to look too far beneath the

---

* However, they stopped short of acknowledging the existence of Tom and Jerry or the specifics of what or who caused the break.

partners' bonhomie to glimpse the agitation between them. Paul's British friends could feel it crackling between them when Artie was with Paul in London. If Artie was in a mood, he turned haughty and insulting. Paul told some friends that he couldn't wait to regain the independence he had as a solo act. It shouldn't have been a shock. The most successful partnerships are often built between two people whose respective strengths and flaws act as counterbalances. So just as Paul's songs were enhanced by Artie's voice, Paul's determination was offset by his partner's more ethereal sensibility, sometimes to the point where Paul couldn't stand it. During one tightly booked tour, Artie turned down a ride on the airplane Mort Lewis had chartered to take them from New York to Boston because he felt like spending the day hitchhiking. It took hours for someone to pick him up in New York City, and he arrived at Symphony Hall with only minutes to spare. Another time, Artie overslept and missed the flight he and Paul were supposed to take to a sold-out show at the Royal Albert Hall in London. By the time he finally roused himself, the only way he could get there in time was to spend ten thousand dollars to book a private plane for the journey. "We had to postpone the concert, return all the money, compensate the promoter," Lewis says. "Paul almost smashed his guitar against the concrete wall at the airport, he was so mad."

Artie the movie star. Mike Nichols telling everyone what a great, natural actor he was. So much presence. So much feeling in his dialogue. And so, so handsome. Movie star looks, they kept saying. And Paul? The shortness, the chubby face that made him look chunky even when he was muscle bound and, increasingly, trim — and just when he thought it couldn't get worse, he started losing his hair. His friends in England could already see it when he was twenty-two, twenty-three years old. Paul became skilled with his comb, developing new and increasingly convoluted patterns to cover the pink top of his otherwise bushy head. No young guy ever wants to lose his hair, but it was worse than ever in the late 1960s, when the length of a man's hair projected everything you needed to know about where he stood on the counterculture–civil rights–Vietnam War–Richard M. Nixon–Generation Gap spectrum.

Teaming up with Artie had relieved some of Paul's anxieties about his looks and his voice; it never hurt to have a sweet-singing heartthrob in your group — right until it hurt you more than you even knew how to express.

By the time Artie got back from Mexico in the spring of 1969, Paul had finished backing tracks for a handful of new songs. Before he started work on their fifth album, Paul's first impulse had been to record it in Memphis, with Booker T. and the M.G.'s as their backing band. He even went down to Memphis to check out the Stax label's studio and talk things over with Booker T. In the end, though, they couldn't make it work, so Paul, Artie, and Roy returned to their usual pattern of dividing the session between Manhattan and Los Angeles, where the musicians they had worked with most often (bandleader/drummer Hal Blaine, pianist Larry Knechtel, guitarist Fred Carter Jr., and bassist Joe Osborn) lived. Setting up for a productive summer in LA, Paul and Artie rented a house in the Hollywood Hills just a few miles from the recording studio. The house on Blue Jay Way, the same place George Harrison made famous with his song "Blue Jay Way," got to feel like a Southern California version of the ambassador's house during the Stockbridge summer, the two of them at the center of a loop of girlfriends, friends, musicians, and occasional celebrity guests. Paul's close friend, and the duo's lawyer, Mike Tannen had relocated to Los Angeles to open a new office for his law firm, so he and Mary were around a lot. Tommy Smothers, of the counterculture-influenced comedy team the Smothers Brothers, came around to smoke pot and flirt with Peggy and Mary, while the actor Charles Grodin, who had befriended

Artie on the *Catch-22* set, also became a regular.

There was still plenty of music to record. Near the start of their LA visit, Artie noticed a Frank Lloyd Wright–designed house on a street nearby, and recalling his collegiate fascination for the architect, he suggested Paul write a song about him. Surprisingly, Paul did exactly that, though he took the tune in an unexpected direction. When inspiration struck in the midst of a late-night party, they used their home reel-to-reel to record a rhythm track built from thigh-slapping, dampened-string guitar strums, and piano bench slamming, and that became the basis for another new song. Paul introduced Artie to the Paris-based Peruvian folk group Los Incas's recording of the South American traditional "El Condor Pasa." Paul had fallen in love with the song when he heard the group perform it during his brief visit to Paris during the summer of 1963, and assigned Mort Lewis the task of securing the rights to use the original recording as a backdrop for new lyrics he had written for it. He also had another song he wanted Artie to sing. It was kind of his "Yesterday," Paul said. And he wasn't joking.

When Al Kooper had played Paul an album by the gospel vocal group the Swan Silvertones, Paul begged to borrow it, if only to relish the hauntingly sweet falsetto of the group's lead singer, Claude Jeter. Kooper let him take it home, and while spinning the disc one evening, Paul connected with a line Jeter calls out in a hail of devotional cries in "O Mary Don't You Weep": "I'll be your bridge over deep water if you trust in my name." Something about that phrase walloped Paul across the forehead. Was it the most powerful assertion of unconditional love he'd ever heard? Still feeling Jeter's words in his chest, he reached for his guitar and, as he described it later, felt his fingers hit some gospel changes, which he repeated while a melody fell into his ears, sweet and restrained at first, then taking flight as if it had set its own course independent of Paul's musical imaginings.

"Like a bridge over troubled waters I will lay me down."

The first time Paul heard what he was singing, when it registered in his conscious mind, tears came into his eyes. The song felt more channeled *through* him than written *by* him, as if Jeter's voice had unlocked a door containing the best melody Paul had ever written. He worked on the tune until 4:00 a.m., which was when the telephone in Kooper's apartment rang. Remember that Swan Silvertones album? It had just inspired a new song, and now Paul needed Kooper to come over and hear it. Right now. Figuring it might be his only chance to get his Swan Silvertones album back, Kooper took a cab from his place in the West Village to Paul's Upper East Side apartment building, walking through his door just as the sun pinkened the distant eastern horizon. The only light in the house came from a couple of candles. Paul started to play and sing. "I was the first person other than him to hear 'Bridge Over Troubled Water,' " Kooper says. When Paul got to the chorus, the other musician nodded and smiled. "I instantly knew where he got the line from." What Paul knew, every bit as instantly, was that the only voice with enough range, power, and feeling to do the song justice belonged to Artie Garfunkel.

When Paul played Artie his homemade demo of the song, Artie liked it immediately — and one thing he really liked about it was how Paul's voice sounded on it. In order to hit the high notes, he had climbed into his falsetto range, finding a rich, flutelike tone he'd never used in public, which Artie thought was a shame. You should sing it, he urged his partner. Artie was trying to be generous: "It *is* a great song. You wrote it, you sing beautifully, you deserve to do it." In the heat of that tense summer, Paul heard this as an insult. "It's my best song and it's not good enough for Artie to want to do it?" It took only a few minutes for Artie to change his mind, but that moment of hesitation — what struck Paul as rejection — took root right alongside everything else Paul had recently come to resent about his partner.

Paul had thought of "Bridge" as a brief, restrained ballad, but the more Artie and Halee thought about the song, the more they were convinced that it had to be enormous: a full production with strings, booming drums, and a cathedral-size ending. They couldn't get all that into a two-verse tune, so now Paul had to write a third verse, hopefully sooner rather than later. Paul scratched out the "silver girl" lines in one sitting, and from there Artie and Halee took over the production. To make sure they'd have an authentic gospel piano sound, Paul got in touch with Marshall Chess, the son of Leonard Chess, cofounder (with his brother Phil) of Chicago's Chess Records,[*] and asked him to send over a dozen or so gospel records. From there, Artie focused most intently on how Larry Knechtel would play the piano part. The relatively simple chord changes Paul had

[*] The Jewish-owned independent label that introduced Howlin' Wolf, Muddy Waters, John Lee Hooker, Chuck Berry, and virtually all of blues and rhythm and blues culture to the world from the mid-1940s, providing a musical education to the teenage Beatles, the Rolling Stones, Bob Dylan, Led Zeppelin, and all who would follow them — which adds up to nearly the entire scope of rock 'n' roll and rhythm and blues from the 1960s onward.

written on his guitar didn't come close to southern gospel piano style, with its jumping left hand, ever-changing passing chords, and elaborate turnarounds, so Artie pulled a stool next to the piano and spent days bent over the instrument with Knechtel. Paul didn't abandon the song to them — when he heard Artie leaving out the octave leap in the first verse, he marched in and ordered him to sing it as written. "You can't take the writer's notes and just *dispense* with them!" he cried. "*I* wrote that note. I'm the writer and that's what *I* wrote!" Artie agreed to sing it to Paul's specifications, and everyone cooled down, for the moment.

And then the sun would rise on another day, and they'd be back in perfect synch. In footage shot during the summer and fall of 1969, Paul and Artie function more or less cheerfully in recording sessions, in tour rehearsals, and in the cars, airplanes, hotel rooms, and crowded hallways leading from here to there and then somewhere else altogether. They talk and joke in one voice, completing each other's sentences, pulling a gag with one breath, serving as straight man in the next. Riding together in a car in the fall of 1969, Artie finished a detailed trashing of a current pop song by ridiculing the far-too-obvious intervals in its vocal arrangement. "When you're in the harmony game," he declared, "you learn to scorn harmonies like that."

Paul nodded, but a small smile tugged at the corners of his mouth. Speaking in a neutral tone, he echoed the most absurd thing his partner had just said. "The harmony game."

Artie let that pass, and a moment later Paul started in on another harmony-based offense, this one performed by Ludwig van Beethoven, when he violated a stricture of his time that forbade musicians from using parallel fifth harmonies in their compositions. Confronted by the inevitable institutional backlash, the peevish German composer, and his twentieth-century interlocutor, were having none of it, and Paul's voice jumped into his dramatic range to really lay it down: "So Beethoven says, *I* say that you can! *I'm* writing in parallel fifths. I say that you *can.*"

Artie shrugged, thoroughly unimpressed. "He was a fool, Beethoven."

With that the conversation was over, the both of them peering through the windshield, eyes twinkling.

The crowning moment of S&G silliness came in May of that year, a day after their meeting Frank Zappa at a Mothers of Invention show in New York. When Zappa, who recalled "Hey, Schoolgirl" from his own adolescence, realized that they were the very same duo as Tom and Jerry, they hatched a plan. They'd accompany the Mothers upstate

331

to their next show in Buffalo and be their opening act — not as Simon and Garfunkel, of course, but as an older and sadder Tom and Jerry, still in their 1950s suits and pomaded hair, somehow oblivious to the passage of time. Unrecognized, they ran through a deliberately rough set of oldies, mixing "Hey, Schoolgirl," "Dancin' Wild," and one or two other T&J songs with a few Everly Brothers covers and a particularly sloppy attempt at the Penguins' "Earth Angel" before limping offstage. Zappa's group did its set next, but when it was time for the encore Zappa brought back the openers for one last, not necessarily welcome, song — which turned out to be "The Sound of Silence," sung as a cheerful doo-wop romp ornamented with plenty of *bop-bop-bop*s and *ooh-lah-shooby-doo*s and a slightly revised chorus that suggested, in typical doo-wop steaminess, "Oh baby, let's do it once in silence." The crowd caught on at that point, just in time to see modern superstars Simon and Garfunkel — it really *was* them! — walk offstage without another word.

When Paul and Artie met with filmmaker Robert Drew to talk about the prime-time special that CBS-TV had just commissioned them to make about their upcoming new album, the celebrated documentarian listened, made a few suggestions, and agreed to coproduce the film. He knew it could be a great documentary, he said a few weeks before his death in July 2014, because it would be about so much more than the making of a pop music album. "They were friends, they were getting along fine, but something was wrong," Drew said. "I got a sense that Paul and Artie were breaking up. It was really a film about Simon and Garfunkel's last stand."

The stars had other ideas for the show. If a major television network was going to give them an hour of prime time to do essentially anything they wanted to do, Paul and Artie figured they'd use CBS's megaphone to project their generation's antiwar, antiestablishment politics into the tens of millions of living rooms that would be tuning them in.

Drew didn't want to direct the film himself — he could tell that Paul would be making all the creative decisions no matter who ended up being the titular director. Drew felt more comfortable serving as the project's executive producer, and given his accomplishments as a documentarian — his raw, unnarrated 1960 documentary about the presidential primary battle between U.S. senators John F. Kennedy and Hubert Humphrey in West Virginia had launched documentary vérité, an entirely new genre of journalistic storytelling — they were happy to accept his counteroffer. After looking at a few other candidates, they ultimately installed Charles Grodin, the actor Artie had befriended on the *Catch-22* set, to serve as director. Grodin had never directed anything — he was a comic actor who played mostly supporting roles — but he had a similar political sensibility, and he made no secret of his admiration for the duo, so off they went.

Whether the CBS television network and primary sponsor AT&T knew exactly what Paul and Artie had planned seems doubtful. Maybe they should have thought about it a little more deeply. Simon and Garfunkel had always had a political consciousness, and the influence of the late sixties counterculture had become all the more pronounced as awareness of the terrors of 1968 took deeper root in the first half of 1969. When they played college shows, Paul and Artie would sometimes invite the audience to gather round the stage after the concert so they could all rap about current events: civil rights, Vietnam, the draft, Johnson, Nixon, drugs, and revolution. Nothing was off-limits. Paul and Artie made a point of listening more than they spoke, as if they were just another couple of guys around the dorm room trying to make sense of the world. They had different plans for the TV show, however. For while Paul definitely loved hearing his music played over sweeping shots of wheat fields, hills, and mountains, he and Artie were most eager to make their own statement about the ugliness of their country — the pollution, the racism, the riots, the assassinations, and the war in Vietnam. So anyone tuning to CBS to hear Simon and Garfunkel music during that hour would be confronted by unsettling footage of filth, violence, and poverty. Yes, there would be poignant shots of the Kennedys and Martin Luther King Jr., and innocence-lost images of childhood heroes Flash Gordon, the Lone Ranger, and good old Howdy Doody. But gloom, cast over everything else, dominated the piece.

When Grodin presented a near-final cut to executives from the network and AT&T, their first reaction was shock, followed by confusion, and then something like outrage. These were old-school American corporations led by old-school American corporate executives, Nixon men, the What's good for Dow Chemical is good for America crowd. According to Grodin, one executive accused them of using AT&T's money to preach "the humanistic approach," a phrase he spat like snake venom. And why were all the political heroes on the screen liberals? Because they had all been assassinated, Grodin explained. No matter. The executives demanded they remove the politics from the film. When Paul, Artie, and Grodin refused, AT&T's executives chose to remove themselves entirely, demanding CBS return the reported six hundred thousand to eight hundred thousand dollars they had invested. CBS agreed, scrambling quickly to convince Alberto-Culver, the maker of VO5 and other women's beauty products, to buy the rights for a fraction of what AT&T had paid.

And what did Alberto-Culver buy? A show so off-putting that once it reached its first commercial break, an estimated million viewers turned it off. Starting with a vaguely cautionary statement by spokesman/actor Robert Ryan — "We think you'll find the next hour to be both entertaining and stimulating" — the fifty-two-minute film veered from those stirring airborne scenery shots set to music to intimate sequences of Paul and Artie moving at top speed between hotels, recording studios, and rehearsals. Paul ran through a Chuck Berry–style political rocker, "Cuba Si, Nixon No," about an airplane hijacker; then the scene shifted to a band rehearsal in the living room at Hal Blaine's house, where Artie ran through the Frank Lloyd Wright song. Scenes of impoverished children outside crumbled shacks played to Coretta Scott King's assertion that the mere existence of hungry children and impoverished families in modern America was just a different form of the violence taking place on the battlefields of Vietnam. "Bridge Over Troubled Water" played on the airwaves for the first time, heard over footage of President John F. Kennedy, Sen. Robert F. Kennedy, and the Rev. Martin Luther King Jr.; then to scenes of citizens crying and saluting their funeral processions.

It's brutal stuff, a deliberate shock to force viewers into recognizing the distance between America's ideals and reality, a message Simon and Garfunkel had up to that point managed to make clear in the delicate terms of their songs. But the biggest surprise in Grodin's documentary is how detached and even incomprehensible it makes Paul and Artie's political statements seem. Artie: "The chaos of what the hell is the whole thing is a violent screaming reaction to the confusion of what *is* this thing?" And when Paul attempts to describe the depth of his frustration with the world, he comes off like Little Lord Fauntleroy on a junk food jag: "We're staying in the Beverly Hills Hotel," he declares, describing how the building's elevators display the front pages of the day's major newspapers. And every day it's the same buzzkill: "I see the headlines and I think, why am I going to make this album? What's the point in making this album? The world is crumbling." Yet Paul seems anything but committed to finding a way to heal the world's problems. Asked if he'd like to try his hand at being the nation's president, he turns instantly silly, predicting that he would take a few months to fix up all the problems, then get back to his career in music. Then again, maybe he wouldn't have the time for even that much distraction.

ARTIE: He wants to develop himself as an artist, Chuck.
GRODIN: You have no time to be president?
PAUL, RECONSIDERING: I feel I'd make the time.

Then Paul's thoughtfulness melts, and he breaks down laughing. Quick cut to "The 59th Street Bridge Song (Feelin' Groovy)," and the viewer begins to sympathize with the AT&T executives. Even in the aftermath of all that shock-and-awful footage of fallen heroes, starving children, and battlefield body bags, Paul, with Grodin's help, plays his own apparent disinterest as a joke. Given that the documentary was intended to serve as a serious statement about the state of the nation at the end of what began as one of the most idealistic decades in history, *Songs of America* stands as the worst product of the Simon and Garfunkel collaboration, an attempt at political advocacy so bungled it actually diminished the people and causes it intended to celebrate.

They had assumed the record would be finished with plenty of time for its scheduled release in the fall of 1969, but as the writing and recording dragged into October, the plan to have it in the record stores in time for the Christmas shopping season faded. Paul, Artie, and their four-piece band played several weeks of shows featuring new songs from an album their audiences had yet to hear. The average Simon and Garfunkel crowd was geared toward quiet, respectful listening, but the anticipation in the air was palpable as Artie introduced Paul's most recent song, the just-recorded "Song for the Asking," which they sang as a duet, Artie's voice turning neat pirouettes around Paul's melody. Some audiences chuckled at Paul's "Architects may come and architects may go" line in "So Long, Frank Lloyd Wright," while "Why Don't You Write Me" registered enthusiastic, if not overwhelming, applause. But the highlight of the show, night after night, was "Bridge Over Troubled Water."

The song always came as a surprise. At Wichita State University in Kansas; at Miami University in Oxford, Ohio; at Carnegie Hall in New York City, it would happen the same way. Larry Knechtel would start the piano intro, and Artie, or sometimes Paul, would say, simply, "This is another new song. It's called 'Bridge Over Troubled Water.' " Then Paul would leave the stage, leaving Artie alone in the spotlight. As Knechtel got to the opening's turnaround, Artie would start singing, and the silence would magnify, all eyes and ears locked on his performance. Artie kept his voice sweet and airy in the first verse, then gathered force with the second verse and the pianistic glories behind the first full chorus. It descended for a few bars in the third verse, and then finally he unleashed all his vocal power on the climactic chorus, holding that one crowning note for three full bars before falling gently back into the gale of applause and cheers erupting around him in the hall. And of course Paul would give him that moment, lingering offstage as his partner absorbed the cheers. From where Paul stood, in the wings with a cigarette smoldering between his fingers, feeling the same envy that burned into him during the fourth-grade assembly. Artie alone in the spotlight taking the crowd for his own. Only now *he'd* written the song, now it was *he,* and not Artie, who deserved to be cheered. Because while Paul could definitely sing "Bridge Over Troubled Water," Artie would never have been able to write it. And Paul had had just about enough of the world's not understanding that.

They were both tired. Paul was tired of having Artie and Halee insist on making his songs so pretty: all those string sections and the layers of echo putting a shimmer on tunes he thought would sound better with a little mud on their shoes. Artie was sick of working within the boundaries of Paul's desires and needs. When Paul came in with "Cuba Si, Nixon No," Artie tried to pitch in some harmonies but then threw his hands up. The song didn't measure up to all the other songs, he said, and he wanted nothing to do with it. Paul didn't want to hear that, but he felt just as unhappy with the "Benedictus"-like Bach piece Artie wanted to put on the album. So there they were, finally, at absolute loggerheads, each determined to wrestle his own song into the one space they had left. Unable to sing either song in one voice, they resolved the conflict by doing neither song. Unable to sing together, they settled for silence.

When they previewed the finished album *Bridge Over Troubled Water* to Columbia Records president Clive Davis and a roomful of family and friends, the reception was overwhelming. Paul, Artie, and Halee had figured that the up-tempo, slightly bawdy singalong "Cecilia" — the song set to the home-recorded piano bench, slack guitar strum, handclap, and dropped drumsticks backing track — would be the perfect lead-off single,[*] but after one listen to the title track, Davis insisted that no amount of industrial strictures against releasing long, slow piano ballads as pop singles could apply to such a strikingly beautiful song. Davis was correct,

[*] Not counting "The Boxer," which had been released as a single the previous spring.

and when the album and single were released on January 26, 1970, the impact was extraordinary. Both were instant smashes, with the song topping the Hot 100 for six straight weeks between February and April, while the album spent an astounding *forty-one* weeks at the top during its three-hundred-week run on the *Billboard* charts, on its way to selling twenty-five million copies. All that talk of Simon and Garfunkel starting to rival the Beatles turned out to be true. *Bridge Over Troubled Water* outsold the Beatles' *Let It Be* by 400 percent that year, and would also sweep the year's Grammy Awards, winning Album of the Year, Record of the Year, Song of the Year, and Contemporary Song of the Year, while the now-estranged John, Paul, George, and Ringo made do with the Best Original Score trophy for the soundtrack of the *Let It Be* movie.

More than revealing the duo's new adult perspective, the album serves as the first pop cultural landmark of the 1970s, the decade when the New Generation, as Ralph J. Gleason had termed it, would assume the independence it had demanded for so long. The songs on *Bridge Over Troubled Water* tell the story in their own way: the title track's declaration of spiritual commitment, echoed lightly in "Song for the Asking," in the upbeat celebrations of the daily grind in "Keep the

Customer Satisfied"* and "Baby Driver"; adult challenges and quandaries fading into memories of youthful abandon; the ageless wisdom in "El Condor Pasa"; the down-and-out fighter in "The Boxer"; the featherweight flirtiness of "Why Don't You Write Me"; the carefree sexuality of "Cecilia"; and the close harmony pleasures of "Bye Bye Love" — all of which take on deeper resonance in the company of the elegiac diptych of "So Long, Frank Lloyd Wright" and "The Only Living Boy in New York," the pillars that form the album's emotional foundation, as well as the key to its mammoth impact not only on listeners who shared their generational and cultural experience, but also on those who lived in completely different circumstances and eras.

From the opening verse of "Bridge" to the final, unadorned note of "Song for the Asking," *Bridge Over Troubled Water* chronicles Paul and Artie's friendship and musical partnership from the first joyful union of their voices to the bittersweet, perhaps inevitable divorce they were beginning to negotiate in the album's songs. The story is neither linear nor directly stated. Only "Frank Lloyd Wright" and "Only Living Boy" address the

* Which could be the story of a grown-up, postlarcenous version of the footloose antihero in "Somewhere They Can't Find Me."

343

separation head-on, but the other songs describe the singers' friendship in other ways. By starting with its title track, the album begins at an emotional climax, the masterpiece Paul knew was the best song he'd ever written. And for all the adoration Paul's lyrics held for his future wife, Peggy, the song is defined even more by his handing it over to the one person he could trust to express his most overpowering feelings with the transcendent force the song required.

"El Condor Pasa" and "Cecilia" foretell Paul's future in shades of cultural exotica and street corner simplicity, while the attempted reggae bounce on "Why Don't You Write Me" falls flat, succeeding mostly as a lesson in why it's best to record foreign grooves when they're being played by the hands that originally defined their sound. The far more successful replication in the song, a feature it shares with the leaping and bounding of "Keep the Customer Satisfied" and "Baby Driver," comes through in the vocal duets, all of which are sung entirely by Paul. This was not because the songs didn't have harmony parts written into their structure — nearly every word of the lead in "Why Don't You Write Me" is written to feature S&G's close harmony — but these were the tracks Paul had recorded when Artie was still in Mexico. Too aggrieved by his absence to wait for his movie star partner's return, Paul had performed all the parts himself, so expertly attuned to the timbre of Artie's voice that most listeners didn't realize they were hearing only half of the duo.

The Paul and Artie blend shines brightly on "The Boxer," Paul's self-portrait as reflected through the cracked mirror of a cheap hotel room. Paul is an unemployed laborer, battered, lonely, and cold, yet determined to keep moving. In the final verse, he sees himself in a different form, as an unsuccessful fighter whose scars and humiliations bend but never break his will. "I am leaving, I am leaving," he cries. "But the fighter still remains." It's Paul's story told in the most personal terms, but he and Artie sing it together, the separate voices locked in the same unison they had been practicing since they were thirteen. They worked with Halee to create the ringing, booming backdrop, each drum strike the slam of a fist, each trombone blast a train shaking the sidewalk, a truck unleashing its air horn. It is a portrait of a desperate, punishing life, but Artie found its grandeur with an upward-bounding countermelody that, through the combined sound of horn and guitar, projected the dirt-stained fighter into silvered light.

The subtext moved in the opposite direction when Artie suggested Paul write a song about his favorite architect. Paul took the idea, but only sort of. Rather than focusing his pen on Frank Lloyd Wright, the leader of the Prairie School of architecture, he turned the designer into a symbol for Artie, and the song a combination salute and farewell. Set to a Brazilian samba with a few modernist touches, the tune moves breezily beneath the singer's gossamer delivery of his bittersweet tale. "So Long, Frank Lloyd Wright" speaks explicitly about moments in the duo's shared lives: harmonizing all night, laughing themselves silly. There's no harmonizing on this song: Artie sings the verses, and Paul comes in for a two-line bridge, celebrating his friend's stubbornness, before handing the mic back so Artie can sing Paul's sweetest acknowledgment to him: "When I run dry / I stop a while and think of you."

The real depth of Paul's feelings for Artie, the years of friendship and interdependence, come through most powerfully in "The Only Living Boy in New York," which rivals "Bridge" and "Kathy's Song" for being the most heartfelt love song in the Simon and Garfunkel catalogue. Singing over a simple one-four chord progression set to an acoustic twelve-string guitar, a church organ, and jumping bass line, Paul's voice is conversational; in the first verse, it's as if he's standing in front of his friend, straightening his tie and handing him his suitcase as the taxi to the airport honks its horn. The second verse sounds more like a letter from home: he's lonely; you can hear the sadness in Paul's voice. At first it's amiable resignation, then sweet impatience. He's happy to wait; he knows it's his turn to be patient. But the more he reflects on their shared life, that disorienting blur of lights and noise and the empty dead of night — what does any of it matter, or mean? The final verse keeps the direct delivery — only now he's speaking much more urgently. Their shared youth is finished. Now they have to become their own men. Paul's parting line, delivered over a vast echoing chorus of his and Artie's multitrack *ahhhhh*s, erupts in a torrent so emotional there's a small but audible sob near the end.

"Hey, let your honesty shine, shine, shine / Like it shines on me."

The conjoined songs that end the album, a bouncy live rendition of the Everly Brothers' "Bye Bye Love" and the brief guitar ballad "Song for the Asking," conclude the story in starker terms. The cheers for the song of Paul and Artie's youth cross-fade into guitar and a string quartet as Paul bids farewell with something between an offering and an apology. The latter is unexplained; the former has been coming through your speakers for thirty-six minutes. And maybe it's not enough. "Thinking it over I'd be more than glad / To change my ways," he sings. As if it could be done that easily.

CHAPTER 14
I'D RATHER BE

When *Bridge Over Troubled Water* was finally finished and they were preparing to launch their fall tour, Artie told Paul a secret he'd been keeping for a few months. When he was in Rome filming the last of his *Catch-22* scenes, Mike Nichols had asked if he'd be interested in playing a lead role in his next film, a drama about two sexually driven men called *Carnal Knowledge*. His costars would be Jack Nicholson, Candice Bergen, and Ann-Margret, all popular young actors, and the shooting would require his attention for most of 1971. Garfunkel said yes on the spot, but had decided to keep the news from his partner until the record was finished, so it wouldn't dampen the mood.

Artie's keeping the news a secret only made Paul more furious: How could he have gone behind Paul's back and taken a solo job without checking first? Didn't he know their first commitment was to their musical partnership? If Paul noticed how closely Artie's secret movie deal resembled his own hush-hush negotiations to leverage a solo contract out of Tom and Jerry's first hit in 1957, he didn't bring it up. They had plenty of other, more recent disagreements to unpack, and once he got going Artie didn't hold back. He didn't even want to see Paul when he was working on the movie. They would be shooting the film in and around New York City, but he ordered Paul to stay as far from the set as possible: no bringing his guitar to demo new songs, no kibitzing with Nichols, no hanging around when Artie was trying to get into character. In fact, don't even come by to say hello — Artie was banning him from the set.

Artie knew Paul's weaknesses as well as he knew how he timed his inhalations before reaching for a high note. Generally, Artie did what he could to cushion his friend's insecurities, complimenting his songs and his voice, hunching his shoulders when they were posing together, standing a step behind or sitting down in photo sessions so he wouldn't seem that much taller than Paul. But now he worked over the insecurities relentlessly. Why should he build his life around pop music when movies were such a superior art form? Film was the most complicated, most fulfilling form of artistic expression, and he was already thriving in the medium. "I'm really only interested in movies," Artie yelled at

Paul. "I work with Mike Nichols and Jack Nicholson, and they're my friends. I'm very good-looking. I *look* like a movie star." Paul was flabbergasted. He was devastated. He was enraged. He'd urged Artie to do something for himself, away from the duo, and now the guy was attacking him with it. He could imagine Artie's internal motivation: "I've always felt like a nobody. Now *you're* going to be the nobody." Paul said, "Part of him saw those movies as an opportunity to fuck me over . . . I mean, he really made me feel bad."

Yet Simon and Garfunkel still had work to do. They had already committed to weeks-long concert tours of America and Europe, where demand for tickets was beyond intense. After all those years of dreaming and working and worrying about this and that, they had reached the top of the top. No matter how pissed off they were at each other, they were still too smart to let a feud get in the way of being the hottest, most celebrated group in popular music.

Dispensing with the backing musicians they had played with during the autumn tour, with the exception of pianist Larry Knechtel, whose sole appearance was on "Bridge," they restored one kind of intimacy to the show. Still, the distance between them could be heard in the increasing number of solo vocals they put in the set. Artie had his star turns on "For Emily, Whenever I Find Her" and the climactic "Bridge," so now Paul got "The Only Living Boy in New York," his guitar workout "Anji," and, most noticeably, a version of "Song for the Asking" that replicated the solo album performance rather than the lovely harmonized arrangement he and Artie had performed the previous fall. They also performed two new songs, "El Condor Pasa" and "So Long, Frank Lloyd Wright," that used both voices but in separate, unharmonized sections.*

The 1970 tour concluded on July 18 with a homecoming show in the ten-thousand-seat Forest Hills tennis stadium. Performing on a pleasant summer evening in a cozy arena that was an easy walk from both their childhood homes, they looked and sounded delighted, joking easily with each other and with the folks in the crowd, all of whom cheered them on like the neighborhood heroes they were. They played "Roving Gambler" and "Put My Little Shoes Away," both traditionals from the Everly Brothers' album of Appalachian standards, *Songs Our Daddy Taught Us,* then responded to someone's request for doo-wop by whipping off a quick cover of the Dion oldie "Why Must I Be a Teenager in Love." Feeling too happy to sing about alienation, they skipped past "The Sound of Silence" for

* Excepting the final verse of "El Condor Pasa."

351

the first time anyone could remember, concluding the evening with one last triumphant "Bridge Over Troubled Water." When it was all over, Paul and Artie shook hands and walked off in separate directions.

Of course they weren't going to break up. Sitting with a British writer in mid-1969, Paul noted that his connection to Artie, and Artie's with him, wasn't a matter of contracts and negotiations. "We'd have to stop our friendship if we were to split, and there's no possibility of that," he said. "We'll always come back together on some venture." Talking to *Rolling Stone*'s Loraine Alterman a year later, well after Artie's *Carnal Knowledge* announcement, Paul barely hinted at their diverging paths. Certainly, Artie was busy with his movies, and Paul had some musical notions that might lead in other directions for a while, but that didn't change anything, really. "We could easily do [a new tour in 1971]," he said. "As far as recording goes that's a simple matter of saying, 'let's make another record.' . . . Probably we will make another record." There was no reason to doubt him. The same week the *Rolling Stone* interview came out in America, England's *Melody Maker* reported that dates for a 1971 Simon and Garfunkel tour had already been booked.

But he and Artie had no plans even to see

352

each other, let alone to do any work together. They had been invited to co-headline the Summer Festival for Peace, a daylong all-star fund-raiser for antiwar political candidates planned for Shea Stadium on August 6, the twenty-fifth anniversary of the nuclear attack on Hiroshima. Paul was eager to do it, but Artie refused even to consider the prospect. So did that mean Paul couldn't do it at all? That hardly seemed right, given how much he believed in the cause, and how much attention the daylong festival would surely receive. So maybe he should go out and play by himself. The promoters were more than willing to book him as a solo. Simon and Garfunkel were so hot that even half the team would be a big draw for New York audiences. But Paul was terrified. He hadn't played a show without Artie by his side for more than five years. Could he hold such a large audience's attention without him? Could he do anything without Artie? No one wanted to hear Paul singing songs by himself anymore, even if they were songs he had written by himself. He'd work himself up like that, but then Peggy would talk him down. They had been married in September 1969, and he had come to depend on her counsel. She was smart, sensible, accustomed to being the boulder in a frantic sea, and she told him to stop being so silly. Of course Paul could do it alone; he'd done it that way for years, all that time in England, where fans had filled the clubs and hushed one another so they could hear every note, so they wouldn't miss a word he uttered. The only thing that had changed since then was that he'd sold millions of records, including the biggest hit album of the year. Paul committed to playing the show.

No one expected it to turn out the way it did. The same mix of peace activists and entertainment pros led by Peter, Paul, and Mary's Peter Yarrow had put on an all-star Winter Festival for Peace at Madison Square Garden the previous winter, and it had been a smash. Jimi Hendrix; the Rascals; Blood, Sweat, and Tears; Peter, Paul, and Mary; and Richie Havens headlined that show, and the lineup for the summer festival was just as lustrous. Paul would share the stage with Creedence Clearwater Revival, Steppenwolf, Miles Davis, Dionne Warwick, Johnny Winter, Joe Walsh's James Gang, and many others. But even the hottest bands can't sell tickets to fans who don't know the show they're playing exists: somehow the show's promoters neglected to publicize the summer festival. There were few advertisements, fewer newspaper stories, and even the chatter in the hippie underground was muffled at best. Also, it was a daytime show scheduled for a Thursday. They eventually sold fewer than twenty thousand tickets for a space built for three times that number. To make matters worse, the sound system wasn't powerful enough to drown out the jet engine blasts of the airplanes on their final approach to LaGuardia Airport, which posed a problem even for the superamplified rock 'n' roll bands. And make no mistake, this was a rock 'n' roll crowd: rowdy New York kids juiced for thunder and screams.

It was not a crowd for one fellow with an acoustic guitar and thoughtful musings on social and romantic alienation. Coming out to light applause and the stubborn rumble of disinterest, Paul did the best he could, strumming and singing the songs that had made him famous, that only a few weeks earlier had inspired ovation after ovation from the ten thousand friends and fans gathered to see Simon and Garfunkel at the Forest Hills stadium. None of those people, it seemed, had come to Shea. These people weren't even looking at the stage. They were talking, shouting, and tossing Frisbees, their occasional glances more impatient than intrigued. Was this real or an anxiety nightmare? Paul could feel the strings beneath his fingers, the lights in his face; and that was his voice, singing and talking, asking for a little quiet so everybody could hear, and then launching into "Scarborough Fair," always a rapturous few moments during a Simon and Garfunkel show. But now it was all airplanes and chatter and laughter and — they were actually *booing.* Then he wasn't playing anymore, and that was it. Turning away from the microphone and the dismal scene, stalking across the stage, shouldering past the throng of whoever the fuck was in the wings, slamming his guitar into his case, stalking wordlessly out of the trash-strewn bowl, into his car, and then — zoom! — a red streak out of the parking lot, out of Queens, back to Manhattan, and locking the damn door.

The bleakness that had stalked Paul since he was an adolescent had never really cleared, the bitter fog drifting behind his eyes, taking hold even in the least likely moments. At the end of one Sunday evening during the Simon and Garfunkel tour in 1969, Hal Blaine had seen Paul leaving the dressing room with his cheeks radiant from the performance, joking and laughing until he glimpsed a solitary custodian sweeping up the garbage that had been left in the arena's empty seats. Paul stopped abruptly. "Did you see that?" Paul asked the others. It's Sunday night; that guy should be home with his family, but now he's all alone picking up garbage all night. It seemed cruel, all the loneliness in the world. His shoulders stooped, Paul shrank inside himself, and when everyone else went for a drink, he slipped into his room and hung out the Do Not Disturb card.

He started seeing a therapist. The actor Elliott Gould had a guy he liked, and Paul grabbed at him like a drowning man, booking four sessions a week to unpack everything he'd been lugging around, just to get to the point where he could have it organized enough to move a little more freely inside his head. He managed to cut it down to three visits a week by mid-1970, but there was still plenty of work to do: the Artie mess, Paul's desperation to strike out on his own, and the terror of what might happen if he did. Maybe he should form a band instead? Or, as his father continued to insist, follow his example and build a more meaningful career in education? *Teach! Teach!* Paul didn't let the old man push him around, but he also couldn't help wondering, especially when it seemed that he'd lost his sense of direction.

Right around the time Artie unleashed his secret about *Carnal Knowledge* during the fall of 1969, Paul had gotten in touch with music department administrators at Columbia University, the New School for Social Research, and New York University to see if any of them would sponsor a workshop class in songwriting that he wanted to teach. Columbia turned him away, but the other two institutions loved the idea, and eventually Paul chose to go with NYU, due in large part to his relationship with David Oppenheim, who had left public television to run the university's arts department.

The memo Oppenheim had his staff post around the arts buildings sketched the specifics. "Paul Simon of Simon and Garfunkel has offered to teach a course in how to write and record a popular song," it began. The class size would be limited, and all students would be selected by the instructor. The uncredited class would start in February and meet on Tuesday evenings until the end of the term in May. You didn't have to be an NYU student to be considered, but only practicing songwriters with music and/or lyrics on hand should apply.

Articles about the class turned up in the *Village Voice,* along with *Billboard* and other music publications, and Paul read through the applications and set up auditions based both on the uniqueness of the students' work and on whether he thought he'd like them enough to spend three hours in their company each week. Oppenheim brought into the meetings (and the workshop) Jeffrey Sweet, a student who had won a coveted spot in Broadway musical composer Lehman Engel's private theatrical music writing class, and he recommended Paul give a listen to some songs written by a recent NYU acting school dropout named Melissa Manchester, and Paul liked what he heard. When a pair of teenage sisters from New Jersey buttonholed him on campus just before the start of the first class, Paul steered them into an empty classroom and let them play a few of their original songs, including one that impressed him so much he invited them to stick around for the class, and then Maggie and Terre Roche were in the course, too.

The class began with the start of NYU's spring semester in January 1970, with the just-released *Bridge Over Troubled Water* rocketing up the album charts. Paul sat on the floor with his students and told them how their class would work. He had no idea what he was doing, he said, so it would be an experiment for all of them. When someone asked if he was getting paid, Paul shrugged — he wasn't sure; he didn't really care. The only thing he knew for certain was that they'd have to take a two-week break in late April so he and Artie could play shows in England and Europe. Other than that, they'd all figure things out as they went along.

Eventually the class found its form. Each week, one or two students would hand around a set of lyrics and then perform their latest work. Paul read along, and when they finished, he'd have them play it again, and sometimes a third time. When he was sure he'd absorbed the song, he'd offer thoughts ranging from the general ("Part of the learning process is to imitate first") to the very specific ("For staccato music you should have more dentalized sounds . . . more *t*'s and *d*'s"). He got bored quickly, and loved being surprised by an odd turn of phrase or a piercing image drawn from real life. When Melissa Manchester sang the phrase "laughing lagoons" in one of her songs, he suggested she change it to "laughing da goons" because it sounded more interesting. When another student's lyrics struck him as flat, Paul told her to get a Bible; it was packed with odd, memorable phrases. "Just steal them," he said. "That's what they're for."

Paul was particularly struck by the Roche sisters. Their song "Malachy's" had leaped out when they played it during their impromptu audition, and the lyric about weathering a tough set in an Upper East Side club rang so true that it brought him back to when he and Artie had to sing above the disinterested crowd at Gerde's. After the first class, he offered to drive the sisters back to the George Washington Bridge terminal so they could catch their bus back to the New Jersey suburbs. He was in his sports car that night, a two-seater with barely room for two people and a suitcase, but they all jammed in, and as they rumbled uptown he alternated slinging compliments and insults in a way that made Terre Roche think he didn't like them very much after all. They were pretty good but nowhere near as good as they probably thought, he said. He turned to elder sister Maggie: Did she think she was as good a songwriter as Paul McCartney? She figured she was, and he gave her a sour look. "You're not." He dropped them at the station without a good-bye, but when they turned up at the next week's class, he greeted them with a smile.

So it went through the winter and spring. Off campus, *Bridge Over Troubled Water* dominated the airwaves and record stores, rapidly moving from being a hit to being a cultural milestone. But the adjunct instructor who came into NYU's music building each Tuesday, dressed most often in jeans, a T-shirt, a sweater, and a heavy hooded parka that looked like army surplus, didn't seem to pay much mind. He'd shuck his coat, find a seat, maybe talk about a song or two that had caught his ear on the radio, then invite the evening's first presenter to play his or her latest tune. One week, he borrowed a guitar to play a fragment of a tune he'd just started to write, talking in detail about how it had come to him and where he thought it might go next. He'd think for a moment and try a chord or two. Did that sound like the right move? He'd try another chord, take it in another direction. What about that? Or how about this? "My sense was that he was searching himself," Manchester says. "He understood that the writer's mind is a muscle. It had to be trained to know how to play, how to get free."

Some weeks, Paul brought in special guests.

One week it was Al Kooper, then the violinist Isaac Stern, who spent much of the time defending the character of classical music, assuming the young students all despised it. For the final session, Paul booked an entire day at the Columbia Records studios on West Fifty-Second Street, complete with an engineer and studio musicians so he could demonstrate how to turn a song into a finished commercial recording. The day was a whirlwind of studio preparations, arrangement scribbling, and overdub after overdub. A small camera crew tracked every move. The camera's lens would hover inches from Paul's face and, as Terre Roche recalled, he'd continue without flinching, without seeming to notice anything beyond the music in his ears and the space between what he was hearing and what he wanted to hear.

As the summer of 1970 fell to autumn, with no Simon and Garfunkel projects or tour dates anywhere in sight, it was hard to figure out what Paul should, or could, do next. He and Peggy were living in a brownstone near Central Park, on East Ninety-Fourth Street, having taken over a three-floor residence once owned by classical guitarist Andrés Segovia. Dark and still, filled with books and Tiffany lamps — Paul collected them — the place was much homier than the modern duplex he'd been in for most of the S&G years.

Peggy read Gloria Steinem and pursued her interests in visual design and photography, but she was also the product of a strict, if troubled, family from a Bible-bred section of Tennessee, and took naturally to the role of the stay-at-home wife — albeit a wife who had no patience for a husband who kept complaining that he didn't have anything to do. "You can't just sit here," she'd tell him. "Go to the office, do *something*!"

If his term at NYU had taught Paul anything, it was that he wasn't ready to obey his father's wishes and toss aside his music career for the life of an academic. The songwriting workshop had its pleasures, but those were less about pedagogy than about being able to hang out with a handful of younger songwriters, hear their work, and, by passing along what he'd learned about songcraft, gain a different kind of insight into his own artistry. Paul had been writing steadily through the year, tapping into a stream of emotionally raw tunes that were faster and funkier than the songs he'd written for Simon and Garfunkel. No longer compelled to steer his songs toward Artie's voice and tastes, he went back to the street corner singers and gospel/soul records that had first spun his head around when he was a teenager, the Latin swing from uptown and the rhythm and blues that had pulled his eyes away from his box score that summer morning when he was eleven.

In late 1970 he went to see Clive Davis to tell him that he was about to record a new album. The only catch was that he wasn't going to be working with Artie — definitely not this time, but probably not ever again. Davis, realizing that Columbia's biggest act (all music's biggest act, actually) had called it quits on him, responded badly. "Well, that's the biggest mistake you could make," he said. "It doesn't matter how good your solo records are, none of them will ever sell like a Simon and Garfunkel album." Paul, already dreading the prospect of not being able to make hits on his own, got just as upset. That might be true, he shot back, but it was also possible that one day Simon and Garfunkel would be a footnote in the story of his solo career. Davis didn't disagree, exactly, but he also knew how the industry, and the world, worked. There were artists, but then there were *institutions,* and the former was never going to add up to anything close to the latter. That was just how the world worked. "I did try to reason with him," Davis says. "Do an occasional solo album, fine. Just keep the institution alive. So there was definitely a disagreement there. But there was never any guile to it, there was never a disguise. He knew that I was always going to be honest with him." And maybe that's what Paul resented the most.

At first Paul thought about forming a band. When he called London-based (but American-born) blues guitarist Stefan Grossman to ask if he'd play on his new album, Paul also mentioned the possibility of starting a long-term collaboration with a couple of other musicians, but the talk ended there. Instead, Paul let the songs dictate who would play them. In December he traveled to San Francisco, where Roy Halee had relocated to set up a state-of-the-art recording studio for the Columbia Records artists who didn't feel like working in New York or Los Angeles. With a top-flight band made up of Stax bassist Duck Dunn, rock/jazz/blues keyboardist Mike Finnigan, and the versatile drummer George Marsh waiting to make music, Paul sifted through his tunes with Halee and got started. He ran through early versions of "Duncan" and "Me and Julio Down by the Schoolyard" with the studio musicians, then spent some time working with Blood, Sweat, and Tears, the chart-topping jazz-rock group Al Kooper had formed (only to be forced out just before they became successful). When *Rolling Stone* writer Ben Fong-Torres came to check in after the first week of sessions, Paul confessed that the days had so far been fruitless. "I've gotten nowhere," he said. "Magic doesn't happen on a schedule."

Paul also didn't hide from Fong-Torres that

he was working on a solo album, his first without Artie since the UK-only *Paul Simon Songbook* in 1965. "Partly I'm looking forward to it just for fun, and partly as a manifestation of Artie's movie commitment," he said, going on to keep the Simon and Garfunkel door ajar, or perhaps to ease Clive Davis's mind for just a little while. "When I finish with this he'll probably be finished with the movie, and I'll think about doing something else." But Paul was much more excited to talk about where he was heading. "Maybe Nashville. Or Jamaica."

Jamaica? That was unexpected, coming from a folk-singing Jewish intellectual from New York City. But Paul had been entranced by the island's offbeat bop since he heard it in London in the mid-1960s. The Skatalites, the Maytals, and Don Drummond had hits on the UK charts then, and their music's chattering *bang-bang* got under his skin. He'd tried to capture it for "Why Don't You Write Me" during the *Bridge* sessions, but while Hal Blaine had no problem mastering the cadence, and the rest of the musicians could follow him anywhere, something about it still rang hollow to Paul — an essence they couldn't capture in the sterile confines of a state-of-the-art studio in Los Angeles. Still itching to feel that pulse in his chest, Paul thought again about "El Condor Pasa," how he'd found the Chilean sound by repurposing Los Incas's original track for his own lyrics and S&G's vocals. Only, instead of using a prerecorded track, he'd sketch out an original tune and take it down to where the sound originated, where he could put it into the hands of the musicians who really lived by the rhythm they wrote and played.

Paul got in touch with Leslie Kong, producer of dozens of hits for Toots and the Maytals, Jimmy Cliff, and Bob Marley, hoping to track down the guitarist who had played on Cliff's 1968 single "Vietnam." That turned out to be Huks Brown, lead guitarist for Toots and the Maytals and part of the house band at Dynamic Sounds, the Kingston recording studio that had produced most of the significant records by Cliff, the Maytals, and Marley. Kong helped him book three days at Dynamic with Brown and a band made up primarily of Maytals members, and Paul was on his way — but not without a few anxieties. How could he, a white American pop star, jet to Jamaica and expect the local musicians to share with him the music style they had invented? It was easy to imagine they'd look at him like a thief, a musical carpetbagger stopping by just long enough to copy the most valuable thing they had, take it back to New York, and add it to his fortune.

Yet when he got to Kingston and walked into Dynamic Sounds, he was greeted with smiles and the traditional celebratory herb.

367

The studio had a fairly rustic setup, but the spirit within the red, orange, and yellow walls more than made up for whatever technical flaws the room contained. To get things started, Paul took his guitar into the studio to show the basic chords and structure of his tune, then retreated to the control booth to run the musicians through a few takes, then a few more. They were making progress, but as the hours passed, Paul couldn't help noticing that Brown and his compatriots had started muttering and scowling. Soon he learned why: in Kingston, musicians got paid by the song, usually somewhere between seven and ten dollars per finished track. Given how quickly most producers wanted to work, it was decent pay. They had never even heard of someone who would want to stay on one tune all day long. Once someone clued Paul in, he called the musicians together and said he'd pay them as if they'd finished three songs each day, and the smiles and herb were back right away. The song still needed work — it didn't have words yet, for one thing — but when he flew back to New York a few days later, Paul had the foundations of a track that sounded nothing like any song he'd ever recorded before, and also a style of working that would lead him in directions no one, including Paul, would have thought possible.

Over the next few months, Paul worked mostly in Columbia's studios in New York, recording a variety of understated tunes in styles ranging from front porch blues to Latin to art pop and beyond. He spent ten days in San Francisco trying to record "Congratulations," and came away with nothing but a drum sound for the tune. Grossman spent more weeks recording in New York and Los Angeles, playing lead guitar parts on songs that included "Paranoia Blues," which, unbeknownst to him, Paul had also recorded with blues/folk guitar and mandolin player David Bromberg playing the lead part. Grossman is featured on the finished track, but nothing else he played over the weeks made it onto the album. Grossman, a seasoned studio player, knew better than to indulge himself with hurt feelings. "He paid for everything and really took care of us. First-class everything. And he's a lovely guy . . . he's trying to get something from you that you didn't know you had."

Flying to Paris to record a new backing track with Los Incas, Paul set up a recording session with the jazz violinist Stéphane Grappelli, Django Reinhardt's collaborator for many years, to work on a song called "Papa Hobo." They had a famous time together, and when Paul went back to listen to what they had recorded he realized that the violinist had stretched out one of his breaks into an eighty-second-long digression that sounded so good he decided to stick it somewhere on the record. Mike Tannen, who had gone with him to France, proposed another idea: Paul could give the fiddle-led vignette a name, credit Grappelli as a cowriter, and it would still earn them publishing royalties as with any other song. Paul liked the sound of that, almost as much as he liked the prospect of having his name on a song with a musician whose name could also be found beneath the titles of some of the most influential music recorded during the twentieth century.

Stacked onto record store shelves on January 24, 1972, *Paul Simon* looked like a homey affair. Cover photographs shot by Peggy catch the newly solo artist peeking out from beneath the fur-lined hood of a heavy winter parka, his lips caught in a small, shy smile. Like the photo Paul McCartney's wife Linda shot for the cover of his first post-Beatles album,* he looks thinner and less burdened than he did on the cover of his group's last album. But while *McCartney*'s one-man band solo music was as homemade as its package, *Paul Simon,* for all its casual-seeming arrangements and performances, is anything but. Each song comes with at least one extraordinary performance set within: a reg-

---

* The back cover, sure, but it's the portrait of McCartney, his baby daughter tucked into his winter coat, that pops into your mind when you think about the album.

gae band here, Peruvian instruments there, Latin percussion, a great bottleneck guitar solo, jazz fiddle, and more.

There was plenty of discomfort at the heart of his new tunes, but the married thirty-year-old Paul had traded the theoretical angst of youth for the real grind of adult life in the modern world. The city is cruel, friends get strung out, relationships fall apart, even your subconscious gets overrun by fascist dictators, but the album is more tense than it is resigned. There are flashes of wit, active resistance, and even hope, as in "Mother and Child Reunion," the finished version of the barely sketched groove he'd recorded in Jamaica. When Paul and Peggy's dog was killed by a car, Paul channeled his grief into a lyric built around the name of an eggs-and-chicken dish he'd seen on the menu of a Chinese restaurant in the West Village. But the mourning in the verses is leavened by the persistent bounce of the rhythm, particularly combined with gospel piano highlights and the passionate voices of the backup singers, who find the uplift waiting just beyond the tragedy, the soul's ascension back into the arms of its creator.

The comfort of faith in "Mother and Child" is lost in "Duncan," which counterintuitively pairs the story of a salt-stained runaway from Maine's fishing piers with Peruvian flutes and strings. While the song is clearly descended from both "The Boxer" and "El Condor Pasa," its title character, a guitar-playing youngster whose full name is the Yankee-to-the-core Lincoln Duncan, finds communion with God in the form of a female evangelist who relieves him of his virginity, leaving him "Just thanking the Lord for my fingers, for my fingers." "Everything Put Together Falls Apart" and "Run That Body Down" describe the perils of overindulgence from two perspectives, the first as a gentle lecture to a strung-out friend; the second, an autobiographical account.

Dystopian visions play out in "Papa Hobo" (life in Detroit), "Paranoia Blues" (life in New York City), "Peace Like a River" (a dream of life in a wicked totalitarian regime), and "Congratulations" (life in a troubled marriage). Throughout, the music leaps and then hangs back. The melodic uplift in the groove of "Mother and Child Reunion" is swept aside by the meandering, nearly a-melodic "Everything Put Together Falls Apart." The joyful bounce of the Stéphane Grappelli track Paul called "Hobo's Blues" makes way for the tinny *skronk* of "Paranoia Blues." The spirit of inventiveness, particularly when it comes to blending sounds in unlikely ways, is as striking as it is unprecedented. Mainstream American radio had never entertained reggae music until "Mother and Child Reunion," the album's lead single, jumped into *Billboard*'s top five. The Latin-inspired "Me and Julio Down by the Schoolyard" did nearly as well a few months later. The vaguely naughty song (the tale of some awful yet never-described scandal that took place between the narrator and his neighborhood pal Julio) made people dance even though its rhythm was made entirely by percussion and the *chunk-chunk* of an unplugged electric guitar, its dampened strings being strummed hard.

As a solo debut, *Paul Simon* does a fine job of stepping away from the Simon and Garfunkel institution without going so far that listeners wouldn't know what to make of it. Some songs are weaker than others ("Everything Put Together Falls Apart" is a trifle, and the gospel grandeur of "Congratulations" feels overblown), but critics sang happily, hoisting the record to No. 4 on *Billboard*'s album chart and moving nearly 1.5 million copies in its first year. Yet Paul was less than happy with the results. When lead *Rolling Stone* critic Jon Landau's celebratory review described the album as a bit depressive, Paul got so upset he delayed an interview with the *New Yorker* for two weeks because, as a Columbia Records publicist explained to the writer, Landau had missed all the irony and humor in the songs. Soon thereafter, though, Paul was happy to have Landau interview him for a lengthy *Rolling Stone* feature, and their talk ran deep enough to read like a kind of public therapy session, particularly when it came to Paul's relationship with Artie. "We get along by observing certain rules," Paul said, explaining that the rules mostly involved each of them avoiding doing or saying things he knew would irritate the other.

Still, even if *Paul Simon* had sold more than a million copies, it was a speck on the face of *Simon and Garfunkel's Greatest Hits,* a single album collection Columbia shipped to record stores in mid-June. Centered on original studio tracks, the album also included four previously unheard live tracks recorded during the 1969–1970 tours, and the combination hits-and-rarities lineup went on to rival *Bridge Over Troubled Water*'s sales, easily outselling Paul's debut in 1972 and going on to sell fourteen million copies in the next decade or so. Paul chose not to mount a solo tour for his album, but when the actor Warren Beatty asked him and Artie to reunite for a benefit concert for the presidential campaign of South Dakota senator George McGovern, the Democratic candidate attempting to unseat President Richard Nixon, they both agreed to do it. Held in Madison Square Garden, the show played off McGovern's campaign pledge to reunite the country by featuring reunions of disbanded partnerships: Simon and Garfunkel, of course; Peter, Paul, and Mary; and most exciting for some audience members, the comedy team of Mike Nichols and Elaine May, both of whom had gone on to big careers in theater and the movies.

As the final act on the bill, Paul and Artie walked out to a standing ovation and, after waiting for the applause to fade, launched into the opening chords of "Mrs. Robinson." Back in their traditional two-voices-and-a-guitar form, their harmonies rang as clear and effortless as ever, particularly in the second song, a close harmony arrangement of "El Condor Pasa." They seemed relaxed, joking to the crowd — Paul got a particular kick when someone requested "Voices of Old People," the *Bookends* montage of Artie's interviews with the aged. They sang the third verse of "The Boxer" ("After changes upon changes we are more or less the same . . ."), which they had edited out in favor of Artie's countermelody, then made a chugging ska arrangement of "Cecilia" into a medley with a harmonized "Mother and Child Reunion" and, a bit more awkward in its new Jamaican getup, "Bye Bye Love." More familiar renditions of "Scarborough Fair" and "The 59th Street Bridge Song" and a particularly resonant "America" came next.

When they started rehearsing for the show, Paul told Artie he wanted to try something different for the inevitable closer, "Bridge

Over Troubled Water." They wouldn't have a pianist for the show, just Paul doing what he could to replicate Larry Knechtel's performance on his six-string guitar. Rather than having Artie sing the song alone, Paul proposed that they sing it together, Artie on the first verse, Paul on the second, and both harmonizing on the third verse and the climactic final chorus. At first Artie didn't know how to respond. Did Paul really think it would sound better, or had he just found another way to shove him aside? "Cut me open and look at all my contradictory reactions," Artie said a few months later. "Do I think that's a good idea? Do I trust? Do I sense his ego trying to subtract from my ego?" No matter. Artie decided to do it Paul's way, just as he had decided to help raise money for a candidate he didn't like very much. After two years away, he was eager to step back onto the concert stage, in sold-out Madison Square Garden, no less, with friends and heroes on the bill. And as they stood on-stage, weaving their voices together in public for the first time in two years, they were heroes, too.

Both their faces tilting to the silver microphones, they looked out at the arena, filled for the evening by a small city of thoughtful liberal urbanites, a gathering of the tribe. "Come home, America," McGovern trumpeted that year. Shed your fears and unbolt your doors; hold out your hand to your friends, your neighbors, total strangers, your rivals, and your enemies, too. They played for half an hour, the crowd with them the whole time, clapping to the rhythmic songs, singing along to "The 59th Street Bridge Song"; then "Bridge Over Troubled Water," that modern hymn to unity, to connection, to the old-fashioned notion that united hearts, hands, and voices can build anything. Remember when people really believed that? It could happen again, and here were Simon and Garfunkel back together, the sound of their voices leading us all home. "We've all come to look for America."

Just a few weeks later, *Rolling Stone* published Paul's interview with Jon Landau. Paul was pictured on the magazine's cover, a mid-distance portrait showing him, head to foot, walking toward the camera palms raised, a cap pulled down close to his eyes — but not close enough to cover the annoyance creasing his brow and, seemingly, erupting from his half-open mouth. He had a lot to say in the article: about how he'd always carried the vast bulk of Simon and Garfunkel's creative burden. All those stories they had told about Artie arranging the songs, or even *helping* to arrange them, were nonsense. "Anybody who knows anything would know that that was a fabrication. How can one guy write the songs and let the other guy do the arranging?" —

an odd argument, considering how often songwriters work with arrangers, and there were many accounts of Artie doing exactly that. Yet maybe Paul was venting something else entirely.

"At a certain point it became very hard to take criticism from each other . . . I felt that if I had to go through these kind of personality abrasions I didn't want to continue to do it." Meanwhile, Artie had abandoned him so he could become a movie star. At that point, they just naturally went their separate ways. "I went to do my album by myself. We didn't say that's the end . . . but it became apparent by the time the movie was out and by the time my album was out that it was over."

"As I stand right now I have no partnership with Artie," Paul said. "I find it a relief."

Louis and Belle Simon in later years. "My father is the person who most influenced my thinking and my life," Paul said.

1

At the height of "Hey, Schoolgirl," old friends and new pop sensations.

3

Tom and Jerry, in their red jackets, white shirts, and black bow ties, rocking a homecoming dance, circa 1958.

2

4   The guitar-thumpin' camp counselor, summer
1958 at Camp Washington Lodge, Long Island,
New York.

Forest Hills High School,   5
class of 1958.

When Paul (right corner, with
guitar) took control of Alpha
Epsilon Pi's Follies entries,
the fraternity won the Queens
College competition every year.

6

During his senior
year Paul (first row,
second from left)
was the president
of Queens College's
chapter of the
Alpha Epsilon Pi
fraternity.

7

8

9

When Paul Simon finished class at Queens College, Jerry Landis
pursued his music career in the recording studios of Midtown
Manhattan. Seen here with ex–Queens College student Carol
Klein, better known as Carole King.

After graduating college
Paul went to law school.
He wouldn't stay very
long.

10

Relocating to
London, Paul
steadily built
a following
in folk clubs
all over the
British Isles.

12

Established in the Greenwich Village music scene, Paul launched a folk-focused song publishing company with musician Barry Kornfeld.

13

11

Reunited as the folk duo Simon and Garfunkel, Paul and Artie juggled their ambitions and identities.

After "The Sound of Silence" made Simon and Garfunkel into stars, Paul's appearance evolved to fit his new status.

Paul and Artie, backstage in the mid-1960s, worked together to make their albums and shows as perfect as possible.

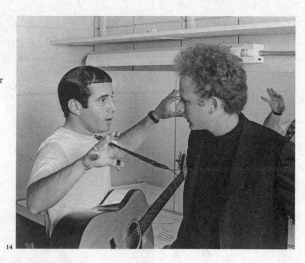

14

15

As Simon and Garfunkel's fame grew in the late 1960s, they were regarded as generational spokesmen and cultural oracles.

After the Simon and Garfunkel breakup Paul made a new life, and a family, with Peggy.

16

Increasingly successful as
a solo performer in the
1970s, Paul made fun of
his brooding reputation on
Saturday Night Live.

SNL producer and new
best friend Lorne Michaels
(middle, with Paul on one
side and George Harrison
on the other) encouraged
Paul to write and perform
in television and movies.

18

By 1975 Paul and Artie were back to being friends. An attempt to collaborate again wouldn't last.

Paul's twelve-year relationship with Carrie Fisher was close, passionate, and ultimately devastating.

The sounds of Ladysmith Black Mambazo and South African pop music would revive Paul's spirits, his career, and his penchant for controversy.

The Capeman premiere, January 1998. The smiles would fade when the reviews came in the morning.

CHAPTER 15
THAT'S IT, THAT'S
THAT GROOVE

When he told the Supreme Court of New York County where his career stood circa late 1972, Paul sounded gloomy. His solo album had, in comparison to *Bridge Over Troubled Water,* been a flop. In the first months of the 1970s, he had set out to make himself into an entirely different performer. "And in effect begin a new career — as Paul Simon," he declared. "No longer can I rely on the great popularity of Simon and Garfunkel but rather must prove to the public and to CBS that the popularity and international acclaim I now possess can be sustained in this new phase of my career." The professional future of the new recording artist Paul Simon, he continued, would be decided by the fate of his second album, which would be released just before he set out to reintroduce himself to concert audiences all around the world.

He was bullshitting, mostly. *Bridge*'s popularity had been so far off the charts of anyone's experience, it would take thirteen years and Michael Jackson to outdo it. *Paul Simon* had been a win by every conceivable measure, and so on and so forth, which was one of the reasons he had to sic his lawyers on the Edward B. Marks Music Corporation. Now that he had become a star in his own right, his former employer and, briefly, publisher had done a deep crawl through its archives in search of the songs Paul had sold them a decade earlier. Having exhumed not only lead sheets but also, in some cases, demo recordings of "Carlos Dominguez," "He Was My Brother," "The Side of a Hill," "Bleecker Street," and the Simon-Garfunkel arrangement of "Benedictus," they recognized the potential of a belated return on their investment and mapped out an *Early Songs of Paul Simon* songbook and an album of Paul's recordings of the songs. And instead of crediting them to Jerry Landis or to Paul Kane, as he'd preferred in those days, they were opting for his real name and therein lay his predictable ire.

Paul won an injunction against Marks, then made a settlement with the company. Then it was back to smooth sailing for Paul's business organization, the daily operations of which he'd entrusted to Mike Tannen, the young associate from Orenstein, Arrow who had made himself an expert on the Simon and Garfunkel account and then a member of Paul's inner circle of friends. It was easy to see why they hit it off so well. Tannen was another physically compact, hotly ambitious Jewish kid with a professional music man for a father, the well-known country music publisher Nat Tannen, who had died unexpectedly when Mike was in college. Nat and Harold Orenstein, whose firm specialized in entertainment law, had been close, and when Mike graduated from New York University Law School in 1965, he had a job waiting for him.

Tannen thrived, and in 1969 Orenstein sent him to Los Angeles to open a West Coast office for the firm. Paul wasn't happy to see him go, but made a point of driving him and Mary to the airport, where he told them not to worry about getting a cab when they got to LA; he'd have a car waiting for them. The limo Tannen had expected turned out to be a new Porsche, a gift Paul intended as a symbol of his confidence in his friend's future prospects. "I think you're the best," Paul told Tannen when his flabbergasted friend called to say thanks. "I wanted you to think you're as good as or better than anyone out there." It was easy for them to keep in touch, given the amount of time Paul spent working in the Hollywood recording studios, and when he started gearing up for a solo career in 1971, just as Tannen had decided to move back to New York, Paul asked the lawyer to help steer the business end of his ventures.

Tannen took the job happily, moving back to New York and setting up shop in a town house on East Sixty-First Street, between Fifth and Madison. Along with the offices for Paul's central enterprises, Tannen also set up a suite for Paul's publishing company, Charing Cross, which had first operated in a space beneath the Orenstein, Arrow offices in Los Angeles. That office was managed by Ian Hoblyn, a former airline steward who worked with a few secretaries to administer the rights to the songs Paul had written.

Already known among insiders for his business savvy — Bob Dylan came to him for advice before he started renegotiating his publishing and recording deals — Paul had built an impressive fortune by his thirtieth birthday. But while he knew it made financial sense to invest his money in real estate or some industry or another, he had little interest in ordinary businesses. He wanted his money to reflect his artistic sensibility and his lifelong involvement with music. Tannen suggested he follow the example of the great songwriter Frank Loesser, who eventually made more money as the publisher of other songwriters than he did as the author of "Heart and Soul," "Baby, It's Cold Outside," and so many other hit songs. Paul liked that idea, so they started DeShufflin Inc., a company they could use to both support emerging artists' careers and get a piece of the hit songs they wrote.

The company's first clients were Maggie and Terre Roche, the suburban New Jersey singing/songwriting duo Paul had welcomed into his NYU class during the winter of 1970. Two years later, the sisters had come from out of the blue, calling his office every day for a week until Paul called back to hear Maggie tell him about all the new songs they'd written since the end of class. Paul sent them to Tannen, who invited them to his family's apartment to play a few tunes. When they were done, he made an offer on the spot, laying out terms that were surprisingly generous. He and Paul would not only give them a cash advance to live on while they readied themselves to record, but also rent them an apartment, get them top instructors to improve their guitar and piano technique, pay all their recording expenses, and then, with Tannen serving as their manager, help them land a deal with a record company. After they settled into a place in Greenwich Village, Paul took Maggie and Terre on a buying spree to Colony Records so they would have cool music to listen to while they prepared to start their careers in the big time. He had them sing on one of the songs for his next solo album, and when it came out months later, they were astonished to find their pictures on its inner cover, a deliberate move to create an instant buzz around the unknown duo. In the wake of some tough childhood experiences, Terre Roche wrote in her self-published memoir, *Blabbermouth,* that the career boost couldn't have come at a more crucial time. "Paul Simon and Michael Tannen gave us a new lease on life."

Although he was happily settled with Peggy, Paul still struggled with depression, though he found some relief when he'd read enough political philosophy to conclude that his gloom was actually the made-up pain of the middle-class intellectual. It was, he said, "a student's fantasy, not the pain of poverty, war or even the tremendous emotional pain that people endure daily." Peggy's interest in feminist theory led Paul to the work of Kate Millett, whose controversial 1970 book, *Sexual Politics,* made him believe that his insecurities and hostility had, in the midst of a male-defined social and political construct, pushed him to the edge of violence. "The whole white male myth makes it imperative that the hero, the winner, be the Great Dane," he explained. "That's why I'm right there with the feminists, because I think the whole thing is debasing. Remember, there was rape long before capitalism."

Peggy learned she was pregnant during the winter of 1972, and when their son, Harper, was born on September 7, 1972, fatherhood grounded Paul all the more. Had he ever felt so relaxed and happy so much of the time? Picking up a nylon-string classical guitar one day, his fingers found a set of sweet, jazzy chords to suit the first unalloyed love ballad he'd ever written, a simply stated declaration to the woman who had inspired it. Singing at first in the voice of a restless traveler, Paul gave the song the title "Let Me Live in Your City." Realizing that he'd already been home for quite a while, he changed it to "Something So Right," in which his customary darkness plays as comic effect. "It's such an unusual sight," he sings of his odd sense of joy. "I can't get used to something so right."

The new songs were upbeat, flooded with the light of gospel praise and the kinetic energy of modern rhythm and blues — faith and frolic, grace and gratitude, all playing out in a highly imperfect world. Listening to the laid-back funk of the Staple Singers' "I'll Take You There" on the radio one day, he heard the church-meets-roadhouse sound he was after. The Staple Singers always worked with a backing group, though, so to figure out who had played what, Paul got in touch with Al Bell at the Memphis-based label Stax Records to see if the black guys who played with the Staples might be available to work with a white artist. Bell laughed: they were certainly available, but they weren't black. The band on the Staples' record, the

Swampers, was the house band at the Muscle Shoals recording studio in northern Alabama, and they were all, to a man, white. A bunch of farm boys who had spent years at FAME Studios playing on so many hits (by Percy Sledge, Aretha Franklin, Wilson Pickett, Otis Redding, Etta James, and others) that they were, without a doubt, the definitive soul band of the era. And all Paul had to do to get their sound on his record was call them up and book some time in their studio.

When Tannen got through to the Swampers, they were between sessions, playing cards in the lounge/office area of the squat industrial building they had made into their studio. Guitarist Jimmy Johnson took the call, holding his hand over the receiver to consult with his partners. Not entirely sure they were speaking to someone who actually did represent such a preeminent rock star, they made their demands increasingly rich, up to the point where they said they would need a producer's credit, and the royalties that went along with it, if Paul *really* wanted to play with them. To their surprise, Tannen, having consulted with Paul, said that would be fine. When Tannen's letter of agreement arrived a few days later, written on Paul Simon's corporate stationery, the musicians got excited. As the appointed week grew closer, one of them brought in cassettes of Paul's first solo album and *Bridge Over*

Troubled Water so everyone could take a close listen. Without a cassette player in the studio, they all came out to the parking lot so they could pile into a car, crank up the volume, and really get a sense of how the guy made records. He was *real* good, they decided — but so were they, and if he wanted to throw a challenge their way, they were going to catch it and throw it right back.

Paul flew down to Muscle Shoals with Phil Ramone, the hit-savvy producer he had hired to work on the new album, discovering that the town's only hotel, a Holiday Inn, had set its marquee with a large sign: WELCOME PAUL SIMON AND PHIL RAMONE. After checking in, they met the Swampers at a nearby restaurant for an introductory dinner where they snuck in enough bottles[*] for everyone to have a few drinks and get nice and friendly. When the waitress asked the musicians which one of them was the star, they pointed to Paul and told her his name. As she absorbed this, Jimmy Johnson, a big boy with curly red hair and a bonus-size gut beneath his overalls, caught her eye and smiled: "And I'm Artie Garfunkel!" When she turned to look, her eyes widened. *Really?* "We all got a big laugh out of that one," says bassist David Hood. When Paul paid the check a little later, he

---

[*] Muscle Shoals, like most of northern Alabama in those days, was in a dry county.

included a tip so generous that the waitress chased him down outside with a fistful of bills, shouting that he had forgotten all his money on the table.

Paul had booked the Muscle Shoals studio for four days, hoping to get a completed take of one song, the plangent "Take Me to the Mardi Gras." Sung in the voice of a man setting out for New Orleans's annual bacchanal, the tune was all cheerful anticipation: a man on his way to his favorite city for its best party of the year. But as Paul told keyboardist Barry Beckett, the words left out one vital detail: "He wants to go, he's gonna go," Paul explained. "Nowhere in the song does it say that he might *not* get to go." That was the trick. Paul needed Beckett's keyboards to project that feeling of doubt. The keyboardist nodded, no problem at all, and they all set out on the trek to the perfect sound that Paul could sense but not quite describe. Like the man in the song, there was always a chance they wouldn't get there in the end.

Two takes and twenty minutes later, the basic track to "Take Me to the Mardi Gras" was finished. Paul listened to the tape once, twice, three times, and had no doubt. Ramone, whose standards of production were every bit as refined as his client's, heard it, too: that song had been *played.* So what next? Paul took out his notebook of songs and leafed through the pages, coming up with

388

"Loves Me Like a Rock." He'd worked with some players in New York to get a gospel lope on this tune, but it wasn't working. He liked his acoustic guitar part, so he had Hood and drummer Roger Hawkins play to that, and there it was again, two or three takes later, another finished backing track.

He went back to the notebook, and out came "Kodachrome," "One Man's Ceiling Is Another Man's Floor," and "St. Judy's Comet" — and by the end of the week, they had tracked half the songs Paul had planned for the album, and all of them with the snappy, soulful charm that flowed through that country-rustic studio as steadily as the current sliding past the banks of the Tennessee River. The Dixie Hummingbirds[*] gospel quintet came in from South Carolina and did such a great job rehearsing their harmonies on "Loves Me Like a Rock" that Paul and Ramone scrapped the real takes to use the one captured when they were standing in a circle practicing with their heads bowed together. The Rev. Claude Jeter, the celestial lead singer of the Swan Silvertones who had helped inspire "Bridge Over Troubled Water," added his high falsetto to "Mardi Gras," and when Paul and Ramone drove to Malaco Studios in Jackson, Mississippi, to record

[*] The Dixie Hummingbirds recorded for Bess and Ike Merenstein at Apollo Records in the late 1940s.

389

New Orleans's Dixieland favorites with the Onward Brass Band, they found the musicians in full parade regalia, from the tips of their caps to the toes of their shiny shoes. Maggie and Terre Roche rode a Greyhound bus down from New York to sing on "Was a Sunny Day" and flew to London to work with producer/arranger (and ex-bassist of the Animals) Paul Samwell-Smith to get a stately string arrangement to go along with the one folk song on the album.

In the wake of his trip to Jamaica, Paul stopped worrying about how he'd be received by the musicians and singers he traveled to work with. They all knew he was a big star and that he paid extremely well for their time and help. If he wanted to project their sound and their names to his enormous audience, how could that be a problem? Better still, Paul didn't hold back his admiration for the other musicians' work. By the time he ventured into someone else's home turf, he'd know their catalogues and be able to cite specific songs and licks from their records. Paul always came in with a sense of the feeling he was after for each song, but also with a willingness to hear the other musicians' ideas on how to get it. And if the backroads studios were less fancy than the ones he used in the city, that was just part of their sound and vibe.

It was raining hard the day he first walked

into the Muscle Shoals Sound Studio, and the musicians had spent part of the morning sticking maxi pads to the control room ceiling in order to keep the building's leaky roof from dripping onto the recording equipment. The baffling they used to focus the acoustics in the studio consisted entirely of burlap bags, and the between-takes goofing and guffawing was a fixture, too, which may have been Paul's favorite part of the sessions. "He liked hanging with just good ol' boys," Hood recalls. "I think he thought of it as like hanging out with the ball team or something, because we were definitely a team."

Paul was so taken with the Muscle Shoals spirit that he had the musicians double as a backing chorus for "One Man's Ceiling Is Another Man's Floor," making sure they were loose enough to laugh and carry on while they did it. Paul expected the musicians to put pieces of themselves into their performances. He never wrote out parts for the musicians to play; he'd just play and sing the song with his acoustic guitar, toss out a few words about how he hoped it might sound, and let them figure out how they could get him there. It was a pretty standard way to work with pop music players, particularly the ones who had as unique a sound as the Muscle Shoals guys did. The big studios in New York and Los Angeles teemed with technical players who could play perfect renditions of every form of music without breaking a sweat. But Paul wasn't after perfect. He wanted the guys whose fingers went naturally to the notes and rhythms any another musician, even the superior technician, wouldn't think to play. The rhythmic and melodic hooks to "I'll Take You There," the Staple Singers hit that had clamped itself to Paul's ear, were both written by bassist David Hood in the midst of a studio jam session. Similarly, the descending piano chords that open and close "One Man's Ceiling" were introduced to the track by keyboardist Barry Beckett. Yet neither Beckett nor Hood (nor anyone else in their organization) had argued for writing credits — and not just because Paul, who paid well over standard session rates and had also given them a coproducer's piece of the royalties, was being so generous. As most studio musicians agreed, if you wanted to get writer's credit, you were welcome to write your own songs and put out your own albums.

Released on May 5, 1973, and titled *There Goes Rhymin' Simon,* a phrase Peggy heard herself saying about her husband in a dream, Paul's second post–Simon and Garfunkel album came dressed for a party, its cover a whimsical mix of a rainbow, with a scattering of stars and confetti, above a mask-wearing mask across a graph paper backdrop like a high schooler's collage. And just in case that wasn't enough to convince you this wasn't the work of a gloomy young intellectual, go to the opening line of the opening song to get the idea: "When I think back on all the crap I learned in high school / It's a wonder I can think at all . . ."

And off he goes, running smooth on a sleek gospel-cum-rhythm and blues groove, the snare drum snapping in lockstep to the bass's liquid propulsion and Paul's acoustic guitar in the middle, revving the engine with a spinning riff that is in turn set off by Beckett's double duty on the keys, comping lightly on the electric and ripping the hell out of a honky-tonk piano, first with rapid-fire chatter, then a succession of eighty-eight-key swoops, one going up, the next going down. That's "Kodachrome," the nostalgia song for anti-nostalgics who know that photos, just like memories, are rarely the best measure of what used to be. "Everything looks worse in black and white," he concludes, and the tune finds a whole other gear as the final chorus segues into a double-time sprint, all hands racing so fast that they blow right through Paul's that's-enough-guys shout "Okay!" and keep on zooming, piano jangling, drums kicking, horns blaring.

From song to song, musician to musician, style to style, *There Goes Rhymin' Simon* runs on exuberance. "Kodachrome" fades into the languorous doo-wop of "Tenderness," Paul singing sweetly above the billowing *oooooh*s of the Dixie Hummingbirds, admitting everything to his estranged friend while still holding out for a little empathy to go along with the bitter truth. "You don't have to lie to me / Just give me some tenderness beneath your honesty." "Take Me to the Mardi Gras" follows, its dreams of New Orleans, along with the Rev. Claude Jeter's honeyed falsetto, intoxicating enough to float you to the city no matter where you're listening. And more: "Something So Right" is unadorned feeling from a lover who has, against all expectations, surrendered his distance. Paul's nylon-string guitar hints at the blues, then falls into line with the doubled basses (one acoustic, one electric) and doubled keyboards (ibid.), vibes, and then a chirping flute to let love speak as directly as possible. Songs about the past, about breaking up, about coming together, about fatherhood, about failing gracefully and feeling sanctified by your mama's embrace — all of them different roads to acceptance, to letting go, to simply *being* without worrying about being something other than who you are.

The outlier on the album, lyrically as well as stylistically, is "American Tune," a folk-style song (Paul's voice, an acoustic guitar, and string quartet) that retells the immigrant's story from the sour perspective of the early 1970s, the time of Nixon, Watergate, and the fraying of the nation's spirit. Adapted from a Lutheran hymn written by the German composer Hans Leo Hassler in 1600, "American Tune" begins with a weary traveler miles away from home and still distant from the glorious city he seeks. And it's not just him. Everyone he knows feels just as lost, as if the road beneath their feet has bent in the wrong direction. When he sleeps at night he sees the Statue of Liberty, the immigrants' beacon for nearly a century, only now she's packed up her torch and taken her leave, bound for somewhere a huddled mass can still catch a break. For the child of an immigrant family, one of the hundreds of millions of citizens whose forebears were delivered to this land on a vessel of some sort, the contrast between hope and reality is almost too stark to contemplate. And still we must accept our fate and our daily burden.

Tomorrow's gonna be another working day
and I'm trying to get some rest
That's all I'm trying, to get some rest.

Commonly cited as one of his best songs, "American Tune" grounds the rest of *There Goes Rhymin' Simon* in the larger story of the nation, particularly in its wholesale blend of cultures and styles. Even if the bleak vision of "American Tune" weren't brightened by the singer's resolve to work another day, the album's multifarious sounds and voices would be enough to call Liberty back to her grimy pedestal in New York Harbor. All the songs work, most quite magnificently. But the most essential moment on the album doesn't come in a song: in the seconds before "Loves Me Like a Rock" begins, Dixie Hummingbirds leader Ira Tucker, still rehearsing in a tight circle with the rest of the group, draws their attention to the magical approach they've all been trying to find.

TUCKER: Mm-hmm, that's it, that's that groove.
PAUL: (in the distance) K.
TUCKER: (whispered) Let go.
THE DIXIE HUMMINGBIRDS: (voicing a re-sounding G chord) Ah-oooohhh!

Paul hits some downstrokes on his guitar, the bass and drums kick in, and they all sing glorious praise to the Jewish boy's solid rock of a mother, though it could be anyone's mother, or anyone's God — and actually it's all of them put together and *mm-hmm, that's it, that's that groove.*

The public fell hard for what they heard. In the United States alone *There Goes Rhymin' Simon* sold more than two million copies during its first year. Released to go along with the album, the lead single, "Kodachrome," spent months on the Hot 100, peaking at No. 2. The follow-up, "Loves Me Like a Rock," was also a smash, and also peaked at No. 2. The album's lighter tone did nothing to change Paul's status as a critic's favorite. "Testifies anew to a major talent that simply will not stop growing," said *Time;* "If I were shipwrecked on a desert island, I'd be happy if I could hear just one album: Paul Simon's . . . *There Goes Rhymin' Simon,*" said the *New York Times.* And so on, in virtually every other major publication that reviewed pop records. Why would anyone want to resist such a joyous yet literate collection of pop songs? The album topped sales charts in Spain and Sweden, and scaled top tens, and sometimes top fives, in countries all around the world.

He had to tour. That was part of the pleasure of being a songwriter, taking your work to your fans, seeing them smile, then hearing their applause when it was over. Even if it got exhausting or boring, and he got to feeling that he didn't want to be anywhere near a stage, it was the only way to keep the buzz going, to keep the records moving in and out of the stores. When *Paul Simon*'s sales ebbed at 1.5 million, he went to ask Clive Davis what had gone wrong. The executive didn't hesitate: "You didn't tour to support it, did you?"

He'd had his reasons, only some of them having to do with his fear of facing an audience without Artie at his side. He'd wanted to have more solo songs to play, and to figure out the best way to present them: Just him and his guitar? Accompanied by a three- or four-piece backing band? Or with guest stars who could take a few turns in the spotlight on their own? Ultimately Paul designed a show that gave him all the above while also resolving the two most daunting questions standing between him and a solo concert tour: Would he perform "Bridge Over Troubled Water"? And if he did, how could he sing it without Artie? As the tour grew closer, Paul started to have nightmares, surrealistic horror shows where he'd walk onstage and find his microphone standing far above his head, or a glass wall separating him from an audience that couldn't hear a note of what he was playing and singing. Typical anxiety dreams — you could unlock their symbolism with both hands cuffed behind your back while in a trunk at the bottom of the East River. But that still didn't relieve his fears, or keep his subconscious from its troubled imaginings.

When Paul launched the tour at the Boston Music Hall on May 6, 1973, he opened the show alone, strumming and singing "Me and Julio Down by the Schoolyard" and "Run That Body Down" before dipping into the

Simon and Garfunkel catalogue with a solo rendition of "The 59th Street Bridge Song (Feelin' Groovy)." Jon Landau was in the audience, seeing Paul's nerves during his solo acoustic songs, then noticing him ease as the band joined for the *Rhymin' Simon* material, a lilting "Was a Sunny Day" that segued into "Cecilia" and then a hushed "American Tune." About fifteen songs into the set, he introduced Urabamba, a Chilean folk group Los Incas founder Jorge Milchberg had formed, to back him on "El Condor Pasa" and "Duncan," then left the stage to let the group play two of their own songs before returning to end the set together with "The Boxer." The structure of the second set was the same, starting with a long solo stretch, then upping the energy with the Jessy Dixon Singers, a five-piece gospel group that included drums, a bass, and Mr. Dixon himself on vocals and organ.

As Landau wrote in his review for the *Boston Phoenix,* this was where the show turned magical. ("Imagine an American gospel group singing backup to a white folksinger's reggae tune," he wrote. "Even more difficult, imagine Simon pulling the thing off as if he was born to do it.") Starting with "Mother and Child Reunion," they moved into a six-voice arrangement of "The Sound of Silence," the group laying their rich harmonies behind Paul's lead. Paul left the stage so the group could perform two of their own songs, then returned for the evening's climax, an arrangement of "Bridge Over Troubled Water" reminiscent of the gospel version Aretha Franklin recorded in 1971, which sounded fiery enough to be a completely different song. Built around Dixon's church organ and Paul's guitar, with the Dixon group's bass and drums playing softly behind, the arrangement is slower than the original, the choir stepping in and out to echo some lines and joining in unison to emphasize others. The group plays in full force for the final verse, then softens into the start of a coda featuring Paul and one of the women repeating variations of "I will ease your mind." Harmonizing here, echoing one another there, spurring Paul to a few shouted repetitions, his voice rising before melting back into the other singers' arms for a round of "I believe, I believe, I believe, I believe I will ease your mind," then "I believe, I believe, I really do believe," and then drifting into one final unadorned "I believe, I believe I really do believe, I will ease your mind." It was, Landau wrote, "a rare, privileged moment, a musical experience of the type I had forgotten takes place on the stages of rock concerts."

Landau concluded his review by noting how different Paul's voice sounded when in the company of the gospel singers on "Bridge." No longer hemmed in by his own seriousness and the restrictions of two-voice close harmony, he'd become a new singer. Free of inhibition, liberated from the complexities of his own mind, so lost in feeling that thinking was beside the point. "Perhaps sometime in the future he will elect to do more with it."

Separated into monthlong (give or take) legs, the *Rhymin'* tour continued for a year, starting with a few weeks in American concert halls in May and then heading to London for a handful of shows at the Royal Albert Hall, then returning to New York in early June for a one-nighter on a larger bill at Long Island's Nassau Coliseum. A set of American college dates ran through the fall, followed in April by Paul's first performances in Japan.

Even from the start, Paul and Peggy made an unlikely match: the New York City–raised artist/celebrity and the church-raised girl from Bybee, Tennessee. Paul's life in Manhattan, including the professional artist part, flowed naturally from his childhood, while Peggy, even after fifteen years of being among (and married to) show business professionals, continued to feel like an outsider in the nightclubs, dressing rooms, and penthouse apartments. As Paul grew more comfortable in his fame, and more familiar with the movie stars he'd met through Mike Nichols in New York and during his own long stays in Los

Angeles, the couple's bond grew strained. Paul was always an attentive father. His job required him to be away from home — Peggy had always known that — but when he was home he treasured his time with toddler Harper. Yet there was a basic incompatibility between husband and wife. The runaway child of the chaotic southern family craved structure, and the dutiful son of the aspiring immigrant family was dying to cut loose.

The split was nearly as amiable as a divorce could be. Paul got Mike Tannen to represent his side in the settlement, and also asked him to help Peggy hire a good lawyer to make her case. It sounds more manipulative than it turned out to be, given that Tannen hired Gertrude Mainzer, a Holocaust survivor known for being a fierce advocate in the courtroom. Paul moved into the Stanhope Hotel for a few months before buying a Central Park West apartment, a close walk from the family's town house on Ninety-Fourth Street, making it easy for them to share custody of Harper. The arrangement also made it easy for Paul to expand his social life, moving into a nighttime circuit of actors, musicians, and writers that ran through spotlit premieres, celebrity-rich after-parties, and Elaine's, the exclusive dining room on Second Avenue on the Upper East Side. On wilder nights he might find himself on the shiny dance floors and shadowed nooks of

Studio 54, fast on its way to becoming the hottest discotheque in the world. Soon Paul's well-known face was spotted in the company of starlets and other enchanting women, including the rising bistro singer/actress Bette Midler, movie actress Shelley Duvall, *Saturday Night Live* performer Gilda Radner, and the celebrity portraitist Edie Baskin, who would lead him into the center of another set of tastemakers. Paul became accustomed to riding in a chauffeured Cadillac limousine, a luxury that made him feel like a character in a film about high society. "You pull up in front of a place, just like in the movies, and when you get out the driver is there waiting for you. It's the New York dream come true."

Many nights, Paul preferred to stay in his apartment, reading and playing with Harper or, if the energy was going his way, discovering the form of a new song. When Paul's grasp on his music slipped, so did he, spinning into days of free-associating gloom, fretting over whatever consumed him at the moment. Maybe it was all a cover for the hot bolts he'd been feeling inside his left index finger, the captain among the five digits that coaxed music from the neck of his guitar. He'd had to take regular cortisone shots to dull the bite during the *Rhymin'* tour, and when he took it to his doctor, the news wasn't good. He'd developed calcium deposits, which not only hurt but also made his finger stiff and clumsy. Back home after the tour ended in mid-1974, he found that the only treatment his doctor could offer was rest, and lots of it. And it wasn't working.

How could he lead a life that didn't have a guitar at its center? For twenty years the instrument had been his dreamcatcher, his coal mine, his pot of gold. Virtually everything that mattered to him came through the mouth of his guitar. In a life built around change, it was the most crucial constant. Yet Paul was surprisingly sanguine. He took singing lessons. He boned up on orchestration. Most significantly, he studied music theory and composition. He had always drawn from a broader palette than the other rock/folk songwriters — being raised in a house filled with jazz and the great symphonies had given him a taste for structural complexity and hepcat intervals that most folk, rock, and blues-inspired writers wouldn't imagine. And that only made Paul keenly aware of everything he *didn't* know about music, particularly when his pen got stuck mid-song and he had no idea where to jump next.

Paul called Phil Ramone, the producer who had been so integral to *There Goes Rhymin' Simon,* asking if he knew an educated musician who could help open some new doors in Paul's songwriting ability. The tiny world being what it is, Ramone put Paul in touch with Chuck Israels, the music camp instructor

404

whom Paul met during his summer in Stockbridge in 1967. Israels was already a schooled musician back then, but his skill and reputation had grown over the years, and Paul was happy to submit to his tutelage. They started meeting regularly at Paul's apartment on Central Park West, Paul paying a hundred dollars a session (a fantastic sum for an hour-long lesson in those days) for Israels to detail the essentials of music composition — repetition, sequence, inversion, retrograde, retrograde inversion, augmentation, diminishment, and so on — to ease his way when his pen got stuck during a writing session. Not that Paul hadn't already incorporated those techniques into his songs; he'd just done it intuitively — which was great until his muse sputtered, reducing him to something like a blind man groping his way through a maze.

Reading music or being able to write in notation still held next to no interest for him. He was after some new writing techniques and a more strategic approach that would help him understand what he already had, recognize its melodic patterns, and let them reveal the way into new sections that grew naturally from themes that had been established in the song's earliest bars. Israels had other tricks, such as knowing when it was best to skip a troublesome section in order to write the end, thereby allowing Paul to return to the tough spot already knowing where it was headed. Appearing on Dick Cavett's late-night talk show in the midst of his studies, Paul took up his guitar to play the start of a song that was so lightly sketched it didn't even have a name. All he had, Paul demonstrated, were two verses about meeting an old girlfriend on the street, going out for a beer, and then going home to reflect on his inability to change. Both verses ended with the same line: "Still crazy after all these years." And while he had no idea where the story would go next, he said, he already knew what his musical choices were, and why they made sense. And he looked really happy about it.

Paul was so delighted with what Israels had taught him, he began to incorporate the bassist/composer into other parts of his life. Invited to a party at Paul's apartment, Israels found himself standing between Shelley Duvall, Mike Nichols, the actor Peter Boyle (then costarring in the smash comedy *Young Frankenstein*), and the British actor/writer Eric Idle, whose innovative troupe Monty Python's Flying Circus was rewriting the rules of comedy on both sides of the ocean. They all seemed nice and welcoming — Israels was Paul's guest; it was clear to them that he belonged — but the speed and complexity of their repartee left him speechless. Israels's parents were important musicians and teachers, too; his kid brother's godfather was Paul Robeson. He came home one afternoon to find Lead Belly sitting at the family's kitchen table, feasting on a chocolate cake that he washed down with glasses of Muscatel. Israels had also been an early protégé of eventual Simon and Garfunkel producer Tom Wilson, who had the college-age bassist play on sessions with Art Blakey, Hank Mobley, and other leading jazz players of the era. It was not a slow-moving crowd. But among Paul's friends that night, it was all Israels could do to keep a handle on his wineglass. "I know I'm smart, I know I'm educated," he says. "Generally I can hold my own. But around those people I'm a blithering idiot."

If Paul noticed, he didn't care. As he continued to write songs for the new album, he turned to Israels repeatedly for help, coming to him with songs that were half-written, maybe just in chunks, using his teacher to analyze what he had and to suggest where he might go next. When the recording started, he'd have Israels come to the studio, and once Ramone got to know him better, the producer grew fond of him, too. They asked Israels to write an arrangement for one of the songs, and though Israels didn't hit the mark, Paul and Ramone kept inviting him to sessions, introducing him to other musicians and producers, and telling them what a great musician and writer he was. It occurred to Israels how eager Paul was to get him hooked into his circuit of successful musicians and producers, to put him in a position where he could work at the top of his game and make the kind of money top-caliber musicians deserve to make. When the album was nearly finished, Paul asked Israels if he wanted co-write status on any of the songs he had helped Paul write. Israels demurred: he hadn't written anything, he'd only shown Paul some options. But the gesture was just as meaningful as it was unexpected.

Most often, Paul's recording process moved at a glacial pace. He'd fill the studio with a handful of New York's best rock and jazz players and do his usual thing of showing them the outlines of the day's song, then describing how he wanted the tune to feel. The players would figure out the rest for themselves, digging into their own sack of riffs to fill the groove Paul yearned to hear. It was never an efficient process, but as long as the ideas flowed Paul was delighted to spend the day hearing his music being shaped by such graceful hands. The musicians were delighted, too; Paul paid far more than union rates, and even if he didn't end up using their work simply having a Paul Simon session on your résumé was a prized accomplishment. Everyone knew that Paul Simon worked only with the best, most distinctive players.

The day's recording sessions were often just the start of the gig. Paul grew close to the people he worked with, and when the sessions ended he and Ramone would sweep up a few folks and take them to dinner at the House of Chan, a cloth napkin Chinese restaurant that had been an institution in Midtown for decades, and which happened to be on the same corner of Seventh Avenue where Ramone's A&R Studios were. They'd stay late, hanging with whatever friends or celebrities happened to drop by, all of them eager to talk in depth about the pursuit of the elusive perfect drum sound, or which studio had truly capable tech guys available at 3:00 a.m., which publicists could get a story on the cover of *Rolling Stone,* and how much Fleetwood Mac really got in that new contract from Warner Bros. And Paul was the center of it all, the most valuable player, the home run king circling the bases with that spark in his eye.

Oh, to be young and rich and famous and admired by Casey Kasem and Leonard Bernstein, Neil Sedaka and Isaac Stern, *People* magazine and E. L. Doctorow. There was nobody else to be, no other city that was better, no better street in a better neighborhood, no speedier private elevator to a better-appointed duplex with a better view of Central Park. Nor a sleeker art deco piano or more tasteful selection of modern art and minimalist, yet comfortable furniture. No cuter son or friendlier ex situated more

409

conveniently, no better recording studios just a short hop, skip, and limousine ride away. And yet, and yet, and yet.

CHAPTER 16
THROUGH NO FAULT
OF MY OWN

The possibility always dangled between them. Whenever they had dinner or trooped together past the photographers outside a premiere or a party, they decided to go to together. It was never just Paul and Artie having a night out. Because look, everyone, it's Simon and Garfunkel! Passersby would stop and point, they'd go away to tell their friends what they had just seen: *I thought those guys hated each other, but I just saw them together outside the Ziegfeld, and it sure looked like they were having a great time . . .* Even when they were alone, hanging around in one or the other's apartment, they'd get in a mood and sing a few tunes, something by the Everlys, Sam Cooke, whatever — and there it was again, that sound they could only make together.

The half decade of independence had eased the friction between them. Paul and Artie had kept in touch for most of the time; it would have been difficult to avoid each other even if they had wanted to, given the many friends and colleagues they had in common. They orbited the same professional loop, too, since they were both still recording for Columbia Records. When Artie performed at a Columbia sales conference at the Century Plaza Hotel in Los Angeles while promoting his first solo record in 1973, Paul, who was there to prime the pump for *There Goes Rhymin' Simon,* chased him down just after his set to tell Artie that he needed to work on his between-song patter. "Paul always gives you a critical rundown," Artie said a few months later.

When Paul had digested Artie's solo work, he fixed immediately on what bothered him the most: the songs were nowhere near as smart as the Artie he knew. Garfunkel had fallen in with pop songwriters and producers who smoothed everything down to a chromium sheen. So pretty, and so empty. What he needed, Paul was sure, was a new song that was just as dark and complex as Artie was. So he set himself to writing just that song.

Actually, Paul had been working on "My Little Town" for months, intending to put it on his own new album. When it seemed the tune wouldn't fit with the rest of the album's tunes, he took it to Artie, who had already heard Paul play it in an earlier form. At first it seemed like Paul wanted to hand off the song and be done with it — do with this whatever you like. But when he was teaching it to Artie, they started to sing it together, slipping into their usual blend, harmonies and all. And when Artie's suspicion that Paul would end up wanting the song back turned out to be right, they started thinking about how they might pull it off together as an old-fashioned Simon and Garfunkel song. Would Paul produce it with Phil Ramone, or would he coproduce with Artie? And if they did that, should they bring in Roy Halee, who had worked on every other song they had recorded? And if they had a finished Simon and Garfunkel song, they'd have to figure out how to release it. Just on Artie's new album, or on Paul's? Should they put it on both their albums, or make it a stand-alone Simon and Garfunkel single? Or maybe it should be part of something else altogether.

Eventually they decided to put the song on both their albums, and to release the records on the same day, so they'd both get the same lift from the inevitable uproar that came from the reunion. That settled, they went with Phil Ramone to three-way-produce recording sessions with the gang in Muscle Shoals. The session went quickly, and almost everyone agreed that it came out sounding exactly as you'd expect Simon and Garfunkel to sound in the mid-1970s: bittersweet, thoughtful, and just a few ticks punchier than the tracks that had made up *Bridge Over Troubled Water.* Released along with their albums in early October with the B-side split between "You're Kind" and Artie's new cover of the Four Seasons' "Rag Doll," the song was an instant add for radio stations across three or four formats and quickly become the latest of the duo's many Top 10 hits. They'd hinted at what was to come by surprising audiences at each other's concerts in recent months, the pair of them stepping out to end the evening with a mini-set of Simon and Garfunkel classics, performed together as easily and cheerfully as ever.

Oh, the life of a wealthy, high-brow pop star in mid-1970s New York City. The parties and the premieres, the ripple that ran through a room whenever he stepped inside. The starlets so pretty and so ripe for the picking. Some days, he glided the streets in limousines; other days, he walked the sidewalks, a white sailor's hat pulled low, the brim shielding his eyes. He went to ball games and scampered through the playgrounds of Central Park with Harper. He supported high-minded civic causes and fit easily among the politically and socially powerful. The whole Richard Cory package, from the common touch to the power, the grace and the style. But no gun. When the gloom came for him, he'd throw himself into his music, diving in as deep as he could get.

Recorded mostly in the last months of 1974 through the summer of 1975, the album Paul called *Still Crazy After All These Years* reveals the artist in songs that are darkly comic, songs that are tentatively hopeful, songs that are down but not quite out, and songs that all but vanish into the gloom. Most of the lyrics are lightly sketched, alluding to things that are never fully explained, then ending while the characters are still in motion, their destinations and fates unknown. The real story comes through the thrum of the chords, the flight of the melody across the rungs of the clef, rising, falling, then somersaulting in the least-expected direction; looking beyond the end of this song to see into the next; recognizing the themes and textures of each tune and then creating a dialogue between them in order to construct the larger narrative. There is so much you can't control in life, but thanks to Chuck Israels's lessons Paul could steer his music lessons, with more precision and delicacy than ever before.

That fragment of a tune he'd previewed on *The Dick Cavett Show* became "Still Crazy After All These Years," the lead song and title track of his new album. The song's title phrase had come to him when he was standing in the shower one day, contemplating his life as a divorced father in his midthirties, moving from one romance to another, still

415

searching for a relationship that could withstand his moods, his schedule, his full-body immersion in his work. The way his life was now, he realized, was the way it had been ten years earlier and, it seemed, the way it would be in ten or twenty or thirty years. He'd nearly burst into tears. But as his pain bent into art, the creative process gave him focus, and his new compositional skills an increased sense of control, which in turn gave the songs a paradoxical nature: tales of emotional chaos written with extraordinary discipline.

Nowhere is this clearer than in the title song, which sets the album in what first seems to be a jazz-rock terrain: the Muscle Shoals guys lay back as the singer's tale unfolds. Meeting his ex on the sidewalk, having a couple of drinks, going home alone. The bridge leaps up the scale, but the singer sinks more deeply into his malaise: life is miserable, and then you die. Star saxophonist David Sanborn gets sixteen bars to elevate the mood and sets up the dark climactic joke: the singer could start killing people without having to fear prison. He'd end up in a mental hospital. Still crazy after all these years.

Turn to the cover of the album to glimpse the misanthrope in the flesh, and he seems to be overstating things. Snapped by then-girlfriend Edie Baskin, the photograph has Paul on a fire escape three floors above

Crosby Street in Manhattan, bending his mustache cheerily from beneath a Stetson that looks far more urbane in SoHo than it would on horseback. His jeans are stylish and snug across his slightly cocked hip, his white linen button-up shirt open to reveal a thick tuft of chest hair. For this moment at least, he's riding high. But when the party's over, the winner's smile fades and the sorrows of the past rise.

As the next track begins, the electric keyboard is replaced by an acoustic piano playing in its lower register. An acoustic guitar and funereal drum arrive, then Artie Garfunkel's tenor rises, Paul joins with a lower harmony, and we're back in time. The excitement of having a new song by the reunited Simon and Garfunkel, the first since *Bridge Over Troubled Water,* deepens the meaning of "My Little Town" and its place in the album's narrative. Their restored harmony is soothing, but also alludes to the tension between them: the swells of jealousy and anger, the knives in the back, the bitter currents in the headwaters of their art, their ambition, their thorny love for each other.

A song titled "My Little Town" could be mistaken as a work of nostalgia, but here it's a horror show, a portrait of a childhood spent in a small town defined by a vengeful God. Rainbows paint the sky black. The weight of the past smothers the future and sends the narrator into the world "twitching like a finger on the trigger of a gun."[*] The song ends in a fury, both singers calling out to the dead and dying as horns blare and walls crumble, and childhood's end becomes the Battle of Jericho, the slaves' eternal pursuit of liberation.

When the scene returns to the present tense, the colors return in garish shades. Introduced by a piercing clarinet, a slurry guitar, and a persistent bell, "I Do It for Your Love" sifts the wreckage of his broken marriage, recalling a rainy day civil ceremony defined by paperwork and a world that can't stop protesting the union. Colors reverse ("The sky was yellow and the grass was gray . . ."), the besotted lovers continually infect each other with a cold. When the narrator buys a rug for their new home, the rains blow in to ruin it before he gets home. An accordion leads a Parisian vignette that is both graceful and sinister, like an approaching street mime. "Love emerges and it disappears," he realizes, and at this point it feels like a mercy.

When the mood turns wicked, "Fifty Ways to Leave Your Lover" tucks adultery into a martial rhythm, then struts shamelessly through the ABCs of abandonment: "Make a

[*] The hint of violence echoes the final verse of "Still Crazy," only without the yuks.

new plan, Stan / You don't need to be coy, Roy." A roguish fantasy for listeners, but not far from the truth of Paul's final months with Peggy. And for this moment at least he's happy to shrug it off. Who's to say it was entirely his doing, anyway? But the rush is fleeting, and as the perspective shifts to interior matters, the breeze chills and the lights go out.

The album bounces from mood to mood, from the louche resignation of "Have a Good Time" to the philosophical self-pity of "Some Folks' Lives Roll Easy" to the gospel ecstasies of "Gone at Last," made all the more majestic by Phoebe Snow's wild co-lead vocal. The cold calculation played for laughs in "Fifty Ways" returns in "You're Kind," in which a gleefully detached fellow inventories his lover's virtues only to rub in how arbitrary his decision to leave her truly is. "I like to sleep with the window open / And you keep the window closed, / So goodbye," he says, already halfway out of the door.

The slinky "Have a Good Time" plays the same way, a footloose man's blues dressed in silky resignation. But the admission that ends the first verse ("I should be depressed / My life's a mess") hints at the darker truth.

The despair defines the funereal tone of "Night Game," which begins with a baseball game at the peak of excitement. It's the bottom half of the eighth inning, the score tied, two outs, and all the world's glory hanging in the balance. But before anyone can cheer for anything, the pitcher collapses and the mound becomes his grave, marked only by his tattered uniform and empty spikes. Winter blows in, the stars become bones, the stadium may collapse. By the end, every form of hope has been extinguished: the third batter strikes out, the season ends ingloriously, the tarpaulin rolls over frozen grass.

Given Paul's devotion to the New York Yankees and to the restorative rituals of baseball, "Night Game" feels that much more mournful, as if he'd come to doubt the central pillars of his consciousness. Things had grown so chaotic by then that even the euphoric "Gone at Last" comes with a troubled backstory, stemming from Paul's initial thought of making the song a duet with then-girlfriend Bette Midler. But their romance was short-lived, and ran aground completely during their attempt to record the song together. The collapse of the collaboration, and the relationship, grew so toxic Paul had to invent three different stories to explain why their duet hadn't worked. "The record companies couldn't agree on the details. That was the only problem," he told *Rolling Stone* just after the record came out. Actually, the problem was the Latin-style arrangement he was trying, *Crawdaddy* was informed a few months later. Or perhaps, as he told the BBC a few

420

years later, Midler's sing-the-hell-out-of-it-and-move-on recording style clashed with his furrowed-brow sensibility. Paul restored order by bringing in the powerful, if less established, singer Phoebe Snow as his co-singer, and when he heard a playback of their joint performance his faith was restored. As Snow recalled the moment to *Crawdaddy*'s Timothy White in 1976, Paul was exulting even before the track was over. "Isn't it nice to win?" he shouted, and she agreed, absolutely: "It really is, for a change." But soon there would be other battles to fight, including the one he was already embroiled in with the actor/director/writer/producer Warren Beatty.

In the thick of producing and playing the lead in his self-written fin de siècle film *Shampoo,* Beatty had asked Paul to write some tunes for the soundtrack. Paul took Beatty into the studio and played him an austere piano ballad that still needed lyrics. Beatty fell for it at first listen, saying it didn't need any lyrics as far as he was concerned; he could use an instrumental version as the movie's closing theme. They shook hands to seal the general agreement, but when Paul not only wrote lyrics but also recorded it for his album, Beatty protested heatedly. They'd had a deal! The song was supposed to be for his movie; Paul had no business recording a different version for his record. But of course Paul protested right back. A deal? What deal?

They had shaken hands on an *idea* and hadn't even started talking about the guts of a deal. Nothing about money, nothing about rights and restrictions. And *that* was supposed to be a binding contract? Paul didn't think so. He also didn't think Beatty had any business telling him what he could and couldn't do with his music. Beatty was just as stubborn, and Paul told his lawyers to start drafting papers for a cease-and-desist order to keep *Shampoo* from using even a note of his song. They made a deal in the end — Beatty got to use the music in his movie, Paul got to record his own version, and everyone got paid — yet the whole affair clarifies the foreboding in the song Paul chose to conclude the album.

It starts on the minor chord, a three-note descent into a vision of Jerusalem, the cradle of the Jewish people: a Jerusalem forsaken, weeping alone, her children scattered across the desert, lost to the wind, blown across the centuries to new lands, new cultures, new selves. The modernized, the secularized, the urbanized and popularized — this is Paul, so far gone from anything that can be called a tradition or a faith that even when he tries to heed her call, he knows he is too far gone to ever come home. And as he has always suspected, the toll for his indulgences will eventually come due.

And we shall all be called as witnesses
Each and every one
To stand before the eyes of God
And speak what was done.

Musically sophisticated, lyrically probing, and yet pop-friendly, *Still Crazy After All These Years* was a pitch-perfect match for its times. While Bob Dylan's landmark *Blood on the Tracks* goes after the breakdown of his marriage like a desperado across a lawless frontier, and Bruce Springsteen's *Born to Run* tears down oil-streaked highways in search of deeper truths, *Still Crazy* documents the cynicism of the post-Nixon era through eyes jaundiced by political disillusion, professional success, and the stultifying comforts of home. It was released on October 25 to the usual praise and a few sharper takes on what some critics saw as Paul's deepening self-involvement, self-pity, and "slick professionalism."

No matter, *Still Crazy* became his first chart-topping solo album, launching four singles into the charts, including the first Simon and Garfunkel release in half a decade ("My Little Town" peaked in *Billboard*'s No. 9 slot), Paul's first No. 1 solo single ("Fifty Ways to Leave Your Lover"), along with lesser hits "Gone at Last" (No. 23 in the fall of 1975) and "Still Crazy After All These Years," which peaked at No. 40 on the pop chart,

423

but rose into the top five of the adult contemporary list. The album sold enough copies to earn a gold record within weeks, and a platinum disc by the end of the year. In the course of its long arc to and from the top of the charts, where it remained for three weeks in the winter of 1976, "Fifty Ways" was nearly as ubiquitous as "Mrs. Robinson" and "Bridge Over Troubled Water" had been in their day. Five years and three albums into his solo career, even in the wake of their one-song reunion, Paul could walk onstage without hearing anyone shout, "Where's Artie?"

Still, Paul and Artie's collaboration on "My Little Town" had touched off a new chain of guest cameos at one another's shows. Most often it came during the encore, a surprise introduction and then two or three songs, "The Boxer," "Old Friends," and maybe "The Sound of Silence." They were all un-billed appearances, however. So when Paul signed on to host the second episode of a new late-night variety show and asked Artie to join him for an extended on-air performance, that was something else altogether.

Paul met Lorne Michaels through Edie Baskin, the photographer he was dating for a time during the *Still Crazy After All These Years* sessions. The thirty-year-old TV producer had hired Baskin to be his new show's chief photographer. Baskin's quirky portraits, along with the whimsical hand-tinting she added to some of them, were a perfect visual representation of what Michaels wanted his decidedly youthful ninety-minute comedy-music-entertainment program to be. The first-ever counterculture-fueled show to be broadcast on a major American television network.[*]

Paul and Michaels clicked immediately; it was hard to figure out what they didn't have in common: both were in their thirties, both assimilated Jews — Michaels's real last name is Lipowitz — raised in families rooted in the entertainment business, both precocious as young men, and both comfortable assuming positions of authority. They also knew how to split the difference between their countercul-ture impulses and their desire to succeed within the structure of established institu-

[*] CBS's *Laugh-In,* despite its hippy-dippy characters and occasionally bawdy jokes, doesn't count. Its producers were establishment professionals who knew that dressing up the usual Hollywood shtick in long hair, sideburns, and body paint would be a clever gimmick. When it started to work, their first impulse was to use the show's popularity to make then-presidential candidate Richard Nixon look with-it. Sure, Lily Tomlin came out of *Laugh-In,* and Michaels was a low-level writer there for a while, but the show's voice was still laced with an older generation's bourbon and cigarettes.

tions. Their friendship grew quickly, and Paul became a regular visitor to the show's offices and to the long dinners Michaels had with a circle of friends drawn mostly from the show's writing staff and cast. Sitting with Michaels and a rotating crew that included Chevy Chase, John Belushi, Dan Aykroyd, Michaels's comedy writer wife Rosie Shuster (a key member of *SNL*'s first writing staff), Paul was present to witness the show's birth. One of the show's most talked-about early sketches bore Paul's mark: when Aykroyd recalled seeing a relative making soup from a whole fish she had dropped into a blender, and proposed doing an ad parody for the Bass-o-Matic blender, Paul laughed so hard the writer-actor went back to his office and wrote one of the new show's most famous sketches. "It's hard to get Paul to laugh, you know, because he's so intellectual, so smart . . . When he started to snort, I said, 'Man, I got something.' "

Paul had wanted to host the first episode of the show (known temporarily as *NBC's Saturday Night* because ABC-TV had secured the *Saturday Night Live* name for a prime-time variety show it launched that same fall), but Michaels asked him to wait for the second go-round: he wanted to give the cast and crew a week to get comfortable before he had a friend take center stage. Michaels tapped the hilariously seditious long-haired come-

426

dian George Carlin to host *Saturday Night*'s October 11, 1975, debut, and when he brought Paul in to start building the next Saturday's show, the atmosphere around the eleventh floor of Rockefeller Center's GE Building became tense, particularly among the cast members. Everyone agreed the first show had gone well. They'd need to tweak a few things, of course, but all the time they had spent working together had paid off. The seven cast members had bonded enough to start playing off one another, while Michaels and the writers (many of whom were performers, too) were well on their way to developing a voice that really did sound like a new generation talking. But the show Michaels and Paul were planning had nearly nothing to do with the comic vibe the others had built.

Obviously Michaels wanted to draw as much attention as possible to his newborn show. Just having Paul as a host was a coup, particularly with his new album on the verge of being released. But toss in the Simon and Garfunkel reunion, their first public performance in three years, and their first national exposure since *Bridge Over Troubled Water,* and it was a big enough deal to ensure not only that the second-week ratings didn't fall off from the first, but also that there'd be a boost in the show's viewership, which would only endear it to the NBC executives whose opinions spelled the difference between a show's long, happy life and a fast, inglorious cancellation. So, at first glance, Paul's commitment to hosting was nothing but terrific. Everyone liked the idea of having guest superstars on the show — until the guest superstar became the entire show. Because Paul had no intention of doing just a few songs with Garfunkel. He wanted to turn the spotlight on other artists, friends, and collaborators, too. Artie needed a solo spot, and Paul also wanted to do at least one song by himself. Add up all that time, translate it into network TV segments, and they had almost no time left for comedy, beyond a taped bit they planned for Paul and a short film by Los Angeles–based comedian Albert Brooks. Other than Chevy Chase, who Michaels thought had the charisma and looks to be a breakout star, the rest of the cast would be seen only in a thirty-second mini-skit with Paul.

The resulting tension made for a long week. Belushi, whose wild-haired onstage persona was not so distant from his real-life persona, told Michaels that "the folk-singing wimp" was derailing their show before it had a chance to really get rolling, and Paul didn't help when he kept disrupting rehearsals by staring into the monitors to make sure his bald spot wasn't too visible to the cameras. When showtime arrived at 11:30 p.m. on

Saturday night, October 18, the scene opened on Paul sitting alone on a stool at the center of the stage singing "Still Crazy After All These Years," the title track to the album that would be released in less than a week. Chase did the first of his soon-to-be-famous show-opening tumbles ("Live from New York, it's *Saturday Night!*) and then Paul was back, this time surrounded by the Jessy Dixon Singers for "Loves Me Like a Rock." Next came Randy Newman to sing "Sail Away," a tune Paul said he wished he'd written. After Chase did his "Weekend Update" news satire, Paul starred in a lengthy taped piece based on the absurd premise of him playing a one-on-one basketball game against the Philadelphia 76ers' Connie Hawkins, then one of the biggest and most fearsome players in the National Basketball Association. Paul did a fine job handling his lines in a gag interview with sports announcer Marv Albert ("I'm spotting him a one-foot, four-inch advantage. I gotta admit that's gonna be a factor in this game. He's got me on shooting ability, but I just have to play my game as I usually play it . . . [and] stay with my strengths. Basically singing and songwriting."). Hawkins responded just as ably when asked to size up his opponent ("He's got a lot of savvy and a lot of chutzpah"), then the game began and the joke spun on its axis. From the opening tip, Paul dominated the game, crushing Hawkins beneath an avalanche of hook shots, outside jumpers, and sneaky lay-ins. Interviewed again by Albert after his easy victory, Paul nailed the punch line with a shrug. "When my outside shot is on, it's *on*."

The Simon and Garfunkel reunion was surprisingly underplayed. About halfway into the show, Paul introduced his old friend, and Artie, who had been sitting with the studio audience, edged through the crowd on his way to the stool set next to Paul's onstage. The familiar needling started immediately.

"So Artie," Paul said. "You've come crawling back."

Artie bent over to laugh, then turned cool: "It's very nice of you to invite me onto your show. Thanks a lot."

"Movies are over now?"

Artie mumbled, "Yeah."

"A little two-part harmony?" Paul asked.

"I'll try it again. See if it works this time."

From there it was like a stream slipping through its banks. The "lie-de-lies" in "The Boxer" falling into "Scarborough Fair," each note trembling with feeling, each syllable laid in its precise position. They moved to the small center stage to do "My Little Town" with the show's band, both singing into handheld mics and visibly struggling to find the balance between moving with the rhythm of the song and dancing like idiots. They kept trying to be serious, but whenever they made eye contact, they couldn't resist the urge to break each other up. By the third verse, Paul started moving closer, edging his partner aside until Artie gave him a little shove back. This only upped the ante for Paul, who stepped right back in, now doing a dramatic finger-point motion that caused his partner to crack up in the middle of a high note.

When it was over, they stood next to each other, a couple of mischievous kids who've just gotten away with something in front of everyone. What could be more fun than that? "I'd still like to do some more stuff with Artie from time to time," Paul told the *Chicago Tribune* a few days after the *Saturday Night* reunion. Artie was just as enthusiastic, talking about how they might make a new record, how nothing was off the table now. But in the weeks that followed, something happened. When *Newsweek*'s Maureen Orth caught up with Paul in mid-December, he said exactly the opposite. "I can't go back and do anything with Artie," he said. "That's a prison. I'm not meant to be a partner." Simon and Garfunkel probably wouldn't be very popular these days, anyway — which was extra-fun to say now that Artie's album *Watermark,* released on the same day as *Still Crazy,* had attracted mostly lukewarm notices and an underwhelming reception in record stores. Fortunately, Artie had Paul to feel sorry for him. "Poor Artie, he's really depressed now," he said, and it wasn't like Paul hadn't tried to help. He'd written him "My Little Town," the elusive song that was as smart as he was, and his public had ignored everything else. And, as Paul pointed out, it wasn't fair. "He just happens to have a voice like an angel and curly hair like a halo," Paul said, pitying his former partner for his boyish good looks. "But he's a *grown-up.*"

What had happened?

Woody Allen called. The writer-director-actor, New York City's most essential movie auteur, was making a movie and was hoping Paul might consider playing a small role: as a music producer type of guy. Big-time. Oleaginous. He could send over some lines. Was Paul interested? He was indeed, but after looking at the script, he went back to Woody. I think I know this character a little better than you do, he said. Can I write my own lines? Well, of course.

The movie Allen was working on turned out to be *Annie Hall,* the first great synthesis of his comedic and filmic sensibilities. Paul's character was named Tony Lacey, his shirt open to reveal the silver coke spoon dangling in his chest hair, his hazy grooviness a pox on the pulsing nerves of Allen's successful but deeply neurotic writer Alvy Singer. Paul's role ran for exactly two scenes, but both were

432

pivotal to the film, and when it was over, his face was as prominent in the film's promotion as those of any of the supporting players. Released in the spring of 1977, *Annie Hall* made the critics spin pirouettes. Audiences cheered, then ran back to the box office to buy more tickets and see it again. *Annie Hall* would go on to win the Academy Award for Best Picture, and launch or expand the reputations of virtually everyone attached to the film, from the young actor Christopher Walken, female lead Diane Keaton, the Broadway actor Tony Roberts, and of course Allen himself.

It was pivotal for Paul, too. He'd evened at least one score with Artie, and found a girlfriend in the actress Shelley Duvall, who also had a small part in the film. Soon they were living together, their relationship pulling him that much closer to the movie crowd he'd encountered through Mike Nichols and Lorne Michaels. He liked them, and he liked their world — the vastness of the productions, the respect accorded to the auteurs. If you had a strong vision, you could follow it as far as you wanted to go, assuming you had enough juice behind you. And given Paul's decade-plus record of nearly nonstop success, plus his surprisingly nimble comic performances on television and in one of the most celebrated movies of the decade, there

433

was no reason for him to think he couldn't conquer this genre, too. He already had a couple of ideas for scripts. In fact, he'd already been writing; the Connie Hawkins sketch had been his idea, and he'd scripted the action and interview segments. Paul also wrote the opening sketch for his next hosting shot on *SNL* in the fall of 1976, an uproarious bit that began with him singing "Still Crazy After All These Years" in a large turkey suit, until stopping it short to say he'd been happy to play along and not be "*soooo* serious all the time," but this was just too much for him to bear.

The turkey suit opening became one of the most talked-about sketches of the season, and when Michaels suggested they collaborate on a prime-time special for NBC's Christmas schedule, Paul signed on to cowrite and star. Michaels brought along *SNL* director Dave Wilson, a clutch of writers, recently departed cast member Chevy Chase, and the widely admired comedian and writer Lily Tomlin. Written almost entirely by Paul and Michaels, the show was set backstage during the making of a completely different Paul Simon special, produced by Grodin's cluelessly assertive character. Paul, looking fit and surprisingly thick on the top of his head, is more comfortable on camera than during his *SNL* turns, playing himself as musically authoritative but vulnerable to anyone with a compliment or dour warning. Friends and colleagues pop in and out. Chase and Tomlin portray themselves. The Jessy Dixon Singers, harmonica expert Toots Thielemans, and sax player David Sanborn reprise earlier performances. Artie shows up to rehearse "Old Friends" and read through a moronic dialogue that Grodin's character has had typed onto cue cards. *The Paul Simon Special* aired on December 8, 1977, scoring reviews that ranged from "a big thumb down" from the *New York Times*'s John J. O'Connor to the enthusiastic write-up from Tom Shales of the *Washington Post,* who thought the sketches weren't bad and found the music sequences, as artfully directed by Dave Wilson, exquisite. The special's ratings didn't add up to much, but by then Paul had other problems to think about.

The hostilities started when Paul released a single-disc collection of his best solo tunes called *Greatest Hits, Etc.* Given that all three of his post-S&G albums had been top sellers with multiple hit singles, the biggest challenge was deciding which tunes to leave out. The CBS brass asked Paul to include a pair of new songs, knowing that hardcore fans would be happy to rebuy old music as long as it came with new stuff, too. Paul did as he was asked, and by the time the album joined the pre-Christmas marketplace, "Slip Slidin' Away," a melancholy gospel ballad featuring

435

backing vocals by the Oak Ridge Boys, was already in *Billboard*'s top five. Knowing that the greatest hits collection Columbia released in 1972 had sold millions without benefit of any new music (apart from a few live renditions), Paul assumed *Greatest Hits, Etc.* would easily find an audience, too. But that's not what happened. The album climbed only to the eighteenth slot on *Billboard*'s album chart, and plummeted from there. How was that possible? When he went to the top office to talk it out with CBS's president, Paul had no doubt about what had led to the catastrophe. Other than buying a few ads in a few magazines and the handful of newspapers in the big cities, the company had done nothing to promote the album: no more ads, no publicity, no push of any kind.

In earlier days Paul would have found a sympathetic ear in Clive Davis, whose adoration of him and his music had never dimmed. But a company putsch in 1973, pinned to a few expense account indulgences that were more foolish than criminal, had led to the president's abrupt defenestration.* His re-

* Intriguingly, the end of Davis's career at Columbia marked the end of Paul's hostility toward the former president. Now they lived in the s̲a̲.̲.̲e building, sent their kids to the same school, and had taken to hanging out together. They have gotten on well ever since.

placement was Walter Yetnikoff, another outer-borough New Yorker, one who'd worked his way through law school and emerged as a uniquely sharp, if socially awkward, lawyer. Davis hired and groomed the younger executive, eventually giving him control over CBS's international division. Perfectly positioned to take the top spot, Yetnikoff reached for it and became one of the two or three most powerful men in the American music industry. And while Davis certainly left him with a winning hand of artists and executives, Yetnikoff was quick to build it up even higher, snatching James Taylor from archrival label Warner Bros. and Paul McCartney from his lifelong home at EMI/Capitol, while nurturing a few established acts (Billy Joel, Barbra Streisand, the Jacksons) to new heights and also encouraging Michael Jackson to relaunch his solo career.

Yetnikoff's new powers, along with his increasing thirst for whiskey and a certain powdered pharmaceutical, conspired to catapult him from an office wallflower into something else entirely. Bull-chested, bearded, and prone to grand displays of chest hair, Yetnikoff sailed the corporate seas as the Blackbeard of Black Rock, shouting and laughing, and hurling paperweights at subordinates who had disappointed him in some small way. Already prone to anger, Yetnikoff had a particular hard spot for Paul, who could fuel his rage just by walking into his office. That Paul happened to be one of his company's most essential artists only made Yetnikoff despise him more. The arrogant little putz was self-involved and somewhere well beyond pretentious, the executive thought. Paul had, in Yetnikoff's mind, screwed over Artie by breaking up Simon and Garfunkel, and done the same to former lawyer Harold Orenstein when he'd followed Tannen, whom Yetnikoff also hated, out of the Orenstein law firm. To hear Yetnikoff tell it, Paul was a caricature of the self-worshipping celebrity, a clown who spent most of their first meeting lying on the sofa while smoking a joint and bloviating about poetry. And did he offer the CBS president a hit off his reefer? No, he did not, and for Yetnikoff that was all he needed to know. "I didn't like the guy," Yetnikoff wrote. "And he certainly didn't like me."

If that weren't combustible enough, Paul's contract with CBS/Columbia was ending and negotiations for a new deal weren't going well. Paul and Mike Tannen had already made clear that they expected Paul's next contract to set new high-water marks for recording deals, and even Yetnikoff could see the logic in it. Paul had been signed to the label for more than a decade. Every album he'd made, including *Wednesday Morning, 3 AM,* once "The Sound of Silence" took off, had made money for Columbia. Most had sold more than a million copies, and several had sold significantly more than that. He was one of the hottest artists in the industry. Still, that didn't mean that Yetnikoff had to let the little twerp dictate his own terms. As Yetnikoff described it, "War clouds were rolling in."

Dollars, clauses, years, whatever — the terms of the struggle could never approach the malevolence both principals in the deal held for each other. It was as if Paul's genteel chill were an affront to Yetnikoff, whose half-mad attempts at intimidation drilled deep into Paul's rich stores of bile. So it got worse.

Nevertheless, Tannen and Yetnikoff, along with top CBS exec Walter Dean, continued negotiating. Sometimes they'd get within a whisker of an agreement, only to have something fly out of whack. For a time in early 1978 it seemed they actually had a deal, until Tannen's written version allegedly came in half a million dollars higher than the CBS team remembered agreeing to. Another time, when Yetnikoff and Tannen happened to be sitting next to each other on an airplane headed to Los Angeles, Tannen proposed that it was time for the two of them to stop the bickering and get to the bottom line, to what was going to work for everyone. It wasn't an unreasonable idea; deals get cut like that all the time. But Yetnikoff went berserk. "How dare you assume what I'm going to do!" he screamed at the stunned lawyer. "There is *no* deal! Paul Simon does *not* have a deal at CBS!"

When he got to LA, a stunned Tannen dialed Mo Ostin, the artist-friendly president of Warner Bros. Records. Ostin, a vocal fan of Paul's work for many years, had never been shy about his eagerness to get Paul on his label. Hearing that his dream artist might actually be available, he invited Tannen over to talk. The deal was finished twenty-four hours later.

Paul owed CBS one more studio album to fulfill his existing contract, but in no mood to give Yetnikoff more than the bare minimum he sent the executive a message telling him that his final record for him would be a collection of cover songs, most of which would be duets or collaborations with other artists. Yetnikoff's response to Tannen, while composed in standard business language and form, still amounted to a resounding *no fucking way*! Paul's contract, he insisted, called for *original* songs, not retreads. Paul and Tannen fired right back: the contract called simply for albums of original recordings — there wasn't a word about who was supposed to *write* them. But neither Paul nor Tannen could find that clause in their copies of the contract. "Tough shit," Paul figured and got to work, only to find that some of the CBS artists he wanted to work with suddenly didn't have the time to record with him. Yetnikoff had made it clear to everyone at the company that they'd be a lot happier later if they stayed away from Paul Simon. And of course Yetnikoff threatened to sue, promising to keep Paul tangled in litigation for so long his career would be over before he had a chance to start working on his first Warner Bros album.

Rarely shy about doing battle in the civil courts, the prospect of going to court against Columbia/CBS jabbed at Paul's more vulnerable spots. He began to wonder if anyone in the company would stand up for him in court. All those executives who had whispered their stories about how Yetnikoff had sworn to destroy him, the ones who had described the incriminating memos, the artists who had seen and heard so much more — they had been so eager to be his friend when he was riding high on the charts. But while it was easy for them to whisper conspiratorially in Paul's ear, it was something else entirely to testify against Yetnikoff, the man with ultimate control over their careers.

No matter. Paul filed two claims against Yetnikoff and CBS on December 21, 1978, the first accusing the company of breaching his contract for threatening to reject his final album and for not publicizing the greatest hits album (*Greatest Hits, Etc.*) properly, particularly after he'd signed with Warner

Bros. in February 1978. The second action demanded financial reparations for all of the above, plus for whatever bad things might happen as a result in the future. The usual threats and recriminations followed, but in the end it didn't take long to reach a settlement: Paul would buy himself out of his deal for (a rumored) $1.5 million. As expected, Yetnikoff played up the settlement as an unalloyed victory, but Paul had already moved on. After two years of work, he was close to finishing his first original movie script. Warner Bros. Pictures had signed him to coproduce and, if he felt like it, play the starring role in a new film. He had entered an entirely new world of creativity, and this time he was in complete control.

CHAPTER 17
SWALLOWED BY A SONG

When *The Paul Simon Songbook* was released in England in 1965, Paul's music publisher, Lorna Music, had issued an accompanying booklet of sheet music. Paul fleshed out the package by adding "On Drums and Other Hollow Objects," an interesting but ham-handed short story about youth and old age. When "The Sound of Silence" broke everything open and he returned to England as a pop star, Paul made a point of telling reporters that prose writing had always been his first love, and that he was already sketching characters and scenes for the novel he'd write once he got the pop music business off his back. Nothing had come of it of course, but working with Mike Nichols on *The Graduate* had turned his head back in the typewriter's direction, this time with movies in his mind.

Paul turned down a chance to write the score for John Schlesinger's *Midnight Cowboy* (reputedly because he didn't want to be mistaken for Dustin Hoffman's personal

443

songwriter), but he never lost his fascination for moviemaking. He talked about the prospect of making a movie to reporters during interviews about his first solo album in 1972, and when he met Lorne Michaels three years later and fell in with a gang of writers, directors, and producers, the idea began to seem more plausible — especially given the unbroken pattern of successes he'd been having since "The Sound of Silence" became a hit. After ten years of not taking a wrong step in the music business, he was getting restless, and more than ready to try his hand at an entirely different medium. It'd be a leap, but not an impossible one. He and Michaels had even won an Emmy for writing *The Paul Simon Special.* A full movie script would be a different matter, but Paul talked over the finer points with Michaels, Mike Nichols, and a few of the other writers he knew.

He was also inspired by his new girlfriend, Carrie Fisher, a young actress whose co-starring role as Princess Leia in *Star Wars* had lifted her to a level of superstardom that was as sudden as it was unexpected. And though she was still six months from her twenty-first birthday when the sci-fi blockbuster was released in the spring of 1977, Fisher was no stranger to the movie business or to fame. Born in 1956 to singer Eddie Fisher and his movie star wife Debbie Reynolds, Fisher weathered her parents' tabloid divorce — Eddie Fisher famously left Reynolds for her closest friend, Elizabeth Taylor, whose recently deceased husband, Mike Todd, had been Eddie's best friend — when she was two and spent the rest of her childhood navigating the twisty roads carved for the children of Hollywood's most spangled grandees.

It was a strange life — gilded and unstable, lonely and crowded with some of the most accomplished and famous artists in the world. Carrie had her first experiences with drugs when she was thirteen. When Reynolds heard that her fifteen-year-old had been talking about trying LSD, she brought in Cary Grant, who had been part of a medical experiment on the drug in the early 1960s, to give her a stern lecture about its evils. Carrie went ahead and did it anyway, but no amount of drugs could dampen her intelligence or dull her natural talent as an actress. Warren Beatty cast her as Lee Grant's teenage daughter in *Shampoo* — her most memorable line, delivered to Beatty's lothario character, George: "Wanna fuck?" — and it was only a matter of months before *Star Wars* producer/director George Lucas came calling.

Young, successful, and witty, Carrie fit easily into the Hollywood-*SNL* circuit and soon became one of the most sought-after women in their circle. She was already being wooed by Mike Nichols, David Geffen, and Richard

Dreyfuss when she met Paul, but once they saw each other, no one else mattered to either of them. And as she prepared to start shooting the next *Star Wars* blockbuster in London, Paul threw himself into his own movie project in the Central Park West apartment the couple now shared.

Paul's muse almost always carried him back to the heart of his own existence, so it was no surprise that the character he envisioned for his movie was a man very much like him. A singer-songwriter whose first single had been an enormous hit in the mid-1960s, but instead of following it up with three more hit singles and a decade-long streak of hit albums, the character spends the rest of his career spiraling away from his initial success. As the movie picked up, he'd be in his midthirties and still on the road, struggling to keep his band moving while also tending to the needs of his estranged wife and their small son. Despite the disparity in their commercial achievements, the musician character he named Jonah Levin had the same core conflict that had gripped Paul for so long: an inability to reconcile the needs of his loved ones and closest companions with a rootless spirit that required the thrum of music to stay alive. Jonah would be good at what he did, too, if only because every note he played and sang would come from Paul Simon. Yet

446

hardly anyone in Jonah's world would be listening — certainly not the men who ran the big music companies. And maybe there was something in Jonah that didn't want him to be successful.

To learn more about the club-to-club grind of most working musicians, while also gleaning something about the psyche of a widely admired yet unsuccessful artist, Paul spent time with the singer-songwriter Dave Van Ronk, whose top-rank reputation in Greenwich Village stretched back before Bob Dylan showed up. Dylan had learned from Van Ronk, too. The Minnesotan lifted Van Ronk's revolutionary guitar arrangement of the blues standard "House of the Rising Sun" for his first record, and was then given the credit, and royalties, when the Animals' cover of the song became a global hit a year later. Many others followed Van Ronk's lead as well, but Van Ronk had never moved beyond the middling ranks of touring folk players, and though he complained about being overlooked, he was a hard-drinking rebel whose dogged resistance to the conventions of the music business struck some of his friends as willful self-sabotage. Paul suffered no such conflicts when it came to business, but that didn't mean he couldn't still taste the ashes that filled Jonah's mouth, the dread that he'd get up one day and discover that the world had lost interest in him.

Paul's work on the script started long before his war with Yetnikoff, but when he started thinking about moving over to Warner Bros., he realized that signing with a label that was a subsidiary of an enormous movie studio could have benefits for a musician eyeing the movie business, particularly for one who had just become the most prized member of its record company's roster. When Paul's script went out to producers, the response was positive, to say the least. In the end it turned into an auction between Anthea Sylbert at Warner Bros. and Paula Weinstein, a producer with Paramount. There wasn't much difference in the money they had to spend, but Weinstein's offer came with a caveat: she wanted Paul to rewrite the script. Sylbert figured it was fine the way it was, so Paul, who had already revised it a number of times, went with Sylbert.

Now he had to find a director and actors. Mike Tannen suggested Mike Nichols, but he was busy, and Alan Parker, whose credits included the acclaimed *Midnight Express* and the popular kid-filled gangster parody *Bugsy Malone,* had a hard time imagining that Paul would give any director enough creative control to truly direct anything. Eventually Paul settled on Robert Young, most of whose work had been in documentaries and news programs. "His ego didn't get in the way," Paul told *People*'s Jim Jerome when the film was released. Choosing a lead actor came with its own complications. None of the leading stars Paul had approached (Dustin Hoffman, Richard Dreyfuss, maybe one or two more) could see themselves in the role, and, frankly, Paul couldn't see them, or anyone else, either. He'd written the movie to include something like half a dozen live performances by Jonah and his band, all of whom would be portrayed by the musicians Paul was recording and playing with at the time. They had already recorded the songs with Paul singing, and as both Hoffman and Dreyfuss figured, it would be ridiculous for anyone to try to lip-synch to Paul's extremely recognizable voice. And why shouldn't Paul play the part himself? As he'd proven on *SNL,* on his own special, and the Oscar-winning *Annie Hall,* Paul had a natural feel for acting. He'd been a stage performer for most of his life. And the semiautobiographical character Paul had created for the movie would hardly be a stretch.

So it was settled: Paul would play Jonah Levin. He hired the Method acting teacher Mira Rostova, who counted Montgomery Clift among her earlier students, to help him prepare. Paul also accelerated his campaign to make himself more physically attractive. Already a consistent exerciser who followed a meat-, sugar-, and alcohol-free diet in order to control the calcium deposits in his hands,

449

he now worked his way below 120 pounds. His reduced weight, along with the passing years, removed the baby fat from his face, giving him a leaner, sculpted appearance. Even more noticeably, his hair had made a comeback, his sparse whorls now rich and fluffy, a development that completed his transition from all too human to Hollywood handsome.

With Mike Tannen serving as the day-to-day producer, the rest of the preproduction details came together smoothly. The rising actress Blair Brown (*The Paper Chase, The Choirboys*) signed on to play Jonah's estranged wife, while the character actor Rip Torn took the role of duplicitous record company president Walter Fox, whose inspiration did not require guesswork. Proto-punk musician Lou Reed played against type as a careerist pop record producer, and some soon-to-be-famous names (Daniel Stern, Mare Winningham) turned up in small roles. Paul's real four-piece band (drummer Steve Gadd, keyboardist Richard Tee, guitarist Eric Gale, and bassist Tony Levin) played versions of themselves, with the outsize Tee, dubbed Clarence Franklin, in the onstage sidekick/offstage protector role that E Street Band saxophonist Clarence Clemons played with Bruce Springsteen.

Shot largely in and around Cleveland during the winter of 1979, the film suffered the usual complications and setbacks. Blair Brown, in the role of Jonah's wife, didn't like how the lighting and staging favored Paul's appearance, while no one seemed to care how she looked. When a late-night shoot at the Cleveland airport stretched to an overnight ordeal, Paul entertained the throng of extras by leading them in a doo-wop singalong of "Why Must I Be a Teenager in Love" between shots. Hoping to attract ten thousand people to fill seats for scenes at an arena show, the team put up flyers for a free Paul Simon concert and attracted only a sparse crowd of thirty-five hundred, a setback that gnawed at Paul's perpetually fragile self-esteem — perhaps in a good way, since the anxiety gave him a direct line into Jonah's dread that his next downturn will be the end.

With his movie scheduled for release in the early fall of 1980, Paul helped design a multimedia publicity campaign of the likes he had never attempted. He gave lengthy interviews to *Rolling Stone,* the *Washington Post,* the *Times* of London's *Sunday Magazine, Melody Maker, Playboy,* and even *People* magazine, whose celebrity profiles have always revealed all the real-life details Paul had spent his career avoiding. No matter. Paul's cover story ("Still Creative After All These Years!") captured it all for public viewing. The ornate tile work on his indoor hot tub, the cost of his in-home gym (five thousand dollars), the make of his car (Mercedes), where he spent his summers (rented homes in the Hamptons), his rigorous diet, his precise weight (117 pounds), and his thoughts on Carrie Fisher, whose second *Star Wars* film, *The Empire Strikes Back,* had dominated the nation's movie screens throughout the summer — said Paul, "She's really got the goods and the Force is with her" — not to mention TV and radio interview shows.

The movie's soundtrack was a ten-song collection: live performances by Paul, Richard Tee, Eric Gale, Steve Gadd, and Tony Levin and studio recordings of the songs Paul had written to reveal the internal life of his main character. The lead single from the album, a Latin rocker called "Late in the Evening," represented another leap in Paul's stylistic meanderings, and a glimpse back to those afternoon dance sessions the Lee Simms Orchestra shared with the Latin bands at the Roseland Ballroom. The song was just as striking on the radio in the summer of 1980, rising to No. 6 on *Billboard*'s Hot 100 and fading off the charts just in time for the release of the title track, "One-Trick Pony," one of the tunes that was recorded live at Cleveland's Agora Ballroom. It was just as striking as its predecessor, slithering funk with a throbbing bass hook punctuated by skalike guitar stabs as Paul's voice traces the image of a performer who can "make it look so easy, look so clean / He moves like God's immaculate machine."

Music itself, its pleasures and its costs, threads through the album, particularly on "Ace in the Hole," the other track recorded live at the Agora. "Ace" rocks harder than anything else on the album, its central hook coming from Gale's guitar, with Levin and Gadd locked in tight and Paul sharing the lead with keyboardist Richard Tee's rumbling baritone, the both of them shouting a musician's credo with a joy that sounds nearly as sanctified as anything you might hear on a Sunday morning.

> You can sit on top of the beat,
> You can hang from the side of the beat
> You can hang from the bottom of the beat
> But you gotta admit that the music is
>   sweet!

The rest of the album, by comparison, feels deflated. Paul's musical inventiveness is de-emphasized in favor of a retiring jazz-pop sound meant to direct listeners to the songs' narratives, all of which describe or comment upon the actions of the movie's central character, this Paul-but-not-Paul singer-songwriter Jonah Levin. But the light jazz setting of the songs (Gadd brushes the skins,

Tee floats pillows from his keyboards, Gale and Levin hang back to make room for the violins, violas, and the occasional bassoon) seem flat in the company of the live tracks. Some of the other songs make bigger waves. "God Bless the Absentee" gets things back on track rhythmically, blending the habitual traveler's isolation with the frustrations and confusion of the road. Does it seem like an endless party out there? It isn't. Not even close. "Highways are in litigation, / The airports disagree / God bless the absentee . . ."

"Oh, Marion," sung directly to Jonah's wife, reveals what he has already concluded: that the real disconnection in their life together resides in Jonah's elusive heart. His life on the road, and the artifice of performing, is where he goes to hide. His voice, he admits, is a disguise. His lyrics don't resonate in his soul: mirrors within mirrors within mirrors. The fiction in Levin's soul reflects the distance between Paul and Levin, the latest in a chain of alternate personae going all the way back to Jerry Landis, whose initials, you might notice, are also those of Paul's latest alter ego.

Scheduled to open in the early fall, *One-Trick Pony* premiered on October 3, 1980, with a murky image. The advertisements and movie posters, like the album cover, featured a big photo of Paul on a city sidewalk at night looking pretty much exactly as you'd expect Paul Simon to look on a winter's night: a guitar case in one hand, a baseball cap on his head, a zipped leather jacket, his lips drawn tight, a hurt/aggravated cast to his eyes. The tagline at the bottom of the movie ads, "Rock & Roll Will Give You Some Laughs But It Won't Do You Any Favors," was both clumsy and confusing. Were they promoting a Paul Simon concert film or an upmarket kind of Elvis movie? Was it a *cinéma à clef* about the music industry or a modern domestic drama about careers, love, marriage, and family? Not many moviegoers came to find out.

The film begins with an abstract shot of lights moving across the screen to the hopeful bop of "Late in the Evening." As the song continues, the verses describing the singer's lifelong fixation on music are animated with flashbacks. All restage moments in Paul's life, first as a small boy singing and plunking at a toy piano in his room,* then as a teenage greaser singing doo-wop with his friends in a tiled subway station, then as a long-haired protest singer playing at a 1968 rally for presidential candidate Eugene McCarthy.

* The younger Jonah is played by Paul's son, Harper. An earlier version of the script restaged the entire sequence of a tuxedo-clad Louis leaning in to compliment the boy's singing, but was replaced by a simpler shot of the kid at his little keyboard.

The lights on the screen are revealed as an airplane descends into the Cleveland airport, and the central action in the film picks up as Paul's character, Jonah Levin, and the four other musicians in his group move from the terminal gate to the city's famous Agora Ballroom nightclub, where they are booked to open for the rising (and real-life) new wave band the B-52s. The band goes over well, but the applause they get is no match for the shrill ovation the B-52s earn just by stepping onstage.

The band members drive from city to city to fulfill their gigs, but it's clear that the group, like the live music industry, is faltering. When a handful of shows get canceled, Jonah returns to New York to see his son, Matty, while also reconnecting with his not-quite-ex-wife Marion. She loves him but can no longer abide his life as a musician. They clearly love each other, and Jonah is just as clearly a warm and loving father to their five-year-old son, but his fixation on his career overwhelms everything else. When he learns that Walter Fox, the president of a large record label, is interested in signing him to make a new album, he makes tracks for Fox's office suite, where he finds the clearly Yetnikovian executive ("Fox" is the English translation of Yetnikoff's Yiddish nickname, Velvel) consulting with the unsubtly named Cal Van Damp, a dim but enormously successful commercial radio consultant.[†] Fox tells the musician that he'd be willing to pay for him to make a comeback album, but only if it's filled with songs slick and danceable enough to become hits. Given no alternatives, Jonah agrees, though the rest of the scene exists entirely to reveal how craven Fox, Van Damp, and the commercial music industry they represent have become.

Fox sets Jonah up with a hot young pop music producer named Steve Kunelian (played by Lou Reed at his aggro-iciest), who wants Jonah to work with studio musicians rather than his own band; Jonah insists on using his guys. His manager calls to tell him that he's been invited to a high-paying industry showcase meant to create a touring market for oldies acts from the 1960s.[*] Jonah is wary of pandering to nostalgia, but he's in good company at the show — Sam and Dave rip the stuffing out of "Soul Man," the Lovin' Spoonful perform a perfect "Do You Believe in Magic?" — and the audience is transfixed as Jonah plays his "Soft Parachutes," the acoustic antiwar ballad that, like Paul's "The

† Based quite obviously on Kal Rudman, whose radio tip sheet *Friday Morning Quarter-back* was enormously influential in the seventies and eighties.

* In 1980, this was a new and somewhat shocking idea. The 1960s rebels stooping to commercialized package tours? No way *that* could really happen!

Sound of Silence," became a definitive document of the 1960s. His appearance is a smash, and the music industry seems to be turning his way again.

Yet the tragedy of Jonah, the part of him that has no connection to Paul, is his contempt for the industry and, even more, for the part of himself that yearns for success. From there, it's all downhill. He gets drunk at Fox's after-show party and insults everyone in sight. He falls into bed with Walter Fox's wife, then after hearing the producer Kunelian's slickened production of his songs, he steals and destroys the master tapes. The opening notes of "Late in the Evening" play, the credits roll, and the screen goes dark.

The early reviews ranged from positive to very good to outright raves. The critic at the *Los Angeles Times,* the hometown newspaper for the movie industry, celebrated every aspect of the film, citing the "acuteness" in Paul's "ruthlessly honest" portrayal of the music industry, then praising director Robert Young's "graceful precision" and his visual portrayal of the industrial Midwest. "One of our most celebrated singer-composers," he concluded, "has become an impressive actor and screenwriter." Janet Maslin of the *New York Times* was less impressed, particularly when it came to the scenes that didn't involve the music industry. Still, she admired Paul's acting (particularly the way he used his "innate air of detachment" to dramatic effect). The *Christian Science Monitor*'s critic called it "a delightful surprise," while the *Chicago Sun-Times*'s Roger Ebert, nationally known as the cohost with his *Chicago Tribune* rival Gene Siskel of what was then called *Sneak Previews* on PBS, called it "a wonderful movie," one of the best in what struck him as a thin year for American cinema.

But all that was swept aside by a torrent of reviews sour enough to make it seem like the critics were talking about a completely different film. *Newsweek*'s David Ansen described Paul's acting as a troika of facial expressions: "Poutiness, archness and arrogance." That last one seemed to be most on Ansen's mind when he dismissed the entire film as "a vanity production." There were a lot of takedowns published that fall, but the most hostile came from Carrie Rickey, a movie critic for the *Village Voice*. A writer with a distinctly political perspective, Rickey built her critique of *One-Trick Pony* into a harsh analysis of Paul's role in American culture over the previous fifteen years. The first paragraph focused on his Jewishness, pairing him with Dustin Hoffman, the similarly short, dark-featured actor who had been his cinematic doppelgänger since *The Graduate*. Separately and together, she wrote, the musician and actor had personified " '60s college-kid alienation, counseling a smug passive resistance to authority," while at the same time creating a vogue on college campuses for "philo-Semitism," and for "legitimiz[ing] Jewish looks."

Rickey seems most intent on hurling brickbats — what exactly does she mean by "legitimizing Jewish looks"? — but a few of her punches land. She sees through Paul's habit of shielding himself within other images and identities. She notes the contradiction of the massively successful rock star making a movie that rails against the same commercial system that fueled his many triumphs over a decade and a half. The previous year had been flooded with films written by and/or starring famous artists whose works seemed deliberately to cloud the difference between author/actor and character. The fame-dodging Woody Allen as the fan-beset comedy writer/ director/actor Sandy Bates in *Stardust Memories*. The recently divorced Dustin Hoffman as the unfairly spurned husband Ted Kramer in *Kramer vs. Kramer.* And now Paul, Jonah Levin, and *One-Trick Pony.* "Shouldn't the dramatic catharsis be in the work, instead of in that trivial limbo between reel and real life?" Rickey asked.

The imaginary Jonah Levin was doing no favors for Paul Simon. The *One-Trick Pony* soundtrack album stalled at No. 12 on the *Billboard* charts, the first original studio record Paul had made that didn't crack the

Top 10 since *Sounds of Silence* in 1966. Even worse, *One-Trick Pony* the movie was a resounding financial flop, grossing less than $850,000 on Warner Bros.' $8 million production budget. His autumn-long world tour with Levin, Gadd, Gale, and Tee offered some distraction, but by the time he played his final three dates in London in early November the strain was showing. Accompanying her mother, Judith Piepe, to visit with Paul backstage before a show at the Hammersmith Apollo theater, Ariel Bruce found Paul looking thin and edgy, not an unfamiliar sight among London's music crowd during the cocaine-dusted early '80s.

Part of the reason for Piepe's visit was to thank Paul for giving her a surprise gift of quite a bit of expensive new furniture, and he was as gracious as ever in receipt of her hug and kisses. Yet Ariel Bruce found the rest of his demeanor unsettling. He asked after Kathy Chitty, the London girlfriend who had so defined his time in the city, and grew particularly exercised as he went along. Where was she now? Did they know how he might reach her? He really wanted to see her again, or at least speak to her. But when Paul left the room for a moment, someone in his management swooped in to ask that Ariel not help Paul in his quest. "It was all a bit unsettling," she says, adding that what happened next was even stranger. "At a concert a bit

461

later, he said, 'Does anyone know where Kathy is?' And the papers got ahold of that . . . I was then telephoned by *Daily Mail, Daily Express* for a job: would I find Kathy? And I said no." No matter, the British papers tracked Kathy down to Wales, camping out on her doorstep until she was close enough to be implored to send a message to Paul in their pages. As independent and willful as ever, Kathy didn't utter a syllable, and Paul went back to New York to face up to what suddenly seemed like a very chilly future.

CHAPTER 18
WHAT DID YOU EXPECT

When the new year began, Paul gave a hard
look at the raw numbers of his ten-million-
dollar-plus *One-Trick Pony* project (production budgets, promotional expenditures, chart
positions, units shifted, and tickets purchased) and went to Warner Bros. Records
president Mo Ostin to apologize. Nothing
like this had ever happened to him, he said.
He'd find a way to make it up to them. Ostin
smiled and waved his hands; he wasn't worried at all. Every artist has his ups and downs;
he had no doubt that the deal would pay off
handsomely in the end. Just let this one go,
turn the page, and look to the future.

Part of the process had started a year or
two earlier when Mike Tannen, Paul's lawyer,
friend, and business partner since the mid-
1960s, left Paul's offices for the last time.
They'd had a disagreement about Tannen's
role in Paul's career, and Tannen withdrew
from his job soon after. Paul had turned to
Tannen to coproduce the *One-Trick Pony*

movie, but with that project finished their day-to-day association ended. In his absence, Paul grew closer to Ian Hoblyn, whose responsibilities in Paul's publishing company had grown throughout his decade-long tenure. Born and raised in England, Hoblyn spoke with the clipped voice of British authority, an affectation (he was not to the manor born) he made real with his intelligence and exceptional skills as a manager, organizer, and problem solver. Intellectually sophisticated, warmhearted, and outgoing, Hoblyn slipped easily into the roles of Paul's chief assistant and daily companion. He accompanied Paul through much of his day and was on call twenty-four hours a day.

Something great was coming next, Mo Ostin had told Paul, but in the late weeks of 1980 and the start of 1981 he found it difficult to believe. If only because he knew that nothing was coming next. He'd been through it before: the weeks and months of silence; the long, frigid winter of the muse. But it had never lasted as long as this, nor been so obliterating. As if he were being punished for his failures by losing his power to make up for them.

It continued through the fall of 1980 and into the winter and spring of 1981. Desperate for relief, Paul called Dr. Roderic Gorney, a psychiatrist on the faculty of UCLA whose influential 1979 book *The Human*

Agenda drew on his unique combination of Freudian practice and humanitarian philosophy. That Gorney was the son of songwriter Jay Gorney, who had cowritten the Depression-era classic "Brother, Can You Spare a Dime?," among many other Broadway and pop hits, as well as discovering the talents of Shirley Temple, was an interesting aside. Paul scheduled an appointment and got on the next flight to Los Angeles. Once he cleared LAX, he jumped into his rental car and drove to the doctor's home office in Brentwood. There he met Gorney, a lanky, gentle-natured man in his midfifties, and considered the doctor's first question: why had he come to see him? It didn't take Paul long to answer: it was all he'd been able to think about for weeks. His problem was that his spirit was so very detached from his circumstances. He was young, healthy, talented, rich, and famous. He was free to do whatever he wanted, nearly all the time. So why was he still so very unhappy? And why couldn't he do the one thing that gave him the most pleasure?

After decades of study and practice, Gorney knew all about the labyrinth of anxiety, pride, and shame that fed the creative drive. The shadowlands of impulse, primal experience, and unconscious association; the symbolic bonds between what must be done and what must never be acknowledged. Gorney's

465

signal case had come in the early 1960s, when he was consulting with practitioners in Leningrad (as St. Petersburg was known in the Soviet era). He was presented with a widely renowned concert pianist who, at sixty-two years old, had grown so terrified of performing that she could no longer lay her hands on the keys of a piano, not even the one in her private studio. Just the thought of it made her dizzy. When she sat at the keyboard, her heart raced; if she raised her hands, her lungs constricted. Disaster felt imminent, escape a necessity. Gorney had seen the same thing happen to Vladimir Horowitz one night at the Hollywood Bowl — the maestro taking the stage, sitting at the piano, and then, after a torturous few moments, bolting offstage. Horowitz fought his demons with varying degrees of success for decades, but the female pianist had been rendered mute, and her Soviet doctors were unable to help her.

Realizing that the Soviets weren't aware of the Freudian principles of psychoanalysis, Gorney helped the pianist uncover a chain of subconscious associations that reached back to when she was nine years old and unexpectedly discovered the tactile pleasure of holding, then swallowing, a gooey raw egg. She had felt ashamed afterward, and got the same feeling at fourteen when her mother gave her a bottle of hand cream as a present. That time, her shame rose almost instantly, and she spent the next fifteen minutes pacing the house with her hands extended away from her body. The primal association, she eventually admitted, stemmed from the pleasure and guilt of masturbation. The egg and the lotion and then the slippery smoothness of the ivory piano keys, the primal joy of creation and the ecstatic release of the music and then the applause, the cheers, the glow in the faces arrayed at her feet — a moment's ecstasy, but always wrapped around that kernel of humiliation; the shame of emptying herself onstage and not just loving her creation but *needing* it. So she, or something in her, shut it down.

Now Paul, for reasons very much his own, had done the same thing.

At the end of the first session, Gorney asked Paul to write at least a few lines of a song about his problems. When he demurred, saying he hadn't brought a guitar with him, Gorney loaned his patient his. Paul couldn't bring himself to touch the instrument on the first night, but the more he unspooled his problems, focusing eventually on his suspicion that his work had no real value to anyone, let alone to society as a whole, the psychiatrist held up his hand. What I'm telling you, he said, is that the way for you to contribute is through your songs. And it's not for you to judge their merits. It's for you to write the songs. "For me that was brilliant. And liberating," Paul said a few years later. When he got back to the hotel that evening, he picked up Gorney's guitar, played two or three jagged chords, and found a melody to skitter across a fistful of words.

My hands can't touch a guitar string,
My fingers just burn and ache
My head intercedes with my bodily needs
And my heart won't give it a break.

It was the start of "Allergies," a song that, just as Gorney had suggested, transfigured Paul's anxieties into music. They continued the intensive therapy for a little longer, but once the doctor helped him kick open his creative logjam, Paul went on a songwriting jag that carried him through the year and into the start of a new album. In the mood to shake things up, he asked Russ Titelman and Lenny Waronker, Warner Bros. staffers who had together and separately produced some of the best albums of the previous two decades, to work on the record. They got started in Los Angeles, and had a few basic tracks recorded when Paul got a telephone call from New York concert promoter Ron Delsener. The promoter had just been on the phone with the city's parks commissioner, who told him about the launch of the Central Park Conservancy, a private nonprofit group that some of the city's wealthiest residents had formed to return the park to something like the clean, well-tended public space it had been before *urban* became best known as a modifier for *blight.* Now the group wanted to launch its campaign with a high-profile event that would draw citizens back to the park while also focusing attention on the new organization. Its leaders had come to Delsener with a special request: could he ask his friend Paul Simon to play a free concert in the park? Paul agreed instantly. He lived across the street from Central Park, and his apartment had an unrivaled view of the place. They talked a bit longer, then Paul rang off and started pondering the best way to pull it off. And that's when he got worried.

Paul had wanted to give a reunion with Artie a chance back in 1975. Writing "My Little Town" for him, then recording it together had been in large part an experiment. Could they work together again? Would they be able to find a new creative balance that would give Paul the control he needed while not shoving Artie completely out of the picture? When they recorded that song, they billed it as they always had, Paul and Artie coproducing, this time with Phil Ramone replacing Roy Halee as the third leg of the stool. But as Artie recalled in the early 1990s, Paul had no intention of allowing his former partner to have any real control over how the track would sound. Artie was welcome to be in the studio and even toss in a thought or two, but mostly his job was to stay out of the way until Paul said it was time for him to sing. Artie, who had hit songs on the charts for much of the seventies, whose 1973 debut solo album, *Angel Clare,* jumped to No. 5 on the album charts, and whose second, the 1975 release *Breakaway,* notched No. 9, had become used to having near-complete control over his solo records, so he chafed against the new arrangement. He did make a few suggestions here and there but kept most of his thoughts to himself. Even that had been too much for Paul, though, as Artie learned when the song was finished and they were flying back to New York. So did you like that balance of authority, Artie asked. Paul shrugged. "Nah. I thought you spoke up too much."

Still, Artie had been happy to join in for the *Saturday Night* reunion, and when *Melody Maker* asked if the success of "My Little Town" might lead to a new Simon and Garfunkel album, Artie didn't disagree. "Yes, it would seem to indicate that," he said. "There is a chance that we might get together to record an album, but I really can't say any more because there is no more answer. [But] it was good to work with him again because I like him and I think he's talented." There was always something off when they talked about each other in public — the faint praise, the patronizing observation, the elbow in the gut, the constant switchback between their brotherly bond and the urge for escape. The burst of cooperation in 1975 ended by early December, and by mid-1977 they could barely look at each other when they sang "Old Friends" on a British music awards show. When a technical screwup made it necessary for them to repeat their three-minute performance, the tension between them eased only because both could turn their ire onto Bunny Freidus, the Columbia Records publicist who had urged them to do the show.

They weren't done with each other, though, not even close. Paul joined James Taylor as a guest on Artie's slowed-down remake of Sam Cooke's "(What a) Wonderful World." The record hit the top of *Billboard*'s adult contemporary charts, though it peaked at only No. 17 on the Hot 100, and Artie appeared in Paul's TV special at the end of 1977, singing a much more cordial version of "Old Friends" and playing in a sketch that ended with Paul alone with an overbearing director (played by Charles Grodin), who takes the opportunity to set him straight. "You know, the sound of you and Artie singing together is *so much better* than the sound of either one of you singing alone that whatever petty differences you have had in the past, I strongly urge that you take a long, hard look at them." Paul, who had written the sketch, thought it was hilarious. But he also knew how much more beloved Simon and Garfunkel was than either of their solo work, even given his own trail of hit singles and albums. Though it was entirely coincidental that Artie's latest movie, *Bad Timing (A Sensual Obsession)*, had been released in the fall of 1980 — and Nicolas Roeg's dark psychosexual thriller had nothing in common with *One-Trick Pony* — some theaters booked the films as a double feature, figuring that billing the show as an evening with Simon and Garfunkel would attract larger audiences.

The whole point of the Central Park show was to attract a large audience. Being at the center of an event that size was part of what made it so irresistible to Paul. He could do something public-spirited while also scrubbing the sour taste of *One-Trick Pony* off his and the audience's tongues. He could play his biggest songs, and the people could remember why they had loved him in the first place. But that would happen only if the show turned out to be as grand an event as he hoped it might be. If anything went wrong, if the show went badly — or, worse, if New Yorkers just weren't interested enough to come out of their apartments for a free Paul Simon concert — that could be fatal. Just imagine the next day's headlines: THE SOUND OF SNORING: SIXTIES IDOL BOMBS IN THE

472

EIGHTIES. The dressing room lecture Paul had written for Charles Grodin in his 1977 TV special didn't seem quite so hilarious anymore.

It didn't take long for Paul to realize that Garfunkel — actually Simon and Garfunkel — had to be in the show somewhere, but how would that work? Paul had little doubt that Artie would be happy to do it — he'd been having a tough go of it over the last few years, too, due in part to the commercial and critical drubbing *Bad Timing* had received. But Artie had been most devastated by the 1979 suicide of the actress Laurie Bird, who had been his live-in girlfriend for several years. He'd been working on the film when she died, and returned to an apartment filled only with absence and grief. It was almost beside the point that his latest album, *Fate for Breakfast,* released a few months before Bird's death, was his first to miss *Billboard*'s Top 40 (though it did hit No. 2 in the United Kingdom). Artie could use a professional triumph even more than Paul, and when Paul called he signed on without reservation. They still needed to work out the specifics, and agreed to work together to make the reunion as smooth as possible.

Paul's first thought was to structure the show chronologically, starting with a set of Simon and Garfunkel tunes, then coming back to do the second half by himself. But as he talked it through with Lorne Michaels, he realized that wouldn't make any showbiz sense — the crowd's excitement would peak during the first set, and Paul's solo set would be an anticlimax. Yet flipping the sets would mean that Paul Simon would be the opening act for Simon and Garfunkel, and Paul couldn't imagine doing that. Then Michaels proposed something else: why didn't he make the whole concert a Simon and Garfunkel reunion? It would be their first full-length performance since the final *Bridge Over Troubled Water* show at Forest Hills Stadium in 1970, guaranteeing the show's monumental status as a full-fledged cultural event. Michaels's production company could capture the whole thing on video, and do an audio recording, too. Maybe they'd get a broadcast deal out of it, and if the show turned out well, they could always release a live album.

Then it was settled. The concert promoter Ron Delsener was delighted, and the parks commissioner and the leaders of the Central Park Conservancy were beside themselves. They set September 19 as the date, and all pledged to keep it a secret until closer, maybe much closer, to the show. Paul and Artie got together to talk through how it should all go, and that's when the disagreements started.

Artie wanted to pick up where they'd left off in Forest Hills, two voices and one guitar, with a pianist to accompany him on "Bridge Over Troubled Water." Paul, noting his advancing years (both were just shy of their fortieth birthdays) and the calcium deposits that had nearly ended his guitar playing days in the early 1970s, said there was no way his hands could withstand two hours of solo guitar playing. Also, so many of the songs, particularly the more recent songs he wanted to do on his own or with Artie, were written with a band in mind; he couldn't imagine trying to play them by himself. Then they disagreed about who should be in the band. Paul wanted to use the funky combo he'd played with on the *One-Trick Pony* album and tour. Steve Gadd, Tony Levin, Richard Tee, and Eric Gale were some of the best players in the business, and he knew they could handle anything he tossed their way. But Artie had his own circle of musicians, and what was wrong with them? There were more fights about which songs to play, particularly when it came to the solo material. Paul had already slated in half a dozen songs from his post-S&G years, but there certainly wasn't time for Artie to play six of his solo songs. They argued about whether Artie, whose forehead had started ascending into regions once filled with curls, should wear a hairpiece. Artie refused at first, but ultimately relented to Paul's insistence. If you went into their trailer between rehearsals, you might have found the four of them together: Paul and Artie in their chairs bracketed by wardrobe busts, one wearing Paul's dark crown and the other Artie's wooly coronet.

When they were done bickering about the band and the set list, they started arguing about the songs' arrangements, disagreements that grew more heated as they began rehearsals at the Beacon Theater during the late summer. But as September 19 came closer and a full-page ad for the show appeared in the September 11 edition of the *New York Times,* there was too much momentum, and too little time, to fight through everything. The week before the show, the action shifted to the park's Great Lawn, where a stage was set up and a small skyline of sound and video towers was ratcheting into the air. A wave of interest, then increasing excitement, swept from the city into the greater Northeast, and then out across the country. The day after the announcement, the New York City Department of Parks and Recreation estimated that as many as three hundred thousand people might attend the show. Five days later they upped it to five hundred thousand. "We're back from the boulevard of broken duos!" Paul told the *New York Times* a day before the show. It wasn't meant to be a permanent reunion, he added, but who knew? "Fun is the key to this whole thing. If this concert in Central Park turns out to be enjoyable, for us and for the people who are there in the audience, then maybe we can plan to do a few more."

September 19 dawned cloudy and cool, one of those end-of-summer days that could tilt back to the sun or fall forward into autumn chill. The determined fans came with the first light, hauling their coolers, their coffin-size portable radio-tape players, their kites and Frisbees, hidden bottles and secret stashes, through the stone walls for a long day of rock 'n' roll communion. The clouds hung low through the afternoon, but the brigades kept coming, New Generation veterans now in their thirties and the younger ones who had missed the original moment and were eager to catch up. By midafternoon the sidewalks near the park overflowed with concertgoers, shutting out the cars, taxis, and buses from the streets within a quarter mile radius of the park. People streamed over the walls and through the trees, a procession of denim jackets, flannel shirts, vintage leather hats, foam rubber trucker caps, sandals, Converse high-tops, down vests, and work shirts. Preppies, corner boys, lawyers, construction workers, brokers, unreconstructed hippies, and concert promoter Ron Delsener, too — all marching into the park, hearts aflutter and hopes high.

The clouds started to fray in the late afternoon, then scattered with the twilight.

When the sky went luminous, it seemed like a sign. The day had indeed tilted back toward summer; now the evening would go back even further. Back to when your friends were all you needed, when the radio sang of a sweeter world and a more naïve time. And what had happened since then? Just walk around the corner to West Seventy-Second Street, where the sallow fat boy murdered John Lennon nearly ten months earlier. Some things were gone for good. But maybe something could be restored: a friendship, a partnership, the shimmer of Simon and Garfunkel harmony. *This* could happen, and at least one thing would be set right. Home wasn't really gone. It was right there; all you had to do was find the door.

At around 7:00 p.m. the lights ignited on a stage built to resemble a classic New York rooftop, with a water tower, spinning ventilation pipes, and a tall chimney. After a quick introduction by Mayor Ed Koch, the spotlights locked on a green rooftop door, which swung open to reveal Artie, both fists raised to acknowledge the crowd, with the guitar-strapped Paul on his heels, a huge grin on his face. Paul wore a black suit coat and pants over a white T-shirt; Artie, a white button-down shirt set off by a black vest and a broken-in pair of denim pants. Arriving at their microphones at center stage, they shook hands, and with that Paul looked over to the bandstand, already strumming the opening to "Mrs. Robinson." Artie's microphone was a bit faint at first, but they righted the mix by the end of the song, and once the cheers died down enough to move into the next, Paul picked out the unmistakable guitar intro to "Homeward Bound," their voices blossoming into harmony, and the evening swelled into something else.

"Well, it's great to do a neighborhood concert!" Paul shouted to the crowd, launching the usual thanks-to-the-mayor-and-commissioner spiel, which he cheekily up-ended by adding even more enthusiastic thanks to the "people that never get recognized for doing good deeds for the city. The guys sellin' loose joints are giving the city half tonight." Big cheers for that, because who said that growing up had to make you a square? Then a passionate "America" and a chipper duet on "Me and Julio." Then came Artie's turn to banter: "What a *night!*" A reverent "Scarborough Fair" with added bass, a little flute, and then cathedral bells chiming from Richard Tee's keyboards. And you could see that they were ecstatic, the both of them together, moving to the music and trading excited smiles and off-mic jokes that kept them laughing between songs, and sometimes during them. Artie's voice still so honeyed, his performance a potent blend of innocence, romantic yearning, and just a hint of a wicked grin. The eleven-piece band they had assembled tread lightly, though you might wonder why keyboardist Richard Tee had to use that squishy underwater effect on his electric piano so constantly, especially on the folk tunes. Paul took center stage for "Still Crazy After All These Years," but Artie was still right there, perched on a stool in the back corner, slapping his thighs to the beat and cheering Paul on. Back at his mic a few minutes later Artie looked deeply into the rumbling darkness ahead and let out a moan. "I'm so in the mood." Paul, taking a page from the Lee Simms Orchestra, barked out " 'In the Mood'!" and snapped his fingers like he expected to hear Glenn Miller's tune right *now.*

Instead, he picked the opening notes to "American Tune," letting Artie sing the verse as if it had been written for him, which, as Paul had admitted, it should have been, before adding his voice to a tightly woven duet that deepened the song's sorrows and gave new life to its fragile dreaminess. The evening continued just like that, a carousel of memories and new possibilities, right up until the unexpected happened, something so unsettling and so out of synch with the moment that, once it was over, it was easy to imagine that it hadn't happened at all. So the show kept right on moving, through a seamless medley of "Kodachrome" and Chuck

Berry's "Maybelline," and then Artie's stunning reprisal of "Bridge Over Troubled Water," with Paul perched just past his shoulder, his face slack. Then came the great parade of the Era Definers, the songs of a generation. "I am just a poor boy" . . . "A newspaper blown through the grass" . . . "Slow down, you move too fast" . . . "Ten thousand people, maybe more" — one after another after another, all perfectly sung and ecstatically received. Then, when the crowd made clear that they would absolutely, positively not leave without one more song, came "Late in the Evening." Then the band left the stage, and Paul and Artie came out for their final bows, faces glowing, arms around each other, faces alight, joking and laughing. They'd spun their spangled thread, and half a million human beings[*] were made to feel joy on a September evening, all of it so heartfelt and so exactly right that you could forget all about the heartbreaks along the way, you could even convince yourself that the clouds had parted for good and all that

* Concert promoter Ron Delsener on the size of the audience: "I forget what the police said, and of course it's always a fake figure, but if you have X amount of acres, one person takes up three square feet. So that's what we figured, X amount of people. They go half a million, I go *I* didn't say half a million, you guys did. But that sounds great to me."

darkness really was in the past.

But the darkness had been there, too. It had come fluttering into view near the end of the main set, after Artie finished with "A Heart in New York" and Paul came back with his acoustic guitar to play "The Late Great Johnny Ace," a song he hadn't yet recorded or performed. It started with Paul describing himself as a thirteen-year-old rock 'n' roll fan with the radio on, hearing that the early rock 'n' roll singer Johnny Ace had just shot himself to death. The first verse is intentionally askew, the tune's key isn't established until the second verse, which covers Paul's happy months in London in 1964. Just months after President Kennedy's assassination, at the early heights of the Beatles, the Rolling Stones, and his own career in music. "And the music was flowing, amazing and blowing my way," he sang. The third verse jumped ahead to the New York of just a few months earlier, in the early Christmas season of 1980. The gloomy chords return while Paul described where he was on the frigid evening of December 8, walking alone when a stranger tapped him on the shoulder to tell him that Lennon had been murdered outside his apartment building just blocks away. He and the stranger went together to a bar to commiserate, and it was just at that point in Paul's performance — "and we stayed to close the place" — when a young man vaulted onto the stage and sprinted at him, shouting frantically as he came.

"Paul! Paul!"

For an instant, Paul didn't see him. He was focused on his singing, bearing down on a convoluted stretch of melody. Then his eyes widened. His voice wavered, and his jaw fell open. It was a kid: eighteen, maybe in his early twenties; handsome, dressed in dark jeans, a bottle-green zip-up sweater, and clean white running shoes.

"I gotta talk to you! I gotta talk to you!"

He seemed frantic, pursued by ill spirits. Eyes wide, Paul slid to his left, at the same time pivoting to keep his attacker in front of him. He kept strumming for a moment and then trailed off, watching a soda machine-size security guard wrap the guy up from behind and carry him off like a toddler, feet kicking as he struggled. A bolt of feedback snarled through the speakers, and Paul stepped back to the microphone to sing the final lines of the song. The entire event caused a two-bar lag before the final line of "Johnny Ace." Moments later, the rollicking intro to "Kodachrome" pulled Paul back into the music, and the segue into "Maybelline," one of his and Artie's shared faves, put a smile back on his face. The rest of the show was nothing but harmony, flowers, and joy, but just off to the side of the stage lurked a wraith: the anguish beneath the love, the stranger with an autograph pen in one pocket and a gun in the other. They spoke its name at the end of the evening, two voices, one guitar, and half a million perfectly hushed fans and neighbors. Artie introduced it by mimicking the distant voices calling from out of the night.

"Soouund of Siii-lence! Sooound of Siii-lence!"

After they took their last bows and walked back through the rooftop door to their trailer, Paul caught Artie's eye. How did he think it went? Artie made a face. *Nightmare!* He didn't like the way he'd sounded; he didn't like how the both of them had sounded. Paul agreed at first. Sure, they could have done better. They had no idea how many people were standing beyond the small section of fans just in front of the stage, or whether they had been applauding or cheering or walking out when the music got going. Most of the preshow buildup had passed them by, too; they'd been working too hard that last week to keep up with the news. It wasn't until the next morning, when Paul saw the headlines on the front of Sunday's *New York Times,* that he got a sense of what had actually happened. Half a million people in Central Park? The newspapers were comparing it to Woodstock: it had been a cultural moment, the reawakening of the sixties generation. Once Paul absorbed that, he dialed Artie at his apartment and they exulted together. All the tension and feuding that had made the rehearsals so fraught vanished from their minds. Maybe the concert hadn't been such a nightmare after all. It was definitely the biggest success either of them had had in the last few years. So what was there to feel bad about? And, for that matter, why stop now?

Not long afterward, Mort Lewis, now mostly retired from the music business and living in an eighteenth-century house in suburban Connecticut, answered his phone and heard Paul's voice. They had spoken just a few days earlier, when Paul called to invite him to Central Park for the show, telling Mort he could sit with Paul's parents and the Garfunkels and it'd be just like the old days. Lewis said thanks but no thanks. He didn't want to drive all the way to New York to get stuck with fifty thousand people in the middle of Central Park. So, have fun, you'll be great, tell me about it when it's over. When Paul called back that Sunday, he had a much bigger idea to pitch. The show had gone so well that they wanted to turn it into a concert tour. And since Simon and Garfunkel had never officially broken up, and Lewis had never officially stopped being their manager, they wanted him to get back to work for them. So come into town and let's have dinner and talk about booking a concert tour. To sweeten the deal, Paul promised that neither of them would have to pay for the meal: "We'll stick Artie with the check." Lewis agreed to make the drive, and by dessert they had sketched the outlines of a two-year world tour that Lewis suggested they launch in Japan. Why there? Easy: they had always sold a lot of records in Japan but had never played a concert there. "They won't hear the mistakes," Lewis said. Paul nodded. "That," he said, "is a great idea."

The life of the Central Park concert went on. The video Lorne Michaels shot would become a concert film directed by Michael Lindsay-Hogg, whose films included the Beatles' *Let It Be* along with scores of shorter promotional films commissioned by the Beatles, the Rolling Stones, and the post-Beatles Paul McCartney. The recording of the show overseen by Phil Ramone and Roy Halee would become a fully produced live album, released by Warner Bros. in America and, because Artie was still signed to Columbia Records, by CBS overseas.* And that

---

* That was the plan until David Geffen, who had become friendly with Paul, took it upon himself to save the musician from Walter Yetnikoff's ongoing wrath by buying the international rights from CBS and releasing it on his own newly launched label. Instead of pleasing Paul, the move infuriated him, possibly because he knew that with the album at

wasn't the only new Simon and Garfunkel record they had planned. As then-coproducer and music industry executive Lenny Waronker remembers, Paul had come into his 1981 recording sessions with a sense that his new songs might work just as well as Simon and Garfunkel tunes. He said the same thing to *Rolling Stone*'s Chris Connelly just after the Central Park show. "The songs are more like stories now," he said. "They're like Simon and Garfunkel songs, but I think they're more sophisticated lyrically." When Artie came in one day to add his voice to one song — just a guest appearance — Waronker, a sensitive soul if there ever was one, was so moved by its beauty that he could barely pull the words out of his mouth to say so. Paul and Artie smiled, and Paul shrugged. "What did you expect?"

The world tour launched in Osaka, Japan, with a pair of stadium shows on May 7–8, 1982, then moved to Tokyo for three nights at the Korakuen. The tour band had evolved from the relatively staid group they'd used in Central Park. Only Richard Tee remained from the *One-Trick Pony* band. The addition

---

CBS Yetnikoff would have no choice but to praise it to the skies, just a few years after pledging to ruin Paul's career. Instead, Geffen snatched away the rights, and Paul's revenge, behind his back.

of guitarists Arlen Roth and Sid McGinnis sharpened the edges, while drummer Dave Weckl, a protégé of Steve Gadd, came with a bank of synth drums that cooed and blurped in a distinctively early 1980s way.[*] Percussionist Airto Moreira, on the other hand, used a junk shop of homemade instruments, including Josephina, a life-size, anatomically correct, if impressionistic, model of a woman that he had constructed from cymbals. They grafted a couple of verses of "Cecilia" at the front of the "Mrs. Robinson" opener, and added "My Little Town," "El Condor Pasa," and a few others. Synthesizers swooped through some tunes. The Simon and Garfunkel–starved crowds swooned and roared, and after a couple of weeks back in New York, the gang reconvened in Madrid, toured Europe for a month, then took the rest of the summer off before playing an enormous stadium show next to the sea in Nice, France, on September 18. The crowds were huge and reliably bowled over; media coverage and reviews were the same. The tension that had vanished in the wake of the Central Park show resumed when they got started on the new projects, but they slipped into that just as easily as they had their old vocal parts, and the prospects ahead were far too exciting to let that get into the way — not at first.

[*] Whether you liked it or not.

When they weren't on the road, they worked to make a Simon and Garfunkel album out of Paul's new batch of songs. Paul had already made basic tracks for many of the tunes with coproducers Titelman and Waronker, so when the joint sessions started in 1982, they set a release date for the spring of 1983, just in time for the launch of their American tour in the summer of 1983. As Paul had made clear from the start, he didn't want Artie to coproduce the sessions. He already had Titelman and Waronker (though the latter had to leave the sessions when he was appointed president of Warner Bros. Records), and he didn't want to destabilize the chemistry by introducing a new set of ideas and priorities into the mix. Artie hadn't wanted to hear that, of course. But what else could he do? The chance to make a new Simon and Garfunkel album, and resume the successful partnership, was too irresistible to pass up. So, okay, he could work like that. Still, in exchange, Artie had his own demand: he wanted to write and arrange his harmonies by himself. Paul wasn't sure about that, but in the interest of partnership and collaboration he agreed to give it a try.

Once again, the push-pull between them started almost immediately, with Artie asserting himself in his passive-aggressive way, showing up late some days, talking at length about a song's particular color or shape, and so on. For a time Paul shrugged it off with a smile. They'd been friends and partners for so long; he knew Artie's foibles as well he as knew his own. Waiting for Artie to show up one day he turned to the assembled producers and engineers and laid it out for them. "This is exactly what's gonna happen when Artie gets here," he said, amiably. "First, he's gonna come in here carrying some incomprehensible math book. Then he's gonna put it right here" — Paul pointed to a spot on the control board where everyone could see it clearly — "where we can all see it. Then he'll pull out a joint. He'll sit down, take a hit, and then hold it out and ask if I want some. Now, Artie *knows* I don't want a hit. But he'll do it anyway. I'll say no, and then he'll shrug and take another hit." That was funny enough, but when Artie walked through the door a little later it took a turn for the riotous. Just as Paul had foretold, there was the math book in his hand. He parked it almost exactly where Paul had predicted, then sat down and, yes, out came the weed. And indeed he took his hit and held it out to his partner. Paul made a no-thanks gesture and shot a knowing smile around the room.

They moved the recording sessions to New York to make it more convenient for Artie, but the tension between them only grew more pronounced. One day when Artie settled in to the studio, he took out a sheet of paper and referred to it as he sang an arc of notes that made Paul sit up straight. He hadn't heard that before. He couldn't remember asking Artie to do anything beyond a basic harmony. Artie added a second and third part, a small chorus of Arties, and, after listening for half an hour or so, Paul finally turned to Waronker. "What's he *doing*?" Something beautiful, the producer thought, but Paul didn't hear it that way. Even when Paul wasn't in the studio, Artie had a way of making things complicated. He resisted guidance from the control booth. A persistent cigarette smoker, he started smoking heavily enough to corrode the delicate folds in his vocal cords. Sometimes it took ages to get a usable track out of him. Other times, it was completely hopeless so the producer and engineers had to send him home to rest until his voice recovered. Weeks would pass, until it seemed that Artie was dragging his feet on purpose. He'd need extra time to figure out what he wanted to sing. Months passed. Nineteen eighty-two ended, and the first weeks of 1983 slid past. Then Artie decided to take a walk.

He'd started making long-distance hikes a few years earlier, after walking across Japan, a relatively short jaunt given the slim geography of the country. Just after Simon and Garfunkel did a brief swing through Australia in early 1983, Artie decided to walk west from

491

his Fifth Avenue apartment to the sandy edge of the Pacific Ocean. He was too busy to walk the whole thing in one go, so he decided to do it in sections, working for a week or ten days, then going to do whatever he needed to do, and eventually returning to where he had left off to resume his adventure. This time he'd make a tape of the songs he still had to work on and do his arranging while he was walking. By the time he got back, he'd have all the parts written, and they could knock out the vocals quickly. So, see you in a bit, Paul, okay?

The tour legs, which interrupted the recording sessions every few months, became increasingly fraught, too. Paul had looked forward to the 1982 tour with real enthusiasm; during the first Simon and Garfunkel tour in the sixties, he'd been so wrapped up in the angst of the moment he barely remembered what their concerts felt like. Now he'd finally get a chance to take in what was going on and really enjoy himself on tour. But once the European shows got rolling in 1982, Artie turned icy. He kept his distance from Paul for most of the summer, and wouldn't say what was bothering him. When Paul finally told him how unhappy it was all making him, Artie told him not to take it so personally. "Don't be hurt by my behavior," he said. "Don't think that I don't like you."

Paul didn't believe it. "On a certain level,

not too far from the surface, he doesn't like me," he said. "I don't even know if Arthur admits that. The same goes for me." But that was only one facet of their baffling brotherhood. "You have to remember that there's something quite powerful between us. This is a friendship that is now 30 years old. And the feeling of understanding and love parallels the feeling of abuse." They both had their reasons. When Artie finally broke down and told Paul why he had been so furious with him during the tour, the conversation wound up right back where their troubles began, on that day in December 1957 when Paul finally confessed that he had secretly recorded a solo record even as their longtime dream of succeeding as a duo was coming true. Didn't Paul see how hurtful that was? How he'd been fucking Artie over since they were kids? Paul couldn't believe it. "I was fifteen years old!" he shot back. "How can you carry that betrayal for twenty-five years?" Let it go, Paul begged. Even if he'd been wrong, how could Artie keep punishing him for a mistake he made when he was a teenager? Artie wasn't moved. "You're still the same guy," he said.

The album they decided to call *Think Too Much* wasn't finished in time for the 1983 American tour. The world would have to wait for another few months to get Simon and Garfunkel's new record. Maybe fall, maybe in time for Christmas. Meanwhile, they focused on the shows, getting the band and themselves back in shape for the July 19 premiere in Akron, Ohio. They had created an enormous show meant for colossal stadiums, with a megawatt, multiplatform sound system and video screens to rival the Central Park extravaganza. Given the hours required to piece it together night after night, they had two identical stages made (a variation on the Central Park rooftop stage, designed once again by Eugene Lee, who had created the stage for the Central Park concert) and two sound/video setups hopscotching one another across the country, with no fewer than 110 crew members keeping it running from night to night. They called it the One Summer Night tour, taking the name from the sugary ballad that sold a million copies for the Brooklyn doo-wop group the Danleers in 1958.

Nearly two years had elapsed since the Central Park concert, which the vast majority of Americans hadn't been able to attend anyway, so by the time they got to the tour opener in Akron, public anticipation was keen, to say the least. Traffic was so backed up on the roads leading to the Rubber Bowl that the band's bus was still a mile from the venue when the radio announced that the concert would begin in precisely one minute. When they finally got onstage, the fans in front of the stage went wild. During "Scarborough Fair" a swarm of crazies hopped the barricade and made it to the stage, where at least one tried to tear guitarist Arlen Roth's shirt off his back. At Patriots Stadium outside Boston a few shows later, fans twirling glow sticks over their heads started letting them fly from their hands, bombarding the stage with a high-velocity fusillade of iridescent missiles. Everyone onstage got hit; Paul took one in the face.*

Anticipating the wild energy of stadium shows, Paul roughed up most of the arrangements, bringing in Roth to toughen the guitar attack, adding surprisingly delinquent guitars and a slam-bang coda to "My Little Town," and taking the pairing of "Kodachrome" and "Maybelline" from a sporty sedan to fire-belching drag racer. They also worked up a handful of the new songs, choosing three or four to play each night. "Allergies," the song Paul started writing on Dr. Gorney's guitar, had turned into a spiky rocker with a vicious guitar solo, a shoes-in-the-dryer rhythmic attack, and intriguingly discordant harmonies from Artie. "The Late Great Johnny Ace"

* They had confronted similarly wild crowds in Europe the previous summer, especially at a beachfront concert in Nice, where enthusiasts started pelting the stage with Evian water bottles, at least one of which clocked Paul in the head.

gained close harmonies during the second verse and lovely double-voiced ending, while "Cars Are Cars" mimicked the red light/ green light pace of the streets with synthesizer honks and interlocked vocals. "Song About the Moon" was a mid-tempo ballad with surprisingly few harmonies. The surreal ballad "Rene and Georgette Magritte with Their Dog After the War" made fuller use of their blend, as did the faster, funnier variation on the album's pair of title tracks.

When the tour got to New York for a show at Giants Stadium and a Queens homecoming in Shea Stadium, the mania took a sour turn. Before the first show, the FBI received a death threat against the duo that it took seriously enough to make Paul stone-faced for the first hour of the show. (After which he realized it had all been a hoax and his life would be spared. "God, I felt great," he told the *Washington Post*. "I sang great. Artie sang great.") It poured rain through the afternoon and evening of the Shea Stadium show, but that was merely a nuisance. For Paul, though no one else onstage knew it, the deluge was another symbol of the reckoning he was facing.

Paul called Waronker, by then the president of Warner Bros., and asked for him and Titelman to come to New York for a meeting. Roy Halee, who had been doing the engineering on the New York recording sessions, was

496

there, too, the three of them turning various shades of surprise, confusion, and distress when Paul said that there was no way he could continue to work with Artie on the new music, that the entire project, the very idea of a modern Simon and Garfunkel album, was misbegotten from the start. Artie was impossible to work with. He'd put them off for so long, more than a year in the end, that they'd blown all their deadlines. What was worse was that nothing they recorded sounded honest to Paul. The songs had come from such a significant turning point in his life, they were too personal to be sung by anyone else. Paul knew it would be terrible news for everyone around him. Noting the particularly baleful cast to Waronker's eyes, he addressed the company president. "You're against this, aren't you?" What could Waronker tell him except the truth? They'd been building expectations, including their own, for almost two years. If there was anything like a guaranteed smash hit in the music business in 1983, a Simon and Garfunkel reunion album would be it. And Paul understood that. But Waronker understood Paul's problem, too. If Paul needed to call a halt to the new Simon and Garfunkel album, that's what they'd do.

Not long afterward, Paul called Artie with two pieces of news. First, he had wiped all of his partner's vocal parts off the album, which would be released in the fall as a Paul Simon solo album. Second, he and Carrie were getting married on Tuesday and they wanted Artie to be there! "I guess I was supposed to conclude that Paul was the cutest guy I know," Artie said later. "I guess that [was] the message."

CHAPTER 19
THESE ARE THE
ROOTS OF RHYTHM

They fought a lot. It's hard to imagine how they wouldn't, this pair of highly creative celebrities, both of them so successful: she since before she turned twenty-one, he since a few weeks past his twenty-fourth birthday. Paul and Carrie burned brightly together and then cratered with just as much force, and not always because something had gone wrong, exactly. "I not only don't like you," she screamed at him in the middle of one particularly explosive encounter. "I don't like you *personally*!" The bizarre assertion ended the fight on the spot — they were both laughing too hard to snarl anymore — but the peace was, once again, short-lived.

Their love was just as combustible. Paul and Carrie were almost exactly the same size, and their bodies fit together so naturally that if they weren't holding hands or draping arms over each other's shoulders, they were often squished up together on the sofa, more or less on top of each other. Carrie added velocity to his life, a kind of wild energy that often set him alight and sometimes made him scream. No, he did not want to roam Greenwich Village boutiques to buy hand-torn T-shirts. He didn't have the energy to pick himself up at midnight and go dancing in Tribeca until dawn. He also didn't want to have to deal with Carrie when she came pinballing home with Christ only knew what powders and pills sizzling inside her feverish skull. Then it would be her turn to crash back to earth, ashamed of her wild moods and indulgences, suddenly convinced she had neither the brains nor the maturity to keep up with her older genius boyfriend.

Carrie's drug use escalated in the late seventies and early eighties, and she spent more time around the likes of *Saturday Night Live*'s John Belushi, Dan Aykroyd, and writer Michael O'Donoghue. She also became close to Penny Marshall, the costar of ABC's *Laverne and Shirley* sitcom. When Marshall was divorced from actor husband Rob Reiner (Mike in *All in the Family*), Carrie set her up with Artie, and they hit it off so well they began a serious relationship soon after. The two couples spent a little time together as a quartet, but it was usually Carrie and Marshall off together, hanging out with Belushi and Aykroyd on a movie set somewhere or on some extravagant, drug-fueled vacation in

Switzerland, the Caribbean, or the Hamptons. The time apart, along with Paul's disapproval of Carrie's supersonic habits, tore at the fibers that held them close. They were so burned out around each other by mid-1983 that they started talking about breaking things off for good. But then they thought again. Breaking up would be too sad. So maybe they should stop talking about that and start talking about getting married. So they did, and that was such a happy prospect they fell in love all over again.

The wedding took place in Paul's apartment on the evening of August 15. Rabbi David Greenberg presided, with Lorne Michaels serving as Paul's best man and Marshall as Carrie's bridesmaid. Artie was there, too, as were Paul's parents and his brother, Eddie, and Carrie's famous parents, Eddie Fisher and Debbie Reynolds, and her born-again Christian brother, Todd. And so many others: Mr. and Mrs. Robin Williams; Randy Newman; the actress Terri Garr; Billy Joel and his new missus, the model Christie Brinkley; George Lucas; Mike Nichols; and a hundred other friends, family, and collaborators. It was a glorious evening, and the fun continued as the tour resumed in hurricane-wracked Houston, where the show had to be canceled due to Hurricane Alicia. Paul ushered his new wife onstage to sing along.

If Artie felt weird about singing his parts on the songs Paul had snatched away from Simon and Garfunkel, he didn't let it slip onstage. What came across most clearly was how thrilled Paul was to be liberated from one partner and officially bonded to another. While they performed in Vancouver, British Columbia, on August 22, the shiny ring on Paul's left hand set the tone for his somersaulting mood. He danced and beamed through the show, and cracked up completely when he and Artie both forgot when to start singing during the intro of "Think Too Much." "We both did it this time!" he shouted just after they'd found their way to the third line. He did it again during his introduction to "The 59th Street Bridge Song (Feelin' Groovy)" during the encores. "Here's a song I wrote in 1966, one day when I was in a good mood," he said, pausing for a beat. "And today here again," he continued, already laughing. "Two good moods! Two decades!" A rare moment, indeed.

The collapse of Simon and Garfunkel's *Think Too Much* came to light on October 8. News that the same material would soon appear as a Paul Simon album called *Hearts and Bones* was, to put it mildly, disappointing. The lead-off single, "Allergies"/"Think Too Much" (the slow version) emerged in early November to very little interest, peaking at No. 44. The follow-up single "Think

Too Much"/"Song About the Moon" (the fast version) didn't sell enough copies to make the charts at all. When *Hearts and Bones* emerged in early November, some critics dished up their usual plaudits while others heard nothing beyond self-pitying naval gazing, and most record buyers opted not to get involved at all. *Hearts and Bones* stalled at No. 35 on the American charts, and climbed only one step higher in England. It barely nicked the Top 100 (No. 99) in Australia, where Paul and Artie had played to hundreds of thousands of fans just a few months earlier. Even the Japanese fans looked the other way. Scandinavian fans, particularly in Norway where *Hearts and Bones* climbed to No. 2, showed a bit more interest. But everywhere else it was a washout.

Maybe the global disinterest in Paul's record had nothing to do with music. Maybe it was the video-fuzzy cover shot of Paul, standing alone in front of a newsstand display of magazines, that didn't read right. Maybe it was the empty space to his right, where Artie had so recently been standing. Yes, the cover picture, along with the inside shot of Paul sitting alone on a train station bench, had come from the same photo session originally commissioned to make a cover for the Simon and Garfunkel album, the once-and-again partners welcoming us to a new adventure.

Instead, the much-anticipated Simon and

Garfunkel reunion album just sort of vanished, leaving the familiar solo Paul and a series of explanations that didn't add up. Artie had had trouble with his voice? For a little while, sure, but he'd just spent two years singing beautifully on stages all around the world. Paul's songs were too personal to be sung by anyone else? It certainly didn't sound that way when they were singing them together onstage. Everything about the last two years of Simon and Garfunkel activity, that great traveling show of personal and artistic reconciliation, had been leading to the real symbol of reunion, return, revivification: the first Simon and Garfunkel album in thirteen years. And now we're hearing that that was just an illusion, a bait-and-switch? Well, fine. Just don't expect your audience to care that much.

And the thing is, Artie had already recorded parts for most of the songs. The piercing harmonies on "Allergies," a shared lead and towering backgrounds for "Cars Are Cars," close harmony support for the more boisterous version of "Think Too Much," and others. What's more, Artie had returned from his walk with detailed notes describing exactly what he still intended to add to eight of the ten songs that were bound for *Think Too Much* only to wind up on *Hearts and Bones*. As ever, he had turned his thoughts into a graph, his precise lettering laying out step-by-step instructions for what he planned to sing in each song, with each entry codified further by bubbles indicating whether the change was absolutely necessary or still being considered. To read along while listening to *Hearts and Bones* and the version of *Think Too Much*** circulating among collectors is to glimpse an alternate version of musical history.

Just as the songs on *Bridge Over Troubled Water* projected the often-conflicting feelings contributing to Simon and Garfunkel's fracture in 1970, the songs on *Think Too Much/ Hearts and Bones* capture the tangled impulses surrounding their reunion. Paul had spent most of his career describing and attempting to resolve conflicts: the primitive authority of rock 'n' roll versus the intellectual nuances of pop and jazz; the internal debate between thought and feeling, between whop-bop-a-loo-bop and the words of the prophets. These conflicts played out in the persistent weaving of musical styles, too, rockabilly with mariachi, the lush "woohs" of doo-wop with the chill atonality of modern classical. To the *New York Times*'s Stephen Holden, the musical and lyrical complexities in *Hearts and Bones* proved the vigor in the

---

* Provenance, mix status, and where it fit into the ongoing stages of the album unknown.

artist's pursuit of "a nobler idea" in popular music. The album was "the most convincing case for using rock 'n' roll as the basis of mature artistic expression," he wrote. On a traditional Simon and Garfunkel record the contrasting thoughts would also be heard in the sound of the singers: the lower, darker voice and its lighter, dreamier companion both contrasting and supporting each other.

They were still re-creating that process when the mixes that appear on the *Think Too Much* bootleg were captured. "Allergies" leads the first side with Artie singing the intro, then adding those spiky harmonies heard at the concerts along with a lower, descending harmony on the chorus. On "Hearts and Bones," the story of Paul's sometimes vexing relationship with Carrie, Artie's voice drifts in, whispers gently, floats off, and then returns, the voices of the angels following the couple's journey together. "Their hearts and their bones / Oh and they won't come undone." The singer didn't record his plans for anything beyond the basic (and very occasional) lines for the playful "When Numbers Get Serious," which takes the logic-versus-belief dialectic to a math class where $2 \times 2 = 22$ and all the other numbers collapse into the most monolithic of all: 1. "Song About the Moon," also performed live in a harmonized arrangement, extends Dr. Gorney's prescription to Paul for beating writer's block ("If you want to write a song about the moon, then do it! / Write a song about the moon") to falling in love.

In "Train in the Distance," Paul's affectionate look back at Peggy, their romance, and their ongoing bond through their son, Artie imagined draping the opening line ("She was beautiful as southern skies the night he met her") with harmonies that would "descend at the top like petals." For "The Late Great Johnny Ace," he added a close harmony for the second verse and a wordless voicing over the top of Philip Glass's bleak orchestral vignette at the end. As the *New York Times*'s Stephen Holden implied, most of the songs describe unifications: mostly romantic but also social, as in the upbeat passages of "Johnny Ace," and cultural, as in "Cars Are Cars." All these threads merge in "Rene and Georgette Magritte with Their Dog After the War." A gossamer ballad inspired by a portrait of the Belgian painter and companions taken during World War II (Paul altered the image's title ever so slightly), the song's verses and chorus imagine the artist and his wife in the New York of the 1950s, discovering the new world as a sensual dreamscape. The extravagance of fashion, the elegant dinners, the gilded corridors of power — all are easily accessible, but none is as thrilling as the time they spend alone, dancing to the music of the great doo-wop singers. Time weaves them together and numbs their passion. But their love continues to throb, forever inside the lush voices of the Penguins, the Moonglows, and the Five Satins. Paul takes the lead vocal for himself, handing off to Artie for the higher reaches of the mid-song digression before resuming the solo for the final verse. The song yearns for the sound of intimacy, for singers breathing as one, the same voice emerging from two throats. Instead, the voices are miles apart, the parts overlapping but never quite touching.

They would never bridge the distance, just as Paul's solo version of *Hearts and Bones* never found its way into the world. It might not have gone over that well if it had come out as a Simon and Garfunkel record. The lyrical conceit of "Allergies" along with the herky-jerky beat and Al Di Meola's porcupine guitar part sit uncomfortably in the ear, while the offbeat imagery scattered through the lyrics of "Song About the Moon" doesn't make up for the song's lack of an emotional pulse. "When Numbers Get Serious" suffers from the same absence: both have the moon-in-jejune chime of songs written on assignment.

Like the Simon and Garfunkel reunion, Paul and Carrie's marriage got off to a lovely public start. As well as popping up onstage for the last few Simon and Garfunkel shows after she and Paul were married, Carrie appeared with him when he hosted one of the first episodes of Lorne Michaels's post-*SNL* — he left his signature program for the first half of the eighties — comedy-variety program *The New Show* in the early weeks of January 1984: they were in one funny skit where he played a henpecked Abraham Lincoln to her dismissive Mary Todd Lincoln. But as the glories faded back into real life, the same problems were waiting just where they had left them. It was only a few months before they broke up again, this time for real, with the help of divorce lawyers.

Alone and bored, Paul went back on the road as a solo act in the summer of 1984. He would visit twelve cities between August 1 and 26, for a handful of dates spread around amphitheaters and auditoriums He didn't take a band with him, either. It was just Paul, a few guitars, and a long list of old favorites, along with a few *Hearts and Bones* songs, if only to keep the album from vanishing without a trace. But, really, he could have played whatever he felt like playing, whenever he felt like playing it. Touring as a solo for the first time since those treasured days in England meant he only had to ask himself. And he already knew how he felt, so he really didn't have to ask at all.

Earlier that spring Paul had met Heidi Berg, a musician who had played in the *Saturday Night Live* band before signing on to be the bandleader for *The New Show.* Unfortunately, *The New Show* failed to find an audience and was canceled by early spring. A week or two later, Michaels started meeting with the show's now-jobless staffers at his Brill Building offices, helping them figure out what they wanted to do next. When Berg came to see Michaels to talk about music jobs on TV, he suggested, among other things, that she poke her head into the offices just up the hall. "You should talk to my friend Paul Simon."

Berg spent a couple of minutes chatting with some ex-colleagues in Michaels's waiting room, and by the time she got to the outer door of the office suite Paul was waiting for her. He was smiling. He heard she was very good. He wanted to hear her songs. After she played him some tapes, he invited her to use one of his spare offices as a rehearsal space, and asked how much she'd need to live on while she got things together to record the album he wanted to produce for her.

The daughter of Norwegian parents, Berg was raised in the heavily Scandinavian Ballard neighborhood in Seattle, where she studied classical violin and doubled on guitar, vocals, and keyboards. Growing up among Norwegians had given Berg a taste for the squeeze box, which she mastered along with her other instruments. In New York in the early 1980s, Berg was riding in a friend's car one day when she found a tape of modern South African pop groups.* She put it into the stereo and was instantly entranced by what she heard. She loved the upbeat slap of the drums and the bopping bass and the jangle of the guitars, but she was truly hooked when the accordion took the lead. It was a kind of rhythm she knew she'd never heard, but which felt completely right the moment it danced into her ears.

Berg started meeting with Paul in his Central Park West apartment, bringing tapes of her demos and talking about how she wanted her record to sound. By this point, she had collected a few South African pop records and was deep in the thrall of mbaqanga, a style of township dance music rooted in tribal songs. When she told Paul how much she wanted to put her own version of the music on her album, he asked her the first question he'd have asked himself if he had been in her position: why don't you go to South Africa and record your songs with the people who made the original

* Marshall Chess, the son of Chess Records founder Leonard Chess and record man on his own, believes the tape originated with him. Turned on by shipments of albums from South African record companies he made many tapes of his favorites and distributed them to friends, who also passed them on.

records? Paul had been doing that for nearly twenty years, but Berg laughed. She didn't know anyone in South Africa; she wasn't even sure who was playing on the tracks, so how was she going to find them? Curiosity piqued, Paul asked a question that turned out to be fateful. Could he borrow the tape? Yes, he could. Berg gave him the homemade tape marked "Accordion Jive Hits Vol. II" with one condition: he couldn't have it for more than a week because it was her favorite; she wanted it on hand all the time. Paul nodded. No problem at all.

It was the spring of 1984, the dawn of the supersized American superstars: Michael Jackson at his military brocaded, chimp-toting height; Madonna in her wedding gown and lace bustier; Bruce Springsteen stomping across the continents in his muscles, work boots, T-shirt, and blood-red bandanna. All three of them flying as high and bright as newborn planets while Paul Simon sat in his apartment counting his ongoing string of high-profile flops: the *One-Trick Pony* debacles, the collapse of the Simon and Garfunkel reunion, the commercial failure of *Hearts and Bones,* his exploded marriage to Carrie, and nothing on the horizon. In earlier years Paul could soldier through heartbreak by focusing on music; it was usually the most stable part of his life. But now his music career was in even worse shape than his

512

romantic life. What could he possibly do next?

For the time being he focused on a piece of property he'd bought in Montauk, the easternmost town in the Hamptons, where he had decided to build a summer home next to the spot where Lorne Michaels and his second wife, Susan Forristal, had built theirs. He hired Paul Krause, the architect Artie had introduced him to in the sixties, to design a sprawling version of a classic shingled beach house with just a few modern touches. (Krause, unlike his client, was a dedicated modernist.) Yet Paul was so intent on perfecting every aspect of the project (including the swimming pool, which was just like Michaels's except, as Paul pointed out, six inches longer) that he made himself a regular presence, driving out from New York every few days to see how it was coming together. It was during one of his drives down the Long Island Expressway when Paul took a second look at the homemade cassette tape Berg had loaned him and fed it into his car's sound system. Soon it was the only music he wanted to hear.

Electric guitars, accordions, saxophones, drums, electric bass, organs, and percussion — all played fast circles through the same two or three chords. And they were always major chords. The minor scale didn't seem to exist for these bands — they didn't even play blue notes in the solos. This was party music, songs to make you slide, spin, and snap your fingers. Some of the tunes were instrumentals; others featured singers vocalizing in an indigenous tongue that made the lyrics sound like chant, an incantation from somewhere beyond the mist. The guitars chimed and chittered, the bass zoomed and pulsed against the *tick-thump-tick-thump-tick-thump* of the drums. The saxophone honked and squealed; the organ burbled. He could hear echoes of nearly everything: early rock 'n' roll music, gospel call-and-response, rhythm and blues, doo-wop, country music, be-bop, "hey-bop-a-loo-bop-a-whap-bam-boom." These were songs from before the dawn of man, sprung from the loam of creation.

Paul dialed Lenny Waronker in Los Angeles. He'd found this incredible music; he'd never heard anything like it and knew next to nothing about where it came from. All he knew was that someone had written "Accordion Jive Hits Vol. II" on it, and the friend who'd loaned it to him said it was from South Africa. Did he know anything about South African music? Who could help him figure out what, and whom, he was listening to? Waronker knew exactly whom Paul needed to speak with. Just the year before, the label had struck a deal with a South African band named Juluka, a biracial Zulu pop group whose recent album, *Scatterlings,* had made some noise on the British charts. Waronker had worked closely with the band's producer, Hilton Rosenthal, and the two men were friendly enough that the South African wasn't too put out when Waronker's call tumbled Rosenthal out of bed late one night to ask a favor. Paul Simon had flipped for a song that seemed to be from South Africa and needed to figure out who the players were.

When he called Rosenthal, Paul could offer a few more details. The song he loved the most was called "Gumboots." That name clicked instantly with Rosenthal: he'd heard the song and knew it was by the Boyoyo Boys, a township group whose driving brand of mbaqanga had made them a regular presence on the South African pop charts. At first Paul wanted only to buy the rights to that one song. He didn't really know what he wanted to do with it; he just knew he could figure something out eventually. But Rosenthal had another idea. Maybe Paul should think about doing a full album of South African music? Rosenthal could pull together a bunch of records by the groups with the best players and the most distinctive sounds. If they caught Paul's ear, Rosenthal would get in touch with the musicians and book them for a few days of studio time. Paul said fine, and a week later he had thirty albums' worth of South African pop in his hands. He spent the next few weeks listening, and then dialed Rosenthal's number again. Make the calls,

Paul said. Book the studio. He and his engineer, Roy Halee, would be arriving in early February.

It was that easy. This miraculous music, pressed into his palm by Heidi Berg, this pretty young guitarist Lorne had steered his way. She'd slipped the "Gumboots" cassette to Paul thinking it was the key to her debut album when in fact it had unlocked something much more significant to Paul: the next stage in his career. Berg had made him an astonishing gift. Or she would have, had she intended to give him anything more than an idea of the sound she wanted for her own record.

From the start, she told Paul that he could have her tape for only a week, tops. If he really liked it, he could dub a copy for himself. All she wanted was for him to give it back so she could get it into her tape player again. Paul did not give it back. According to Berg, when they met at his apartment to talk music, he'd tell her he'd left it at the office. But when Berg called the Brill Building, no one there had any idea: he must have taken it home, they supposed. She didn't see him much that summer; he was either out at Montauk or off to one of the amphitheaters or concert halls he was set to perform in during his August tour. Berg caught up to him backstage at the Saratoga Performing Arts Center in upstate New York, where he had invited her to see the show and say hi. She asked about her "Accordion Jive" tape then, too, and though he didn't have it on hand there, either, he had great news: he'd just bought the rights to the recording of the "Gumboots" song. Now he could plug in one of the melodies he'd been singing over the track, write his own words, and blend his own sensibility into this music from the distant, dusty South African townships. Wasn't that great?

Berg did not think it was great. Berg thought that Paul, her putative mentor and would-be producer, had isolated her best idea and snatched it away for himself. She still regrets what she did next, thrusting out an empty palm and asking, sharply, "Where's my end?" That's all it took for his corneas to ice over and for him to pivot away from her, launching a conversation with someone else a few heads away. But she also remembered what he'd said to her when she first told him about the South African music she treasured. "Why don't you just go there?" He had been completely serious when he said it. He told the same thing to every musician with ears tuned to a faraway sound: figure out where the spirit of the thing lived and go there. Paul hadn't even heard the music when they had that conversation. But once he did, he knew where he was going next, and he didn't care if getting there was going to be complicated.

■ ■ ■

Paul knew there would be trouble. The South
African government, which enforced the racist system of apartheid, had been condemned
by the United Nations and most of the
world's civilized nations both for its inher-
ently unjust national structure and for the
brutality it employed to keep the country's
nonwhite majority under heel. Many nations
refused to trade with or even acknowledge
the authority of South Africa's apartheid
government. The U.S. government took
another course, justifying its mutually profitable relationship with the racist nation by
pointing out the ties between the black South
Africans' central opposition party, the African
National Congress, and the Communist
governments of China and the Soviet Union.
That argument held no sway in Europe,
though, especially in England, where the
struggle against apartheid gathered force
through the 1970s and the early '80s. By the
mid-'80s the antiapartheid movement had
gained a solid foothold in America, where
campus protesters shut down numerous colleges and universities to force administrators
to rid the institutions of every stock, bond, or
mutual fund with any connection to South
Africa. For many activists from the 1950s and
'60s, the war against apartheid had become

the next front in the civil rights movement, particularly for Harry Belafonte, the storied musician/actor/activist who for decades had stood as a pillar of inarguable moral clarity.

Paul had known Belafonte since the 1960s, when both were friends and supporters of the family of Andy Goodman, the murdered Freedom Rider from Queens College whom Paul had come to associate with "He Was My Brother." The two artists had stayed in touch over the years, and when Paul called to talk through his South African plans, he was at first relieved to hear the older singer's enthusiasm. He could already imagine how beautiful the music would be, Belafonte said, but he also knew how complicated the politics of South Africa, and especially the antiapartheid movement, could be. So if Paul wanted to make it as easy as possible for himself, he had to do one thing before he left: get in touch with the leaders at the African National Congress and other groups in the Pan Africanist Congress and tell them what he was planning to do. Pay your respects, keep the line of communication open. Paul, ever the defiant soul, wasn't enthusiastic about checking with anyone about anything, but Belafonte said he could make it easy for him. "I can introduce you to the powers that prevail to let them know what you're doing, [and] you can have all the necessary passes." It would have been easy: a couple of telephone conversations, a clear statement of what he had in mind. Given Belafonte's recommendation, Paul would have faced few, maybe no, real questions.

But Paul was an artist, not a politician. He had no interest in the thoughts of governments, political activists, or opposition organizations. He wasn't out to subvert anything or to make himself a part of anyone's movement, and he definitely didn't want politics to become a barrier to the struggle to make music. But when Belafonte mentioned that phrase, "the powers that prevail," Paul's eyes glazed over, just as they did when Quincy Jones, the other music industry activist with the moral gravitas to steer opinion, told him the same thing. Paul didn't want to put himself, or anyone, in the sights of armed and angry insurgents. As long as no one stood a chance of getting killed, he didn't need to know anything else. As far as Paul was concerned, the only person in the world with the power to tell him where he could make music or whom he could make music with was Paul Simon. The other musicians always had the power to say no to Paul; that went without saying. But when it came to begging a political leader's pardon before he did his work, to have to bow down and acknowledge some other person's authority before he could open his guitar case — well, that wasn't going to happen. Belafonte figured that out before the end of their telephone call. "I saw right then and there that Paul resisted the idea," he said. "[He] declared that the power of art and the voice of the artist was supreme, and . . . to beg for the right to passage was against his instinct."

They left the conversation unfinished; they weren't talking about the same thing. Belafonte's head was in politics, while Paul's thinking began and ended with what he'd heard on the "Gumboots" cassette. Paul had originally told Belafonte that he'd wait for him to get in touch with his contacts at the African National Congress before he went anywhere. But the more he thought about it, the less he wanted to wait. He could have called Belafonte to tell him that. His friend was using his own name and reputation to gain Paul the trust of the organizers who could give his project the patina of righteousness. All he had to do was wait just a bit more. And Paul would not wait. He'd made his plans and now he didn't want to put them off. "It's like having your dad tell you not to take the car on a date you really want to go on," he said later, with a teenager's not-quite-apologetic smile. "You take the car anyway."

When news of Paul's impending visit reached the South African musicians' union, its leaders were instantly wary. Less than two years earlier they had stood by while Malcolm McLaren, the British impresario who had

521

given the world the Sex Pistols in the mid-1970s, then started his own career in the '80s, had come to South Africa to record his 1983 album, *Duck Rock,* with the help of mbaqanga stars, including the Boyoyo Boys, whose song "Puleng" impressed the British provocateur so much he repurposed its most memorable parts to make his hit single (No. 3 UK) "Double Dutch," for which he claimed full authorship. The Boyoyo Boys sued for copyright infringement and got their money eventually, but only after they chased McLaren through the courts for more than a year. How could the Musicians Union know that this Paul Simon fellow wasn't planning to steal from them, too? Rosenthal clarified the situation: Simon had committed to paying the musicians (who usually earned about fifteen dollars for a day's work) three times the two-hundred-dollar daily scale union musicians earned in New York City. Simon had also promised to share writing credit on any song that included any original musical or lyrical contributions from the local musicians. It was the best deal any of them had ever heard of, and it got only better when they considered what would happen when the recording was over. Simon was a big star all over the world; he could introduce South Africa's music to millions of listeners who wouldn't otherwise know that they existed. When the leaders of the Musicians Union of

South Africa asked their members if they should send Simon an official invitation to come record, the resolution passed by a large margin. Paul Simon, they decided, could turn out to be the best thing ever to happen to South African pop music.

Paul and Roy Halee got to Johannesburg in early February. During the first week of the sessions in Ovation Studios, Paul and Halee, with Rosenthal there to bridge the gap in languages, cultures, and technical practices, worked with the mbaqanga and Township Jive bands that Paul had heard on the "Accordion Jive" tape. The Boyoyo Boys were there, along with the bands Tau ea Matsehka and Stimela, whose fleet-fingered lead guitarist, Ray Phiri, developed an especially good ear for Paul's musical sensibilities. As in Jamaica during the "Mother and Child Reunion" sessions fifteen years earlier, the atmosphere was a bit strained at first, particularly among the musicians who didn't speak English. They ironed out the misunderstandings soon enough,[*] though, and after that the mood stayed productive and sunny.

Sometimes Paul would play guitar; other times, he'd slap at a drum or just dance around the studio, his cheeks tilted up to feel

[*] And avoided them for good after that by working with only English-speaking musicians. They made a few exceptions later, but not many.

523

the music across his skin. During the first week, the musicians played the songs they had brought in. If Paul had an idea, they'd find ways to make it fall together. Township Jive was by definition crossover music, a blend of South African tribal chants and the speedy rhythms of the city streets; and the adaptations during Paul's sessions weren't just musical. When General M. D. Shirinda came in to record the basic track for the song that would become "I Know What I Know" (a variation on some of the music Paul had heard on one of Shirinda's albums), he came with fifteen members of his family, including the two brothers who played in his band, his five wives (billed on his records as the Gaza Sisters), and a small throng of his children, some of whom were nursing from their mothers, with enough toys to keep them busy. They were still setting up when Paul arrived for the day, eyes open and wondering, aloud, what *this* was supposed to be. General Shirinda wore a crimson silk shirt with a metallic gray bow tie. His brothers dressed more casually, white shirts and black pants, but the wives wore matching purple, gold, and royal blue dresses with striped teal blouses and yellow, brown, and black headdresses. Paul, who just happened to show up in a crisp teal-and-white button-up, matched the band's palette. So they all sang and played and danced, the babies and toddlers watching from the corners as the day of work became a party.

After the first week, Paul told Rosenthal that, during the second week, he wanted to build his own backing band from the short list of players he'd enjoyed working with the most. That would be Ray Phiri on guitar, Bakithi Kumalo on bass, Vusi Khumalo on drums, and a few others. Rosenthal had also booked the Soul Brothers, an mbaqanga band centered on a thick Hammond organ sound, but a few days later their manager, Stanley Corsi, called back to tell Rosenthal that something had gone wrong. When he'd mentioned the Simon sessions to a friend from the African National Congress, the guy had stopped him cold. No one had told them that a white artist from a country that still did business with the apartheid government was recording with black musicians in Johannesburg. Without the ANC's knowledge or acceptance, he said, the Soul Brothers, who were members of the organization, could not play. Corsi was both apologetic and chagrined. It would have been a great gig for the band; they were all looking forward to it. But they were ANC supporters, and in the spirit of the struggle, they had to line up with their leaders. Rosenthal told Corsi not to worry about it. Instead, he started to worry himself. It had seemed so obvious to Rosenthal that recording sessions were not mentioned in terms of cultural boycott. The other bands had come in, worked, and left without anyone mentioning the boycott or the ANC. Now Rosenthal knew there would be a problem. But they could worry about it later. They were making beautiful music, and they weren't about to stop now.

The spell Paul fell under in Ovation Studios held through the second week of recording. Jamming over a quick shuffle beat with Ray Phiri, bassist Bakithi Kumalo, and drummer Vusi Khumalo one day, Paul was surprised to hear Phiri reach for a minor chord, a sound that didn't exist in the South African pop vocabulary. As Phiri told Paul, he'd heard enough of Paul's earlier songs to know how often he went to that very change, and he figured Paul might like to use it there, too. Paul found a similar connection with Lesotho-raised accordionist Forere Motloheloa, whose *famo* style of music came through the migrant laborers who worked, and sometimes died, in the diamond mines. Their tribal sounds gained the accordions and concertinas of the cities, and the combined tribal/urban sound fed into a driving chord pattern that became the central progression in "The Boy in the Bubble," a vision of an increasingly mechanized planet. On another day, Phiri's guitar fired off a simple one-five-four progression, one of the most basic moves in the canons of rock 'n' roll, folk, and soul, or any form of popular music. But set to an eight-eighths rhythm, a bubbling, mbaqanga bass line, and the mid-neck chittering of another guitar, it became something else entirely — not a meeting of distant cultures as much as a family reunion, a sidewalk collision of strangers who look up to see they're both wearing the same face.

The common melodies and rhythms seemed profound, mystical. Even if the music was different, even if they played instruments tuned to different scales and sang in separate languages, they still shared that heartbeat rhythm, that same yearning for melodic flight and resolution. The early rock 'n' roll twang in mbaqanga, the *chukka-chukka* pulsing through township jive and rockabilly, the tribesmen's call and gospel's response, the Zulu hunter's whoops with the swoons of doo-wop. If you needed to talk politics, that was in the philosophical core of what Paul was doing — the same thump in every chest, the same dreams and aspirations, the irrepressible tilt toward joy. How could there be a more powerful statement against apartheid? Yet the common sounds also spoke of the centuries of European colonialism, imperialism, and slavery that had been inflicted upon the people of South Africa for more than four hundred years. Founded by Dutch traders in the mid-seventeenth century, the port now known as Cape Town served as a spillway that worked in both directions. While the European traders and colonialists came to collect South Africa's minerals, fabrics, and crops, they also brought slaves from India, Malaya, and other regions in Africa. The cultures mixed, and all came to bear the mark of the Europeans' society, too. The colonialists brought along their music, dances, and instruments, which were absorbed, adapted, and adopted by South Africa's natives.

The advent of recorded sound made just as large an impact on South African culture at the turn of the twentieth century, and by the 1910s the ragtime and jazz created by the Africans in America echoed back to Africa, where the music lit up the dance halls and house parties like nothing Reuben Caluza, a young Zulu choirmaster with an ear for popular sounds, had ever heard. Caluza had formed the Royal Blue Singers in 1910, intending to perform traditional music. But as his interest in African American spirituals, jazz, and ragtime grew, so did the size of the choir's audience. Perhaps the greatest cultural synthesist of his day, Caluzo was beloved throughout South Africa, and as other musicians pursued the same cross-cultural weave, their shared sound developed into a style called *marabi,* which folded African polyphony into the three-chord structure of

Western pop forms. Caluzo's sound, along with his overwhelming success, inspired Solomon Linda, another Zulu bandleader, whose choral band, the Evening Birds, started blending traditional tribal chants with elements of Western music. When Linda combined a hunting chant he'd learned as a child with the banjo and sped-up rhythm he'd heard on American jazz records, the song he'd titled "Mbube" became a smash, selling more copies across Africa than any previous record ever had.

Who knew that centuries of imperialism could have at least some heartening benefits? And as "Mbube" would prove, the cultural wind blew in both directions. When preeminent South African record label Gallo sent a box of records to the New York offices of Decca Records, in the hope of getting some of them released in the United States, the folk archivist/Decca executive Alan Lomax passed the Evening Birds record to the folk singer Pete Seeger, who recorded it with the Weavers under the title "Wimoweh" — he had misunderstood Linda's pronunciation of "Mbube" on the original — and they scored the biggest hit of their careers. A dozen years after that, the Tokens found the song, by then affixed with English lyrics and retitled "The Lion Sleeps Tonight," and turned the ancient Zulu chant into a million-selling No. 1 hit.

The revolving popularity of "Mbube"

wasn't always a good thing, particularly for Solomon Linda and his often impoverished family. But it set more than a few American heads spinning, including the teenage Paul Simon's.

Twenty-five years later Paul no longer had to fake his way to the exotic sounds that caught his ear. Even after the Ovation Studios sessions ended and he returned to New York, he could call back to Johannesburg and get a handful of South Africa's most distinctive musicians to record with him in New York or London or anywhere they felt like going. Paul paid for everything and made certain they had first-class airfare, rooms in five-star hotels, meals in the best restaurants — whatever they wanted. When they gathered in the Record Plant studio, they did their best to ignore their state-of-the-art surroundings and re-create the loose energy they had all felt in Johannesburg's Ovation Studios. Often they'd return to tracks they had started in South Africa, adding horns, a heavier drum sound, and more modern synthesizers to Phiri's majestic three-chord riff tune, which Paul had expanded into "You Can Call Me Al." They laid down a couple of new songs Paul had written in the thrall of his South African visit, and added horns and synthesizers to enhance some other tunes.

A month or two after the first New York

sessions ended, Paul flew to London to work with Ladysmith Black Mambazo, a choral group from the Natal region in South Africa's northeast. Paul and the group's leader, Joseph Shabalala, had met in Johannesburg that winter. Many of the musicians who had played on the Ovation Studios sessions were well known in South Africa, but Shabalala and Ladysmith Black Mambazo were like superstars. A ten-person group built from members of two Zulu-Swazi families, LBM sang traditional-style songs with an edge that cut through to the modern era. Signed to Gallo Records in the early 1970s, the group became the label's best-selling act due both to the resounding force of its harmonies and to leader/lead singer Shabalala's ability to perform his music in a voice as cunning as it was melancholy. During the depths of apartheid, Shabalala and Ladysmith Black Mambazo were the people's reigning tricksters, appearing to sing gently of remote villages and lonely migrant laborers (a job Shabalala held as a younger man) while actually addressing larger injustices. The message didn't get through to everyone, especially not to English-speaking activists who didn't understand the Zulu language. When Paul heard their records, he heard something else, too. "Almost like the greatest doo-wop group you could hope to sing with."

Gathered in Abbey Road Studios, they set

531

out to record "Homeless," a chant Paul had written in the group's style. The original composition was a simple melody over two chords, its two-line verse "He homeless, her homeless / Moonlight sleeping on a moonlight bay." Shabalala adapted the words of a Zulu wedding song for an introduction, then embroidered the rest with his own Zulu lyrics, the chorale singing the central refrain and then shifting to a call-and-response for a brooding Shabalala lyric about a storm that has torn down homes and left twisted bodies. A lyric that says nothing and everything about the reality of life under apartheid. It took a couple of days for the song to start to feel right, an unsettling process for a master chorus accustomed to nailing it almost immediately. But when Paul heard it coming together, he left the control room and skipped into the circle of singers around the microphone. The singers were astonished. They were brothers and cousins and friends who had been singing together for years. To them, singing together was an act of intimacy, a fraternal ritual. And here was Paul Simon, a white man untouched by the racist brutality they had spent their lives under, stepping among them to add his voice to their chorus. "I am thinking, *Who is this guy?*" Shabalala said later. "He is my brother. What is he doing in New York? I call him brother."

The *Graceland* album was released in

August 1986. It made an immediate impact, compelling Paul's favorite critics to summon new linguistic powers in order to declaim the record's beauty, ingeniousness, and glorious humanity. The album marched quickly into the Top 10, reversing the ebb tide that had dragged Paul's new records so far from the action during the first half of the 1980s. Paul debuted the music on *Saturday Night Live.* After a quick introduction by Robin Williams, the camera swooped over to find Paul with sixteen musicians and singers, all of them dark-skinned, some in suits, others in the electric purples and yellows of modern Africa. The band kept to the back. Paul, in a sporty blue suit with a red-blue-and-white-checked shirt buttoned to the neck, stood at the very front. The ten members of Lady-smith Black Mambazo stood in the middle, lined up in matching golden dashikis and white soft-soled shoes. They began to chant, their voices deep and sweet and spellbinding, all the more so for their dancing, feet moving, knees bending, hands rising, and falling. Paul, his hair glossy under the lights, his eyes sparkling, joined in. "She's a rich girl, / She don't try to hide it, / Diamonds on the soles of her shoes."

It was an incredible moment. The line of dancing Zulus, then the watery tumble of Phiri's guitar, the zooming bass, the staccato horns and chattering percussion. And the gold-shirted chorale continuing their ritual dance throughout the song, waving and kicking in unison, swinging their hips. They were singing, too, voices spread across the octaves in a spine-rattling *ta-na-na-na-na*. And Paul in the front, moving with his black-wood guitar, riding those three chords, singing and glowing, catching an eye off-stage, and nearly laughing with delight.

"And I could say woo, woo, woo / And everybody would know what I'm talking about."

Talking about love, talking about music, and talking directly to Richard Milner, the classmate at Queens College Paul had taken aside twenty-five years ago to tell about his miraculous hour of singing doo-wop with the black quartet he'd encountered in the uptown subway station. He was radiant then, too, describing how they'd opened the circle to welcome him in. How they were black and he was white and from a completely different part of town, but how none of that mattered when their voices were in tune like that. Milner recognized that familiar grin on his TV screen twenty-five years later and knew exactly what had put it there.

"The niggas were letting him sing again!"

CHAPTER 20
I'VE GOT NOTHING
TO APOLOGIZE FOR

At first the fellows at Warner Bros. didn't know what to think. When they got the first few tracks Paul sent to them in 1985, Waronker, Titelman, and the other top executives ran to the nearest sound system, slammed the door, and hit the Play button. And there it was: the herky-jump beat, the bleating bass, the choral chants, weird-strung guitars, and everything else. Then they smiled and nodded and agreed that, yeah, this was pretty fuckin' cool, Paul was really into something here, it really was like nothing they'd ever heard before, and wow, wow, wow. But then they tried to imagine how they could get it into the marketplace. Whose radio station was going to play Paul Simon's version of South African dance music? Where would the record stores display it? After all, it wasn't rock 'n' roll, it wasn't folk, and Paul Simon wasn't a world beat artist. Small questions in the grand scheme of art, but Paul knew as well as anyone that commerce mattered, too. The more they heard over the next few months, the more they realized they had only two courses of action. They could release it quietly and hope that Paul's core audience would pick up on it and start a word-of-mouth tidal wave, or else they could dig deep and put together a massive publicity campaign that would, if nothing else, ensure that every sensate human in the United States knew that Paul Simon's new album represented a major turning point in Western popular culture. They opted for the second approach.

Graceland lived up to the hype. It's not a flawless record, given the pair of non-African tracks Paul slapped onto the end, the remnants of an early notion that the album would be an around-the-world-with-Paul-Simon record. "That Was Your Mother," recorded with Rockin' Dopsie and the Twisters, and "All Around the World or The Myth of Fingerprints," with the rising Cali-Mex band Los Lobos, are both wonderful tunes, both powered by great bands and by Paul's probing, imaginative lyrics. But it's the joyous spirit of the South Africans that elevates the album into something more than a collection of catchy world music.

The record opens with the accordion of Forere Motloheloa, squeezing out the first chords of the Sotho folk tune that had grown into "The Boy in the Bubble," a portrait of a global society laced together by technology as miraculous as it is terrifying. "These are the days of lasers in the jungle," Paul sings. "Staccato signals of constant information, / A loose affiliation of millionaires, billionaires, and baby . . ." The lyrics are elliptical, drifting from vision to vision: a terrorist attack, nuclear fallout, an entire orbit of cameras surveilling everything, all the time. But there are also wondrous things: medical miracles, the next great hero perpetually one jump shot away from changing the world again. A gripping start — and from there the party begins. "I Know What I Know," the bouncing, slapping General M. D. Shirinda tune with the female chorus chanting something Paul first heard as a caustic "I know what I know, I know what I know," and so that's how he'd written the lyric, a high New York love affair built on status, money, sex, and the toe-tingling rumble of the next uptown express. Paul's version of the Boyoyo Boys' rim-slapping "Gumboots," the siren song for this whole journey, is an urban slapstick of neurotic friends, romantic come-ons, and wise-ass comebacks. "Diamonds on the Soles of Her Shoes" rises from the earthy rumble of Ladysmith Black Mambazo to the glittery tumble of joy that made Paul laugh with delight on *Saturday Night Live*.

Unleashed by the jiving beat, Paul spins crazily through New York's uptown society, the empty hiss of the private elevator, and the bespoke blues of the empty Central Park West triplex. When the narrator in "Crazy Love Vol. II" sulks about his divorce, he floats down on a pillow of keyboards and angel's harp guitars. He's fat, sad, and crumpled, but what the hell. "She says the joke is on me, / I say the joke is on her . . . Well, we'll just have to wait and confer." He's on the move from song to song, one foot in disaster the other bound for glory, and every tune unfolding a new surrealist tableau. "You Can Call Me Al" teems with dogs, cows, changelings, scatterlings, angels, crimes, and misdemeanors set to Ray Phiri's towering riff, fast-slapping congas, a bubbling bass, click-boom drums, synthetic twangs and whooshes, all of them merging into a sound that brings heaven down to the dung-scattered boulevard and drapes our man in an ecstasy. "Spinning in infinity / He says Amen! and Hallelujah!"

The feeling is amplified by the title track, in which the scene shifts to the southern United States, a car ride to Elvis Presley's Graceland estate, the ceremonial seat of rock 'n' roll, the spiritual mecca for every kid who turned on the radio and heard the sound of an unimagined world. The song is a classic American vision set to the clickity-clack of an express train, just like Elvis's cover of Junior Parker's "Mystery Train," one of the most hallowed songs in Paul's sonic pantheon. It has what seems like a straight rockabilly beat, but this one flows from tribal drum slaps. Bassist Bakithi Kumalo bounces around the scale, and pedal steel player Demola Adepoju twists notes into animal calls. The Everly Brothers glide in, and now this train is coming from every direction, from north and south and distant shores. The Graceland they're approaching is no longer in Memphis, no longer a palace built for the man in the pink Cadillac: "Maybe I've a reason to believe / We all will be received in Graceland."

And that's everything, right there, the point — what Louis Simon would call *the purpose* — of not just this astonishing, troublesome record, but also Paul's career, his life, even. The train to heaven running on music, with everyone on board and every heart singing in divine, syncretic harmony. And in this vision Paul is exalted. And his record is a triumph. And it soars around the world, a multimillion-selling mega-hit, the biggest solo album he'd ever made. And what a pure and beautiful thing it would be, were the artist not so fragile, so battered, so hardened, or so beset by such raw and stubborn needs. But he is, so it was also an international incident, the cause for demonstrations, official denunciations, a terrorist bombing, and Paul's spot at the top of at least one radical anti-apartheid group's hit list.

■ ■ ■ ■

The first hint of trouble came on August 24, 1986, the day before *Graceland* was released. Dozens of stories about the album came out that Sunday, many based on interviews Paul had granted to reporters from magazines and newspapers all around the country. Most of the pieces focused on the extraordinary idea of the collaboration itself: the sophisticated urbanite Paul Simon taking on African music. They also said it was the best thing he'd done in years. But a few of the stories dug into the muttering coming from just behind the music: about apartheid, about recording in one of the most repressive nations on the planet, about the morality of a white American celebrity finding inspiration among the victims of one of the world's most vicious governments.

Tough questions, but Paul had his answers. He'd been working with the South African producer Hilton Rosenthal, who had collaborated with the black musicians for years. All the artists playing on the album had been there willingly. And how about that official invitation from South Africa's black musicians' union? And his pre-visit discussions with Quincy Jones and Harry Belafonte, the latter of whom, Paul noted, worked closely with the South African music community?

"They both encouraged me to make the trip," he said, neglecting to mention that Belafonte had also requested that Paul not go anywhere until he had alerted the African National Congress, advice Paul had deliberately ignored, and that Belafonte hadn't spoken to him since.

Paul explained how much he had paid the South African musicians, how he handed out writing credits and royalties to every musician who contributed to the songs. And, yes, he knew all about the cultural boycott enforced by the African National Congress and the United Nations Special Committee Against Apartheid. He noted that its dictum keeping entertainers and athletes away from performing for the segregated audiences of South Africa said nothing about recording *with* black musicians. "I wasn't going there to take money out of the country," he'd say. "I wasn't being paid for playing to a white audience. I was recording with black groups and paying them and sharing my royalties with them." And he had treated his black collaborators as equals: they had shared music, food, drink, and friendship. Now he was projecting their music to the vast audiences that apartheid had kept them from reaching. At first Paul's explanations seemed to work. The music mostly drowned out the politics through the end of the year, but as the worldwide *Graceland* tour moved closer to its

January 1987 launch, the political static grew louder. When Paul flew to Washington, DC, a week after the New Year to talk it all over in a public forum, the controversy burst into flame.

It would have been Elvis Presley's fifty-second birthday: January 8, 1987; icy blue skies over Manhattan as Paul flew to Washington, DC, where he was set to meet with students at the historically black Howard University. Shadowed by a handful of journalists, he had come prepared to face criticism, which made it both exhilarating and strange for him to learn, via a telephone call from his office a few minutes before his talk, that *Graceland* had been nominated for four Grammy awards, including Album of the Year. The album had officially passed a million in sales a few weeks earlier, and was selling just as well in Europe and, of course, South Africa, where it was in the midst of its residency at the top rungs of the national sales charts. But while they greeted their guest politely, the forty students who met with him in the school's Gallery Hall were not in a congratulatory mood. First Paul spoke about his time in South Africa, hitting his usual notes about the musicians' union and so on, but when he asked if anyone had any questions, the choler in the room erupted. A student in an orange sweatshirt leaped to his feet.

"How could you go over there and take their music? It's nothing but stealing!"

He was Mark Batson, a sophomore who came out of a housing project in the blighted Bedford-Stuyvesant section of Brooklyn. Batson, a music major studying piano, had a solid grasp on the injustices in American cultural history. He'd learned it all, he'd heard all about it, and now he was done listening.

"How can you justify taking over this music?" he demanded. "For too long, artists have stolen African music. It happened with jazz! You're telling me the Gershwin story of Africa!"

Batson shouted about cultural diffusion, about the generations of white musicians who absorbed the sounds and feelings of black music and took it over so thoroughly that the black hands and hearts that actually invented it vanished from sight. Did Batson know it was Elvis's birthday? He surely knew that the so-called King had made his fame perched on the backs of black songwriters and performers whose work he had adapted for his own purposes. And it was infuriating, even more so for a young musician who knew how hard it was for a black man in a white man's world. Batson kept going, unleashing gouts of fury that got wilder as he lost himself to his anger. Paul couldn't have been to South Africa, not to the real country — he wouldn't be alive if he had been. And there was no way Paul could understand the music he'd been playing at. He didn't understand the musicians; he just paid them off, plain and simple.

Paul shot back, angrily at first, but then calming himself, trying to find his balance in a room tilting steeply toward anger. Attempting to regain control, he asked Batson a question: "You don't think it's possible to collaborate?"

Batson shook his head. "Between you and them? No."

Batson sat down, but even if the other Howard students were less visibly enraged, most had strong opinions about their famous guest's cultural, political, and artistic trespasses. They felt that he had violated not just the ANC's boycott, but also the United Nations' strict policy of isolating South Africa, and that he had created another everything's-cool-here ruse for the South African government and also provided it with a distraction from the violence taking place every day in the country.

As the event lurched to a finish, Paul seemed dazed. "Well, it has been an education," he said.

The *Graceland* wars were only just beginning.

How could he have made nearly an entire album with South African musicians, recorded largely in South Africa, without including a single song about apartheid? Was he wicked or just that naïve? How had he fooled Stimela, the Boyoyo Boys, Ladysmith Black Mambazo, and all the other musicians into surrendering their music to him? And what showbiz hex had he cast to make them all seem so happy about it? These questions led to others: Why had his most significant works of the 1980s become tangled in anger and bitterness? How could he be so beloved and also so loathed? Why didn't Ray Phiri get any composer credits for the songs he so obviously cowrote? Why were the guys in Los Lobos, the band Paul used for "All Around the World or The Myth of Fingerprints," so very furious? Why had Paul refused to sing on Steve Van Zandt/Artists United Against Apartheid's protest song "Sun City"? Why was the most famous guest vocalist on *Graceland* one of the first artists to perform at the moral void of a casino that had inspired the song? And had Paul really called Nelson Mandela, the imprisoned spiritual leader of all black South Africans, a Commie? And would you be surprised by that if you'd seen what he said about the leader of the racist nation of Rhodesia (now Zimbabwe) back in 1966?

Paul never cared that much about politics. You could count on one hand the times he'd taken a public stand about anything beyond love, literature, moral quandaries, and the entertainment industry — with a finger or two to spare. Even at the height of the civil rights movement in the early 1960s, he limited his thoughts to his songs, except for the one time he led the effort to integrate the nationwide Alpha Epsilon Pi fraternity. He played his first post–Simon and Garfunkel solo show for a peace concert in 1970, then staged the first Simon and Garfunkel reunion to benefit George McGovern's presidential campaign in 1972, but that had less to do with McGovern's brand of liberalism than Paul's deep loathing of the shifty, anti-intellectual president, Richard Nixon. By the time Ronald Reagan was elected to the presidency on a staunchly conservative platform in 1980, Paul wished him good luck, even if he didn't share Reagan's militarism or his nostalgia for the apple-cheeked America of pre-1960s America. "Reagan has my best wishes," he said. "I just hope he gets it right."

The bulk of Paul's explicitly political songwriting was finished after *Wednesday Morning, 3 AM.*[*] He rarely faced political questions

---

[*] The song "7 O'Clock News/Silent Night" doesn't really count, given that the headlines about the Richard Speck murders, the death of Lenny Bruce, and so on are less political than simply bad things that happened in America in 1966.

or made statements beyond the most generic antiwar and antiracism proclamations. On the rare occasions when he did talk about current events in the first three decades of his career, he was significantly less radical, or even liberal, than virtually all the other musicians of the era. In perhaps his most explicitly political interview, with the unnamed writer of *Melody Maker*'s Pop Think-In column in 1966, Paul refuted the then-popular money-is-the-root-of-all-evil philosophy ("Money should be the road to freedom . . . it's neither good nor bad") and disapproved of Muhammad Ali's (still called Cassius Clay) branch of black Muslimism ("I don't buy racial supremacy, black . . . or white"). And when asked about the racist governments of South Africa and Rhodesia, which had recently declared its independence from the United Kingdom due to the British government's insistence that the country allow its black citizens to vote, Paul took a most unexpected position for a hip young musician.

Certainly, he said, the apartheid government in South Africa was "an anachronism," but he shared little of the outrage that the similarly governed Rhodesia's rebellion had spurred in Britain. To justify its existence, Rhodesia's white minority government and its sympathizers warned of its opponents' violent tendencies, and the possibility that a radicalized majority government could allow the nation to become an African foothold for the Soviet Union or the Chinese. "Rhodesia," Paul said, "causes a lot of emotion but not a lot of thinking." Ian Smith, the leader of the country's racist white government, "was sincere and I don't think he had any choice" but to abandon the British empire. Yet it would be a tragedy, he continued, for the new country to "develop into a situation like South Africa . . . I certainly think the African in Rhodesia should have a voice in Government" — but, it seemed, not immediately. He never said why exactly, or if he did, his thoughts didn't make it into *Melody Maker*. Still, even after his strong support of the American civil rights movement, something about the black resistance to white-run governments in Africa put him on edge.

He felt the same way twenty years later, when Steven Van Zandt, then on hiatus from his role as guitarist/consigliere for Bruce Springsteen, asked Paul to contribute a vocal part to an antiapartheid anthem "Sun City." Van Zandt had visited South Africa in 1984 to experience the place for himself, and his time among the activists and radicals in the black townships had been catalytic. Back home, he teamed with the writer and activist Danny Schechter to start an organization called Artists United Against Apartheid, and wrote "Sun City" in the mold of fund-raising choir-of-superstars singles like Band Aid's

"Do They Know It's Christmas?" and USA for Africa's "We Are the World," both of which were intended to raise money to help victims of the drought-created famine. But while those songs were feel-good affirmations about making a brand-new day and feeding the world, Van Zandt's "Sun City" made plain the horrors of apartheid, called out the villains, and demanded immediate action, particularly from the entertainers who had taken the loot to sing and dance on that shiny stage in Bophuthatswana. As the chorus made explicitly: "I, I, I, I, I ain't gonna play Sun City!"

Dozens of the era's most popular and influential artists, including Bob Dylan, Bruce Springsteen, Miles Davis, Lou Reed, Kurtis Blow, and the members of Run-DMC, committed to performing on the song, but when Van Zandt sent Paul the lyrics, he refused on the spot. The lyrics he saw (an earlier draft Van Zandt later revised) called out the names of the stars who had performed at the resort, including Paul's friend Linda Ronstadt, and there was just no way he was going to be a part of that. The next time Van Zandt recalled seeing Paul was at a birthday party for Peter Parcher, an entertainment lawyer who had worked with both of them, and when the guitarist-activist started talking about his experiences with the anti-apartheid groups in South Africa, Paul dismissed them all as Communist puppets. The African National Congress, he said, was a front for the Soviet Union, while the Pan-African Congress, the anticolonial organization formed in 1919, was hand in hand with the Chinese government. "Why are you defending that Mandela guy?" both Van Zandt and the writer Dave Marsh recalled Paul saying. "He's obviously a Communist." He knew this because he'd been talking to a friend who knew about these things. That friend was Henry Kissinger, the controversial secretary of state to both President Richard Nixon and his successor, President Gerald Ford. For the moment, Paul seemed to have forgotten about his deep loathing of Nixon and everything his administration symbolized in the late 1960s and early '70s. At that point, Van Zandt figured they should agree to disagree. A proud son of the working-class towns of central New Jersey, the former and future E Street Band guitarist had a distinctive way of saying this. "You and Henry Kissinger," he said, "can go fuck yourselves."

The "Sun City" single was released in the fall of 1985, nearly a year before *Graceland* emerged, and though it barely cracked the Top 40 in *Billboard,* it made heads spin across Europe and on American college campuses, where the song's frontal attack on the apartheid-friendly Reagan administration, along with anyone else amoral enough to jump into bed with the South African government, crystallized the terms of the antiapartheid movement and spurred a rise in antiapartheid activism in America. But Paul had his own statement to make. In the thrall of his rapidly deepening collaboration with Joseph Shabalala and Ladysmith Black Mambazo, he had written "Under African Skies," a cross-hemisphere vision of music as the essence of all humanity, the deepest and most profound manifestation of the human spirit. Here is the dark-skinned Shabalala walking beneath an African moon while a girl child in the Southwest American city of Tucson, Arizona, her eyes on a different horizon and ears locked on different sounds — the two a world apart but still bound together by music's power to soothe, to inspire, to transform. With the Tucson-raised Linda Ronstadt as his duet partner, it's clear that she is the girl Paul has described. Unsurprisingly, Ronstadt sings beautifully, her voice at the height of its power and sensitivity. Yet there's a sour note hanging over her performance.

Ronstadt was one of the elite Western entertainers who had played at Sun City. The booking came near Sun City's opening in 1979, and as per the South African government ruse behind the whole thing, she was told the resort wasn't actually in South Africa but in a native homeland/independent state called Bophuthatswana, where blacks were welcome to visit the resort and do everything the whites did. Ronstadt accepted the booking and regretted it immediately, issuing a quick apology to the ANC, which forgave her on the spot. Even so, Ronstadt's history made her an awkward addition to the album. Even though she had never said or done anything before or since that even hinted at her being racially insensitive, her presence on the record looked provocative at best, and at worst a deliberate jab at the ANC/activists' insistence that politics and appearances were more significant than art.

But just as Paul refused to ask for political clearance to make music in South Africa, he wasn't going to apologize to any political or government authority for having done so. "Authoritarian governments on the right, revolutionary governments on the left — they all fuck the artist," he told the *Village Voice*'s Robert Christgau. "What gives [politicians and governments] the right to wear the cloak of morality? Their morality comes out of the barrel of a gun." And what would happen when all those righteous guns started loading for action? What kind of morality would that create? "Let's keep pushing to avoid the battle. Millions of blacks could get hurt."

Still, the struggle against apartheid wasn't over yet. If anything, it was growing more jagged by the day. And Paul Simon's multi-continent *Graceland* tour was about to start.

Planning to take *Graceland* on the road in 1987, Paul recruited Ray Phiri and the core of his *Graceland* studio band to be the show's musical heart, with Ladysmith Black Mambazo on board to re-create its performances on his songs and to perform a few of its own songs without him. To give the shows even more emotional impact, he turned to two long-exiled heroes in the antiapartheid struggle, the jazz trumpeter Hugh Masekela and the singer Miriam Makeba, both of whom had left their benighted homeland more than twenty-five years earlier to pursue music careers. Paul had known the pair of them for some time: Makeba was close to Harry Belafonte, Masekela had shared the Monterey Pop Festival stage in 1967, and both were sympathetic to him and to the *Graceland* album, even as other antiapartheid activists had condemned it. Pledging that the show would be less about him than the culture of South Africa, Paul dubbed the tour Graceland: The African Concert, and sketched a six-month itinerary that would take the group from Atlanta to Zimbabwe (formerly Ian Smith's Rhodesia), as close to South Africa as they could get without actually playing in South Africa.

The presence of Makeba and Masekela

girded the tour's political bona fides, but given the ongoing controversies with the ANC and so much of the rest of the anti-apartheid movement, Paul went back to South Africa in early January 1987 to iron out details with the musicians and try to figure out how to keep the Graceland tour from becoming overwhelmed by politics and protests. Here he got in touch with Johnny Clegg, the co-leader of the racially integrated South African band Juluka. Indeed, if anyone knew how complex the dynamics of the African National Congress and its cultural ban could be, it was the most famous white (honorary) member of South Africa's Zulu tribe.

Born in Britain to an English father and a Rhodesian mother, Clegg was also Jewish — his mother's family had immigrated to Africa from Poland. Like Paul, Clegg had wanted nothing to do with Judaism when he was growing up, even after spending an early year in Israel. Relocated to South Africa as a grade-schooler, he developed a love for Celtic music during his early adolescence, then fell just as hard for Zulu music and dance when he was fourteen. A friendly black street guitarist took the youngster under his wing, and it was only a matter of months before the South African police first arrested Clegg for consorting with the natives after curfew. Two years later, Clegg met a Zulu migrant worker/musician named Sipho Mchunu. They made themselves into a traditional Zulu duo, performing tribal songs and dances that became increasingly original, and increasingly Celtic-influenced, as Clegg and Mchunu found their unified voice.

The different colors of the partners' skin did not escape the attention of the local authorities, and soon the police took to crashing their shows with attack dogs and canisters of tear gas, doing their best to scatter the crowd and silence the multicultural music. Mchunu and Clegg grew accustomed to having 30 to 40 percent of their concerts either canceled or shut down in mid-performance by the authorities. For their white fans in the cities and their black ones in the townships, however, that made the music only that much more precious and the musicians more heroic. The group thrived, gaining additional racially diverse members and changing their name to Juluka.

Clegg had always been an activist — it was impossible to run a biracial band in South Africa without being an activist. He was also an avid student of social anthropology, earning an undergraduate degree at the University of Witwatersand, then joining the faculty as a lecturer. Clegg understood the social and political dynamics of apartheid, and had built a life and career that stood in opposition to the notion that races and cultures should be walled off from one another. Yet his lessons on the unintended effects of the African National Congress's cultural boycott came in 1979, when Juluka scored a surprise hit in England with Clegg's song "Scatterlings of Africa." Showered with offers to perform on television and in London's concert halls, Clegg, Mchunu, and the other members of Juluka went north, eager to build their audience and take their message of racial inclusion to Europe and beyond — but that was before the ANC, working with the London branch of the British Musicians' Union, stepped in.

The more politically progressive communities in England had boycotted exports from South Africa ever since the white government wrote apartheid into the nation's constitution in the 1950s. Labor unions and cultural organizations joined the struggle with little prompting, and by the end of the 1970s the British Musicians' Union enforced the principles of the ANC cultural boycott with singular determination. Given the apartheid government's persistent attempts to present its state-sponsored arts groups and sports teams as symbols of a healthy, not-the-least-bit-monstrous society, the British union's vigilance paid off. No matter who had invited a South African group to perform in England, for whatever reason, the show wouldn't go on anywhere that a member of the union or its partners was working. Union members would walk off the job and return with picket signs. The ANC's cultural boycott would be enforced to the letter.

The problem was that the letter of the ANC's rule didn't always represent the spirit of the antiapartheid movement. So when Clegg and Juluka went to England in 1979 to promote "Scatterlings of Africa," the fact that they were a racially mixed group whose existence was an affront to the apartheid government didn't matter. They were from South Africa and thus would not be allowed to perform. Once again, Juluka's shows were broken up. Their television appearances and concerts were all canceled. Eventually the group left England without playing a single note for anyone. As one writer said, the British ANC succeeded where South Africa's racist government failed: it had successfully silenced Juluka.

Sitting with Paul in his Cape Town hotel suite in early 1987 to describe the complexities of cultural boycott, Clegg launched into a detailed analysis of the antiapartheid movement's politics, and how each chapter of the ANC had its own way of interpreting and enforcing the boycott, and how you might be welcomed heartily into one country only to be treated like a pariah in the next. The South African musician got through only a few minutes before Paul, his face gone blank, asked him to stop. "This is very complicated," he told Clegg. "I can see that you're talking. I can hear words coming out of your mouth. But I have no idea what you're saying. Hang on a sec— I've got to smoke a doobie." Paul jumped to his feet, went into his bedroom, came out with a joint, took a hit, and handed it to Clegg. They passed it between them until it was finished, and then Paul, looking revived, asked Clegg to continue. As Clegg remembered, "I started again, and he asked me very penetrating questions about how one navigates through this."

There was plenty of navigating to do. The United Nations antiapartheid committee had placed Paul on its 1987 list of South African boycott violators, putting him in league with the lowest of the racist sympathizers. Understanding how much trouble this would create for the tour, Paul sent a letter to Joseph Garba, the Nigerian ambassador who chaired the UN Special Committee Against Apartheid, and on the eve of the tour's February 1 opening in Rotterdam, Paul stopped in London to hold a press conference. He started the session by reading the letter he'd just sent to Garba, describing himself as "an artist completely opposed to the apartheid system in South Africa" who was "working in my field toward this goal [of ending the racist system]." Clarifying that he had refused all offers to perform in South Africa and would continue to do so until apartheid had been dismantled, Paul felt he'd smoothed the waters with the UN and ANC officials enough to report that they had cleared him of whatever wrongdoing he was accused of, and thus he would be free to take the Graceland tour around the world without risking condemnation. But when a reporter noted that United Nations sources had referred to his letter as an apology, Paul bristled. "I've got nothing to apologize for!" he insisted. The ANC responded with its own statement, declaring that Paul's "apology" had made it possible for them to "welcome his commitment to support the cultural boycott and total isolation of apartheid South Africa."

Paul's refusal to appear even a little bit contrite, if only for miscommunicating with the leadership of the antiapartheid movement, blew back on him immediately. Amer Araim, the senior political affairs officer at the UN Centre Against Apartheid, dismissed Paul's original letter as "cleverly worded" and described his London press conference as consisting of "funny statements" and "nonsense." And Joseph Garba, no longer convinced that the musician's intentions were entirely honorable, sent a letter back to Paul spelling out the official terms of the United Nations' cultural boycott of South Africa, and informing him that until he could say that he understood and was willing to respect the rules of the code, his name would stay on the violators' list. Paul responded in some satisfactory way: the committee removed his name from the list three days later, citing his commitment not to perform in South Africa, which he had established in his first letter, but the anger in the antiapartheid movement persisted.

As Linda Ronstadt had discovered, all they wanted was an apology. They didn't even care about the money the boycott violators took home with them. As long as you said you were sorry, you could keep every dime. They cared just as little about what you said to clear the books. As long as you acknowledged their authority and said you were sorry for whatever you'd done, everything else was forgiven. But Paul would not, could not, do that, no matter how righteous the cause. He would bow to no one's authority, particularly when it came to his music — and once again there would be a price to pay.

As plans for the first months of the Graceland tour came together, Paul and his advisers decided to make the final leg of the journey, an eight-stop swing through North America during the summer, into a series of benefit shows to raise money for a variety of African and African American causes. The tour's promoters, along with Miriam Makeba, proposed leading off the charity shows with a free concert at the New York headquarters of the United Nations. To gain support from inside the United Nations, Paul's tour managers recruited the United Nations African Mothers Association (UNAMA), an advocacy group created by the spouses of the UN's African ambassadors. But while Evelyn Garba, wife of Joseph Garba, had at first been eager to participate, her enthusiasm faded when she realized how bitterly Paul had feuded with her husband. That ended UNAMA's cooperation before it began, and prompted Joseph Garba and the rest of the Special Committee Against Apartheid, none of them happy that Paul's representatives had seemed to attempt an end run around them, to restate their opposition to Paul and the tour. This directed even more attention to the antiapartheid demonstrators massing outside the doors of London's Royal Albert Hall, where Paul was set to play six nights in early April. Unlike Johnny Clegg and Juluka, Paul was too well known, and the public demand for the shows too overwhelming, for the protesters to shut him down entirely. Still, their shouts and anti-*Graceland* pamphlets cast a shadow over the entire week.

Paul had supporters, too, including some of the antiapartheid movement's most influential figures. The Rev. Allan Boesak, who led Children of Apartheid, had been a prominent figure in South Africa since he founded the

United Democratic Front in 1983, spent a day in New York to hail Paul and the Graceland tour's campaign to raise world awareness of apartheid's many abuses, particularly on the country's black children. The archbishop Desmond Tutu felt exactly the same way, Boesak said. Asked for comment, the UN's Amer Araim was quick to point out that the antiapartheid committee basically agreed. "But Simon should reply to the letter of the chairman of the Special Committee. If he would do that, we have no problem with his tour or any of his activities." A reply to a letter. Just that. "We think the whole episode could be closed when he has made a proper formulation . . . to the Special Committee," wrote ANC secretary of culture Barbara Masekela in her part of a special issue of the American news magazine *Africa Report.*

Again, there were things Paul wouldn't do. He wouldn't write the letter. And though he had been generous, to a point, with songwriting credits for the African musicians, he didn't do the same for the two American bands with whom he'd worked on two of the album's other tracks.

It was galling, particularly for Los Lobos, the critically beloved Los Angeles–based Mexican American group whose debut album with Warner Bros., 1984's *How Will the Wolf Survive?,* had earned them a national audience and the admiration of their label mate from the Upper West Side of New York City. As saxophonist Steve Berlin recalls, he got a call from Warner Bros. president Lenny Waronker saying how big a fan of the group Paul had become, and that he really wanted to record a track with them when he was in LA in a few days, Berlin was delighted. He'd grown up in Philadelphia; he knew all about Paul's music. The band's other members, though, David Hidalgo, Cesar Rosas, Louie Perez, and Conrad Lozano, came from a culture defined by Mexican and Latino music. "They knew 'Sound of Silence,' but they really couldn't care less," Berlin says. Warner Bros. Records ran family-style in those days: the lobby was full of musicians and friends; everyone's office, including those of Waronker and Mo Ostin, had an open door and a warm welcome. So if Waronker asked them to play a session for another member of the Warner Bros. family, they were there, no questions asked. So the band left it to their manager to sort out the details, and when the day came, they went to Amigo Studios in the San Fernando Valley ready to work.

Paul was there with engineer Roy Halee, who showed them around the studio, but Paul was surprisingly chilly, giving the most perfunctory of hellos before vanishing into the control booth, where he could peer down through a window and communicate through

the studio intercom, lending him an omni-
scient voice-from-the-skies effect as he directed the band through the day. Not that he
had much in the way of specific directions to
give. He launched the session by telling the
group to "just play something," leaving them
to meander from one unstructured jam to
the next, churning away for five or fifteen or
twenty minutes at a time before the intercom
would crackle. "Nope, that isn't it," Paul
would say. "Try a six-eight. Nope, try a blues
groove." They'd spend the next ten or fifteen
minutes on a twelve-bar blues piece only to
hear the static and then Paul's "Eh, no, that
ain't it, either. Try something else." Ten
minutes later and — "Nope, nope, nope.
Sorta close but still not there. What else you
got?" And on it went, much to the mounting
anger of the band members, none of whom
was the least bit interested in coming back
for a second day of this kind of monkey-in-a-
cage shit. How the *fuck* did this guy have no
ideas? What the hell was this supposed to be,
anyway? Let's just get our gear and go home.
Berlin made a quick call to Waronker, telling
him that it wasn't working and that now the
guys were in revolt and had no intention of
returning. Waronker begged Berlin to get the
band back into the studio. "You've gotta get
them back, you gotta hang in there, we gotta
make this happen." Berlin was wary, but
again, family was family; he'd get the band to

come back. Waronker gushed with relief. "I swear I'll make it up to you," Berlin recalled hearing him say.

As Berlin recalled, when he relayed all of this to Hidalgo, Rosas, Perez, and Lozano, they finally threw up their hands and said sure, fine, whatever, let's just get this fuckin' thing over with already. They all showed up the next day, took up their instruments, and heard the voice from the ceiling telling them to play something, whatever they had. They spent another futile hour or two achieving nothing, until Hidalgo started playing some chords the other guys recognized from recent band rehearsals and jumped in after him, playing a driving two-chord progression that jumped into a simple but catchy chorus with contrasting rock and Mexican-style guitars, a nice accordion riff, and Berlin's saxophone adding texture to the lower registers. They had already put some time into it; everything about the tune came straight from the same well that had sprung the title track of their first album. So of course that was the point where everything turned around.

"Wait, what's that? What are you playing there?"

Now the voice from the ceiling was intrigued. Hidalgo looked up to say it was something they'd been working on.

"Okay, how's it go?"

Hidalgo led the rest of the group through

the tune, all of them so relieved to glimpse a glimmer of light at the end of the tunnel. Paul was sold. "Let's work on that," he said, and two or three takes later, he declared himself happy, and the Los Lobos guys were out the door, then back in their cars headed for home. Paul wrote some lyrics to go with the tune and called Hidalgo and Perez in to sing it with him. And that was the last they heard from him until *Graceland* came out and "All Around the World or The Myth of Fingerprints" was credited as a solo Paul Simon composition.* At first the LA band was sure the printer had made a mistake, that they'd get a call from Paul's office offering profuse apologies and the next printings would be more accurate.

But that didn't happen, and no wonder: Paul disputes the Los Lobos musicians' entire account of their collaboration, claiming that he'd just been after a "generic Los Lobos dikka-de-dikka guitar sound," and that he had helped shape the music they recorded.

But a similar story seems to lie beneath the album's other non–South African track, recorded with the New Orleans zydeco band

* Paul's lyric is an abstruse analysis of fame, identity, and the myth that anything or anyone can't become something or someone else at will. Or, as the famous talk show host says about fingerprints, "I've seen 'em all, and man they're all the same."

Rockin' Dopsie and the Twisters. "That Was Your Mother," as Paul titled the tune, is a light-footed zydeco shuffle that boasts another great lyric, a tongue-in-cheek lecture to a child about how much better his dad's life was before he was born. The track is great, too, a hippity-hop zydeco shuffle built around an ear-grabbing accordion riff, with a great sax solo that takes the tune to another level. Seven years earlier, a strikingly similar set of chords and central accordion riff were part of a Dopsie song called "My Baby, She's Gone," which was credited entirely to Alton Rubin Sr., Rockin' Dopsie's legal name. Granted, Dopsie's original has a bluesier melody and a slightly crooked beat, and the sax solo is different from Paul's version. But the heart of the tune bears a distinct resemblance to the 1979 recording. And yet *Graceland* credits only one writer for the song: Paul Simon.

Maybe Dopsie figured that was a small price to pay for the global exposure and additional work he and his New Orleans party band would undoubtedly receive for being on an album with one of the music industry's biggest stars. But Los Lobos weren't quite as hungry for the Paul Simon bump. *How Will the Wolf Survive?* had sold far better than they imagined it would; their label was behind them and they were sifting through a pile of offers, including the one that would net them a No. 1 single in the theme song to the Ritchie Valens biopic *La Bamba.* But they also knew that they made themselves vulnerable. The group's manager, a dedicated, hardworking young woman named Linda Clark, had been an assistant publicist at Slash Records when they met. She signed on to be the group's manager and the arrangement worked perfectly when they were a regional band touring clubs and making records for independent labels. But when they launched themselves into the big time the terms of Clark's job changed dramatically. But Clark had little experience in the rough-and-tumble of big money entertainment and, like her clients, had gone into the Paul Simon session figuring that they would all work on a handshake and trust the fraternal feeling between Warner's artists. As a result they had made no presession agreements beyond the understanding that they would earn double the union's hourly scale for playing the sessions. Writing credits and royalty splits never came up, and in the end he took them all for himself. The members of Los Lobos were understandably outraged, but once again Paul felt he had nothing to apologize for.

With the company riding high on *Graceland*'s global success, Waronker asked Berlin to convince his bandmates to keep their displeasure to themselves: the last thing the label needed was more controversy around their biggest hit of the year. When a couple of band members couldn't resist grumbling in public, Waronker was adamant: *Don't do this, guys, don't speak ill of Paul, it's bad for the family.* He'd make it up to them, he'd make it good, Waronker swore he would. And they had no doubt that he would. They wanted to be loyal to Warner Bros. and Lenny really was a great guy. A gentle soul who cared deeply about music and musicians. Still, Linda Clark felt obligated to confront Paul, to tell him and his management that the members of Los Lobos felt that the song was at least half theirs and were pissed off about what Paul had done, and that if he didn't do something to make it right, the next call they would get, she promised, would be from a lawyer. According to Berlin, the response from Paul's office was unapologetic.

You don't like it? Sue me. See what happens.

And that, according to Muscle Shoals Rhythm Section's bassist David Hood, was more or less the same thing they had heard a decade earlier when they inquired why the production royalties they were supposed to earn for the tracks they had played on *There Goes Rhymin' Simon* stopped coming.

See what happens. See Graceland: The African Concert tour roll into Rufaro Stadium in Harare, Zimbabwe: Paul in his immaculate white T-shirt and black jeans, his all-African

569

band bloused in yellows, golds, black, multi-hued stripes — all moving, ducking, and rolling to the rhythm as the ten orange-bloused singers of Ladysmith Black Mambazo dance across the stage; a smaller line of women singers in black skirts and silver glinting tops; then Hugh Masekela with his brass horn and jazzbo brim. They're playing "Township Jive," a feel-good jam that the main musicians, Paul, Ray Phiri, Masekela, and Joseph Shabla-lala, came up with for a show opener. An overture of sorts, a party starter — it works like magic, the floor of the stadium alive with motion, raised hands and open, smiling faces; and here the colors are just as varied and just as vivid: black faces, brown faces, white faces, babies on their shoulders, children dancing at their sides. And they're writhing out of the bad juju of "The Boy in the Bubble," then jumping like street partiers through "Gumboots," which segues sweetly into the Del-Vikings' "Whispering Bells." Then here's Masekela again, righteous and joyful as he sings and plays his horn through his "Bring Him Back Home," a plea for the release of Nelson Mandela, still locked in his bare cell on Robben Island. Coming from a black man whose words are amplified by tens of thousands of black, white, and brown male and female voices, it's as pure an affront to apartheid as could be created anywhere. And no one needed to get anyone's permission to make it.

See Paul at the Grammy Awards in Los Angeles a week later, running onstage to collect his Album of the Year trophy from actors Whoopi Goldberg and Don Johnson, and the guy is so happy, just bursting with it, it's like he's shining, gleaming in the spotlight and just kinda dreamy as he thanks good old Roy Halee, studio genius, and then of course Mo and Lenny. Paul calls out to Los Lobos from East LA, and Rockin' Dopsie in New Orleans, and then, with a serious face now — this is a statement he truly must deliver correctly — his African compatriots in music.

"They live, along with other South African artists and their countrymen, under one of the most repressive regimes on the planet today, and still they are able to produce music of great power and nuance and joy." He pauses, seems to choke something back. "A-A-And I find that just extraordinary, and they have my great respect and love."

CHAPTER 21
THE WHOLE WORLD WHISPERING

Graceland sold more than six million copies around the world during its first year, making it the highest-selling solo album that Paul had ever made. By the time the album collected yet another Grammy in 1988 — the title track won Song of the Year honors due to its being released as a single in late 1987 — he had ascended to a sphere of fame and influence he hadn't seen since Simon and Garfunkel's *Bridge Over Troubled Water* peak in 1970. And he had done it in a style so exotic that virtually no one in the pop mainstream had known it existed. There was no one in pop music to compare with him, or in all of popular culture, for that matter. He had refashioned himself into a completely different kind of artist with what seemed to be a completely different career. And again, he had made it look easy.

He revived Graceland: The African Concert for a European tour in the summer of 1989, and when South Africa's apartheid government released political prisoner Nelson Mandela after twenty-seven years, Paul was the most prominent artist invited to perform at the 325,000-strong welcoming rally held in Los Angeles when Mandela got to the United States in the early summer of 1990. Paul came with Ladysmith Black Mambazo and spoke of Mandela not as the Communist he'd dismissed in 1985, but as one of the world's last heroes. "To me, the message is that a moral position cannot be broken and will prevail," he told reporters backstage. "We are lacking that moral conviction in the world today." Whatever anger remained in the antiapartheid movement, and in the scrum of political groups vying for authority in the looming postapartheid South Africa, kept out of sight. For the time being, anyway.

Standing on the big stage in Los Angeles that day, arm in arm with the living saint of the antiapartheid movement, Paul hovered above all the protests, the shouted diatribes, and the published canings. He'd been proven right again, both as a moral actor and as one of the modern era's most daring artistic visionaries and most successful popular artists. His ambitions now leaped to all-new heights. Thirty years after breaking in with "Hey, Schoolgirl" and twenty years after reaching number one with "The Sound of Silence," he felt he was finally finding his artistic stride. There was still so much to discover, so much life to live, so much music to make. And he was already headed to the jungle, some labyrinthine river valley near the southern tip of South America, Roy Halee at his side and a new musical vision steeping in the medicine man's magical pot.

Paul got the idea while chatting in the New York nightclub SOB's with Puerto Rican pianist Eddie Palmieri and jazz trumpeter Dizzy Gillespie. Palmieri brought it up first, half-jokingly. *Graceland* was so great, he said, you should keep going. South Africa may have the continent's great singers, but Africa's great drummers were on the continent's West Coast, which was the launching pad for the African diaspora, first to the lower reaches of South America, then through Brazil, and up to the Dominican Republic and Cuba on its way to Miami and New Orleans. Paul was intrigued. He'd already worked with the Senegalese singer/drummer Youssou N'Dour and with Nigeria's dynamic singer/showman King Sunny Ade, so he knew something about Africa's many sounds and cultural styles. The one thing he lacked was a starting point, someone to step into the role Hilton Rosenthal had played in Johannesburg, the local expert who could clear his way, bring in the right players, and make the crucial introductions.

A few weeks later he got a call from Quincy

Jones asking if he'd be up for singing a duet with Milton Nascimento for the new album the great Brazilian pop singer was recording in Los Angeles. Paul was already a fan, so he went to California,* and when they were finished with the track he asked if Nascimento could help get him set up with drummers in Brazil. The singer took his guest up to the control booth, where his producer, Marco Mazzola, one of the central figures in Brazilian music at the time, had been working. They had a nice chat about the drumming traditions that followed the Africans from Guinea to Puerto Rico and beyond, so Mazzola was surprised to pick up his home

* Nascimento sent Paul a recording of the song and asked if he could write a part for himself with original English words, a task Paul found impossible to perform. He became so panicked about having to let down Nascimento that he became feverish and exhausted and convinced himself he had the dread tick-borne Lyme disease. But when he told this to Warner Bros. uber-boss Mo Ostin, the executive proposed that Paul's symptoms were entirely psychosomatic and he should focus on writing his part. Paul rejected this diagnosis — "I don't *do* psychosomatic," he assured Ostin — but when he brought what he had to the studio and Nascimento told him it was beautiful, Paul soared through the all-night session. "Lyme disease," he noted, "completely and miraculously cured."

telephone a few weeks later and hear Paul's voice. It took a few minutes for Paul to convince him that he wasn't some wise guy playing a prank, and once they sorted that out, Paul told him his plan. He'd be flying down in just a few weeks. Would Mazzola have time to work with him? If so, could he pull together some interesting music and musicians for him to listen to when he got there?

Paul arrived at Mazzola's studio in Rio de Janeiro with engineer Roy Halee and friend and sometime coproducer Phil Ramone. Given the size of the country and the low-to-the-ground ways of its best drummers, Mazzola knew they wouldn't be able to corral the musicians in a big-city recording studio. Instead, he packed up his visitors for a two-hour flight to Salvador, a small city in the northeast of the country, where the Banda Olodum drumming group worked out of the cultural center they had set up in the old town's Pelourinho Square. The group had a staunch commitment to protecting the perennially threatened rights, lives, and culture of the nation's dark-skinned African Brazilian community. It was a struggle, particularly given the currents of tribalism, racism, and corruption in the region, so they pursued their calling with fiery eyes and gun-heavy belts.

After hearing the fourteen-strong drumming group perform in Pelourinho Square, Paul went to Olodum's leaders to arrange a recording session. The guns stayed holstered, but the talks grew tense, particularly when Paul explained that along with their services he needed to buy the rights to everything they played when they were recording for him. At first that was a problem — what was business as usual for professional musicians was something else to activists whose entire mission was built around keeping their traditions in the hands of the people whose forebears spoke through the skin of their drums. In the end, though, the prospect of being featured on an American superstar's next hit album was too compelling to pass up. They signed Paul's contract, he wrote a significant check, and they set a time for the next day.

Olodum had too many members to fit into any of the recording studios in Salvador, so Paul and his helpers arranged to have a portable eight-track recorder flown up from Rio de Janeiro, setting it up on the edge of Pelourinho Square, where it would connect to the microphones Halee hung from strategically placed wires, light posts, and balconies. The group got started on one of their standard patterns, a nearly martial beat that took on new layers that gradually bent the rhythm into a juju that pulled at the ankles and migrated up into the hands and chest. Paul, Halee, and Ramone caught forty minutes of it, then took the recording back to Rio and then up to New York.

When Paul returned to Brazil six months later, he recorded the work of Uakti, an instrumental group led by Marco Antonio Guimarães, a classically trained cellist whose handmade instruments were constructed from specially cut PVC tubes, foam rubber, and other found objects. Inspired in part by a South American myth about a hole-filled creature who beguiled the local ladies whenever the wind blew through his body, Guimarães's creations were tuned instruments that came together into a melodic rumble that was a cross between a mbira, a marimba, an electric bass, and a bag of hollow coconuts and gourds. Quite a bit gentler than Olodum's thunder of the gods, but every bit as mesmerizing.

It was that spell, the hypnotic charge in the ecstatic pounding, that drew him in in the first place. When Paul followed the drummers' trail to Brazil, he hadn't come with any songs or even *ideas* for songs. The inspiration for his next album would spring from the rhythms the musicians created when he was with them. That's why he kept going back, back to the land of the musical trees, the thrumming water bowls, the agogo bells, the talking drum and dancing bongos, the congas and the bow, the arrow and gourd-built *berimbau*. Each time, he worked with a different set of players, a different set of instruments, all invoking the voices of the spirits, the ancient ones and the timeless ones, too. He was looking for anything that could gather him up and give him vision, show him his path forward.

The divorce from Carrie hadn't taken. They spent a few months apart, then started talking again, then seeing each other. Then they were back to living together in his apartment when she was in town, and in her Beverly Hills cottage when he was in LA. There had always been something perfect about them when they were getting along: the way they huddled together, the way he grounded her, the way she could make him laugh so easily. And he loved her, with a desperation that sometimes frightened him. Then he'd say something too cutting, or she'd move like a tornado for days or weeks, a ball of energy raking the countryside until it ran itself into the ground, so tangled in its own wreckage it could be days or weeks before she righted herself. In the mid-1980s, Carrie had taken herself to rehab to shed her drug habits, but drugs were only symptomatic of the manic-depression she'd suffered her entire adult life. She'd recognized it in her father when she was younger, the outlandish moods and compulsive habits that had consumed her throughout her adult life. Her depths were unimaginably deep, and Paul's were nothing to sneeze at, either, so they clung to each other with a passion that could both soothe and abrade.

Maybe the jungle held more spells for him, and maybe for Carrie, too. When she joined him on a float trip down a remote stretch of the Amazon, Paul got to talking to one of the boat hands and learned that the river would take them through a village close to a *brujo,* a spiritual healer whose magic called to unwell and unhappy people from miles away. Invited to walk the half mile to the *brujo*'s house, Paul and Carrie set out in the late afternoon and arrived to find the doctor tending to other clients with his tribal cures, applying herbs, speaking incantations, praying to the gods in the air and in the bush. After dark, the *brujo* began an ayahuasca ceremony, a spiritual cleansing ritual that begins with a long *icaros,* a song-like incantation meant to enhance the visionary effect of the thick, brown tea he was brewing from a combination of caapi vine and the leaves of psychedelic plants known only to the *brujo.* Once they'd consumed the tea, the doctor, speaking through an interpreter, prepared his patients for the visionary experience they would encounter that evening. "The anaconda will appear to you in a vision," he said. "But don't be alarmed — it's a vision." The appearance of the snake would herald hours of seeing into their deepest spiritual selves, and communing with a higher power, a divine, all-knowing presence that would reveal the essence of their souls and uncover where they had been broken and perhaps, if they were lucky, how they might dispel the bad energy that had fixed itself to their spirits.

Paul and Carrie settled into one of the doctor's treatment rooms, actually a rustic shack near his house, and fell into the spell of their hallucinations. The *brujo* came to check on them (with an interpreter) and asked if they had specific problems they hoped to resolve. Carrie said she did have a problem, and the *brujo* nodded and said he already knew what it was, and he knew where she would find her solution. When he turned to her companion, Paul could only say that one of his elbows had been bothering him lately, maybe just a little bit, which only earned him an aggravated glance from the *brujo*. "He said, 'Oh, that's nothing.' Like, don't come here with an elbow problem, we're dealing with serious problems here!" Paul recalled a few years later.

After the *brujo* left, Paul lay back, resting his head on Carrie's lap, while she stroked his hair and then laid her hand across his forehead, first just feeling his warmth, but then becoming aware of an odd vibrating sensation. "It felt like it was pulsing and growing," she said. "Like . . . WAAHHHH-

WRRR!" Just another sizzle-brained fantasy, or a transcendent flash from somewhere beyond the inky jungle night? As close as they were, Carrie still talked about feeling pinned beneath Paul's ever-spinning, ever-controlling brain; about the way he, like so many powerful men she knew, assumed his expertise and control over every situation. When Carrie complimented him for having so much self-discipline, Paul got cranky because, he said, discipline had *nothing* to do with it. He was just *well organized.* "It's not an argument, more like debate club," she said. "It's not that you disagree with [him], you just didn't agree in the *right way.*" He was mercurial: sunlit and laughing one day, consumed by his work the next, then wandering blindly around the moors the day after that, kicking his fools and bellowing into the murderous gale.

They had spent most of twelve years together, driving each other wild in all the best and worst ways. When they came down from the ayahuasca tea and found their way back to the boat and the stretch of river that would take them to Rio and their flight back to New York, their joint adventure was finished. She spun away from him and didn't come back, leaving him feeling withered and defenseless. Soon Paul would listen to one of his Brazilian drumming tracks and hear the story of a man pinned beneath the rubble of his shattered heart. "Abandoned and forsaken," he wrote. "As if she'd captured the breath of my voice in a bottle / And I can't catch it back."

His voice was still very much his own. After four trips to Brazil, Paul worked with the drum tracks in New York, listening to the tapes with a pen in his hand, a sheet of paper filling with whatever came into his head.

"If I have weaknesses / Don't let them blind me."

Something like that, and he'd feel his way into the beats and bangs and the sharp *rat-a-tat* of the congas, and look for a melody, humming and *la-la-ing* and scatting this or that, something from the sheet of phrases or something bound for it.

The man was wearing jacket and jeans,
The woman was laughing in advance.
Song dogs barking at the break of dawn.
Effortless music from the Cameroons
The spinning darkness of her hair.

As he'd hoped, everything came through the drums: the anxiety and the wonder; the anger and the surrender; the steady current of imagining and laboring, dreaming and carving, pulled him forward. He'd take his chords and lyrics to the Hit Factory recording studio on Fifty-Fourth Street, thread in the tape, and figure out which sections were the most interesting and then get Halee to slice and dice, matching one section to a verse, another to a chorus — cutting and trimming, mixing and matching. Then they'd call in other musicians: old New York favorites Randy and Michael Brecker on trumpet and saxophone, keyboardist Greg Phillinganes, and Paul's most trusted drummer, Steve Gadd. *Graceland* players Ladysmith Black Mambazo, Ray Phiri and Bakithi Kumalo on guitar and bass, and new discoveries from West Africa and the diaspora route, including guitarists Vincent Nguini and Rego Star, and the Cameroon brothers Felix and Armand Sabal-Lecco, on drums and guitar, respectively. High-profile visitors included blues guitarist J. J. Cale, Fabulous Thunderbirds singer/harpist Kim Wilson, zydeco hero Clifton Chenier on accordion, and Milton Nascimento, the singer who set Paul's most recent journey in motion. Paul would play them the original drum and percussion track, then sketch his chords on his guitar, sing a bit of melody, and let the musicians invent their own parts as he listened, sifting what he liked from what sounded wrong or what maybe would be best used in another song. When they were done, Paul and Halee would do more editing and revising, building, reconsidering, rewriting, and then start the process again. The sessions went on for months, then a year, two years, then three.

The budget hit the seven hundred thousand dollars it had cost to make *Graceland,* and kept rising. When they finally finished in the spring of 1990, Paul had spent a million dollars on the project.

He called the album *The Rhythm of the Saints,* referring to how the traditional African drumming ceremonies had to be altered for post-Columbian South America, where the Europeans' religious authorities tried to force the natives to abandon their deities for Jesus. Instead, the immigrants dressed their deities in the robes of Catholic saints and held their sacred drumming and chanting ceremonies as they always had, only with different names. It didn't matter. The spirit power in the music remained. Paul carried no brief for anyone's god or saint, but he felt the spirit in the rhythm pull him deeper into his subconscious, only to emerge with one of the most haunting works of art he had ever created.

The record starts with a sharp report from Olodum's fourteen drummers, a fast *rat-a-tat* from the snares, then a sturdier pulse from the bass drums, a rolling beat that propels the opening strums of one of Paul's chipper schoolyard melodies, a variation on the "Me and Julio" theme, anchored to a multigenerational tale called "The Obvious Child." He'd started singing that phrase, "the obvious child," as fill-in syllables when he was wiring

585

the song. But as the verses strung into a story of parents, children, and the passage of time, the abstract phrase, along with the pregnant assertion "the cross is in the ballpark," became the most meaningful lines in the tune. Paul thought he was writing about stadium-size Christian rallies, but his characters had their own concerns, and reminded themselves that their burdens weren't quite as impossible, and their rewards not nearly as remote, as they assumed.

> Some people say the sky is just the sky
> But I say
> . . .
> The cross is in the ballpark
> Why deny the obvious child?

The liquid pulse of the Uakti group's tuned PVC instruments sets the uneasy mood of "Can't Run But," a fresh variation on the techno-dystopianism of "The Boy in the Bubble," with the meaning and marketing of art, contrasting again with the mystical sounds of the South American jungles and rivers. It's that very spirit that illumines the jangling guitars and rattling gourds, bells, and shakers in "The Coast," a sparkling benediction for musicians and their creation, the essence of beauty in a world riddled with loneliness and need. The even livelier "Proof," a fast-moving contraption built of bongos, talking drums, *chakeire,* synthesizer, electric guitar, and accordion, pushes the buoyancy even higher, its anticipated triumphs (a fortune, a marriage, and endless luck) claimed in the here and the now because "Faith! / Faith is an island in the setting sun / But proof, yes, / Proof is the bottom line for everyone."

The worrying thump of the bass drums, soon joined by gourds, congas, bongos, and bata, set the backdrop for "Further to Fly," the first of two songs haunted by Carrie and the end of their love affair. Here, thoughts about the end of love weave with aging and death, a grief so deep it could be insanity or, as Paul sings, "a morbid little lie." He summons the rose of Jericho (a self-renewing plant that dies in drought, only to be reborn in rain), but ends with a more realistic if still impossible-seeming wish for "the strength to let you go." "She Moves On" tells the same story in sharper terms, its anxious guitars and throbbing bass revealing a woman ravenous for speed and distance. You can sense Carrie's illness in the woman's midnight fevers, but the singer can't help seeing her restlessness as hostility. "You have underestimated my power," she whispers, and is gone again.

"Spirit Voices" appears like a jungle waterfall, a rain of chiming guitars, triangles, and synthesizers recalling the Amazon *brujo* and the power of his spells. Through sparkling eyes, the natural world trembles with meaning. A bright green lizard appears; a spider weaves a perfect web; water sings from the river, mingles with the sea, and returns as holy water. "Then the sweetness in the air combined with the lightness in my head / And I heard the breathing in the bamboo," which emerges in the heavenly voice of Milton Nascimento, promising that no matter what the morning brings, it will definitely come, and it will be powerful.

If Paul ventured into the jungle in search of immortality, he came close to his target. For the length of *The Rhythm of the Saints'* nearly forty-five minutes you could believe that he'd hit it exactly. The music is that full, the artistic spirit that generous. The ancient music had connected him to something deeper than his busy, busy brain could ever perceive. Like the *brujo*'s tea, the rhythm had ushered him into the darkness and shown him his demons. They squirmed through the songs, a parade of beasts and usurers, lost lovers and waning powers, all massing into the verses of "The Cool, Cool River," where love is anger, where justice is corrupt, where prayers are little more than memories of a vanished deity, and where hope still persists, where suffering will end, and where a resilient heart can still make a difference. The song, and the album, climaxes with a ringing fanfare of horns, guitars, and bass and a shouted declaration:

"Hard times?
I'm used to them.
The speeding planet burns
I'm used to that.
My life's so common it disappears."

Miracles come and go; even music falls short. But just as the rhythm revealed his own hidden spirit, it also uncovers the divinity of simply being alive, with the most essential rhythm in heaven and on earth pulsing in your chest.

This time no one at Warner Bros. had to wonder if Paul's latest safari into the wild would find an audience with American record buyers. Once again, the radio was probably a lost cause, but as they had discovered with *Graceland,* you could sell millions of records without even approaching *Billboard*'s Top 40 singles chart. Paul might be closing in on his fiftieth birthday, but a lot of the fans he'd collected during the 1960s and '70s were into their forties and still buying records. And given the popular momentum he'd amassed with the South African record, Paul's equally exotic follow-up drew more attention than any record he'd released since the record he and Artie didn't release after the Central Park reunion tour.

The Rhythm of the Saints made its entrance on October 16, 1990, riding a surge of television and newspaper stories that was soon swelled by a rush of reviews that were just as ecstatic as the notices attending *Graceland.* The new record might not be the global wingding the previous one was, but as the critics noticed, that's because it was deeper and more complex in its music and lyrics. In the afterglow of *Graceland,* the public might not have needed convincing. *Saints* jumped up the charts in double time, reaching No. 4 (*Graceland* had peaked at No. 3) and selling its first million copies within the first month of its life. The record did even better in the United Kingdom, where it topped the album charts while climbing nearly as high in countries ranging from Finland to Australia and Japan to Hungary. News of a year-plus-long global tour of sports arenas and stadiums created box-office mob scenes where long-time fans jousted with youngsters to score the best tickets. And when there was a little public dustup about how the tour's commercial sponsor, American Express, was hoarding some of the best seats for its elite Gold Card customers, Paul apologized quickly and unequivocally, and all was forgiven.

The tour opened on the second day of 1991 with a stop at the Tacoma Dome, outside Seattle. It was the first time Paul had performed in the Pacific Northwest since the Simon and Garfunkel swing in the fall of 1968,[*] and the sold-out crowd stayed on its feet for most of the evening. The ensemble spent the next week polishing the show, then started the tour in earnest with a show in Vancouver on January 9, followed immediately by a night in Portland. Paul performed with a seventeen-member band (including the three members of the vocal group the Waters) he'd built from the same mix of old accomplices, *Graceland* veterans, and the West African and South American musicians he'd met on the *Rhythm of the Saints* sessions. The show was held on a multilevel platform that descended to meet the fans at the front of the stage. As thunderous as they were delicate, the concerts led off with "The Obvious Child," "The Boy in the Bubble," and "She Moves On" before an mbaqanga arrangement of "Kodachrome" established how the night's older songs would be reinvigorated by Paul's globalized sensibility — which had also reinvigorated Paul, elevating him to new levels of perception and musical imagination that had less relaunched his career than started it again, as if his older songs were the work of a completely different artist. The opening chords of "You Can Call Me Al" and "Diamonds on the Soles of Her

[*] While also composing "The Boxer."

Shoes" spurred bigger ovations than "Still Crazy After All These Years," while the final notes of the just-released "Proof" and "The Coast" incited roars bigger than what came after Simon and Garfunkel standards "Cecilia" and even "Bridge Over Troubled Water" (due also to the gospel-reggae arrangement that played against the original's emotional grandiosity, but still). The audience preferred the new stuff to the classic hits. Had any other fifty-year-old pop star come close to being able to claim that?

The Born at the Right Time tour would continue to the end of 1991, but the climax of the year, and of the *Graceland–The Rhythm of the Saints* era, came on August 15, 1991, on a cloudy day in the Sheep Meadow in Central Park, not far from Paul's living room windows on Central Park West. It had been ten years since Simon and Garfunkel's reunion spectacular in 1981, and a decade later Paul no longer worried about being able to draw citizens out of their apartments on his own power. Because it wasn't just him; it was *Graceland* and it was *The Rhythm of the Saints,* the hearts and hoofbeats of half a dozen cultures all twirled into one massive, irrepressible sound, with Paul's melodies and words draped over the top. They bowled over crowds, shook the stands, and detached roofs from arenas night for night for night, sending the patrons back into the street three hours later with feverish cheeks and tingling feet. So a summer night in Central Park? This show was built for that.

Offstage, Paul became wound tighter as the day drew nearer. Most artists get edgy before playing New York and Los Angeles, the big industry towns where the crowds are so much more jaded and easily bored. Toss in the homecoming stakes and the back-in-his-own-footsteps and the many pitfalls of playing an outdoor show in the middle of a big city, and it could all seem overwhelming. When Chris Botti, a late addition to the band on trumpet, asked Paul how he could bear the pressure of such a massive event, Paul projected the entire affair into the ballpark. Playing on a smaller or more remote stage, he explained, he'd come onstage hoping to nail a single or a double. But when you're a born slugger and you work your way to Yankee Stadium with everything at stake, there's only one thing you know how to do: swing for the fences.

In New York, the dawn came in humid murk. Early forecasts declared that the bad weather would hold through the day, then take a turn for the worse with the sunset. Rain for nearly certain, possibly lightning and thunder. Still, the stage had been built, the video screens and sound towers standing as high as the trees. To account for the sound lag in the back, they'd engineered a digital delay long enough to fill two stadiums with crystalline sound. Once again, the people flooded into the park from every direction. The skies lightened with the afternoon, then broke apart into a puffy blue ether. Streets crowded and choked; the coolers and blankets spread from Seventy-Second Street into the Nineties. When the show began, Paul came out at a jog, guitar in hand, skipping down the stairs to his microphone three steps from the bottom. The Olodum drummers, flown in specially from Salvador, Brazil, stretched across the top row at the back, and with Paul's signal they fired off the first drum beats of the evening, launching "The Obvious Child" into Sheep Meadow, over the reservoir, through the trees, and beyond — everywhere there were ears, 750,000 sets of them, according to the city's crowd estimators.

There were no stage rushers, no demonstrators, no denouncements from the United Nations or any other governing body — just a delirious crowd, a stage peopled by South Africans, Brazilians, Cameroonians, white Americans, black Americans, Latinos, rock musicians, soul musicians, jazz players, the classically trained, and Third Worlders whose first instrument was a rock and a stick; a montage of color and sound and not an angry ex-partner among them. Halfway through the set, Paul raised a hand in the middle of "Proof," snapping the band into an abrupt silence. "Proof!" he shouted. "The sun came out, it was a cloudy day, they thought there was gonna be a rainstorm, and it's a perfect night. In New York City!"

Artie could have seen and heard the whole thing from his living room sofa if he'd been home that night, but he wasn't. He'd left his house, and the city, for the weekend specifically because he didn't want to have to deal with the commotion outside his Fifth Avenue windows. "I'd rather wish Paul well from afar," he said. Actually, Paul's good luck was the last thing on his mind because Artie was furious. How could Paul return to the site of their most triumphant night a decade later and not ask him to come out for a few of their songs? "I'm not good enough to be invited," he grumbled in a *New York Times* interview published the day before the 1991 show. "My guess is that it would hurt his sense of his stature." Note the expert design of those two sentences, a master class in passive-aggression presented in nineteen words. Artie had more to say, particularly about how HBO was promoting its simulcast of the concert with clips of Simon and Garfunkel's 1981 concert, as if promising that Artie would be at the new show, too. But Paul wasn't in a sharing mood, so that was that, and off Artie went, not to return until all remnants of the show had been swept away.

So, fine. Paul was used to Artie. It was easy to let his public complaints go without comment or even a public eye roll. Other issues were more disturbing. When the *New Musical Express* writer Gavin Martin came to talk about *The Rhythm of the Saints* in the fall of 1990, he posed a few questions about how Paul had distributed writing credits and royalties to the musicians on the album. And though Paul seemed thoroughly unflapped and happy to detail it all in a tone of voice that was every bit as chummy as when they started talking, he cut off the magazine's hour-long photo session after just three minutes, leaving the photographer with a furious record company publicist, who said that Paul was so upset about Martin's interview that he had decided to cancel the two television appearances they had scheduled for the next day. Someone from the record company called later to say that it had all been a misunderstanding, but as Martin knew, nothing else he'd said could have been even remotely upsetting to Paul.

Soon there would be more for Paul to freak out about. The freeing of Nelson Mandela in 1990 and the steady crumbling of apartheid inspired Oliver Tambo and the other leaders of the African National Congress to cancel the cultural boycott at the end of 1991, clearing the way for anyone and everyone who wanted to tour South Africa to feel free to do so. And who would be a more appropriate first booking than Paul Simon and his multinational, South African–inspired band? South African concert promoter Attie van Wyk booked the Born at the Right Time tour for five shows, and off they went for what Paul figured would be a victory tour for everyone in the band, the antiapartheid movement, and all of South Africa. What he didn't anticipate was that the country was still in the final throes of white rule, with power very much up for grabs and the opposition fractured into a dozen separate organizations, each with its own constituencies and leaders. The Azanian People's Organisation (AZAPO), formed in 1978 from three different black consciousness groups, had pursued a more militant path through the years, with a military wing that most definitely didn't make peaceful resistance a priority. So while the ANC embraced Paul and the tour, AZAPO did not, and neither did the Pan African Congress. Both groups talked about mounting demonstrations at the concerts, but the members of AZAPO's youth-focused subgroup, AZAYO, one of its more military-minded branches, decided to get their message across in a more vivid way.

Paul and the rest of the touring party got to South Africa a few days into January, mak-

597

ing his first public appearance in the country at a tour-launching cocktail party whose guests included future president Nelson Mandela. It was a big affair, in one of Johannesburg's swankier hotels. Paul came in a black suit and a royal blue button-up, doing all the right chatting and hand shaking, and then posing for photos with Mandela, their hands held high, black and white fingers knotted in a symbol of brotherhood. And it was such a lovely affair and a beautiful celebration, and everyone went home, and Paul back to his hotel room, with nothing but fond memories and buoyant hopes for the future. Right up until three hand grenades were hurled into the offices of tour promoter Attie van Wyk, blasting the place into a fiery ruin. Greetings from AZAYO.

It happened just before 2:00 a.m., so no one was injured, but what did it portend? Soon van Wyk and the rest of the tour managers gathered in Paul's suite, where they found him in a panic, walking circles in the room and talking about pulling the plug on the whole thing before someone got killed. Van Wyk, who had called in security expert Rory Steyn, tried to talk Paul down. They knew who was who in the radical movements; AZAYO comprised mostly big talkers — "Three guys and a fax machine," van Wyk said. Even a few hand grenades through a window was beyond their usual capabilities.

And the group had already made clear it was happy to negotiate a settlement. The government was prepared to step up its security efforts. So the smartest thing to do was to stick with the tour and, if possible, smooth things with AZAYO. Working through back channels, they set a closed-door meeting between Paul and AZAYO leader Thami Mcerwa, at which Paul agreed to donate some money to the group and include it in a press conference where, along with AZAPO, it could state its views, including its decision to join the ANC in welcoming the tour to South Africa.

The deal eased Paul's mind considerably, at least until the press conference on January 9, where Mcerwa informed the press that neither he nor anyone in AZAYO had any intention of welcoming the tour after all. "We have always pointed out that should his show go on, there is the potential for violence," Mcerwa said, to Paul's obvious unhappiness. Yet the tour would go on, and though ticket sales fell through the floor and though demonstrators did stalk the band — many carrying signs with AZAYO's slogan that Paul would end up with blood on the soles of his shoes — the five shows came off without a bomb hurled, a shot fired, or even a politically inspired punch thrown. The only real victim turned out to be van Wyk, who had added extra shows based on early demand, only to have sales fall off a cliff after the hand grenades landed.

They ended the African swing with one night in Botswana, which also marked the end of the Born at the Right Time tour and the *Graceland–The Rhythm of the Saints* era, save for two stadium shows in Miami that fall and a one-off stadium concert in Uruguay in December. Along with giving worldwide exposure to the music of Brazil and the African diaspora countries, the *Saints* project changed the course of Olodum, whose struggles to pay the rent on their offices ended when Paul bought the building and donated it to the organization for keeps. He also changed the life of the tour's trumpet player Chris Botti, whose playing and writing he admired enough to sign him to a publishing deal with a $250,000 advance — enough money for the musician to form a band and launch his career as a jazz interpreter and songwriter. Botti stayed a part of Paul's touring band for the next nine years, along with guitarist-arranger Vincent Nguini, who also became one of Paul's closer friends. Marco Mazzola, the producer Paul first contacted to prepare for the project, also became a lasting friend. "I think he showed his true self through his music," Mazzola says. "By working with him, I realized he is exactly what he shows. What you hear is what you get."

CHAPTER 22
PHANTOM FIGURES
IN THE DUST

For more than a decade Paul and Ian Hoblyn, his closest and most trusted assistant, had been inseparable. Hoblyn did everything for him, from directing Paul's house staff and keeping his social calendar to planning and managing the day-to-day details of his international concert tours. Charismatic, erudite, with a passion for visual art as profound as his employer, Hoblyn soon became one of Paul's best friends — in his 1984 interview with *Playboy* Paul listed him as one of his two closest male friends, second only to Lorne Michaels. When Paul went on vacation Hoblyn went with him, and not just as his helpmate, but as another one of the friends who were there to eat, drink, and hang out. If Hoblyn wanted to bring a friend that was usually okay, too, though it didn't stop Paul from abruptly directing his assistant to leave the circle and run an errand. Hoblyn would do what he was told, but not before putting on one of his long-suffering smiles and, perhaps, making on affectionate eye roll for the benefit of the others.

Their social circles started to blend. Paul got to know some of Hoblyn's better friends, and welcomed his boyfriends as he did any of his non-professional friends' spouses. He'd invite one or another to join the rest of his gang to go on his latest adventure, and when AIDS cut a brutal swath through Hoblyn's circle of friends Paul did what he could to be supportive, attending memorial services, including one that he organized and paid for.

It was all a pleasure for the first ten or so years. But then Hoblyn, who had become a sophisticated connoisseur of the finer things during his tenure with Paul, had gotten accustomed to living like a man with extraordinary means. Paul paid very well and had no problem if they got to the end of a long tour and Hoblyn wanted to hole up in some luxe hotel to unwind with a friend or two for a few days. But Hoblyn took to stretching his privileges a bit, then a bit more than that, and it was never a problem because Paul trusted him too much to question his expenditures. But then things started to add up. A newly hired accountant showed Paul a tally of Hoblyn's expenses, and when another inventory revealed that several of his paintings (Paul's collection was far too large for all of his pieces to be on display, even given his three homes) had gone missing, and it turned out that Hoblyn had borrowed them to decorate his apartment, Paul blew up. More than fired, Hoblyn was exiled from his life. No more calls, no more long talks, not a single word. Hoblyn, his friends say, was never the same after that, particularly given his guilt over his own lapses of judgment. When he learned he had terminal cancer a few years later Hoblyn hoped his old employer and friend might reach out to him before he died. He didn't.

When Paul happened to visit Lorne Michaels at a broadcast of *Saturday Night Live* in October 1988, he was bedazzled on the spot by Edie Brickell, the lead singer for the Texas neo-hippie band the New Bohemians, whose single "What I Am" was high on the charts. Tall, slim, and shy, Brickell beguiled Paul so thoroughly that he stood just offstage during the group's first performance and started waving his hands to catch the singer's attention. At this, he succeeded so well that viewers could see and hear Brickell waver, muffing a word or two before snapping back into focus. "We can show the kids the tape and say, 'Look, that's when we first laid eyes on each other,'" she said later.

The daughter of a professional bowler and a receptionist who were divorced when she was three years old, Edie grew up in a chain of apartments around Dallas, Texas, moving to whichever working-class neighborhood was closest to her mother's latest job. Drawn to music and art as a child, she picked at a guitar for a while, pursued an interest in songwriting, studied art at Southern Methodist University for a year and a half, then dropped out to focus on her music and songs. Although painfully shy, she fell in with a Grateful Dead–inspired band called the New Bohemians. Three years after she joined, she was performing with them on *Saturday Night Live* while an oddly familiar-looking man waved at her from the side of the stage.

Paul Simon's season of glory had begun even before *The Rhythm of the Saints* landed in the fall of 1990. In late 1989, the twenty-fifth anniversary of the release of *Wednesday Morning, 3 AM,* Simon and Garfunkel became eligible to be inducted into the Rock and Roll Hall of Fame. Like Chuck Berry, Elvis Presley, the Beatles, and the Rolling Stones before them, Paul and Artie were granted the honor the moment they were eligible. And so began the traditional pre-induction ceremony parlor game. Could the estranged partners bear to stand on the same stage? Would they sing together? Could they step back into the shoes of the sweet, melancholy oracles they had been a quarter century ago?

Of course they could. There was no way those Alan Freed disciples, their lives built upon the twin towers of Elvis and the Everlys, could resist their turn in the spotlight that had shone on so many of their greatest heroes. When the evening of January 18, 1990, arrived and the most elite of elite musicians and their many helpmates from the corner offices gathered in the grand ballroom of New York's Waldorf-Astoria Hotel, Paul and Artie stood to get their due. It was a big year for the Hall of Fame, with entrants including Louis Armstrong, the Who, the Platters, the Kinks, the Four Tops, and two of the most influential songwriting teams of anyone's era: Motown's Holland-Dozier-Holland and the Brill Building's Carole King and Gerry Goffin. Epic company, to say the least.

Presented by the celebrated seventies singer-songwriter James Taylor, Paul and Artie came to the stage wearing proud grins and keeping a polite distance from each other until they turned to shake hands, each projecting the slightly stilted friendliness common to global leaders whose cities are still mapped into their nuclear launch orders. Artie took a moment to fiddle with the podium microphone, tossing off a quip that doubled as a shot at one of his partner's most sensitive spots ("It's mic height! That's what broke up this group!"); thanked their manager, Mort Lewis, and Roy Halee; then complimented the Hall of Fame itself in the slightly jumbled elocution he tended to adopt when making a significant statement: "It has my total credibility and there's not too many of those things around." To conclude, he turned to the other fellow standing a few feet back from the podium and thanked "the person who has most enriched my life by putting these great songs through me, my friend Paul, here."

Paul stepped to the podium, a wicked grin on his lips. "Well, Arthur and I agree about almost nothing," he said. "But it's true. I *have* enriched his life quite a bit, now that I think about it." He made another crack about the Hall of Fame needing to add a special wing for feuding partners — Simon and Garfunkel, Ray and Dave Davies from the Kinks, Mick and Keith, Ike and Tina Turner — then turned serious, recalling how Artie's voice rang across their neighborhood, how rock 'n' roll had brought them together and delivered them to unimaginable places via the playlist of New York's dominant pop station WINS-AM, which showcased a rainbow of artists, including Ray Charles, Johnny Cash, Frankie Lymon, Ruth Brown, the Moonglows, and Elvis, Elvis, Elvis. "We used our imaginations to figure out what were the connections," Paul said. "It became the dominant interest in our lives, and to this day it's still fascinating . . . all this time in my life I've never been bored." The erstwhile partners' reunion, such as it was, waited for the traditional show-ending jam session with a sloppy, all-hands try at "Bridge Over Troubled Water" and "The Boxer."

It wasn't much to spin the pinwheel of even the most excitable S&G fan. Meanwhile, Paul's solo Central Park show in 1991, coupled with Artie's high-pitched complaints about being left out, seemed to mark a new low in the shadow story of their lives together. Yet, the following spring, they joined with Mike Nichols and Elaine May in Los Angeles to play an eight-song set at a reunion-centric benefit for cancer-stricken children. And when Paul decided to mark the thirtieth anniversary of the start of his post–Jerry Landis career with a monthlong stand of retrospective concerts in New York, Artie became a part of that, too.

Plans for the career-spanning shows began with *Paul Simon 1964–1993,* a triple-CD, Paul-curated box set of highlights from his three decades at the forefront of popular music. And though the Simon and Garfunkel period amounted to less than a third of the time he had spent as a solo artist, those seven years had been too extraordinary to play down, particularly in a staged career retrospective. When Paul announced the first batch of what had been titled Concert Event of a Lifetime* shows at the Paramount Theater in October, the Simon and Garfunkel reunion was a centerpiece of the news, along with the duo's commitment to perform together at Neil Young's Annual Bridge School Benefit Concert in November. They'd probably make a television special about the reunion, too, though that didn't mean they were actually reuniting; no, they were merely "recapturing as purely as possible what was, not working out something new or recording again." Just in case fans (or Artie) were tempted to assume anything else.

Paul built the Concert Event of a Lifetime into a thirty-five-song chronicle of his creative journey, starting with an hour-long set with Artie, presenting nine of the "The Boxer"-size jewels in the S&G crown along with a wry, music-enhanced retelling of their earliest days together that ended with a near-full performance of "Hey, Schoolgirl (In the Second Row)." An intermission followed, then a set of Paul's solo works presented in

* Even given the double entendre — it's the concert event of *Paul's* lifetime — the title, particularly the "Event" part, seems much more appropriate for a Streisand-Liza-Celine-caliber show that would involve dancers and rockets and probably bubbles or lightning bolts and would require the construction of a specially designed concert hall on the Las Vegas Strip.

608

loosely chronological fashion from "Me and Julio Down by the Schoolyard" to "Hearts and Bones" to a handful of favorites from the *Graceland* and *The Rhythm of the Saints* years, climaxing with a wild rendition of "You Can Call Me Al," lately made even more famous as an unofficial theme song for newly elected vice president Al Gore. The only way Paul could top that was by sending Artie out for "Bridge Over Troubled Water." Paul rejoined him for more of those heart-squeezing harmonies. Then the curtain came down, and there went three thousand people back onto the streets as the last echoes of the show merged with the honks, screeches, and many-tongued curses of New York City.

It was the same onstage: the ten-member band built from musicians drawn from Africa, South America, Europe, New York and Oregon, all bending to fit Paul's peripatetic vision. Each of the major works was informed by still other musicians, traditions, and muses: Artie's harmonies during the first half of the show; then the many-hued second set, starting with the Los Angeles–based Mighty Clouds of Joy bringing the gospel to "Loves Me Like a Rock," New Yorker Phoebe Snow doing the same for the urban-secular gospel of "Gone at Last," then Ladysmith Black Mambazo bridging the African American traditions to the roots of the African veld, the headwaters for so much of the music that

609

had flowed through Paul since he opened his eyes and ears five decades earlier — a lifetime of influences and inspirations, of collaborators and creative partners.

All Paul's collaborators had influenced his music, but none could claim anything like the power Artie held over him. As much as Paul tried to deny it, the partnership had marked him, and not just because a world of fans couldn't get past it. At first Paul reveled in their resumed harmony — mostly. "I felt a lot of affection for [Artie] from the audience," he said after the first few shows. "It feels great when I see that." Did that sound, in the midst of Paul's extraordinary popular comeback, just a little bit patronizing? When a *New Yorker* magazine writer called to talk a few days later, Artie sounded something less than loving when he shared his thoughts on "America": "That's Paul Simon taking a posture of disappointed world-weariness," he said of a song many people had come to see as a vital document on the post-idealist America of the late 1960s. "It is sophomoric, inflated talk when you're just out of college. Now I'm older, and I know honor, money, love, loss, competition. I have a child. I don't feel I'm lost . . . it behooves me not to accept that. I live in a troubled country, but I won't cashier it. Make something better of America, or else drop the subject."

Then it was happening again: the averted

eyes, the stiff atmosphere backstage, the toxic silence. It went on like this for weeks, all the way until just after the third-to-last show, when something set them off so badly during the encores that they stormed back into a dressing room, slammed the door, and ripped it all open again, the decades of hurts, and the grudges: harsh tones growing into shouts, holding there for a while and then rising into sustained bellowing and then, good God, full-on *screaming*. And even though the door was shut and locked, you could hear it everywhere: down the hall and up the stairs, and then the throats went, vocal cords knotting, fraying, and popping. Neither could speak the next morning. They had to cancel the next show to recover their voices. Amazingly, the final shows were every bit as smooth, their between-song patter just as warm, as they had ever been.

They were teenagers in the late 1950s, a pair of young immigrants set loose in a frigid, steely city. Like Paul and Artie, they took to the street corners to meet their compatriots in teenage hijinks, affected fancy clothes to maximize their impact, and found their way to the west side of Midtown to make their stand. But instead of taking a song to Tin Pan Alley, Sal Agron and Tony Hernandez went to a street corner park in Hell's Kitchen known as a hangout for the Norsemen, an

Irish street gang that had recently thumped a friend of theirs. Agron and Hernandez, both fifteen years old, were members of the Vampires, a Puerto Rican gang from uptown. At least a few of the guys in the park were members of an Irish gang, and it didn't take long for trouble to start. When it was over, two of the Irish kids were mortally wounded, stabbed repeatedly by Agron and left to bleed to death on the concrete.

A tragedy by any measure, but in the New York City of 1959, when street gangs (including the Parsons Boys, who tormented Paul and Artie on their way to and from Parsons Junior High) had become the urban menace of the moment, the crime became an instant sensation, and not just because it involved teenage members of a street gang and not just because Agron and Hernandez had committed their crimes while clad in a black cape and wielding a black umbrella, respectively. It was also because they were Puerto Rican, the fruit of the latest wave of immigrants whose darker faces, foreign accents, and inscrutable ways clashed with the upstanding values of the New Yorkers who had the common decency to be descended from one of the earlier waves of immigrants. And if all of that wasn't enough tinder for a blazing tabloid series, think again of those costumes.

Agron and Hernandez had vanished on the night of the bloodshed, so the saga of THE

CAPE MAN MURDERS (which is how it always appeared on the front page, in all caps, 24-point type) began as a mystery. They were captured soon afterward, but the newspapers kept them in the headlines for more than a year, through the investigation, to the trial, to their sentencing hearing. A few things didn't add up. Agron's knife was unmarked by blood, as were his cape and shoes. But how could you reconcile those facts with his glee at being identified as the murderer? Found guilty, the sixteen-year-old was the youngest person ever to be sentenced to death by the American judicial system. New York governor Nelson Rockefeller commuted the death sentence a few years later, at the behest of Eleanor Roosevelt, among others, and Agron went on to become something like a model prisoner, earning high school and college degrees and developing a passion for social justice, particularly when it came to the inequities of race and class. Paroled in 1979, he had seven years of freedom before dying of a heart attack in 1986 at forty-two. Once past the initial rush of infamy, he declared himself innocent and never displayed much sympathy for the surviving family of the boys who died that night in Hell's Kitchen.

Tracking the story in Kew Gardens Hills, Paul had felt a kinship with the murderer. The middle-class honor student Paul was in many ways the opposite of the impoverished, uneducated ghetto kid. But Agron's look and attitude — at the time, he told the reporters that he didn't care if he burned for the crime — thrilled the good boy from Queens. The Puerto Rican gang member was an outsider, young and wild in the streets, with no interest in anyone's expectations of how nice boys were supposed to behave. And what buttoned-down high schooler doesn't secretly yearn for the weight of the leather? "There were gangs in Queens . . . I felt the typical middle-class aspiration to be [in one]," Paul said. "I was in a couple of fights." Thirty years later, Agron reminded Paul of early rock 'n' roll: the curl of his lip, the absence of remorse, the raw power of not giving a fuck. At the same time, Paul could hear the echoes of the Latin dance bands he'd seen sharing the stage with the Lee Simms Orchestra at the Roseland Ballroom and the Latin rhythms and voices coming from the fringes of the radio dial, the sound of his youth, the essence of the New York that had created him and then, like his youth, slipped away. Between his memories of the crime, the echoes of the music, and the deeper implications of Agron's jailhouse rebirth, Paul recognized a multilayered tale that was dramatic and exciting, tragic and hopeful, a New York story that spoke as clearly about America as it did about any one man's life. It was a story shot through with rock 'n' roll, with doo-wop, with the passion of Latin dance: music, murder, and redemption — a perfect night in the Broadway theater.

The marquees in Midtown had beckoned Paul for years. In late 1967 he had signed up to compose the music for *Jimmy Shine,* a Broadway show about a struggling Greenwich Village artist that the playwright Murray Schisgal had written for Dustin Hoffman. Paul's first shot at theatrical songwriting didn't last long. Overwhelmed by Simon and Garfunkel work, he stepped aside and was replaced by Lovin' Spoonful leader and songwriter John Sebastian. The allure of the theater didn't leave him, though. Still, as he often did, Paul revealed the distance between his ambition and his confidence in tones of disinterest and contempt. Speaking to Jeffrey Sweet, the theater-focused student in his New York University songwriting workshop in 1970, Paul said he could never get past the artifice of theatrical music — especially, he said, when the characters onstage burst into song in the middle of a conversation. It was absurd; nothing like that ever happened in real life. Sweet countered that it was just as unrealistic for Shakespeare's kings and knaves to chat in perfectly composed iambic pentameter, but Paul was having none of it. "If I ever write a musical," he told Sweet, "there will be a big radio upstage, and when it's time for a song, they'll go upstage and turn on the radio, and that's where the music will come from." Wanting to show his famous teacher a more contemporary form of musical, Sweet offered to take Paul to a second-night performance of Stephen Sondheim's innovative musical *Company,* and at first Paul seemed interested: "I might do that," he said. Sweet gave him one of his tickets, but when showtime arrived Paul's seat was empty.

His wheel of fascination/scorn continued to spin. In 1973, Paul declared that the score of the supposedly revolutionary hit *Hair,* despite its long-haired cast, flashes of nudity, and knowing references to drugs, sex, and revolution, was a pale imitation of real rock 'n' roll. "That's because the best writers of popular songs never wrote for the stage," he said. "Consequently you get people who did poor imitations getting the big hits." Still, he said he was eager to get to know Joseph Papp, who ran New York's purposefully offbeat Public Theater. Maureen Orth noted similar statements in *Newsweek* a few months later, but only a few weeks after that, Paul dismissed talk about pursuing theater as "bullshit," adding, "I have absolutely no plans for something like that." But, he added, "I'm not saying I wouldn't be willing to do it someday." By 1980 he put writing a musical on the very short list of projects he wanted to finish by the end of the decade.

■ ■ ■

That didn't quite happen, but he did settle on the Capeman murders as a subject, sketched a plot about the life of Sal Agron, and composed a handful of songs before putting the project aside to focus on the *The Rhythm of the Saints* album. Other than the Concert Event of a Lifetime shows in 1993, once *Rhythm* was done, he devoted himself to the Capeman, diving into the facts of the story: Agron's birth in Puerto Rico, the fight in the playground, his rebirth in prison, and then his premature death in the mid-1980s. Paul couldn't see why he needed to fiddle with the story. It would be as exciting as the tabloid stories that had thrilled him as a teenager and as beautiful as the music at its core. That it was also entirely true would give it exactly the kind of literary gravitas Broadway hadn't seen in generations: a murder story with huge social and moral implications.

But Paul also knew that a Broadway musical wasn't just music. It was a story and a script. Directing, set designing, casting, acting, singing, and dancing — each practice had its own traditions, rules, ideals, and vocabulary. If writing, producing, and performing music required a community of talents, staging a full-blown musical demanded the skills and commitment of an entirely different set of people working jobs Paul didn't understand, applying skills he didn't have, and enacting visions that weren't necessarily his own. For a fiercely willful man intent on not just joining but actually reinventing an artistic medium that he kind of despised, it would be a herculean undertaking. Paul knew he'd need help, but he also needed to keep enough control so that the final product would be the fully formed version of his creative vision.

Eager to consult, and possibly collaborate, with someone whose work he respected, Paul took his script-in-progress to the novelist E. L. Doctorow, whose *Ragtime* had recently been adapted into a popular and acclaimed musical. Doctorow wasn't interested in collaborating on anything, as it turned out. And after reading the "Capeman" manuscript, he had one piece of advice for Paul: throw this out and rewrite it as fiction. The facts were interesting, sometimes even thrilling, but they didn't add up to a *story,* with the deeper emotional and artistic truths that reality could rarely touch. Paul and Doctorow talked for a while after that, and Paul thanked him for his advice. But he had already mapped the stars, and he wasn't going to change course now. Still hoping to find a collaborator to shore up his story for the stage, he went to Derek Walcott, the Saint Lucian poet whose blend of formal language and Caribbean imagery had earned him a 1992 Nobel Prize and a global reputation as one of the world's best living writers. An admirer of his work, Paul had befriended Walcott in the 1980s and turned to his poems for inspiration when he was writing the songs for *The Rhythm of the Saints.* Later Paul dedicated "The Coast," one of the most beautiful songs on the album, to the poet. Walcott, who also wrote and directed his own plays from time to time, was happy to be asked, and they started working together immediately.

They made a good creative match. Eleven years Paul's senior, Walcott had also succeeded early in life, and had nurtured a world-beating reputation ever since. A mixed-race child, one of twin boys whose grandmothers were Caribbean-born black slaves and whose grandfathers were British slave owners, Walcott was raised in opposing cultures, strung between the classical literature of his imperial grandfathers and the brilliant colors and lofting breeze of his grandmothers' Caribbean. While he proved a brilliant student as a child, the African strain in Walcott's mixed blood shamed him no end. "He had prayed / nightly for his flesh to change," he recalled in verse. Inspired in equal measures by shame, anger, self-loathing, and self-assurance, Walcott was both an insightful observer of the world and an enthusiastic chronicler of his own life. He was still in his thirties when he wrote the explicitly autobiographical *Another Life* (published in 1973) and spoke often of the torments of writing and of simply being himself. "Caught between two races and two worlds," wrote critic William Logan in 2007, "[Walcott] has sometimes succumbed to pride or self-pity, or to that pride indistinguishable from self-pity." Still, when Walcott took pen in hand, all these emotions fueled one of the most illustrious bodies of literature of the twentieth century.

At first collaborating wasn't easy for either of them. Both were stubborn. Neither was accustomed to having a coauthor. The more he read about Agron, the less Walcott could stand him. Paul refused to write music to fit Walcott's verse, insisting that it had to be the other way around. When Walcott had an idea, Paul would grab his guitar and play snatches of the tunes he had yet to match with lyrics. The rhythm is too fast? How about this one? Does it sound like this melody? It was an eccentric and often creaky process, but they made it work. A reference to St. Lazarus tucked into one of the songs about Agron made Walcott realize that the heart of the story was about redemption and the progress of Agron's soul. Had his crime been imprinted on him before he was even born? A childhood visit to a Puerto Rican Santero, a priest in the blended Yoruban/Catholic religion, seemed to reveal the darkness in Sal's future, spirituality draped all over the facts of Agron's life.

Meanwhile, Paul worked on the music, writing song after song after song in a litany of styles. Doo-wop, *plenas,* rockabilly, a *bomba,* and more. As the pieces fell together, Paul happened to have lunch with his old friend, lawyer, and partner Mike Tannen, and ended up inviting him over to hear the new music and take a look at Walcott's hand-drawn sketches of the scenes they had written. It had been a long time since Paul sought his counsel, but Tannen felt obligated to tell his old friend two things: the music was jaw-dropping, maybe the most powerful set of songs Paul had ever written, but the story, he said, would be a problem. The character of Agron was unsympathetic at first and unredeemed at the end. Audiences accustomed to experiencing stories through the eyes of a likable protagonist would find it difficult to root for a character as troubling as Agron. "The whole project's on a razor's edge," Tannen told his former client. "I can see it going either way."

Paul wouldn't budge. For all that he valued the thoughts of his friends and compatriots, he couldn't let them push him away from what felt right. Did they think he was a pop star who had wandered out of his depth when he'd made a left turn onto Broadway? Well, he was finished with being a pop star — no more records, no more tours, no performing of any kind. To symbolize the decision, he got rid of his lush brown hairpiece, covering his nearly naked pate with either a baseball cap or, if he felt like it, nothing at all. He hated all the fuss of being a star, he said, and he was finished with doing things he hated to do. Was Paul Simon making himself clear? Forty years of stardom was enough. Take him or leave him; just don't expect him to alter a note or change a word.

From the sketching out of the story, the writing of the songs, the pursuit of investors, and all the way to the final curtain call on opening night, they have a way of doing things in the theater. Paul had no intention of doing them like that. Rather than make a demo reel of the songs in the score, he worked in the recording studio for more than a year, creating a fully produced album of finished songs. Rather than pursue investors with the expertise to help shape the production, he and close advisers Peter Parcher and Dan Klores, a lawyer and publicist respectively, got their seed money from investors who worked in music and television. The one exception, James L. Nederlander, came from a long line of theatrical investors and producers, but unlike most of his family members James was strictly a moneyman, with next to no experience working on a developing show. When one of his investors convinced Paul to meet with a few producers from the successful Dodger Theatricals outfit, Paul heard their advice to hire a seasoned Broadway director as an insult. "You're telling me I don't know what I'm doing," he said. That kind of talk could destroy his confidence, he added angrily. And given the sorry state of Broadway, why would he want to let them push him into making another show just like the ones he already didn't like?

News that Paul's next major work would be a Broadway musical called *The Capeman* broke in early May 1995, pegged to the announcement that Paul would hold an open audition for teenage doo-wop singers in a talent contest with ten thousand dollars in prize money at stake. He pursued potential directors with care, seeing shows, getting in touch, visiting for a while. A lot of names came up. At one point in 1995 he sat down with Susana Tubert, an up-and-coming Argentinian director who had moved to New York in 1980. Tubert's career was on the rise following a prestigious 1991 National Endowment for the Arts directing fellowship that had allowed her to work with leading directors from the avant-garde opera director Peter Sellars to Harold Prince, who was then developing his enormously successful musical adaptation of *Kiss of the Spider Woman.* By the midnineties Tubert had staged plays and musicals at theaters across the country, most often to great acclaim. When Paul called he invited her to his Central Park West apartment to play her the *Capeman*'s music on his guitar, then asked her to pull together some singers who might be right for the show. With a dozen performers scheduled, Paul, Tubert, and Walcott spent a day running auditions, and when the afternoon ended they had all hit it off. "I will see you again," Walcott told Tubert when they were saying their farewells.

Was Tubert the front-runner to be *The Capeman*'s director? Sort of, but not really. Paul interviewed other directors. He talked at length with the rebellious choreographer Mark Morris and tried to hire him to direct the play, but Morris had a dance company to run, and there weren't enough hours in the day for him to also direct an ambitious Broadway musical. Morris did agree to create the play's choreography, helping attract talented performers while also drawing fans to the ticket window. The cast would have to be almost all Latinos, primarily because the Agron family, like virtually everyone else in the show, was from Puerto Rico. Better, a nearly all-Latino show would be a first for Broadway. Finally, the city's millions of Latinos would have a big, splashy musical to tell their American story beneath the brightest lights in New York.

Paul's reputation and checkbook made it easy to woo prominent actor-singers to lead the cast: Panamanian actor-musician Rubén Blades to play the older Agron and the rising twenty-seven-year-old Latin pop star Marc Anthony (born in New York to Puerto Rican parents) as the younger version of the character. They were great additions, but also an affront to the show's eventual director, who would have to work with stars who might not fit into his or her conception of the show and its script. Paul hung on to as much authority as he could. He hired an experienced stage designer named Bob Crowley to create the sets. He hired Priscilla Lopez to play Agron's mother. He made more decisions. In the late winter of 1996, he finally called Tubert again. "I just spent a year and went all the way to Puerto Rico looking for a director," he told her. "Only to realize that the perfect person was back in New York City." Tubert took the job.

After a set of introductory meetings, Paul sent Tubert and stage designer Crowley to Puerto Rico to absorb the texture of Agron's homeland. Tubert held some auditions; she and Crowley both met with Agron's sister and other relatives, then visited his grave. They spent time with a santero, a priest in the Santeria faith — the mystical blend of Catholicism and Yoruba spirituality followed by Agron's family. Back in New York, Tubert set to work with the script, searching for visual and dramatic devices that would not just serve the script and songs, but also project the work's animating spirit into a kind of visual poetry; a chain of images that would not only underscore the action but also symbolize its deeper meanings. The task presented several puzzles, not the least of them being that the younger and elder Agrons barely encounter one another onstage. As a result, the show's two central characters, and its two biggest, most dynamic performers, wouldn't have a chance to play off of each other. Tubert proposed using the thread of magical realism running through the script — the spiritual element set forth by the santero — to open up more possibilities. When the younger Agron prowled the stage, the spirit of his older self would be onstage, too, observing and commenting on the action. The dynamic would reverse in the second half, the spirit of the Capeman continuing to stalk the older, reformed Agron.

Paul and Walcott seemed dubious when Tubert mentioned the idea in passing, so she let it go, confident that it would make sense to them when she staged her vision for the entire show during rehearsals. It was still early days in preproduction, new faces coming in to contribute their own talents, skills, and ideas; a time for blue-sky thinking, shared creativity, more possibilities than limitations. Tubert, Paul, Walcott, and the other main players worked together easily. Tubert had one small problem: although she had been working on the project for several months, her agent and Paul's representatives still hadn't worked out the terms for her contract. The problem boiled down to one point: as the youngest and least-established member of the creative team, Tubert wanted to make sure that her contributions to the show would be acknowledged, even if she wasn't the titular director on opening night. She was still building her career; her résumé needed all the high-profile credits she could get. Paul already had enough professional credits to float ten careers; nonetheless, her request became a sticking point. When it began to seem that their agents would never find common ground, Paul went to Tubert directly. Let's get rid of the business guys and work it out between the two of us, he said. Tubert, who had yet to be paid for any of her services, agreed, and they met after work on a Friday.

As Tubert recalls, she made her case strongly. By hiring her Paul had made Tubert a key member of his creative team. And in an industry where credit for developing shows is so often misassigned, she needed to be sure that her contributions to *The Capeman* would be recognized both contractually and publicly. Paul didn't see it that way. In the music industry he could hire and fire musicians without having to worry about what they did or didn't contribute to his songs. But, as Tubert knew from all of her experience in the theater, the director's vision of a show is the foundation for all of the many components in a production. Paul didn't, or couldn't, see it like that. It was a perfectly amicable conversation, but in the end they agreed to disagree. When it was over, he sat next to Tubert on the sofa and put his arm around her shoulder in a kindly way. "What made you think you wouldn't be the director when we open?" she recalled him asking. "Why worry?"

He had made none of the concessions Tubert wanted, but she came away feeling like he had opened up and revealed his confidence in her. When she got outside, Tubert called her agent and said she'd take Paul's offer as it stood. Everything seemed normal when she went back to casting the show on Monday morning, but in the late afternoon she learned that her meeting with Paul had somehow morphed into a catastrophe. Paul's publicist and coproducer, Dan Klores, called Tubert's agent to say that Paul had left his office on Friday afternoon feeling unsettled, and then angry, by what happened during their meeting. Now Tubert would need to take back what she said if she wanted to continue working on *The Capeman.* At first Tubert couldn't believe what she was hearing. How could they suddenly be at such an impasse? But Paul had drawn a new line in the sand. And so did Tubert. They'd had a disagreement and she'd made her case. She had nothing to apologize for. So that was it; Tubert left the show.

When the Born at the Right Time tour got to Chicago in 1991, Paul had invited Stephen Eich, managing director of the Steppenwolf Theatre Company, to see the concert, then come backstage to talk about his ideas for a new kind of musical. Four years later Paul called back and asked Eich to join the *Capeman* project. One of Eich's closest compatriots at Steppenwolf was a young director named Eric Simonson, who'd worked on a variety of productions for the company, most notably *Jacob Zulu,* a play about South Africa that featured the singing and dancing of Ladysmith Black Mambazo. *Jacob* had made it to Broadway and done well. Paul had liked it quite a bit, too, and when Eich suggested Simonson would be a good director for *Capeman,* Paul paid attention. Simonson had been in the running before Tubert was hired, and when she left in the summer of 1996 Paul hired him to take her place.

Simonson had a lot of experience in the theater, but he hadn't experienced anything like *The Capeman* before. Everything was complicated, including the casting of the minor characters. Paul insisted that the performers be great singers. Morris demanded good dancers, but Simonson needed actors who could embody their characters. The lines of authority in the show snared around Paul's ankles, and just to make things even more complex Derek Walcott, who had written and directed his own plays in the past, made no secret that he was sure he could direct *The Capeman* better than anyone else. Asked to keep his thoughts to himself during rehearsals, the poet did so, but given his Nobel-grade charisma, the displeasure hanging over his being was impossible to ignore. Ordinarily the director of a play is the uncontested leader of the production; his or her word is the law of the theater. But Paul came from a professional culture where the first sour note ended everything on the spot. He thought nothing of cutting off an entire scene the instant he saw or heard something that irked him. The whole company would be midway through a complicated scene and Paul would come rushing onstage waving his hands. "Stop! Stop!" The trumpet player hadn't hit his note on the pickup, so they'd have to go back and get it right. In one incident that quickly became legend, Paul halted a full-cast rehearsal because he didn't like the sound of the tambourine. After half an hour of scooting the guy from one corner of the stage to the other, Paul allowed the rest of the cast and crew to get back to work. Simonson might have been the director but, as everyone knew, Paul's word superseded everything. Simonson would take the stage to explain exactly how he wanted a scene to work, and it would take only a minute for his actors' eyes to seek out Paul's face, waiting to see what *he* thought. They all knew who was really calling the shots.

Even if Paul didn't have expertise in theater, his intellectual and perceptive powers could be stunning. Simonson was particularly impressed by his ability to grasp a person's character and motivations. "I think actually he's a great psychologist," the director said. "He really gets to the core of what a person is about almost immediately. He's got really great instincts, and can sense things." Simonson could sense how powerful a show *The Capeman* could be. The raw material, no matter its flaws, was inordinately rich with possibility. All he needed, he figured, was the space to do his job in the way he always worked. Yet, so far, Paul wasn't eager to let that happen. Simonson's top priority that fall was to whip the show into shape for a workshop performance for friends and investors in December. A scratch version of the production, no costumes or sets, but an important step in the process. When the day finally arrived, the preshow stress in the Westbeth Theatre Center was overwhelming. But when it was over, the audience stood and cheered, and triumphant smiles lit faces all around the theater — except for Paul, who rose from his chair scowling angrily. The music hadn't sounded right. He had noticed other mistakes onstage too, blown steps and ill-timed entries, the usual early production foul-ups. But Paul thought of it as a catastrophe, though, and Simonson was fired by the end of the next day.

Mark Morris finally agreed to take over the director's chair, but news that Paul Simon's show had spat out two directors in less than a year clanged alarm bells all across the city. The *New York Times* ran a story. Was the self-proclaimed reinventor of Broadway finding the job a bit more difficult than he imagined? Flocks of dancers and other cast members were sent away. The show's budget swelled, then burst through the ceiling. Investors got antsy. Jimmy Nederlander reduced his family's stake from six million dollars to one million. Klores, the producer-slash-publicist, took to the media to declare that all was well; new investors were beating down the door, stuffing wads of cash through the mail slot, desperate to be a part of the *Capeman* team. It made for a nice story, but Klores didn't have any names to offer, and it took months for them to surface in public. To save money, they canceled the show's out-of-town tryout, a crucial opportunity to gauge audience reaction and fix or revise accordingly. Originally set to open in the fall of 1997, the show was pushed back to the winter. If you were looking for signs of trouble, *The Capeman* bristled with them. The sound of sharpening knives rang across Midtown.

What else could go wrong? The *New York Daily News* published an item about *The Capeman* that would have been harmless except for the reminder that the show's hero had been a real New York City street punk and a murderer. The word *Disgraceland* featured in the headline. In September, *Newsday* ran a Broadway establishment–friendly story headlined "A Neophyte Capeman: Simon Musical Relying on Untested Talent." The story described *The Capeman*'s creative team as thoroughly inexperienced in the theater. Walcott, it sniffed, had only ever written and directed for *regional* theater. The piece was riddled with errors, including its central premise — "the creative team includes a number of Broadway veterans," read the published correction — but there was plenty more criticism to come, and most of it was far too accurate.

Tickets for the show went on sale in early September 1997. Sales weren't bad at first, but also not spectacular. The *Daily News* noted *The Capeman*'s imminent arrival with a story called "Teen Slay Caper Nearing Stage" that included the outraged complaints of the victims' survivors. "Why would anyone want to write a show about a guy who killed two boys?" the uncle of one of the victims asked. "Is he going to sing and dance?" Paul and Blades responded as sensitively as possible, pointing out that the heartbreak of the victims' mothers would be explored in one of the show's stand-out songs. It didn't matter, another *Capeman* controversy had blossomed. In mid-September a different Agron play, this one by a writer named Fred Newman, who had befriended Agron while serving as his psychologist following his 1979 parole, opened in an Off-Off-Broadway theater in SoHo. The story centered on a romance Agron had with a leftist political activist in the Southwest, but also addressed the strange celebrity visited upon him due to the murders, and his unexpected rehabilitation and release. "Salvador was forever concerned with other people commercializing his life," Newman said. Oh, and one of the characters in the Newman play was a famous musician/aspiring dramaturge named Paul Simon. "He represents the commercialization of pop music," Newman explained.

In October, hoping to stir up buzz for the show, Paul released *Songs from the Capeman*, his performances of thirteen tunes from the show's score. Ranging from doo-wop to early rhythm and blues to Puerto Rican *bomba* to something like theatrical lieder, the album was rhythmically diverse, melodically engaging, and expertly performed — everything you'd expect from a new Paul Simon album — and generally celebrated as such, despite a few critics who couldn't fathom hearing a wealthy white-skinned fifty-six-year-old musician singing in the voice of a teenage Puerto Rican gang member. "Act your age (and class advantages)," demanded the *New York Daily News,* a newspaper that seemed to harbor a distinct enmity for *The Capeman.* At the same time, the *New York Times Magazine* published Stephen J. Dubner's cover story "The Pop Perfectionist on a Crowded Stage." Invited to write about the inner workings of the production just as it was getting started, the author had observed nearly everything along the way: the hirings, firings, breakthroughs, breakdowns, and every other form of Sturm und Drang *The Capeman* had created over the years. Starting with the cover portrait of a nearly hairless Paul, Dubner's report was most striking for its portrayal of its subject's descent from cool confidence to grim forbearance. Asked about the many controversies erupting from the play's story and characters, Paul made like *The Capeman* narrative was all but irrelevant. "If you're asking *me* this is about an incredible love of sound. This is *all* about music," he said. "This is about how I fell in love with music and who I was when that love happened."

Imagine the scene in that Hell's Kitchen playground in 1959: a couple of kids looking for trouble, a couple of other kids more than happy to provide it. The neighborhood boys against the invaders; white skin against brown; the Irish against Puerto Rican, Micks against Spics. It's about turf, about keeping the outsiders where they belong — nowhere near here. Move the setting, and even if the faces and details change, the story remains the same: about anti-Semitism, about slavery and Jim Crow and South African apartheid, too; about purity, authenticity, and the promise/threat of assimilation; about the politics of folk music in Greenwich Village and the politics of folk music in England; about the generation gap in the 1960s and apartheid in South Africa; and about rock 'n' roll and Broadway, too; about who you think you are and who you know you aren't. "I was in some fights," Paul had claimed of his own delinquent ways back in the studded-leather days of Baldies, Demons, Vampires, and Norseman. And as *The Capeman* headed to its playground rendezvous, Paul's blade was sharpened, oiled, and ready for action.

"I couldn't care less what the theater com-munity, or whatever it is that they call themselves, think about this [*The Capeman*]," Paul snapped to *Vogue*'s Bob Ickes. "I didn't write it for Broadway. I wrote it for me." Paul had been dropping similar bombs since he started talking about the early reaction to *The Capeman,* but never so bitterly. Set into type in the pages of a popular national magazine, Paul's dismissive words ignited all of the anger that had been gathering around the play. The families of the victims, flanked by leaders of victims' rights groups, complained and led demonstrations. Still, some Puerto Rican immigrants and their families anticipated that *The Capeman* would be an enormous breakthrough: a showcase for their joyous culture and difficult history in America. But other Nuyoricans, as they had come to call themselves, saw yet another version of the violent stereotype that had reigned since Leonard Bernstein's *West Side Story*. As Vampires leader Tony Hernandez tells Agron in the play, "What home of the brave? This is a fuckin' war zone!" Indeed. Soon after, complaints from the cast and crew bubbled into view, with one anonymous source telling the *New York Post* that the atmosphere inside the production had become "almost intolerable."

Could anyone make it stop? Paul's old friend and super-successful director Mike Nichols spent a day or two watching rehearsals and meetings, coming back with a frank and useful opinion that prompted quick action. Paul and his theatrical partners tossed *The Capeman*'s directorial keys to Jerry Zaks, a top-drawer Broadway director whose ten-year hot streak of smash productions included the likes of *Six Degrees of Separation, Smokey Joe's Cafe,* and Neil Simon's *Laughter on the 23rd Floor.* Zaks greeted the beleaguered cast and crew with thousand-watt gusto: "You are the best of the best!" he proclaimed. "This will be a fantastic show!" Twenty years later, he looks back and laughs. "I was very sick at the time," he says. "I had a very bad case of hubris."

The scheduled January 3 opening was pushed back another four weeks to give Zaks enough time to tighten some scenes and fix a few others, but soon enough it was 8:00 p.m. on January 29. The lights went down, the curtain came up, and *The Capeman* came to life.

The first act began with Agron as a child, an open-eyed Puerto Rican boy with no idea where New York City was, let alone what lay in store for him there. He was soon joined by Blades as the grown-up Salvador, just out of prison and addressing his mother. "There's a truth that still needs to be spoken," he sings, and a moment later Anthony as the teenage Sal appears, running around a playground in the company of some other boys, joined by Blades's late-life Salvador, both describing the sweep of their existence with the lyrics of "I Was Born in Puerto Rico." A flashback showed Agron as a small boy in Puerto Rico, a spirited child with a sunny smile. Yet when his mother decides to move to New York, she takes him to visit a santero who looks into his eyes and sees only darkness. Indeed, Agron will be battered, he will be tormented, he will be seduced, he will commit a horrible deed and spend the rest of his life paying for it. Blades and Anthony were in top form, the younger performer doe-eyed and spring-heeled, an innocent from the toes of his sneakers to the highest notes in his sweet tenor vocal range. Blades played the older character in shades of quiet anger, persistent faith, and moral confusion. The world had set him up: the cruelty of the nuns and his wicked stepfather; racism, poverty, and class-ism. Society spent his first fifteen years dehumanizing him, then threw him into a prison because they thought he'd done something inhuman? In his mind, the Salvador who committed the murders no longer existed. He spent twenty years in prison growing into a man who had nothing to do with that bloody night in the playground. And maybe the younger Sal wasn't really to blame, either.

The songs were generally beautiful; so

639

many of them really do stand up to Paul's greatest works. Bob Crowley's sets were quietly spectacular, particularly the setting for Salvador's New York: the street corners, housing projects, and buttonhole playgrounds a geometric wonder of triangles, rectangles, and distorted perspective. There were video screens, photos, and film clips of the real Agron and the New York City of the rock 'n' roll 1950s. The show's first act zipped by in a rush of songs, colors, and motion, all of it bedazzling and all of it cursed. The Vampires were beautiful, mordantly funny, and lightly sinister. They danced and sang their way from the projects to a gleeful shoplifting expedition at a clothing store to the chain-linked concrete grounds of Hell's Kitchen, where the steps became a frantic death ritual. The knife tore into flesh, blood flowed, and as Salvador sang in "Adios Hermanos," the song that closes the first act, "it's time for some fuckin' law and order."

The second act began with a video montage of headlines describing Agron's progress through the next fifteen years: the death sentence; the pleas for clemency from Eleanor Roosevelt, among many others, that convinced New York governor Nelson Rockefeller to reduce the sentence to life. If the first act was a 1950s delinquent fantasia gone bad, the second was a 1970s sociologist's lecture on the social and economic factors

that can transform an innocent boy into a
killer: the physically abusive stepfather who
wielded God like a cudgel; the racism faced
by all new immigrants; the poverty it creates;
and the street violence that is echoed by a
vengeful justice system. Being locked in a cell
opens Agron's mind and then frees his soul
as he explores poetry, philosophy, and leftist
political theory. The New York State Department of Corrections dressed prisoners in
white, which gave Agron a saintly look underscoring his spiritual rebirth and, more important, the fact that he had always been a vessel
that others used to carry their shame, their
schemes and hatreds. The musical visited the
families of Agron's victims and registered the
never-ending tragedy of their lives, but the
socioeconomic biases facing the Irish immigrants pale in comparison to those that
shaped Salvador and his people.

Here again Salvador Agron feels like a vessel, only now he's carrying Paul Simon's fears
and fantasies: the innocent youngster
wounded by circumstance and fate, hardened
by his subculture, made into a celebrity, and
then made to pay for other people's inability
to understand who he really is. Asked to summon sympathetic or even apologetic words
for the parents of his victims, Agron can only
say that if they treat him in a forgiving manner, he'll treat them humanely — which
doesn't really cut it when you're addressing

the parents of the children you've been convicted of murdering. Yet with so many political and economic factors working against him, how can Agron accept full responsibility, let alone apologize for anything? With no redemptive breakthrough available in his true story, the play digs deeper into its spiritual narrative. Did the young Agron ever have the power to change his fate or did the santero's vision mark him for life? Was his inability to atone for his crimes balanced by his subsequent ability to comprehend the forces that slipped the blade into his hand? When the world failed him, Agron pinned his hopes to the spirit of St. Lazarus, to whom Jesus restored life after four long days in his tomb. For a while it seemed that the saint had done his job, but when Agron's heart froze in place two days before his forty-third birthday, he was locked into his tomb, just as the santero foretold.

Paul had reinvented himself continually since he was fifteen years old, and though he had taken himself further than anyone might have imagined, he still could not land the jump to Broadway — possibly because he never really wanted to. He'd gone in with no idea how Broadway worked and every confidence that he didn't need to find out. As if he had discovered a new door, locked it shut, and then put his head down and tried to sprint through the solid wood. You didn't need to be a santero to predict how that was going to end.

"But he can't leave his fears behind." St. Lazarus sang those words during *The Capeman*'s final performance, just sixty-six nights after it opened. "Phantom figures in the dust / Phantom figures in the dust."

CHAPTER 23
THE TEACHER

The Capeman made its premiere in front of an audience packed with investors, families, and celebrities including actors Julia Roberts, Mark Wahlberg, and Jimmy Smits, *Saturday Night Live* star Molly Shannon, and comic actress, director, and old friend Penny Marshall. Salvador Agron's sister Aurea was there, accompanied by four of her children and a grandchild. The audience stood and cheered at the end, and then the cast, crew, and a mob of friends walked the short distance to the Marriott Marquis Hotel, where the opening party was soon in high gear. The guests juggled plates of paella and champagne glasses, while Tito Puente's band played and the months and years of anxiety melted away, at least for a few hours. Paul, the *New York Times* Style section reported, showed up with his usual baseball cap "look[ing] almost happy." His moderate cheer wouldn't last much longer.

The morning newspapers ran with blood.

" 'The Capeman' is a dud," declared *USA Today.* "A sad, benumbed spectacle," growled the *New York Times.* "Damp, sputtering logs of received non-wisdom" sniffed the *New Yorker* a few days later. Not all the reviews were quite that brutal. *Variety* pointed out that Paul's score "ranks among the best Broadway scores of this or any recent season, an exquisite glen of salsa, 1950s American doo-wop and Simon's own impeccable artistry." Dan Hulbert from the *Atlanta Journal-Constitution* set the evening into full perspective, praising the score and Bob Crowley's sets before acknowledging that the haters were right. "It's as if the world's best engineers were so busy designing the coolest race car body, they forgot to put in the engine."

Ticket sales, which had been sinking since *The Capeman*'s troubles came to dominate the preshow news coverage, fell by an additional 30 percent. Dan Klores, coproducer and spokesman, said the show, in the highest Broadway tradition, would go on. "We're ready to swing our fists," he said. "We'll be here for the Tonys." Yes, the notices had been unkind, but the critics didn't represent the tastes of most theatergoers, he argued, or even Broadway insiders. Surely the real pros would recognize the amount of talent and work that had gone into the show's acclaimed score and sets. And wouldn't they want to draw attention to the work of celebrated non-Broadway, nonwhite performers Blades and Anthony? Possibly, but that would also require the Tony Awards Administration Committee members to forget all the times Paul dismissed their genre for being so predictable and stupid for so many years. Oh, dear. When the investors, already ten million dollars in the hole, pulled the plug on *The Capeman* on March 29, the Tony Award nominations were still five weeks away. It wouldn't have mattered if they'd waited: the show earned a total of three nominations, one for Paul and Walcott's score, another for Crowley's set design, and the third for the year's best orchestrations. It didn't win any of them.

If you watch the New York Public Library's DVD of the original production — part of the organization's collection of recordings of first-run Broadway shows — you'll see one of the show's final performances, a Wednesday matinee less than a week from the show's demise. You can sense the disappointment in the actors' faces, just as you can pick up the excitement in the significantly Latino audience. There is at least one group of grade-schoolers in the orchestra section, and a few organized clusters of Puerto Rican social groups and retirees. When an offstage announcer mentions that the performance will be preserved for the ages on video, there is applause, then cheers. It is, the announcer says, quite an honor. When the curtain rises on a stage full of Latino performers, Latin music, and the vibrant culture of Puerto Rico, the audience cheers again. Heads bob to the familiar rhythms and melodies. Every so often a wide shot of the stage will reveal a beaming brown face, eyes sparkling with bittersweet recognition. Yes, it's a sad and jagged story with an indistinct conclusion, but if all the people who stood up to cheer the final curtain hadn't lived their own version of that story, you have to think they either knew or were related to someone who had.

The end arrived when the curtain came down on the Saturday evening performance on March 29. Paul had kept his distance from the show for most of its run, but he was at the Marquis Theater for the day's 2:00 p.m. matinee, walking the backstage areas, then rallying everyone for a pre-curtain talk. He started haltingly as he thanked the cast, the musicians, the crew, and everyone else for all their hard work. By the end, he was in tears, barely able to get the words out. He left quietly; no one expected to see him at the evening's show. Yet he was back that evening, too, this time in a sharp-cut blue suit and a new baseball cap. The audience jumped to its feet when he came up the aisle to his eighth-row seat, and Paul happily signed his name for all the fans who came to shake his hand during the intermission. He joined Marc Anthony and Rubén Blades for the final bows, and when the cast returned for their bows, more than a few came out with fists held over their heads. Handed a full-size Puerto Rican flag, Anthony wrapped it around Paul's shoulders and stood back to lead everyone in another round of cheers. When the ovation quieted, Paul gestured around the stage and the crowd and shouted back, "If this is a failure, what's success?" That touched off another ovation, another few moments of exaltation, before the house went dark for the last time.

Louis Simon found his resting place in January 1995 at ninety years old. The end had been coming for some time. He'd lived his life, done his work with care, and raised two fine boys, both of whom had followed his steps into the music business. Younger brother Eddie was the first to take up the guitar, and became the better player of the two boys, then continued Louis's path into education by starting and running the Guitar Center, a place for lessons and theory he founded in 1972 with an investment by Artie Garfunkel. Louis had a more difficult time coming to terms with his elder son, the one whose musical talents outstripped his own by many factors, and whose earliest wave of success was profound enough to fulfill the dreams of a hundred immigrant families. Sometimes it seemed that Louis would never abide the life Paul had chosen for himself. He'd listen to the records and come out for a show, but the lights and the noise and the cheering still put him off. Such ostentation, and for what? Paul had accrued so much knowledge over the years; he could find a classroom somewhere and make a real difference in some students' lives.

It had nothing to do with love or lack thereof. Louis loved both his sons as all good fathers must, beyond reason, beyond measure. Yet he still couldn't be satisfied with Paul. Success, money, and fame were easy. So everyone loves you, he said. Who cares? Lou had left the music business for teaching and quickly concluded that that was the purpose of life. "Teach! *That's* the purpose." He was near the end of his life before he found the words to tell his son that he had always been proud of him, that he knew he had achieved rare and mighty things. Paul took it to heart, but it's the things your dad tells you when you're five or fifteen or twenty-five that shape your internal geography, not the addendum that comes when you're in your fifties.

In the fall of 1997, when there was still cautious optimism around the production offices of *The Capeman,* Paul confided to the *New*

York Times Magazine's Stephen Dubner that his father's thoughts on the transcendent value of being an educator had given him a new sense of what the purpose of his elaborate musical truly was. "I'm starting to think, without getting maudlin and psychological, that this whole 'Capeman' thing is about teaching."

As his struggle over *The Capeman* became all-consuming, Paul swore that his recording and performing days were over. He'd already moved on; he had found deeper, more satisfying things to do with his life. Of course, he said that sort of thing a lot, going as far back as the days of Tom and Jerry, when he and Artie both told reporters that pop stardom was just a goof on their way to college and graduate school. Paul had repeated it multiple times during the height of the Simon and Garfunkel era (fiction writing was his first love, etc.), reaffirmed his pledge when he went solo in 1971, and again at the end of his tours in 1973, 1975, and 1980. He'd seemed committed to the idea when he was promoting his new Broadway career during the mid-90s. "I'm thinking of 'The Capeman' as a very big ending," he said, going on to say that he was done making records, too. It sounded pretty definitive, even if he did end up carving himself just a bit of wiggle room ("That's sort of my thinking at the moment . . ."). By the time the play closed in late March, he had decided that he was done with Broadway shows, too.

He was leaving, he was leaving. Best friend Lorne Michaels had stopped taking it seriously years earlier. "Since I met Paul, he's been saying that he's getting out of show business." It was a tactic, a defensive mechanism, a way to say, I'm above all this anyway, so why should I care if you like what I do? He'd pretend to go, linger by the door for a while, then pop right back in with a big smile and a brand-new record, a brand-new tour, a brand-new Paul.

Paul stuck with his retirement vow for slightly more than a year. An offer to co-headline a concert tour with Bob Dylan, Paul's perpetual influence, rival, friend, and enemy, in the summer of 1999 proved irresistible. The two musicians convened in New York for a few days to work through some ideas for duets. Dylan was hoping to do "The Only Living Boy in New York" and "The Boy in the Bubble," and Paul talked about trying out "To Ramona" and "Forever Young." Ads and posters for the tour, built around a painting of two locomotives thundering down two parallel tracks, alluded to the separate paths the two singer-songwriters had followed through the world. The dream of the onstage collaboration was prettier than the real thing. Barnstorming arenas and amphitheaters, the two folk-rock icons took turns opening and closing the shows, with one end intricately prepared and exuberantly played and the other rough-edged and blazing. Critics noted that the artists' mutual admiration didn't necessarily equal onstage chemistry. As much as Dylan got into singing with Paul on "The Sound of Silence," his inability to master the lyrics or sing the same combination of notes in the same way from night to night made their harmony something less than silky. Knowing all attempts at reining in his fellow bard would be pointless, Paul stood back and reveled in the moment. In the wake of a particularly shaggy go at "Helllooo darkness mah ol' freee-yennnnnn / I come to talllk to yewwww agai-yennn" near the end of the tour, Dylan leaned across the microphone and shouted into his fellow icon's ear, "On a scale of one to ten how do I compare to Artie?"

Paul was so convulsed with laughter that it was a wonder he didn't fall down.

A similar tour with Brian Wilson in 2001 dispensed with the duets, even though Paul's beautifully deconstructed guitar-and-voice cover of "Surfer Girl" had been one of the high points of a Wilson tribute at Radio City Music Hall a few months earlier. Wilson and his band opened the shows with ninety minutes of his greatest songs (from "Surfin' USA" to "Good Vibrations" to "Love and Mercy"), one finely cut gem after another.

Then Paul would come with his band and "The Sound of Silence," "Kodachrome," and "You Can Call Me Al," and the party would get even wilder. Fifteen years later the *Graceland* songs had ascended into the pantheon of pop music, the sounds hard-wired into the synaptic receptors for joy and comfort.

Paul played plenty of his familiar songs, but he couldn't imagine spending this new phase in his career as an oldies act. Bits of new songs started to come to him in 1998, and though the pace was closer to a seep than a flood, he managed to get a handful of instrumental tracks recorded before breaking for the Dylan tour in 1999. By mid-2000 he'd produced enough music to fill an album of deceptively tranquil love ballads, narrative story-songs, and explorations of the end of life and the start of what might come next. Working with the core of his globally sourced band (drummer Steve Gadd, bassist Bakithi Kumalo, guitarist Vincent Nguini, percussionist Jamey Haddad, and the many-handed guitarist Mark Stewart, who doubles on every other stringed instrument plus horns and vocals), Paul crafted tracks that incorporated nearly all the sounds that had entranced him over the years: the restless percussion and tinsel-stringed guitars of South America, the bouncy beats of South Africa, the banjos and Dobros of American folk and blues, the processed sounds and drones of the modern

653

avant-garde. Throughout the album, he sings with an actor's grasp of character, speaking some lines and singing others in a voice that bends from sweet to sarcastic to hushed with the enormity of life and the finality of death. He called the record *You're the One* and released it in the early fall of 2000, less than a year and a half after *The Capeman*'s collapse.

Nearly sixty years old, Paul had achieved a kind of domestic tranquility that seemed like a scene from someone else's life. Married in 1992, he and Edie started their family as soon as the fertility gods allowed, welcoming a son named Adrian in 1994, a girl named Lulu in 1995, and their youngest, Gabriel, in 1998. It was a fresh start that seemed charmed. They moved to a large but homey house in exurban New Canaan, Connecticut, and basked in the same wonder that puts so many parents in mind of life's great pleasures and terrors. "This is near enough to bliss," Paul sings in "Look at This," before acknowledging the other end of the parental bargain: "If you're looking for worries, you got 'em."

Harper, the son he had with Peggy in 1972, had given Paul plenty of worries over the years. He suffered the usual adolescent struggles, compounded by all the temptations of children of the rich and famous and, worse, his own bouts of depression. Even as a young teenager, Harper became a regular at CBGB, downtown, drinking heavily and fooling around with weed and LSD. Paul and Peggy weren't naïve; once your son starts getting kicked out of schools, the situation becomes clear. Raised in part by Carrie, who had come into his life when he was five, Harper asked to live with her in Los Angeles, but by the time he turned twenty-one he was out of control, using heroin, Demerol, speed, and morphine until, as he recalled, the mixed-up powder was tumbling out of his pockets and nose. "Like Rainbow Brite in a nasty mood." He eventually got the help he needed and family order was restored.

You're the One takes on love and contentment with a realist's eye for the meteor plunging from the clear blue sky. "Darling Lorraine" follows a long marriage from romance to separation to reconciliation and death, while "Quiet" anticipates a senescence peaceful enough for the singer to "lie down on my blanket / And release my fists at last." "The Teacher" sinks deepest to its creator's bone. Equal parts awed and bitter, the song describes a life spent in the shadow of a great and wise man, a philosopher-king of sorts, who leads a tattered group of immigrants over raw hills to a paradise he can describe but never quite reach. Still, they follow because "it's easier to learn than unlearn / Because we've passed the point of no return." The teacher grows older and stronger; his appetites strip the hills and drain the rivers. His words come inscribed upon tablets, and though his acolytes know his flaws, they can't resist his authority, or the memory of being carried away from danger in his arms. "Carry me home, my teacher / Carry me home."

Released in September 2000, *You're the One* lacked the energy that defined virtually all Paul's previous records, but its rise to No. 19 on the *Billboard* list (twenty-three slots higher than *Songs of the Capeman* had reached three years earlier), along with a chorus of encouraging reviews, was a step in the right direction. The album earned Paul his sixth nomination for the Album of the Year Grammy, and though he eventually lost to Steely Dan's reunion album, *Two Against Nature,* simply being included felt like a welcome-back hug from his many friends, colleagues, and admirers in the music industry.

Another new album came in 2006, this one a jaunt into the electronic textures of Brian Eno, the British producer who had helped the likes of the Talking Heads, David Bowie, and Robert Fripp create some of their best-known albums. With Eno's metallic whooshes and clicks as a sonic landscape (as described in the album credits), Paul worked with small combos of mostly rock players to craft a steelier set of songs for the post-9/11 America of the Bush-Cheney years: songs about conflict, about desperation, about love, prayers, and escape. Called *Surprise,* the album veered from modern pop to the deliberately obscure to the sweet and delicate ("Father and Daughter"). The last was actually a bit of a retread, a slightly enhanced version of a song Paul had written about his daughter, Lulu, then contributed to the soundtrack of the animated movie *The Wild Thornberrys.* Built around a tumbling guitar riff reminiscent of "Diamonds on the Soles of Her Shoes," the song resonated deeply enough to score an Academy Award nomination for Best Song, and a nod in the same category at the Golden Globes. *Surprise* sold better than its predecessor, debuting at *Billboard*'s No. 14 slot before dropping out of sight.

Paul's music had been one of the defining cultural forces during the last thirty-five years of the twentieth century. But the dawn of the twenty-first century launched a fifth era in his recording career, the point where his storied achievements both gilded and deflated his new work. He'd spend two to four years producing a set of songs and then present it to the world in a downpour of excellent reviews. *His best in a decade! His best in twenty years! His best since* Graceland! He'd play a couple of the new tracks on *Saturday Night Live* and sit for some interviews, talk about the new songs, the good old days, and, with varying degrees of patience and crankiness, the bad old controversies. His fans would run to the local record store or hit the Buy button on Amazon or pick it up at the Starbucks counter along with their grande macchiato and slip it into the car's CD changer to listen to on the way home. *It's actually really good,* they'd tell their friends at a Saturday night dinner party. *Well, it's no* Graceland, *but it sounds just like him.*

As Paul knew, the modern pop mainstream had no room for a legacy artist in his sixties, a man old enough to be the average pop radio listener's grandfather. It didn't bother him, he said. He would have been shocked if the kids of the day paid attention to what he had to say. So he would say what he felt, make it sound good to his own ears, and get it out there for whoever wanted to hear it. He'd sell a decent number, enough to put him in the Top 20 for a week or two, but it was a different game now. When his contract with Warner Bros. ended with *Surprise* in 2006, he became a free agent. It didn't bother him that much. The morning after the deal expired was the first day he hadn't been subject to a recording contract since the fall of 1963, when he was twenty-two years old.

Now was the time for more inductions and awards, for even greater tributes, for fancy-dress evenings in columned stone buildings. In 2001 he was welcomed into the Rock and

Roll Hall of Fame again, this time for the solo career he had launched amid so much anxiety in 1972. Wearing a white suit over a black T-shirt, he sat patiently at his table in the Waldorf-Astoria ballroom and took in Marc Anthony's loving, if teasing, induction with a flickering smile, the light fading a little when Anthony joked about their both being in federal witness protection since *The Capeman.* The crowd responded lightly to Anthony's praise, and didn't warm up very much when Paul took the stage. He played it humble, mentioning so many friends, colleagues, and compatriots that the Rock and Roll Hall of Fame's record keepers noted that his fifty-name list set a new record for the most thank-yous in one speech. When Artie's name came up, Paul first turned plaintive: "I hope that one day before we die, we'll make peace with each other." Then, with a sly smile: "No rush."

The applause was polite, the cheers measured, the sound of respect, as opposed to a rush of affection. Was it the lingering effects of the *Graceland* controversies weighing down their hands? The reports of back-alley tactics used to snatch up what his collaborators, and many others, assumed was theirs? Or maybe it was the criticism he'd dealt to so many of his fellow travelers over the years. Or maybe they were just envious of everything he'd achieved, and how easy he had made it look. No matter: Paul was named the Grammy Awards' MusiCares Person of the Year a few months later, as a tribute to his charitable work, particularly with the Children's Health Fund, an organization devoted to caring for the children of impoverished families that he'd cofounded with Dr. Irwin Redlener, who, coincidentally enough, was related by marriage to Paul's first mentor and manager, Charlie Merenstein. Kennedy Center Honors came a year after that, and in 2007 Paul was the first recipient of the Library of Congress's Gershwin Prize for excellence in popular song. He was inducted into the American Academy of Arts and Sciences in 2011, and in 2012 the Royal Swedish Academy of Music gave him a Polar Music Prize, an award for great contributions to music whose previous winners included Bob Dylan, Karlheinz Stockhausen, Ravi Shankar, Led Zeppelin, Isaac Stern, and the Baltic states.[*] Then came honorary degrees and doctorates from his alma mater Queens College, from Berklee College of Music and Yale University, and from ten times others that he turned down because who wants to listen to that many speeches? It was more

[*] Not a band, but the governments of Estonia, Latvia, and Lithuania, in honor of their support for national music culture and publishing rights organizations.

than he'd wanted, more than he ever could have dreamed.

Heading to England for the *You're the One* tour in the fall of 2000, Paul dug out some of his old diaries and made a short list of names of the friends from his London era, when they all lived the day-for-night lives of young musicians, trading sets during the evenings and then staying up until dawn sharing their riffs, songs, and stories. The older he got, the more he understood that those precious few months in the mid-1960s, the last days before the fame struck, were the happiest of his life, when he was so young and unencumbered, surrounded by friends and music and then resting in the arms of Kathy, the love of his soft-cheeked young life. Their romance hadn't ended happily. Pulled away by the sudden success of "The Sound of Silence," Paul had sworn he'd be back within a few months, half a year at most. But then his life spun in a very different direction, and when the six months were over he was on an orbit Kathy could never have entered. She went in the opposite direction, back to the hills of Wales and to a husband, kids, and the quiet family life she was born for. When Paul finally got through to her in the late 1990s, she greeted him warmly and they chatted for a long while.

Paul also spoke to Martin Carthy, the folk

guitarist who showed him how to play his distinctive finger-picked arrangement of "Scarborough Fair," only to be shocked when Paul adapted it to Simon and Garfunkel's style and, with the benefit of Artie's "Canticle," made it into a cross-national hit, crediting himself as arranger and making no mention of Carthy. Carthy, who soon became one of the most admired folk guitar players in England, with an influence that extended to blues aficionados Jimmy Page, Eric Clapton, and countless others, had spent years feeling bitter. Paul had made a fortune and never so much as acknowledged Carthy's contribution. "I really became the full-fledged victim," he said. "And that's a very comfortable place to be."

Until it wasn't, until that was one of the only things people asked about when he'd rather have been talking about his music, a ritual he started thinking of as, in his words, "trudging the grudge." Carthy had already stopped feeling upset about "Scarborough Fair" when Paul called from Stockholm in mid-October 2000 to say he'd be playing London at the Hammersmith Apollo and wanted Carthy to play the song with him, at last. Carthy accepted the invitation even before Paul told him his side of the "Scarborough Fair" story, how he really had been paying royalties all that time with no idea that Carthy's manager hadn't been forwarding his client his fair share. That night, Paul and Carthy performed the song together for the first time, and stayed up for hours after, talking about old friends and old songs.

Paul had been kicking it around for years, trying to work out exactly what went wrong with *The Capeman,* and why. He had talked about the show in the decade since its collapse in varying tones of regret, mea culpa, and flashes of anger. He'd complain that the journalists and critics had come in disinterested in Puerto Rican culture, that they had it in for him personally. That terrible *Vogue* story, the one where he'd said, supposedly, that he didn't give a rip about what the Broadway community thought about anything, was totally phony, he said. "I never said any of those things." That neither Paul nor his managers had ever demanded a retraction and had made similar assertions to other reporters must not have registered[*] in his memory. But then, a few breaths later, he'd think again. "Okay, maybe it didn't flow slickly. Maybe it was a little static. Okay, it wasn't a perfect thing by any means." A few weeks later he was ready to accept that *The*

[*] As Paul should have remembered, the entire interview had also been captured on tape and been vetted by several layers of editors before being published in the fall of 1997.

Capeman really had been kind of, well, substandard. "I made a lot of mistakes. I didn't know anything; I only knew what people told me. Different people told me different things, and I picked a piece of information that I thought applied, and it was wrong."

Then again on the other hand he could think it through a million times and what would it matter? All he could do was let it go and have faith that someday, somewhere, someone would dust off the *Capeman* and give it another chance. Maybe that's when people would be able to really listen and finally figure out what he had been trying to do.

Almost exactly ten years after the final curtain fell, Paul and *The Capeman* got their chance. The Brooklyn Academy of Music put on a monthlong series of shows focused on Paul's music. Billed collectively as Love in Hard Times, the series consisted of three separate programs, each featuring a different set of guest stars performing Paul's works. The first, "American Tunes," covered the singer-songwriter days, with half a dozen artists (pop-classical singer Josh Groban, the Roches, alt-country singer/guitarist Gillian Welch, multi-instrumentalist Olu Dara, guitarist Amos Lee, and Brooklyn's own indie-rock heroes Grizzly Bear) performing Simon and Garfunkel and Paul's songs from his pre-*Graceland* solo years, and with Paul performing "How Can You Live in the Northeast?," one of the highlights from his then-current album, *Surprise.* The "Under African Skies" shows covered the *Graceland–The Rhythm of the Saints* period with the help of Ladysmith Black Mambazo, David Byrne, and a few younger African and Brazilian singers. Paul and members of his band performed on about half the songs in both programs. But he sat out all but one of the songs in the third and most daring program, an evening dedicated entirely to the music of *The Capeman.*

The passage of time had a miraculous effect on how New York audiences and critics perceived *The Capeman,* particularly in the oratorio form in which it was performed at BAM. Divorced from the play's book and the awkward turns in its staging, Paul's songs soared. The show received enormous ovations each night, and a new generation of critics couldn't say enough to celebrate what they'd heard. " 'The Capeman' might be [Simon's] most important and enduring work," the *New York Post*'s Dan Aquilante wrote, describing "a classic tragedy firmly rooted in modern times." The *New York Daily News*'s Jim Farber, one of the most venomous critics from the show's original run, tried to pick up where he left off ("It's still a tepid, ponderous and repetitive affair"), but he had to admit that the show's new iteration worked much better than the original production, particularly given such moving performances by the singers. The *New York Times*'s Ben Ratliff was also restrained in his praise, but still acknowledged the beauty of the music, particularly in the pair of albums (Paul's and a belated only-on-iTunes release of the original cast album), which, as he noted, were now usually described in print with the prefix "the underrated."

The Capeman's redemption tour continued in the summer of 2010, when New York's Public Theater, best known for its Shakespearean productions in Central Park, presented a three-night staging of the show, once again minus the book, at its open-air Delacorte Theater in the park, again in oratorio form, the singers performing a streamlined version of the show from behind music stands. The show enraptured the eighteen-hundred-strong audience on all three nights, spurred even greater praise from the New York critics, and not-so-hushed talk about how the last revived Broadway show to follow the path from Off-Off-Broadway to the Delacorte and then back to Broadway was the late-sixties hippieish show *Hair*. Would *The Capeman* make the same leap? Maybe someday. Stranger things had happened.

"It's over. Long over. I can't even imagine why people would be interested."

That was Paul in 2000, and you already know what, and who, he's talking about, and which age-old question he had just been asked.

When are you and Artie Garfunkel going to get back together?

Paul could get pissy about the topic, but it was hard to blame him. They had already tried it twice, once in the early 1980s and then again in 1993, and each time had been disastrous — not musically disastrous: their voices had always slipped back together so easily, their unified sound rich and dense with feeling. But then there was that other thing, the nearly lifelong connection, the bond that sank so deep it felt like an invading presence that could turn malignant at any moment. That had to be expelled at all costs.

Sometimes Paul would tell his friends that he didn't even *like* Artie. They were brothers, sure, but a lot of brothers can't stand each other, and that's the kind of brothers they were. He couldn't talk to him anymore, couldn't talk about the weather without it triggering a nasty crack about something that had been said, or not said, decades earlier. At one point in the mid-1980s they were so estranged that they refused to stand close enough together to take a portrait for the cover of a greatest hits collection for the European market, and they eventually came to one of the more absurd compromises in the history of rock 'n' roll: the European record label could find a pair of Simon and Garfunkel–esque models, put them somewhere scenic, and photograph them from afar. Then the real Paul and Artie, in their separate rooms on their separate sides of Manhattan, would try to agree on which shot was best, and that would be the cover.

Still, their connection, and their friendship, continued. When Artie turned forty-eight in 1989, Paul, with the assistance of then-girlfriend Carrie Fisher, sent Artie a birthday package of new clothes. "New outfits for a new decade . . . the 'new you,' the 'new G,' so to speak," Paul wrote in his accompanying note. Scrawled across a torn-off sheet of wrapping paper, Paul's thoughts meandered from there.

I have not managed to quite grasp the "old you," so you might consider them as a means to explain yourself to your old friend who loves you. Loves you as a guy, well not as a guy but a friend, sort of a person, well not exactly a person but more as a voice. A strange voice. Yeah, a strange voice.

They had reconciled for the Concert Event of a Lifetime shows in 1993, but that hadn't ended well, and as Paul made clear to *Newsday* in 2000, they kept their distance into the new millennium. During Paul's reunion with Martin Carthy at the Hammersmith Apollo in 2000, he confessed that the one relationship he had never been able to restore was his oldest one: "There's one person I can't reconnect with, and it really bothers me," he told Carthy. "And that's Artie."

The distance continued until the National Academy of Recording Arts and Sciences tapped Simon and Garfunkel for a Career Achievement Grammy in early 2003, and they were touched enough to perform "The Sound of Silence" on the Grammy broadcast, the first time they had sung together in public in nearly a decade. Performing in their old two-voices-and-a-guitar arrangement, they sounded just as they had forty years before, and as the audience stood to applaud, Artie draped an arm across Paul's shoulder in a gesture as familiar, and easy, as the harmonies they had just sung.

They announced the new world tour in early September 2003 and, in Auburn Hills, Michigan, six weeks later, premiered a two-hour show that included a guest set by the Everly Brothers, more than twenty Simon and Garfunkel favorites, and a warmth between the two stars that hadn't been evident since their *Bookends*-era shows in 1968. Playing with the best band they had ever toured with, a seven-piece ensemble of players led by Paul's usual music director, Mark Stewart, the duo breathed fresh life into their familiar songs with new arrangements that tightened some tunes while stretching out others (particularly "Homeward Bound" and "The Sound of Silence") and drawing out the exotic rhythms that had once been only alluded to in "Mrs. Robinson," "Cecilia," and others. Artie added more energy with new twists on his harmonies on most of the songs, but the deeper source of the crowd's sometimes tearful enthusiasm stemmed as much from the emotional subtext of the show, emphasized so cannily in the montage of nostalgic glimpses back to the America that had both inspired and been inspired by the familiar old songs — songs that had accompanied so many members of the graying crowd through their youth and young adulthood, through graduate school and into careers, and then into parenthood. For an evening, at least, it was a homecoming, a reassurance that no amount of time, acrimony, or terrorist-borne disaster could ever bar the door that led back to the way it used to be, when there was still a home to go to, where your friends were still waiting, where the darkest night could brighten with warmth and harmony.

They joked with each other — scripted jokes mostly, but still — and resisted the subtle little digs they'd thrown at each other at previous reunions. Artie was clearly more interested in recording a new album than Paul was (Paul: "I think this is more about what we *were*"), but the possibility — well, who could rule anything out now?

The tour ran for nearly a year, climaxing with an enormous crowd at the Colosseum in Rome, but the friendliness persisted through the rest of the decade. Artie sang a beautiful "Bridge Over Troubled Water" at the ceremony for Paul's Gershwin Prize in 2007, and they sang a handful of songs together at the Rock and Roll Hall of Fame's twenty-fifth-anniversary concert in October 2009. By then they were already in the midst of a planned two-year world tour that had begun with a month of stadiums and arenas across Australia, New Zealand, and Japan earlier that summer. The shows, which included separate-but-equal sets for each of them to perform his solo work without the other, went as smoothly and played to the same acclaim as the 2003/2004 shows had. The tour was to continue through North America and Europe in 2010, and to start the season off with a bang they accepted a headlining spot on the second day of the annual New Orleans Jazz and Heritage Festival. And this was where the recent years of happy collaboration came to an end.

For months Artie had been aware of a stiffness in his vocal cords, a physical block of some sort that had made his rich voice go ragged. He'd aim for notes well within his range and miss by a mile, his voice ricocheting away in a thin, sad squeak. The problem was intermittent at first, and he went to New Orleans expecting to soldier his way through, then find a way to nurture it to health in time for the start of the tour a few weeks later. Instead, he found himself standing in front of a vast crowd, completely unable to perform. Paul picked up on his partner's distress quickly and did what he could to shore him up, making sure the crowd knew Artie wasn't feeling well, bringing them onto his side, checking in from song to song, asking if he was up for "My Little Town," cheering him on when he pulled off a song without too much trouble. When they finally got to "Bridge Over Troubled Water," Paul reached over to rub Artie's back while they sang together, then led the cheers for Artie's brave, if ultimately disastrous, attempt at the climactic verse. When it was done, Paul stepped back to applaud, then stepped up to throw his arms around his partner's shoulders, wrapping him in a long hug that ended with both of them laughing, then clasping their hands together over their heads like prizefighters.

When Artie was diagnosed a few weeks later with vocal cord paresis, a temporary paralysis in his vocal cords, they had to cancel the tour, promising to reschedule the dates when he was cleared to sing. When the paresis proved more stubborn than expected, Paul continued work on a new solo album, then scheduled a solo tour to promote its release in 2011. A brief tour marking the twenty-fifth anniversary of *Graceland* followed in 2012, but as Artie reported in October of that year, Paul made it clear he was ready to resume Simon and Garfunkel business whenever Artie felt strong enough to get going. "He called me a few weeks ago and said, 'When you're ready I'm very happy to bring the guitar around the house and let's try "The Boxer." Let's warm up, let's see where we're at.' So he's definitely rooting seriously for me . . . It shows you the core of Simon and Garfunkel is a thing of beauty."

More time passed. Artie's vocal cords remained frozen, and then the tone got frosty again. Artie took to sniping at Paul in the media, complaining that he'd never received his due credit for the Simon and Garfunkel years, that it was his voice that had made Paul's songs into hits. Paul didn't respond directly, but when the prospect of another reunion came up in 2013, he responded coolly. "It's a very complicated relationship. And at the moment, we're not in contact." In another conversation that year, Paul expanded on the thought. "We are currently in one of our breakup phases," he said. "But that could change at any moment. Possibly at one of our funerals."

So Beautiful or So What, Paul's first original album in six years, came out in the early spring of 2011. The album's liner notes, composed by Elvis Costello, got straight to the point: "I believe that this remarkable, thoughtful, often joyful record deserves to be recognized as among Paul Simon's finest achievements." That was quite a thing to say about a nearly seventy-year-old artist more than fifty years into such an ambitious and busy career. But Elvis wasn't that far off the mark. The album is an audiophile's candy store, each note of every song tweaked for maximum textural intrigue. No longer satisfied by the sound of a naked instruments, Paul had taken to embroidering one sound with the ghost of another. The sound of a wildebeest cry infiltrates a guitar note here. The ghost of a bell shores up the retard of these other notes. Samples from a 1941 homily by the minister J. M. Gates, along with the shouts of his congregation, underscore the rhythm of one track; another begins in an electronic haze created by Chris Bear from the outré Brooklyn band Grizzly Bear.

The songs, as probing and barbed as anything he's ever written, confront life and death with the snap of a high schooler facing down the fearsome principal. In "The Afterlife," a dead man wakes up in a heaven that runs like the DMV, with lines to stand in and forms to fill out and pretty girls to flirt with, until he finally lands at the foot of his creator, only to discover that the secret of existence is Gene Vincent's "Be-Bop-a-Lula." When God and Jesus reappear on earth in "Love and Hard Times," God can take only a few minutes of it before ditching for less befouled terrain. But the dark comedy pivots to reveal what God leaves in his stead: the love that keeps spirits alive even through a scourge of pain. It's an album about life and death, angels and Jay-Z, fate and self-determination — with lyrics that are dense with thought and reckless with passion.

The critics agreed with Elvis Costello's evaluation of *So Beautiful or So What,* and though it's hard to call it a comeback, precisely, the album jumped into *Billboard*'s Top 5, Paul's highest chart placement since *The Rhythm of the Saints* made the No. 2 slot twenty years earlier. Six months' worth of American and European concert dates ran from mid-April through the end of 2011, a chain of ninety-minute sets that displayed Paul's strengths as a live musician, singer, and performer. Given a guitar and a stage full of musicians, he moved easily and happily, his entire being vibrating to the pulse of the music filling the air around him.

CHAPTER 24
SEE WHAT'S BECOME OF ME

Without a guitar in his hands, Paul wears his legend like a heavy cloak: a ceremonial garment embroidered with his many achievements, but woven from a darker fabric of his sorrows and his wounds. It's so difficult for him to write. When he records his songs, he's like a molecular physicist, stripping the chemical bonds from each sonic atom, altering their charges and then painstakingly stringing them together into intricate patterns few human ears could ever detect — and it takes so long, and nobody *understands*.

"I've only completed two songs in the last three and a half years," he told the faculty, students, and other rapt observers who filled a church hall at Emory University in September 2013. "People ask quite often, 'What took you so long?' as if it were a pizza delivery. The answer is I was trying to write the whole time."

Paul was at Emory to present a series of talks as the university's prestigious semiregular 2013 Richard Ellmann Lectures in Modern Literature. The lecture series' previous celebrants include Seamus Heaney, Mario Vargas Llosa, Umberto Eco, and Salman Rushdie — not a pop star in sight until the series extended an invitation to Paul, whose acceptance triggered complex systems of mutual exaltation. Dubbing Paul a legitimate genius, English professor/lecture series director Joseph Skibell pointed out that he had enough "literary gravitas" to qualify for this lecture series that "gives the writer a chance to make a major statement."

I got to the three-day lecture series at the start of the second day, in time to see Paul's "public conversation" with Billy Collins, the popular poet who was President George W. Bush's poet laureate. Sitting in matched armchairs on the stage of Emory's Glenn Memorial Auditorium, the two writers bantered about themselves and the burdens of professional creativity in the self-deprecating-yet-self-aggrandizing tone that I hear myself using when someone asks more than one question about what I do. The stage and the stakes were much larger that afternoon, and it was interesting to see Collins, whose poetic voice is so very tuned to the common person's frequency, hit the stage with such laureated swagger. The poet was very quick to point out that he and Paul are not only friends and peers, but also, he said, stars who, o irony, don't really know where they're going.* Paul's expression flickered a little when Collins pronounced himself a straight-up peer, but they are indeed friends in real life, and the musician was just as focused on staking his claim to Collins's, and his hosts', academic exceptionalism. He complained about contemporary music, particularly how the kids these days are so happy "settling for vulgarity and unsophistication as easily as the loss of privacy." The line drew an ovation from his largely middle-aged audience, which Paul seemed to anticipate. And it didn't seem like a coincidence that he was essentially sampling the lectures about rock 'n' roll his father had tormented him with in the mid-1950s. But Paul had a larger point to make that afternoon at Emory, which was how certain he is that the next generation of truly important musicians will be highly educated music students who, he predicted, will go back to the great masters because they're bored with commercialized, "crappy" music. Once again the middle-aged audience, consisting largely of highly educated academics who have devoted their lives to creating the next generation of highly educated academics, cried out their approval while Paul nodded beatifically, perfectly at home in a place he'd

* The reference to "Me and Julio Down by the Schoolyard" was obviously intended.

never been.

Just a few months later, Paul found himself in another place he'd never been, only this time he was standing with Edie in front of a judge in Norwalk Superior Court, near their home in Connecticut, trying to explain why the disagreement they'd had a couple of nights earlier had ended in a scuffle so loud and seemingly violent that one of them — Paul, it turned out — had dialed 911. The police arrived to find a low-bore domestic confrontation: the couple was in the guest-house they used as a recording studio, where, Edie told the police, Paul had done something to "break [her] heart." She had had a few drinks, and things went south from there: some pushing and slapping (her hand, his cheek), and so on. It all ended up on the public record, which meant that it also played in the newspapers, along with paparazzi shots of the couple strolling to court where they hoped to convince the judge that they truly did not need or want a protective order keeping each safe from the other. The judge couldn't find a reason to doubt them and they walked off together holding hands, heading to their youngest son's Little League baseball game. Another sunny day in upscale suburban America.

Even the younger kids in Paul's family with Edie are mostly grown up now. The couple's eldest son, Adrian, a singer, guitarist, and keyboardist, released a record with his band, the Ivy League, when they were still in high school. Graduated from college in 2015, Adrian is just a couple of years ahead of middle child, Lulu, who has shared the stage with her father at benefits and other special shows in recent years. Gabriel, the youngest child, still lives at home. Paul and Peggy's son, Harper, now in his forties, fell in with a circle of avant-pop performers based mostly in Los Angeles, a group that includes the talented offspring of some of the more famous musicians of the sixties, seventies, and beyond, including the children of John Lennon, Yoko Ono, Lowell George, Kate Mc-Garrigle, and Loudon Wainwright III. He also formed a group with stepmother Edie called the Heavy Circles, which released its first, and so far only, CD in 2008.

Edie and Paul keep their family life to themselves, though simply existing around New York City puts all well-known faces within range of paparazzi cameras and the lenses of any of twenty million cell phones being wielded every minute of every day: Paul and Adrian sitting courtside at a Knicks game; Paul and the kids standing on a street corner; Paul and the kids walking into a movie theater. Even when caught by surprise, Paul usually wears a proud smile, like any other dad thrilled to be spending another day watching his children in the act of walking, thinking, joking, singing, living.

On the verge of his seventy-fifth birthday Paul still moves gracefully. He has made peace with his hair, which he now keeps close-cropped and white, with just a bit more on top than he revealed on the cover of the *New York Times Magazine* in 1997. He exercises daily, keeping his chest and arms fully loaded and his gut under control. He's partial to fedoras, T-shirts, jeans, and blazers, which puts him somewhere between a domesticated rock star and a stylishly hip literature professor, which seems exactly right. The sounds he explores now are the ones he can find or invent in his home studio, where he produced the bulk of his latest album, *Stranger to Stranger,* released in the spring of 2016. The first song to surface from the album was "Wristband," a conga-slapping acoustic funk number that starts as a wry story of a musician locked out of his own gig, trying to convince a skeptical security guard to let him back in. What starts as a funny backstage confusion (even the star can't get into his own dressing room without the right pass) eventually transforms into something larger and more sobering, a symbol of outrage for the millions of the underprivileged "whose anger is a shorthand / For you'll never get a wristband." It is an archetypical Paul Simon move: bridging the personal and the social, the silly with the serious, the frivolous and the absolutely essential.

When he's not making it look easy, he's nearly buckling under the burden. In the early twenty-first century, Paul suffered another creative block, this one finding form in a blustery internal voice that wouldn't stop condemning him for misusing his talent and, worse, for perpetually gathering up God's gifts to sell at the marketplace. Paul got past it eventually, and there has always been somewhere else to go, some other frontier to travel, some new song he can put under the microscope, pick apart, and put back together in a new and uncanny way. Whether his labors will resonate with anyone other than himself and a handful of his smarter, cooler friends doesn't seem to matter to him — or he says it doesn't matter, anyway. Look, *So Beautiful or So What* popped into *Billboard*'s No. 4 slot the week it was released in 2011. When his next album emerged five years later, it was preceded by a multiplatform publicity campaign, including online previews, comic video appearances, a concert tour, and high-profile interviews. The full-bore assault pushed *Stranger to Stranger* to a No. 3 debut on *Billboard*'s album chart, making it his highest charting album since *Rhythm of the Saints*.

Paul's bizarre public relationship with Artie

Garfunkel, by turns his oldest and best friend and a guy he can barely stand to be near, remains one of the most essential fables of the sixties generation. The boyhood chums turning themselves first into harmonizing teen idols and then a folk duo, then rock stars, then cultural oracles, all the while remaining best friends, only to fall into a decade-long feud, then back into harmony, then back into another decade of feuding, only to resume again, only to fall apart again, only to come back together and collapse again, each time their harmonies sounding just as luminously perfect as they ever did. Six decades later an observer might wonder if the never-ending Simon and Garfunkel saga is the longest-running installation in the history of conceptual art or perhaps the most successful inside joke they ever concocted. *And the winner of the Fattest Girl in the School Contest turns out to be . . . the whole world!* Whatever, it's definitely a deeply symbolic story about youth and maturity, innocence and experience, the importance of leaving home and the even greater importance of coming back and finding your old neighborhood just as it was, all your friends and your younger self waiting to resume the life you left behind.

Assuming you can stand the idea that you had an old life.

■ ■ ■ ■

I got to Emory University's Glenn Auditorium early Monday afternoon and found a place about halfway back in the pews — the building is a restored church — and settled in. After digging a notebook and pen from my bag, I saw that Paul was already sitting quietly in his chair on the stage alone, waiting for things to get started. We hadn't met, but as I knew he knew, I was already working on this book.

When I looked up from my notebook and pens, I had just enough time to think, *Oh look, there's Paul Simon sitting by himself on the stage,* before his eyes seemed to fix on my face. There was no one else near me, and he was looking really hard, in that unblinking, stare-you-down way. Or that's how it seemed to me. I had contacted Joseph Skibell to see if I could attend the lectures, and he had been most helpful in clearing my way, and I supposed he might have told Paul I was going to be lurking around the campus. Like most published writers, I'm easy to find on the Internet. Maybe he'd taken a glance so he'd be prepared in case I came marching up to confront him?

What could I do? I looked back at him, and he kept looking back at me. Were we having a staring contest? Was he engaging with me or was he seething at me? Was I imagining the whole thing? I doubt this went on longer than fifteen seconds, but as it turns out that's a lot of time to think when the subject of your new book is giving you the once-, twice-, and thrice-over in a church in Atlanta. He hadn't authorized my book. He had no enthusiasm for biographies, I learned. But since I was enthusiastic enough for the both of us I got to work anyway. I heard from his co-manager brother Eddie a few times, and received a phone call from Jeff Kramer, the other co-manager, who made it clear that the prospect of my book was causing some anxiety around certain Brill Building offices. I've worked closely with other subjects, less closely with others, and was happy to talk about my approach and address their concerns, but they weren't interested in that.

He didn't look angry. Stern, maybe. Impassive, definitely. Eventually, he raised his hand and turned away. Not just sort of away, but forty-five degrees away, like, *I'm not looking at you anymore. I'm looking this totally different way now and so we're done.*

Just above face level, his palm flat and perpendicular to the floor, like a stereotyped movie Native American going "How!" Or a traffic cop saying, "Stop!" Or maybe a guy signaling his uninvited biographer to keep his distance — which is understandable on a human level, but less so in the wake of fifty-plus years of public life. All that self-revelation in his music — in the hundreds of thousands of words of interviews he's given, talking about his wives; his lovers; his astonishingly screwed-up relationship with the friend/musical partner he will sometimes insist had no real impact on him at all, and then turn around and say that their lives have always been woven together; and his father; his creative blocks; his anxieties; his therapists; and more.

Still: *Don't look at me.*

Or not, at least, at what I don't want you to see.

Don't notice that Paul really was Jerry Landis, just as he was also True Taylor and Paul Kane, even if his early folk songs were a little overblown. *One-Trick Pony*'s Jonah Levin was a mash-up of all three, given his own Paul Kane folk song ("Soft Parachutes") and Jerry Landis's one-hit track record. Levin also shared Jerry Landis's initials, as per the Jewish tradition of giving a newborn a name with the same initials as a deceased relative. But the film is full of hints about Paul and the undergirding of his most essential self.

The most telling sequence in the *One-Trick Pony* script didn't make it into the completed movie but was significant enough for Paul to use it as the final scene in a draft of the script dated 1979: the moment when Jonah takes his son in his arms and tells him all the reasons for the things he's done, going a step further than the absentee father described in "Slip Slidin' Away," who can only kiss his sleeping child before vanishing back into the darkness.

The scene begins as Jonah and his all-but-ex-wife, Marion, discover that their late-night arguing has woken their young son, Matty. The boy asks his dad for a bedtime story, so Jonah carries Matty back to bed and starts telling him a story about a boy exactly his age, a dedicated Yankees fan who could also make up magic songs that made other people so happy when they heard them that they needed to sing along. Paul's own life, divided into three faces and retold as a hero's journey.

The story begins at Yankee Stadium, in the bottom of the ninth inning, when the hometown club can either win big or lose it all. Key slugger Reggie Jackson is at the plate with the bases loaded and with two strikes already against him. As Jonah tells his sleepy son, the struggling hero may finally be meeting his match. But when he slaps a foul ball into the boy's grasp, the boy sings his magic song to the ball then tosses it to Reggie, who hears the music and sends it back to the mound. The pitcher winds up and speeds it back to home. Jackson's mighty swing makes contact, sending the ball entirely around the planet before finally landing at the feet of the road-worn Jonah, who picks it up on his way to the stage in a Cleveland nightclub. He hears the song just in time for his son to appear next to him. Jonah and his son perform the song together, lulling the crowd, along with the father and son sharing the stage, into an ecstatic slumber.

Unification.

The sweet boy with the inexplicable talent; the big-time hero slugger standing tall at the plate in Yankee Stadium, taking his biggest swing ever just as he is on the threshold of his darkest moment; and also the isolated traveling musician whose dedication to his son is rivaled only by his yearning for a new song. And back to the son, who is, in this story at least, finally able to satisfy his father so much that they can put down their instruments and fall asleep in each other's arms. The camera pulls back to show Marion sitting on the floor, watching Jonah with the sleeping Matty in his arms. The anger in her eyes replaced with love, she reaches out to her husband, her fingertips about to reach him when the image freezes on the screen and the opening notes of his "Late in the Evening" play.

And it was late in the evening
And all the music seeping through.

NOTES

1 Real and Assumed

"I enjoy singing and rock and roll": Tracy Thomas, *New Musical Express,* April 8, 1966.

2 The Tailor

"I never saw the point": Josh Greenfeld, "For Simon & Garfunkel All Is Groovy," *New York Times Magazine,* October 13, 1968.

"Lou," he said, "was really quiet": Author interview with Al Caiola, April 8, 2014.

"I would add Lee Simms": "Inside Stuff — Music," *Variety,* September 30, 1959.

"I felt there was enough suffering": Quoted, minus attribution, Joe Morella and Patricia Barey, *Simon and Garfunkel: Old Friends* (Secaucus, NJ: Birch Lane Press, 1991), p. 8.

3 Our Song

"the most famous singer": Simon and Garfunkel joint interview, *USA Today,* September 14, 2003.

"You've got a nice voice": Timothy White, "Public Pitches and Stolen Moments with Pinin' Simon," *Crawdaddy,* February 1976.

"God, that's *awful*": *60 Minutes,* CBS-TV, January 6, 1991.

"I just sat back": Ibid.

"Because it's really *dumb*": Ibid.

"I would sit and examine": Paul Zollo, *Songwriters on Songwriting* (Cincinnati, OH: Writer's Digest Books, 1991).

"I'm sure Paul's father": Author interview with Jerry Garfunkel, April 2013.

"You keep it the same": Rehearsal tape for Art Garfunkel's bar mitzvah service. Queens, NY, 1954.

"He was a very good ballplayer": Author interview with Ron Merenstein, November 2014.

"slovenly in dress": From *Jewish Messenger,* quoted in Irving Howe, *World of Our Fathers: The Journey of the East European Jews to America and the Life They Found and Made* (New York: Touchstone Books, 1990), p. 230.

"You're the winner": Ben Fong-Torres, "Arthur Garfunkel: The *Rolling Stone* Interview," *Rolling Stone,* October 11, 1973.

"pretty and built": Art Garfunkel letter to Paul Simon, summer 1957, in the possession of the Rock and Roll Hall of Fame and Museum's library.

"You can imagine": Paul Simon letter to Art Garfunkel, summer 1957, in the possession of the Rock and Roll Hall of Fame and Museum's library.

"a fuck, though": Ibid.

"so pitifully stupid": Ibid.

"I never went to camp": Author interview with Norman Strassner, May 11, 2015.

4 Nowhere to Go but Up!

"I wanna talk": Fong-Torres, "Arthur Garfunkel: The *Rolling Stone* Interview."

"Who are those *jerks?":* Ibid.

"I'm from Macon, Georgia": The Richard Ellmann Lectures in Modern Literature, Emory University, September 25, 2013.

"But that's what it was": Paul Simon interview with Craig Inciardi, Paul Simon: Words & Music, exhibit at the Rock and Roll Hall of Fame and Museum's library, October 30, 2014.

"Man, they sound exactly": Author interview with Robert Lieberman, June 2014.

"Since we couldn't agree": Victoria Lee, *New York World-Telegram and Sun,* February 1958.

"want to crack-up [*sic*]?": Letter from Paul Simon to Art Garfunkel, New Jersey, August 9, 1957.

"He was a little fella": Author interview with Chester Gusick, June 6, 2014.

5 Two Teenagers

"Best Men on Campus": Alpha Epsilon Pi, fraternity advertisement, Queens College 51 *Rampart,* 1958–62.

"You gotta hear this!": Author interview with Brian Schwartz, January 12, 2015.

"We're gonna get this right, okay?": Author interview with Ron Pollack, 2015.

"Huge Harold, a hostess": Ibid.

Jerry Landis is going places: Gloria Stavers, "Jerry Landis Is Going Places!" *16 Magazine,* February 1960.

they formed the Cosines: Author interview with Marv Kalfin, April 26, 2015.

he signed with Wemar: Paul Simon, affidavit in Paul Simon and Arthur Garfunkel v. Big Records, Inc., Sidney Prosen, Keel Manufacturing Corp. and Pickwick International, Inc., Supreme Court of the State of New York, County of New York, 1967.

something fewer than one hundred copies: Ibid.

"out of the common groove": "Reviews of this week's singles," *Billboard,* October 10, 1960.

One detail Pizzarelli doesn't recall: Author interview with Bucky Pizzarelli, March 31, 2014.

"Landis! Git in here!": Author interview with Al Contrera, June 11, 2014.

"I wasn't aware of Jerry Landis": Author interview with Ron Pollack.

"The niggas let me": Author interview with Richard Milner, June 8, 2014.

6 The Freedom Criers

Paul looked for glimmers: Author interviews with Marty Cooper and Mickey Borack, 2013–2015.

The seed of "Wild Flower": David Coplan, *In Township Tonight!* (Chicago, IL: University of Chicago Press, 2008).

Cooper didn't really need: Author interviews with Marty Cooper, 2013–2015.

Paul moved on: Ibid.

"You've gotta start singing": Ibid.

"I was reaching out": Author interview with Mark Levy, February 7, 2015.

"we speak Middle English": Author interview with Brian Schwartz.

Like many others on campus: Robert Christgau, "The Supreme Achievement of the Second Industrial Revolution," *Cheetah*, 1968.

"Don't listen to the *singing*": Author interview with Al Kooper, March 10, 2014.

"It's the most alive": Author interview with June Tauber Goldman, February 2, 2015.

7 What Are you Searching for, Carlos Dominguez

It was late spring: Paul Zollo, "Breakfast with Art Garfunkel," *Songtalk,* 1993; Paul Simon interview with Tony Schwartz, *Playboy* 31, February 1984.

tricks of the busker's trade: Michael Kay interview with Paul Simon, *Center Stage,* July 14, 2009.

the Pont Neuf: Paul Simon interview with Tony Schwartz, *Playboy.*

had any grass on him: E-mail to author from John Renbourn, March 11, 2014.

"Didn't I just see you in Amsterdam": Paul Simon interview with Pete Fornatale, n.d., 1986.

Those were the names they used: Tom Wilson interviews, *Paul Simon Songbook,* BBC Radio Series, prod. Frank Wilson, London, UK, 1991; Patrick Humphries, *Paul Simon: Still Crazy After All These Years* (New York, NY: Doubleday, January 23, 1989).

drove some colleagues to despise: Interview with Hale Smith and Bill Banfield, *Musical Landscapes in Color* (Lanham, MD: Scarecrow Press, January 29, 2003), p. 63.

"Focus on your music": Author interview with Brian Schwartz.

Usually he'd switch off: Paul Simon interview with Betty Rollin, *Look,* November 29, 1966.

"So I told David": Author interview with Martin Carthy, January 31, 2014.

"It's good to be here": Paul Simon live at Brentwood Folk Club, 1963/64, Brentwood, Essex, recording in possession of Essex County Records Office, Chelmsford, England.

The fucking guy knows: Author interview with Martin Carthy.

It was hard to resist: Banfield, *Musical Landscapes in Color,* p. 63.

Paul offered something else: Paul Simon interview, iTunes Originals, 2006.

"this is completely backwards": Michael Kay interview with Paul Simon, *CenterStage,* July 14, 2009.

8 The Voice of the Now

They'd had a few drinks: Robert Shelton, *No Direction Home* (New York: William Morrow and Company, 1986), p. 177.

Dylan and Paul had met: Author interviews with Barry Kornfeld, 2013–2016.

"an encounter typical": 'Shelton, *No Direction Home,* pp. 177–78.

Simon and Garfield it was: Tom Wilson interview, *Paul Simon Songbook,* BBC Radio.

There were hardly any anti-Semites: Ibid.

"Gentlemen, it's 1964": Ibid.

"This terribly well-written song": Author interview with Bill Leader, February 11, 2014.

"I also record for Columbia" Paul Simon letter to "Ted," June 12, 1964.

Born as James Henry Miller: Michael Brocken, *The British Folk Revival 1944–2002* (London: Routledge, 2003), pp. 31–35.

"were becoming quasi-Americans": Ibid., p. 34.

"I'd never heard anything": Author interview with Harvey Andrews, February 2014.

So off he went: Ibid.; Harvey Andrews interviews, *Paul Simon Songbook,* BBC Radio; J. P. Bean, *Singing from the Floor* (London: Faber and Faber, 2014).

In London, the hipper musicians: Author e-mail interview with John Renbourn, March 2014.

Artie spent much of the summer: Art Garfunkel letters to Jack and Rose Garfunkel, September 1964.

"This was the bloke": Judith Piepe interview, *Paul Simon Songbook,* BBC Radio.

9 He Was My Brother

"The people in this city": Andy Goodman, postcard to parents, June 21, 1964, viewed by author courtesy of David Goodman.

The same couldn't be said: Jacob Tanzer, "1964: My Story of Life and Death in Mississippi," *The U.S. District Court of Oregon Historical Society Newsletter* (Spring 2010); Seth Cagin, *We Are Not Afraid* (New York: Macmillan, 1988), pp. 1–2; Jesse Kornbluth, "The '64 Civil Rights Murders: The Struggle Continues," *New York Times,* July 23, 1989.

"We close our eyes": Andrew Goodman, "Corollary to a Poem by A. E. Housman," *Andrew Goodman: 1943–1964* (Long Island, NY: Peter F. Mallon Inc., 1964).

"One of them is the song": Paul Simon, "Chez/For Kathy," record, autumn 1964.

"I've already done the whole introduction": Ibid.

"So that was a bomb": Tom Wilson interview, *Paul Simon Songbook,* BBC Radio 6, 1991.

between *Housewives' Choice:* Judith Piepe interview, *Paul Simon Songbook,* BBC Radio 6, 1991.

Paul got a British publishing deal: Author interviews with Michael Tannen, 2013–2016; Victoria Kingston, *Simon and Garfunkel: The Biography* (New York: Doubleday, 1998), p. 29.

"He was the favored child": Author interview with Ariel Piepe Bruce, February 26, 2014.

Along the way, she had traded: Ibid.

"He was creating a package": Author interview with Harvey Andrews, March 10, 2014.

"He was very friendly": Author interview with David Rugg, February 2014.

"If I'm not a millionaire": Geoff Speed quoted in J. P. Bean, *Singing from the Floor* (London: Faber & Faber, 2014), p. 176.

Paul responded to the producer's: Author e-mail interview with Melanie Ezekiel, winter 2014; Humphries, *Paul Simon: Still Crazy.*

"Very American! He used to": Paul Simmons, "Interview with Bert Jansch," *The Ptolemaic Terrascope Magazine,* 1996.

"He had a reputation": Ralph McTell interview, *Evening Standard* (UK), July 14, 2004.

He spent a third: Author interview with Stephen Bromfield, February 2014; Humphries, *Paul Simon: Still Crazy;* Kingston, *Simon and Garfunkel.*

"I start with the knowledge": Paul Simon liner notes, *Paul Simon Songbook,* CBS, 1965.

"Who wrote this junk?": Ibid.

"Sorry, this guy is trying": *Melody Maker,* July 24, 1965.

"A small, dark, intense man": "Two Views on Baez," *New Musical Express,* July 30, 1965.

"rehashed Ginsberg": "The Great Dylan Row," *Melody Maker,* October 5, 1965.

"Typical brash Americans": Author interview

with Hans Fried, February 2014.

"So you have the Byrds": Simon and Garfunkel club show in London, September 1965, included in *Paul Simon Songbook,* BBC Radio 6, 1991.

when Stan Kavan: "Col Relay System Puts 'Silence' Over," *Billboard,* February 19, 1966; Jim Melanson, "Col/Epic 'Q' Product Gains Momentum," *Billboard,* November 10, 1973.

a very simple calculus: "Col Relay System Puts 'Silence' Over"; interviews with Tom Wilson and Mark Weiner, *Paul Simon Songbook,* BBC Radio.

"I was mildly amused": Zollo, "Breakfast with Art Garfunkel."

"No, more than sort of successful": Paul Simon interview, iTunes Originals, September 6, 2006.

What the fuck is that?: Author interview with Al Stewart, February 11, 2014.

"So that's when": Ibid.

"I don't feel it": Paul Simon interview from 1965, *New Musical Express,* August 10, 1968.

I wasn't violently against": Jim Delehant, "Inside the Mind of Paul Simon," *Hit Parader,* August 1967.

In 2006, Paul described: Paul Simon interview, iTunes Originals.

Paul spent the time: Ibid.

"I said, *'Shiiit'* ": Ibid.

"I remember this": Ibid.

"I'd rather not have a hit": Author e-mails with Harry Knipschild, February 2014.

10 It Means Nothing to Us

reigned at No.1: Paul Simon interview with Pete Fornatale, 1986.

"You've really got a hit record": Author interview with Ron Merenstein.

"What's the name of": Author interview with Mort Lewis, 2013.

"To Morty, I hope": Ibid.

"It's that easy?": Ibid.

"To show people": Zollo, "Breakfast with Art Garfunkel."

"Dylan or somebody would": Author interview with Bob Johnston, June 2014.

"rather intense, though hardly": Columbia Records publicity handout, January 1966, in the possession of the Rock and Roll Hall of Fame's library.

"How could this happen": Ralph J. Gleason, "Then There Was 'Silence' with a Red Bullet," *This World,* February 20, 1966.

"to, and perhaps for": Robert Shelton, "Folk-and-Pop Duo in Recital Debut," *New York Times,* May 2, 1966.

"Pop music is catching up": Robert Shelton, "A Law Firm They're Not," *New York Times,* August 28, 1966.

"Pop music is the most vibrant": "Rock 'n' Roll: The New Troubadours," *Time,* October 28, 1966.

"Their intellectual prowess": Tracy Thomas, *New Musical Express,* April 8, 1966.

"No matter how successful": Ibid.

"Do you know how much": Keith Altham, "Now They All Want Paul Simon Songs!," *New Musical Express,* April 22, 1966.

"Sing!": Bruce Woodley and Judith Durham, quoted, minus attribution, "Seeks on the Simon Sound Trail," *Melody Maker,* April 23, 1966.

"Paul Simon is getting": Interview with Bruce Woodley, *Melody Maker,* January 29, 1966.

"I haven't had any real need": Paul Simon interview, *New Musical Express,* August 10, 1968; Greenfeld, "For Simon & Garfunkel All Is Groovy."

"who used to be": Simon and Garfunkel, live at Tufts University, March 11, 1967, recording in author's collection.

For all that British critics: Paul Simon interview with Timothy White, *Goldmine,* 2001.

"What kind of image are": Interview with Norman Jopling, *Record Mirror,* April 22, 1967.

"I think it strange": Altham, "Now They All Want Paul Simon Songs!"

"Unfortunately, I'm always being": Ibid.

"A linebacker-size fellow": Blair Jackson

interview with Roy Halee, *Mix Magazine,* October 1, 2001.

"People say I'm a dollar": Penny Valentine, "Simon & Garfunkel: It's a Lonely Life at the Top," *Disc,* March 23, 1967.

11 Some Dream of What I Might Be

"I said, 'Yeah' ": Stephen J. Dubner, "The Pop Perfectionist on a Crowded Stage," *New York Times Magazine,* November 9, 1997.

"That's the *only* important": Dubner, "The Pop Perfectionist."

"They're not yelling at me": Tracy Thomas, "Enter the Intellectual Simon & Garfunkel!" *New Musical Express,* April 18, 1966.

"I don't know how": Jim Delahunt, "Inside the Mind of Paul Simon," *Hit Parader,* August 1967.

"The people who call you a poet": Greenfeld, "For Simon & Garfunkel All Is Groovy."

"Simon and Garfunkel are fictitious": Ibid.

"He *should* have been": Paul Hendrickson, "Paul Simon: Two for the Road; In Town on Tour with Garfunkel," *Washington Post,* August 13, 1983.

"Can you imagine girls": Ibid.

"It's like the greatest put-on": Greenfeld, "For Simon & Garfunkel All Is Groovy."

"Okay, you made all this money": Dubner,

"The Pop Perfectionist."

"My father," he said: Ibid.

"my many neuroses": Simon and Garfunkel, live at Tufts University.

"a cul de sac": Greenfeld, "For Simon & Garfunkel All Is Groovy."

"Rock 'n' roll for people": Christgau, "Supreme Achievement."

"is neither a poet": Jann Wenner, "Doin' the Thing," *Daily Californian,* Fall 1966.

fifty thousand dollars seed money: Michael Lydon, "Where's the Money from Monterey?," *Rolling Stone,* November 9, 1967.

The trip was a success: Joe Morella and Patricia Barey, *Simon and Garfunkel: Old Friends,* p. 65.

Columbia president Goddard Lieberson: Author interview with John Simon, September 16, 2014.

Hendrix . . . with whom he played a little: Paul Simon interview, *Paul Simon Songbook,* BBC Radio.

"We'd like to introduce": *Monterey Pop,* dir. D. A. Pennebaker, Leacock-Pennebaker Inc., London, 1968.

"Ah, you dig the red lights": Ibid.

"Make sure to tell 'em!": Author interview with Keith Altham, February 2, 2014.

As reenvisioned by Mike Nichols: Sam Kashner, "Here's to You, Mr. Nichols: The Making of the Graduate," *Vanity Fair,* no. 571, March 2008.

"Jewish *inside*": Ibid.

Nichols was born in Berlin: Bruce Weber, "Mike Nichols, Urbane Director Loved by Crowds and Critics Dies at 83," *New York Times,* November 20, 2014.

Paul and Artie were initially dubious: Kashner, "Here's to You, Mr. Nichols."

they agreed to provide: Peter Bart, "The Back Lot," *Variety,* May 16–25, 2005.

At long last, a trickle: Kashner, "Here's to You, Mr. Nichols"; Peter Bart, "The Back Lot."

Except for that there was: Zollo, "Breakfast with Art Garfunkel"; Kashner, "Here's to You, Mr. Nichols; Peter Bart, "The Back Lot."

As Davis knew: Author interview with Clive Davis, December 3, 2013.

"Not the way Paul": Ibid.; author interviews with Mike Tannen.

12 Bookends

When the successful British pop band: Graham Nash, *Wild Tales* (New York: Crown, 2013).

In the spring of 1967 Paul rented: Author interviews with Mike Tannen; author interview with Chuck Israels, August 7, 2013; Greenfeld, "For Simon & Garfunkel All Is

Groovy."

Talking to a reporter at the Stockbridge: Greenfeld, "For Simon & garfunkel All Is groovy."

In the recording studio: Morgan Ames, "Simon & Garfunkel in Action," *High Fidelity,* November 1967, p. 63; Greenfeld, "For Simon & Garfunkel All Is Groovy."

"It's no good": Ames, "Simon & Garfunkel in Action."

"Almost as if it's not there": Ibid.

When bassist Bill Crow: Author e-mail interview with Bill Crow, March 24, 2014.

Looking for a mod new sound: Ibid.; author interview with John Simon, September 16, 2014.

"They were concerned about": Clive Davis and James Willwerth, *Clive: Inside the Record Business* (New York: William Morrow and Co., 1974).

Davis knew it was coming: Author interview with Clive Davis.

"They are both college boys": Letters from David Oppenheim to Boris Sedov, 1968, in the possession of New York University library.

Plus a Soviet intelligence agent: U.S. Department of State, *Foreign Relations of the United States, 1969–1976,* vol. 12, *Soviet Union* (January 1969–October 1970), doc. 1.

"two of the finest singers": Kevin Kelly, "Simon and Garfunkel, Poets, Balladeers," *Boston Globe,* January 30, 1968.

"Nobody is talking for this generation": "Rock: What a Gas!" *Time,* April 19, 1968.

"It looks like somebody's lunch": Recording of concert at Hollywood Bowl, August 23, 1968, in the possession of the author.

"There's been a change of identity": Ibid.

13 So Long Already, Artie

Nicols called Paul: Paul Simon interview with Craig Inciardi, *Paul Simon: Words & Music,* The Rock and Roll Hall of Fame and Museum's library, October 30, 2014.

Paul had plenty of other things: Author interviews with Mort Lewis, May 2013.

"I liked people": Ibid.

"We're divorced": Author interview with Hal Blaine, May 16, 2013.

"Little and poor": Paul Simon original lyrics, *Paul Simon: Words & Music,* The Rock and Roll Hall of Fame and Museum's library, October 30, 2014.

"I am but a poor": Ibid.

such a deliberately wounding way: Paul Simon interview with Tony Schwartz, *Playboy.*

How could Paul begrudge: Jon Landau, "Paul Simon: The Interview," *Rolling Stone,* July 20, 1972.

He wrote letters telling Artie: Zollo, "Breakfast with Art Garfunkel."

"dig-yourself competition": Columbia Records publicity handout, January 1966.

Paul's determination was offset: Author interview with Mort Lewis.

"We had to postpone the concert": Ibid.

His friends in England: Author interview with Keith Altham.

Before he started work: Ben Fong-Torres, "Hello Darkness, My Old Friend," *Rolling Stone,* February 7, 1971.

"When Al Kooper had played Paul": Author interview with Al Kooper.

The first time Paul heard: Chris Ingham, "Paul Simon: Still Crazy?," *MOJO,* November 2000.

as if Jeter's voice: Paul Simon interview with Craig Inciardi, The Rock and Roll Hall of Fame and Museum's library.

"I was the first person": Author interview with Al Kooper.

"It *is* a great song": Zollo, "Breakfast with Art Garfunkel."

To make sure they'd have: Author interview with Marshall Chess, February 10, 2016.

"You can't take the writer's notes": Zollo, "Breakfast with Art Garfunkel."

"When you're in the harmony game": *Simon and Garfunkel: Songs of America,* dir. Charles Grodin, CBS, November 30, 1969.

The crowning moment: Frank Zappa, *The Real Frank Zappa Book* (New York: Poseidon Press, 1989); "Simon and Garfunkle on WFUV," *For What It's Worth* (blog), July 4, 2011, christopherfountain.wordpress .com/2011/07/04/ simon-and-garfunkle-on-wfuv/.

When they played college shows: "Folk Duo, Students, Talk Pot and the Police," *Wichita State University Sunflower,* November 4, 1969.

"humanistic approach": Charles Grodin, *It Would Be So Nice If You Weren't Here* (New York: William Morrow and Co., 1989).

When Paul, Artie, and Grodin refused: Loraine Alterman, "Paul Simon: The *Rolling Stone* Interview," *Rolling Stone,* May 28, 1970.

"The chaos of what the hell": *Simon and Garfunkel: Songs of America.*

"We're staying in the Beverly Hills": Ibid.

"When Paul came in": Jon Landau, "Paul Simon: The Interview."

When they previewed the finished album: Author interview with Clive Davis.

14 I'd Rather Be

When he was in Rome: Paul Simon interview with Tony Schwartz, *Playboy.*

"I'm really only interested in movies": Ibid.

"he really made me": Ibid.

Performing on a pleasant summer: Audience recording, Forest Hills Tennis Stadium, Forest Hills, NY, July 18, 1970, in the possession of the author.

"We'd have to stop our friendship": Royston Eldridge, "What Friendship Means to Simon & Garfunkel," *Melody Maker,* June 7, 1969.

"We'll always come back": Alterman, "Paul Simon: The *Rolling Stone* Interview."

"We could easily do [a new tour]": Ibid.

Paul committed to playing: David Browne, *Fire and Rain* (Cambridge, MA: Da Capo Press, 2011).

It was not a crowd: Ibid.

"Did you see that?": Author interview with Hal Blaine.

He started seeing a therapist: Alterman, "Paul Simon: The *Rolling Stone* Interview."

Paul had gotten in touch: Author interview with Jeffrey Sweet, October 2, 2014; author interview with Melissa Manchester, December 13, 2014; Terre Roche, *Blabbermouth* (New York: Terre Roche, 2013).

"Part of the learning process": Heather Winett, "An Interview with Paul Simon," *Washington Square Journal* (April 13, 1970).

"laughing lagoons": Roche, *Blabbermouth.*

"Just steal them": Winett, "An Interview with Paul Simon."

Paul was particularly struck by the Roche sisters: Ibid.

Did she think she was as good: Roche, *Blabbermouth.*

"My sense was that he was searching": Author interview with Melissa Manchester.

"You can't just sit here": Author interviews with Mike Tannen, 2013–2016.

"Well, that's the biggest mistake": Author interview with Clive Davis; Davis and Willwerth, *Clive: Inside the Record Business.*

"I did try to reason with him": Author interview with Clive Davis.

At first Paul thought about forming: Author interview with Stefan Grossman, December 5, 2014.

"I've gotten nowhere": Fong-Torres, "Hello Darkness, My Old Friend."

"Partly I'm looking forward to it": Ibid.

Paul got in touch with Leslie Kong: John Sebastian, "A Conversation with Paul Simon," *Radio Today Entertainment,* January 30, 1991; Paul Simon interview with Jerry Gilbert, *Sounds,* 1973.

Yet when he got to Kingston: Paul Simon interview with Inciardi.

He spent ten days in San Francisco: Author interview with Stefan Grossman.

"He paid for everything": Ibid.

"Cut me open": Fong-Torres, "Arthur Garfunkel: The *Rolling Stone* Interview."

"Anybody who knows anything": Jon Landau,

"Paul Simon: The Interview."

"At a certain point it became very hard": Ibid.

"As I stand right now I have no partnership": Ibid.

15 That's It, That's That Groove

"And in effect begin": Paul Simon, affidavit in Paul Simon, Charing Cross Music, Inc., and CBS Records v. Edward B. Marks Music Corporation, Supreme Court of the State of New York, County of New York, 1972.

"I think you're the best": Author interviews with Mike Tannen, 2013–2016.

The company's first clients were Maggie and Terre: Roche, *Blabbermouth.*

"Paul Simon and Michael Tannen gave us": Ibid.

"a student's fantasy": Sandra Shevey, "Simon Says: Pop Singer Paul Simon Talks About Women, Psychoanalysis, Being Short and Life Without Art Garfunkel," *Chicago Tribune,* May 7, 1972.

"The whole white male myth": Ibid.

The new songs were upbeat: Author interview with David Hood, July 5, 2013.

Not entirely sure they were speaking: Interview with Barry Beckett, *Paul Simon Songbook,* BBC Radio, 1991.

"And I'm Artie Garfunkel!": Author interview

with David Hood.

"He wants to go": Interview with Barry Beckett, *Paul Simon Songbook,* BBC Radio.

He went back to the notebook: Author interview with David Hood, July 5, 2013; author interview with Richard Blakin, June 13, 2014; author interview with Paul Samwell-Smith, May 1, 2014.

"I think he thought": Author interview with David Hood.

"The joint custody arrangement": Paul Simon interview with Paul Cowan, "The Odysseus of Urban Melancholy," *Rolling Stone,* July 1, 1976.

"You pull up in front of a place": Ibid.

Paul called Phil Ramone: Author interview with Chuck Israels; interview with Phil Ramone, *Paul Simon Songbook,* BBC Radio, 1991.

"Generally I can hold my own": Author interview with Chuck Israels.

16 Through No Fault of My Own

"Paul always gives you": Fong-Torres, "Arthur Garfunkel: The *Rolling Stone* Interview."

heard Paul play it in an earlier form: Chris Charlesworth, "Art Garfunkel: Art for Art's Sake," *Melody Maker,* October 1975.

Some days, he glided the streets: Cowan, "The Odysseus of Urban Melancholy."

"The record companies couldn't agree": Wayne Robbins, "Simon & Garfunkel Reunite: It's Paul, but Is It Art?" *Rolling Stone,* December 18, 1975.

"Isn't it nice to win": White, "Public Pitches and Stolen Moments with Pinin' Simon."

"slick professionalism": Paul Nelson, "Pinin' Simon: Still Slick After All These Years," *Rolling Stone,* December 4, 1975.

when Aykroyd recalled seeing: Dan Aykroyd interview with Terri Gross, *Fresh Air,* NPR, November 22, 2004.

"It's hard to get Paul to laugh": Ibid.

"the folk-singing wimp": Doug Hill and Jeff Weingrad, *Saturday Night: A Backstage History* (New York: William Morrow and Company, 1986).

make sure his bald spot wasn't too visible: Ibid.

"I'd still like to do some more stuff with Artie": Lynn Van Matre, "The Pen Is Mightier Than the Stage to Songsmith Simon," *Chicago Tribune,* November 9, 1975.

"I can't go back": Maureen Orth, "Simon Says," *Newsweek,* December 15 1975.

"The hostilities started when Paul": Author interview with Clive Davis; author interviews with Mike Tannen; Frederic Dannen, *Hit Men: Power Brokers and Fast Money Inside the Music Business* (New York: Crown, 1990).

The arrogant little putz: Walter Yetnikoff, *Howling at the Moon: The Odyssey of a Monstrous Music Mogul in an Age of Excess* (New York: Broadway Books, 2004), p. 92.

"I didn't like the guy": Ibid.

"War clouds were rolling in": Ibid.

"How dare you assume": Author interviews with Mike Tannen.

Paul owed CBS one more studio album: Yetnikoff, *Howling at the Moon,* pp. 96–98.

reach a settlement: Dannen, *Hit Men,* p. 125.

17 Swallowed by a Song

"His ego didn't get in the way": Jim Jerome, "Still Creative After All These Years," *People,* November 30, 1980.

None of the leading stars: Dave Marsh, "What Do You Do When You're Not a Kid Anymore and You Still Want to Rock and Roll?," *Rolling Stone,* October 30, 1980.

Paul also accelerated his campaign: Jerome, "Still Creative After All These Years."

"She's really got the goods": Ibid.

" '60s college-kid alienation": Carrie Rickey, "One-Trick Pony Review," *Village Voice,* October 8–14, 1980.

"Shouldn't the dramatic catharsis": Ibid.

"It was all a bit unsettling": Author interview with Ariel Bruce.

18 What Did You Expect?

Something great was coming next: Author interview with Lenny Waronker, June 2013.

Paul called Dr. Roderic Gorney: Author interview with Rod Gorney, November 21, 2014.

He was young, healthy, talented: Paul Simon interview with Tony Schwartz, 254 *Playboy.*

At the end of the first session: Ibid.

"For me that was brilliant. And liberating": Ibid.

telephone call from . . . concert promoter: Author interview with Ron Delsener, December 13, 2014; author interview with Lenny Waronker, May 2014; author interview with Russ Titelman, November 2014; Paul Simon interview with Tony Schwartz, *Playboy.*

"Nah. I thought you": Interview with Art Garfunkel, *Paul Simon Songbook,* BBC Radio 6, 1991.

"Yes, it would seem": Chris Charlesworth, "Art Garfunkel: Art for Art's Sake."

they could barely look at each other: Author interview with Bunny Freidus, December 12, 2014.

Paul's first thought: Author interview with Ron Delsener.

Artie wanted to pick up: Ibid., and Paul Simon interview with Tony Schwartz, *Playboy.*

"We're back from the boulevard": Robert Palmer, "Simon & Garfunkel Take on Central Park," *New York Times,* September 18, 1981.

"Fun is the key": Ibid.

"We'll stick Artie with the check": Author interview with Mort Lewis.

"That," he said, "is a great idea": Ibid.

That was the plan: Thomas R. King, *The Operator* (New York: Random House, 2000).

"The songs are more like stories": Chris Connelly, "Simon and Garfunkel Reunite in Central Park," *Rolling Stone,* October 29, 1981.

"What did you expect?": Author interview with Lenny Waronker, June 2013.

As Paul had made clear: Paul Simon interviews, Art Garfunkel interviews, *Paul Simon Songbook,* BBC Radio 6, 1991.

"This is exactly what's gonna happen": Author interview with Lenny Waronker, June 2013.

"What's he *doing*?": Ibid.

He resisted guidance: Author interview with Russ Titelman, November 2013.

"Don't be hurt by my behavior": Paul Simon interview with Tony Schwartz, *Playboy.*

"On a certain level": Ibid.

"How can you carry that betrayal": Ibid.

When they finally got onstage: Author interviews with Arlen Roth, 2014–2015.

"God, I felt great": Paul Hendrickson, "Paul Simon: Two for the Road; In Town on Tour with Garfunkel," *Washington Post,* August 13, 1983.

"You're against this": Author interview with Lenny Waronker, May 29, 2013; author interview with Russ Titelman, April 2, 2014.

"I guess I was supposed to conclude": Art Garfunkel interview, *Paul Simon Songbook,* BBC Radio.

19 These Are the Roots of Rhythm

"I not only don't like you": Carrie Fisher, *Wishful Drinking* (New York: Simon and Schuster, 2008), p. 97.

Greenwich Village boutiques: John Swenson, "Simon's Rhymin', This Time to a Soweto Beat," UPI, January 12, 1987.

Carrie's drug use escalated: Tim Appelo, "Carrie Fisher Spills the Beans," *Savvy Woman,* September 1990; Tim Appelo, "Still Crazy," *City Arts,* April 1, 2009.

close to Penny Marshall: Penny Marshall, *My Mother Was Nuts* (New York: New Harvest, 2012).

"We both did it": Audience tape of concert, August 22, 1983.

"Here's a song I wrote in 1966": Ibid.

"the most convincing case": Stephen Holden,

"Paul Simon Uses Rock as a Springboard for the Mature Act," *New York Times,* October 30, 1983.

"descend at the top": Art Garfunkel's handwritten notes for "Think Too Much" harmonies, Rock and Roll Hall of Fame and Museum's library.

"You should talk to": Author interview with Heidi Berg, December 12, 2015.

why don't you go to South Africa: Ibid.

Waronker knew exactly whom: Author interview with Hilton Rosenthal, July 9, 2014.

Rosenthal had another idea: Ibid.

Make the calls: Ibid.

"Where's my end?": Author interview with Heidi Berg.

"I can introduce you to": Harry Belafonte interview, *Under African Skies,* dir. Joe Berlinger, A&E Television Networks, 2013.

"I saw right then and there": Ibid.

"It's like having your dad": Paul Simon interview, *Under African Skies.*

Stanley Corsi called back: Author interview with Hilton Rosenthal.

Founded by Dutch traders: Coplan, *In Township Tonight!*

The advent of recorded sound: Ibid.

When preeminent South African record label: Ibid.

A month or two after: Ibid.

"Almost like the greatest": Charles M. Young, "Paul Simon: The Soweto Factor," *Sunday*

Times (UK), August 24, 1986.

"I am thinking, *Who*": Joseph Shabalala interview, *Under African Skies.*

"The niggas were letting": Author interview with Richard Milner.

20 I've Got Nothing to Apologize For

"They both encouraged me": Stephen Holden, "Paul Simon Brings Home the Music of Black South Africa," *New York Times,* August 24, 1986.

"I wasn't going there": Randy Sue Coburn, "Ambassador of Music Paul Simon's New Album a Bridge Over Troubled Cultures," *Chicago Tribune,* August 24, 1986.

Shadowed by a handful: Jennifer Allen, "The Apostle of Angst," *Esquire,* June 1987; James C. McBride, "Paul Simon, Under Fire at Howard; Irate Students Protest SA Album," *Washington Post,* January 9, 1987.

"How could you go over there": Ibid.

Batson shouted about cultural diffusion: Ibid.

"You don't think it's possible?": Ibid.

"Reagan has my best": Roy Coleman, "Paul Simon Breaks the Sound of Silence," *Melody Maker,* 1980.

"an anachronism": "Paul Simon/Pop Think-In: The Biggest Thing Dylan Has Got Going for Him Is His Mystique," *Melody Maker,* April 30, 1966.

"Rhodesia," Paul said, "causes a lot": Ibid.

He felt the same way: Steven Van Zandt interview with Dave Marsh, *Kick Out the Jams with Dave Marsh,* Sirius/XM E Street Radio, 2014; Dan Solomon, "Steven Van Zandt Tells the Story of 'Sun City' and Fighting Apartheid in South Africa," *Fastcocreate,* December 13, 2013, http://www.fastcocreate.com/3023454/steven-van-zandt-tells-the-story-of-sun-city-and-fighting-apartheid-in-south-africa.

Dozens of the era's: Steven Van Zandt interview, *Kick Out the Jams with Dave Marsh.*

"Why are you defending that Mandela guy": Ibid.

"You and Henry Kissinger": Ibid.

Ronstadt was one of the elite: Aaron Latham, "Linda Ronstadt: Snow White in South Africa," *Rolling Stone,* August 18, 1983.

"Authoritarian governments on the right": Robert Christgau, "South African Romance," *Village Voice,* September 26, 1986.

Born in Britain: Author interviews with Johnny Clegg, September 2014.

"This is very complicated": Ibid.

"an artist completely opposed": Michael Maren, "The Sins of Paul Simon," *Africa Report,* July 1, 1987.

"I've got nothing to apologize for": Ibid.

"funny statements": Ibid.

"We think the whole episode": Ibid.

It was galling: Author interview with Steve

Berlin, February 4, 2014.

"just play something": Ibid.

"Nope, nope, nope": Ibid.

"I swear I'll make it up to you": Ibid.

"Wait, what's that?": Ibid.

Hidalgo led the rest: Ibid.

You don't like it?: Ibid.

"They live, along with other South African": Paul Simon acceptance speech for *Graceland,* Album of the Year, Grammy Awards, February 24, 1987.

21 The Whole World Whispering

"To me . . . a moral position cannot be broken": Ken Franckling, "Mandela Rally Draws 325,000," UPI, June 23, 1990.

Paul got the idea while chatting: Paul Simon interview with Craig Inciardi, Rock and Roll Hall of Fame and Museum's library.

he got a call from Quincy Jones: Ibid.; author e-mail interviews with Marco Mazzola, October–November 2013.

"Lyme disease" he noted: Paul Simon interview with Craig Inciardi, Rock and Roll Hall of Fame and Museum's library.

Paul arrived at Mazzola's studio: Author interview with Marco Mazzola.

The group had a staunch commitment: Dubner, "The Pop Perfectionist"; Carol Cooper, "The Noise from Brazil," *Elle,* August 1989.

After hearing the fourteen-strong: Phil Ra-

723

mone with Charles L. Granata, *Making Records: The Scenes Behind the Music* (New York: Hyperion, January 1, 2007), p. 168.

When Paul followed the drummers' trail: Paul Zollo, "Recording with Roy Halee," *Songtalk,* April 1990.

The divorce from Carrie hadn't taken: Ed Bradley interview with Carrie Fisher, *60 Minutes,* CBS, January 6, 1991; Susan Wloszczyna, "Fisher's Mother Lode: Hollywood's Raconteur Strikes Gold," *USA Today,* September 12, 1990; Diane Sawyer interview with Carrie Fisher, "Carrie's Story: Carrie Fisher Discusses Battle with Drugs and Manic Depression," *ABC News,* December 21, 2000.

Maybe the jungle held more spells: Timothy White, "The Rhythm Method: Paul Simon's Solo Expeditions," *Goldmine,* April 3, 1992; Carl Wayne Arrington, "Carrie Fisher: A Spy in Her Own House," *Time,* October 15, 1990.

"He said, 'Oh, that's nothing' ": White, "The Rhythm Method."

"It felt like it was pulsing": Arrington, "Carrie Fisher: A Spy in Her Own House."

"It's not an argument": Tim Appelo, "Carrie Fisher Spills the Beans," *Savvy Woman,* September 1990; Tim Appelo, "Still Crazy," *City Arts,* April 1, 2009.

Paul had spent a million dollars: Stephen Holden, "Paul Simon's Journey to Brazil and Beyond," *New York Times,* October 14, 1990.

"When Chris Botti": Author interview with Chris Botti, November 19, 2013.

"I'd rather wish Paul well from afar": Douglas Martin, "About New York; Just Simon in the Park, to Garfunkel's Disappointment," *New York Times,* August 14, 1991.

"I'm not good enough to be invited": Ibid.

When the *New Musical Express* writer: Gavin Martin, "When the Saints Go Cashing In," *New Musical Express,* October 27, 1990.

It happened just before 2:00 a.m.: Author interviews with Attie van Wyk, September 22, 2014; and Rory Steyn, September 2014.

"Three guys and a fax machine": Author interview with Attie van Wyk.

"We have always pointed": Tom Cohen, "Militant South Africans to Protest Paul Simon Concerts Peacefully," Associated Press, January 10, 1992.

"I think he showed his true self": Author interview with Marco Mazzola.

22 Phantom Figures in the Dust

"We can show the kids the tape": Colleen Long, "Edie Brickell Releases Her First New Album in a Decade," Associated Press, December 29, 2003.

"recapturing as purely": Sheila Rule, "The Pop Life," *New York Times,* June 16, 1993.

"I felt a lot of affection": Greg Kot, "Still Crazy After All These Years; Paul Simon Looks Back — and Ahead — After 3 Musical Decades," *Chicago Tribune,* October 10, 1993.

"It is sophomoric, inflated talk": "Talk of the Town: (Still) Looking for America," *New Yorker,* October 11, 1993.

Then it was happening again: Author interview with Chris Botti, November 19, 2013; author interviews with Jerry Garfunkel, April 23–24, 2013.

"Neither could speak the next morning": Author interview with Chris Botti.

"There were gangs in Queens": David Hinckley, "Homeward Bound — In 'The Capeman' Paul Simon Returns to the NY of His Youth," *New York Daily News,* November 16, 1997.

"I was in a couple of fights": Larry McShane, "Paul Simon's Controversial 'Capeman' Hits Broadway," Associated Press, December 12, 1997.

the sound of his youth: Timothy White, "The Secret History of Simon's 'Capeman,' " *Billboard,* November 3, 1997.

In late 1967 he had signed up: Sam Zolotow, "Dustin Hoffman to Try Broadway; Star of 'The Graduate' Cast in a Schisgal Musical," *New York Times,* May 20, 1968.

he could never get past the artifice: Author interview with Jeffrey Sweet, September 28, 2014.

"If I ever write a musical": Ibid.

"I might do that": Ibid.

"That's because the best writers": Paul Simon interview with Jerry Gilbert, "Paul Simon," *Sounds,* May 19, 1973.

"I have absolutely no plans": Paul Simon interview with Timothy White, *Crawdaddy,* February 1976.

By 1980 he put writing a musical: Jim Jerome, "Music Keeps Coming," *People,* November 3, 1980.

Paul took his script-in-progress: E. L. Doctorow story as told by friend Eric Alterman to author.

"The whole project's on a razor's edge": Author interviews with Mike Tannen, 2013–2016.

Well, he was finished with being a pop star: Dubner, "The Pop Perfectionist."

"You're telling me I don't know": Ibid.

"I will see you again": Author interview with Susana Tubert, January 18, 2016.

He talked at length: Dubner, "The Pop Perfectionist."

"I just spent a year": Author interview with Susana Tubert.

Paul sent Tubert: Ibid.

Let's get rid of the business guys: Ibid.

"What made you think?": Ibid.

Everything seemed normal: Ibid.

Born at the Right Time . . . got to Chicago: Author interview with Stephen Eich, September 10, 2014.

Paul hired him to take her place: Author interviews with Eric Simonson, 2014–2016.

Everything was complicated: Ibid.

"Stop! Stop!" Ibid.; Dubner, "The Pop Perfectionist."

Paul halted a full-cast rehearsal: Ibid.

Paul's word superseded: Author interviews with Eric Simonson, 2014–2016

"He really gets to the core": Ibid.

When the day finally: Dubner, "The Pop Perfectionist."

Simonson was gone: Author interview with Eric Simonson, 2014–2016.

The show's budget swelled: Dubner, "The Pop Perfectionist."

What else could go wrong?: Patricia O'Haire, " 'Capeman': Sounds of Violence Paul Simon Musical Looks at Gang Leader's Life in Disgrace-land," *New York Daily News,* June 11, 1997.

In September, *Newsday:* Patrick Pacheco, "Play by Play/A Neophyte Capeman/Simon Musical Relying on Untested Talent," *Newsday,* September 4, 1997.

"Why would anyone want to write a show": Michael Riedel, "Teen Slay Caper Nearing

Stage," *New York Daily News,* September 7, 1997.

"He represents the commercialization": "Rob't Dominguez, Rival Play Raps Simonized 'Capeman,' " *New York Daily News,* September 19, 1997.

"If you're asking *me*": Dubner, "The Pop Perfectionist."

"I couldn't care less": Bob Ickes, "The Capeman Cometh," *Vogue,* January 1998.

"almost intolerable": Ward Morehouse III, "Is Nichols Tailor-Made for 'Capeman' Alterations?" *New York Post,* December 11, 1997.

"You are the best of the best!": Author interview with Jerry Zaks, April 28, 2015.

"I was very sick at the time": Ibid.

23 The Teacher

"We're ready to": Greg Evans, "Gang of Crix Knife 'Capeman,' " *Variety,* February 2, 1998.

"If this is a failure": Tara George and Dave Goldiner, "Simon 'Cape' Crusader at Closing," *New York Daily News,* March 29, 1998.

"I'm thinking": Dubner, "The Pop Perfectionist."

"Since I met Paul": Alec Wilkinson, "The Gift," *New Yorker,* November 25, 2002.

"On a scale of": Author interview with Chris Botti, 2013.

"Like Rainbow Brite": Harper Simon interview with Sabine Heller, "Harper Simon: Singer and Songwriter," *Purple,* 2012.

"I hope that one day": Neil Strauss, "In Jam-Filled Ceremony, an Eclectic Mix Joins the RRHoF," *New York Times,* March 20, 2001.

"I really became": Author interview with Martin Carthy, February 2014.

"trudging the grudge": Ibid.

"I never said any": Ingham, "Paul Simon: Still Crazy?."

"Okay, maybe it didn't": Ibid.

"I made a lot": Letta Tayler, "He's the One," *Newsday,* December 3, 2000.

"It's over. Long over": Letta Tayler, "He's the One," *Newsday,* December 3, 2000.

"New outfits for a new": Note from Paul Simon to Art Garfunkel, 1990, located in the Rock and Roll Hall of Fame and Museum's library.

"There's one person I can't": Author interview with Martin Carthy, February 2014.

"I think this is more": David Bauder, "Simon & Garfunkel Heading Out on the Road Again," Associated Press, June 7, 2004.

"He called me a few": "Who Am I If I Can't Sing? It's My Identity," *Daily Telegraph,* October 18, 2012.

"It's a very complicated relationship": Paul Simon interview with Craig Inciardi, located in the Rock and Roll Hall of Fame and Museum's library.

"We are currently in": Scott Freeman, "Review: At Emory, Paul Simon Lectures on Songwriting and Performs an Unforgettable Concert," *ArtsATL,* September 26, 2013, http://www.artsatl.com/2013/09/review-paul-simon/.

"I believe that this": Elvis Costello liner notes, *So Beautiful, So What,* Hear Music, April 12, 2011.

24 See What's Become of Me

"literary gravitas": Rupsha Basu and Stephen Fowler, "Simon Delivers Lectures on Songwriting, Decline of Art," *Emory Wheel,* September 24, 2013.

"break [her] heart": Steve Kobak, "Details Emerge About Paul Simon Arrest," *New Canaan Hour,* April 29, 2014.

ACKNOWLEDGMENTS

I started thinking seriously about writing a book on Paul Simon in mid-2012, just as I was finishing work on my previous book. My connection to his music went back as far as the summer of 1968 when the transistor radios in our Seattle neighborhood played "Mrs. Robinson" six or eight times a day, every day, while I pushed my trucks through my parents' backyard. Simon's early solo hits were all over the radio when I was in grade school, and I started collecting his albums when I got to high school. I bought each new record as it was released over the next forty years. It was clear to me that Simon's music had become an essential part of the American cultural experience in the late-twentieth and now early-twenty-first centuries.

I started writing a proposal for this book in the winter of 2012–13 and began work on the book itself in the spring of 2013 and devoted the next three years to researching and writing about Simon's work, his life, and his times. As always, I benefited from the work and kindness of many smart, cool, and generous people along the way.

First: My agents Dan Conaway and Simon Lipskar, along with Taylor Templeton and Caitlin Ellis at Writers House. Thanks also to Gillian Blake, who brought me to Henry Holt & Co, and Eleanor Embry, both of whom contributed so much to the book during its creation.

Thanks also to my friend/wingman/transcriber Craig Williams and my New York–based research assistants Emily Kaplan and Greg Hanlon, all of whom made invaluable contributions to this work. Also to Mike Tannen, Barry Kornfeld, Mort Lewis (RIP), Rob Oudshoorn, Raymond F. Kearney and Eric Alterman, and Jim Carlton, all of whom withstood more than their share of calls, visits, and emails. The same goes for my friends at the Rock and Roll Hall of Fame Museum + Archives: Greg Harris, Lauren Onkey, Andy Leach, and Jennie Thomas and everyone else at the RRHoF's research library.

I also owe thanks to the staff of the Essex Records Office in Chelmsford, UK; the New York Public Library for the Arts in Lincoln Center; the British Library; Malcolm Taylor and everyone at the Vaughn Williams Memorial Library at the English Folk Dance and Song Society; Principal Saul Gootnik and everyone at Forest Hills High School; the staff of the Queens College Library; the staff of the American Federations of Musicians, Local 802; and the staff of New York University's Tamiment Library.

For their recollections, insights, suggestions, and so much more: Jerry Garfunkel, Ron Merenstein, Steven Merenstein, Chester Gusick, Morton Craft, Bucky Pizzarelli, Marshall Chess, Bert Skolsky, Art Gatti, John J. McDermott, David Goodman, Ron Pollack, Judith Flanembaum, June Tauber Golden, Mark Levy, Brian Schwartz, Gerry Solomon, Mike Barkan, Harvey Kushman, Norman Basner, Richard Milner, Stuart Hochman, Robert Lieberman, Marv Kalfin, Marv Goldberg, Mickey Borack, Marty Cooper, Al Caiola, Al Contrera, Neil Sedaka, Roderick Warner, Al Stewart, Ariel Bruce, Martin Carthy, Stephen Bromfield, Rick Norcross, John Renbourn (RIP), Hans Fried, Miranda Ward, Bruce Woodley, Wizz Jones, Harvey Andrews, Rupert Hine, David W. Rugg, Geoffrey Speed, Dolly Terfus, Rick Norcross, Melanie Ezekiel, Bill Leader, Bredda Roberts, Spencer Leigh, Jim Abbott, Andre Ceelen, Harry Knipschild, Clive Davis, Bunny Friedus, Michael Pillot, Paul Samwell-Smith, Susan Curry, Janice Lagunoff, Will Trinkle, Linda Grossman Garfunkel, Frank Reina, Norman Strassner, Bill Crow, Bob Johnston, John Simon, Al Kooper, Morgan Ames, Chuck Israels, Hal Blaine, Melissa Manchester, Stefan Grossman, David Hood, Richard Blakin, Dr. Rod Gorney, Ron Delsener, Lenny Waronker, Russ Titelman, Fred Lipsius, Arlen Roth, Attie Van Wyck, Hilton Rosenthal, Jabu Ngwenya, Johnny Clegg, Rory Steyn, Ray Phiri, Steve Berlin, Heidi Berg, Chris Botti, Randy Brecker, Graham Hawthorne, Paul Levant, Dean Parks, Marco Mazzola, Joseph Skibell, Susana Tubert, Eric Simonson, Jeffrey Sweet, Stephen J. Dubner, Stephen Eich, Jerry Zaks, and Paul Zollo.

More thanks to the small but crucial group of sources who spoke, often at length, off the record, on background, and without attribution. They know who they are.

Thanks also to colleagues and friends: Brad Rosenberger, Patrick Humphries, Victoria Kingston, Paul Du Noyer, Loraine Alterman, Jeffrey Melnick, Ben Sidran, Tim Riley, Jim Cullen, Ryan White, Bertis Downs, and Patterson Hood.

For places to stay, places to write, places to hide: Claudia Nelson and Rory Dolan, Brendan and Christe White. Thanks also to the artists residency program at the Sou'Wester Lodge, Seaview, Washington.

More thanks to the King: "So it's settled. That's what you're doing."

As ever, forever, for Sarah, Anna, Teddy, and Max.

ILLUSTRATION CREDITS

1. Time & Life Pictures / The LIFE Picture Collection
2. Photofest
3. ZUMA Press, Inc. / Alamy Stock Photo
4. Norman H. Strassner / Strassner Family Collection
5. Author Collection
6. Queens College Archives
7. Queens College Archives
8. Michael Ochs Archives
9. Queens College Archives
10. Archant CM Ltd. / Norfolk
11. Donald Hunstein / Hunstein Art Services
12. Author Collection
13. Pictorial Press Ltd. / Alamy Stock Photo
14. Pictorial Press Ltd. / Alamy Stock Photo
15. *New Musical Express*
16. Peter Simon
17. NBCUniversal
18. Richard E. Aaron / Redferns
19. Time & Life Pictures / The LIFE Picture Collection

ABOUT THE AUTHOR

Peter Ames Carlin is the author of several books, including the *New York Times* bestseller *Bruce,* a biography of Bruce Springsteen, published in 2012. Carlin has also been a freelance journalist, a senior writer at *People,* and a television columnist and feature writer at the *Oregonian.* A regular speaker on music, art, and popular culture, he lives in Portland, Oregon, with his wife and three children.